Coming Back Brockens

by the same author

OUR GRANDMOTHERS' DRUMS

Coming Back Brockens

A Year in a Mining Village

MARK HUDSON

JONATHAN CAPE
LONDON

First published 1994

1 3 5 7 9 10 8 6 4 2

© Mark Hudson 1994

Mark Hudson has asserted his right
under the Copyright, Designs and Patents Act, 1988
to be identified as the author of this work

First published in the United Kingdom in 1994 by
Jonathan Cape
Random House, 20 Vauxhall Bridge Road, London SW1V 2SA

The writing of this book was assisted by a bursary
from the Arts Council of Great Britain and an award
from the Authors' Foundation administered by the
Society of Authors.

Random House Australia (Pty) Limited
20 Alfred Street, Milsons Point, Sydney,
New South Wales 2061, Australia

Random House New Zealand Limited
18 Poland Road, Glenfield,
Auckland 10, New Zealand

Random House South Africa (Pty) Limited
PO Box 337, Bergvlei, South Africa

Random House UK Limited Reg. No. 954009

A CIP catalogue record for this book
is available from the British Library

ISBN 0–224–04170–3

Printed in Great Britain by
Clays Ltd, St Ives PLC

for Julia

In the old 'bord and pillar' system of coal extraction pairs of hewers drove roadways into the coal, fifteen feet wide. Every twenty yards, new roadways were struck off to the left and right, creating a grid-like network of tunnels, with *stooks* – pillars of coal twenty yards square – holding up the immeasurable tonnage of rock overhead. This was called *coming yehl*.

When they'd reached the furthest extent of a district – and there might be twenty pairs of hewers working in a district on each of the three shifts – they'd start to work back towards the shaft bottom. Where there were areas of habitation, roads or particularly churches on the land above, the stooks were left in place. Otherwise they went for total extraction. They began moving – 'coming back' – towards the shaft bottom, slicing out the pillars of coal as they went. And the 'roof', the incalculable weight of rock, was allowed to collapse in behind them, 'as it liked'. This was called *coming back brockens*.

Contents

1

Hudson Avenue

I NEVER CREST the brow of the hill out of Peterlee, catching my first glimpse of the village of Horden – the rather mean roofs sticking up against the blank, implacable mass of the North Sea – without feeling that there must be something or someone there for me.

Horden. The name reverberated through my childhood like a dull gong. Harden. Hwoden. Huerden. Conventional orthography is inadequate to convey the nuances of the different ways I heard the name pronounced during my youth. But mostly I heard it as my father said it: coming down hard and nasal on the first syllable as though trying to crush the life out of it. Horden was my father's place and it was understood from the satisfyingly dry and resilient sound of those two syllables that in Horden everything a man needed to be a man was already in place.

My father's family were miners, working the narrow seams five miles out under the North Sea, lying in spaces only eighteen inches deep, often in water, hacking into the coal with picks or a primitive coal cutting machine called a nig-nog. They had to walk the miles from the pit bottom to the coalface, bent double for much of the way, and they weren't paid till they got there. Bob, the eldest of my father's uncles, was the first to get out, invalided with pneumoconiosis. Charlie, the next, went south to work on the railways, Hal to a factory in the Midlands. Only Jack stayed on. But they all died young – in their late thirties or early forties – mostly of heart attacks, and this, we were given to understand, was because of the strain imposed on them by the punitive physical labour they had undertaken since they were hardly more than children. It was only my grandfather, the one who, I was led to believe, was a bit cleverer, had a bit more vision than the others – Percy, the socialist, the 'great' trade unionist – who had managed to get a job at the surface and lived on into his sixties.

As a child, Horden – the dignity with which the miners bore the cruelty of their labours, the richness of its communal life, the beauty of the countryside through which my father had roamed as a boy, his schooling, which had mixed the excitement of intellectual discovery with what I perceived of as a Dickensian darkness and brutality – was part of my inner landscape, inculcated into me by my father with the same visceral narrative intensity with which he described not only his own experiences of the Second World War, but his father's during the Great War. For me, it was all part of the hardship and cruelty of earlier lives; of the inescapable discomfort, the essential horror of the existences of people who had lived before me. But if Horden was part of the world from which we were now escaping into brightness and modernity, the dignity and the resourcefulness and the sheer physical resilience of its inhabitants were to be remembered, and to be drawn on.

And yet Horden itself remained physically remote. I suppose when I was a young child we must have called on my grandparents, but on our visits to the North-east we stayed with my father's sister Mollie and her husband Fred, both teachers, at their house in Easington Village – the nearest thing to a middle-class enclave in that world of pit heaps and colliery rows. My sole memory of Horden was of driving through pouring rain on a winter's afternoon, trying to find the house in Fifth Street where my father had been born, only to find that the entire street had been demolished a few months before.

Even then the raw Durham world was uncomfortably alien. My sister and I always felt far closer to our mother's family – modest, old-fashioned farming people from North Yorkshire – than we did to the loquacious combative Durham folk, who all knew each other, and assumed they knew you too whether you liked it or not.

Through the subsequent years, which saw our parents' divorce, we had less and less to do with this world. It became increasingly vague and remote, till it was hardly more than a memory. Indeed the whole of the country outside London seemed to recede until, although we had both been born in Yorkshire, we could hardly even claim to be Northerners any longer.

My father now lived on the Pacific coast of Canada. But on each of his visits to Britain, once every one or two years, he would make a visit to the North, to Horden, and each time he would find it more changed. Horden colliery had closed in 1986, and there were now only two working pits in the area.

Afterwards in London, he would make it almost an article of faith to tell the old stories, to recreate in words, usually in some Soho trattoria, the world of his childhood – and each time he told it, the story became more idealised. In the Horden of his mind, there had been no crime, and such were the persuasive skills of the union leaders – exemplified by his father – there had been little need for strikes. Such men were dedicated to the elevation of their class, who as far as one could gather had little need of being elevated, since men and women lived in a condition of mutual harmony and respect, the women being not only paragons of domestic order, but capable of producing simple local dishes such as pease pudding and pickled pork salad to a standard that would grace any Parisian table, while every man was a connoisseur of Italian opera. There was some drunkenness, but that was only among 'a few idiots'. People had to make their own entertainment, but that was not difficult since people did not have the desire for incessant amusement they did today.

While listening to some of the grimmer details of the pit work, it would occur to me that I should try to write something about my forebears, that there was 'good material' here that should not be wasted. But then I would remember that these people had been 'Geordies', the sort of people who in my southern chauvinism I now characterised as 'ignorant Northerners' – the sort of people who could be seen scurrying in packs on the London underground, loudly, and no doubt drunkenly professing their inability to understand the tube map, giggling as they braved the snapping carriage doors. The sort of people whose endless domestic prattle filled the hours of the weekday soaps, the very sound of whose voices carried a weight of injustice, a sense that they had suffered more than anyone else – and if you weren't careful they would tell you all about it. Geordies, I reflected sadly, were nearly as bad as Scousers, and there was no way I was interested in writing about *them*.

One Christmas, however, two or three years ago, I found myself suffering from a viral infection, from which I seemed for a time unable to recover. In my weaker moments, I began to have visions of hallucinatory vividness, in which I revisited places far from the capital that had been of importance to me during my childhood and adolescence. I felt as though I were walking again beneath the crumbling limestone cliffs of South Wales, the hard wet sand

and the huge expanses of grey mud glowing silver in the winter
stillness. I saw again the place where we made fires on summer
evenings from the detritus washed up from the docks across the
bay – cable drums bigger than we were, rolled up over the rocks,
pieces of rope a foot thick, half-rotten packing cases plastered with
tar and paint that puckered and bubbled in the heat, sending sudden
flashes of strangely coloured flame into the darkening sky. I decided
suddenly that I must revisit these places as soon as possible – felt,
in fact, in my state of feverish intensity that I had been damaging
myself in some way by allowing myself to become estranged from
them.

One afternoon, several weeks later, sitting in the sepulchral
dimness of a London basement, still fairly weak, I had the idea of
making a journey through Britain that I would record in words – a
journey that would have no purpose other than to 'find something
for myself'.

In my mind's eye, our country beyond the suburbs of the capital
had dissolved into a perpetual detour of ring roads and retail parks,
studded with 'heritage sites' selling sanitised, prepackaged concep-
tions of the past. Britain was a country where people were rapidly
losing any sense of a shared life and culture other than was granted
them through the mass media, yet lived in places that were, at the
same time, becoming more and more the same; where one suburban
street densely lined with the cars of its invisible inhabitants would
be the same as another hundreds of miles away; a country the length
and breadth of which could be travelled without having to interact
meaningfully with anyone, without having to feel anything.

Now, however, it was time to go beyond this sense of a country
that was itself derived at least in part from advertising and the
summations of newspaper journalists, to go beyond the usual clichés
by which British people try to define their cultural identity, to find
things with their own flint-like validity that would re-establish my
emotional and spiritual connections with the land I came from. It
would be a journey not only through time and space, but imagination and memory, a journey which it seemed to me at that time of
'moral malaise' and national crisis in identity, every British person
should try to make. And as a writer I had the opportunity to do
it.

I decided then and there that since everything had, as far as
I knew, begun for me and my family in Horden, I would start
the journey there. I also had the thought that as my father's sister
Mollie, whom I had seen only twice in the preceding ten years,

had died the previous summer, there might be much that should
be recovered now, before it disappeared for ever.

It was mid-March before I set out on what I conceived of as an
exploratory foray to the North. Mollie's husband Fred met me at
the station in Durham. With his ruddy, clear-browed features and
his thick hair that had been silver even when I was a child, he seemed
hardly to have changed at all. It was pouring with rain.

As we were negotiating one of the roundabouts around the centre
of Peterlee, the new town ten miles east of Durham in which Fred
now lived, I noticed a sign pointing off to the left. 'Horden' was all
it said. Although I had come here with the express purpose of visiting
Horden, it still came as a slight shock to me that this name, which carried with it such deep and profoundly personal resonances, also had
a physical existence so tangible that people had actually put up road
signs pointing to it. Not only that – we must have been very near it.

'How far is Horden?' I asked.

'About a mile,' said Fred, in his changeless imperturbable tones.
'I'll take you there in the morning.'

So, next morning, twenty years after my last visit, I found
myself in the car with Fred, cresting the brow of the hill – the
bank, as they called it – catching my first glimpse of the leaden-grey
roofs of Horden. The sky, radiating a troubled brilliance as the sun
tried to break through the grey disorder of cloud, was, after the
cramped vistas of London, dauntingly immense. But the roofs of
Horden and the houses beneath them, seemed in their drab colours,
their inverted, inscrutable plainness to be looking inwards, only on
themselves. And I received from that first glimpse a curious frisson
of both foreboding and familiarity, before we descended the bank
and the buildings began to tuck themselves into a fold in the land
beneath the bare fields that rose beyond them towards the sea and
the inklike horizon.

Then suddenly we were bowling along the streets of the village. The sun had come out, which made one more aware than
ever of the presence of the wind; the dark pavements glimmered
intermittently as the shadows of the great clouds passed over the
village, the surrounding headlands seeming to shudder, their bright
grasses rippling furiously, as we moved quickly, perhaps too quickly,
between the different parts of the village. 'There's the Co-op,' said
Fred, pointing to a broad brick building that dominated one of the
most prominent corners of the village, 'where your grandad always
insisted everyone did their shopping.'

On the right were interminable rows of low terraced bungalows, made like most of the village from a red brick – not the rich and reassuring orange of the South, but a dour and mottled brown, stained to a liverish purple by decades of coal dust. 'That end house,' said Fred, pointing to the end of a row so exactly like the others I could never have found it again, 'that's where your great-grandfather lived, up until he died.' My great-grandfather! He had always been for me a figure of the remote, irrecoverably distant past, described either as 'a real Victorian patriarch, absolutely unshakable in his convictions' or 'a very stubborn and stupid man', depending what mood my father was in. I could still remember the shock I had felt on learning that a member of my family, a miner indeed, had been a Conservative. The story was that he and my grandfather, Percy, had quarrelled violently about politics, only days before my father was due to be born, and the old man had cast Percy, and his heavily pregnant wife, Jenny, from the family home, out into the howling night. The two men had never spoken again. I was surprised now at the smallness and the relatively suburban appearance of the house in which this bogey-man had ended his days.

But I had hardly time to reflect on this before Fred was pointing out another landmark. 'That's where Mary lives. You remember Mary?'

Of course. Mary. Percy's second wife. I could hardly recall my grandmother, who had died when I was three, but I could remember Mary. A cheerful round-faced woman, she had always seemed somehow more tractable than my other Northern relatives. I was looking forward to seeing her.

We visited various other sites of family interest: the council house on a rather bleak estate above the north end of the village where my grandfather had spent the latter part of his life; the council house in a quiet cul-de-sac near the Co-operative Store where my father had grown up. What struck me most was not so much the ageless, styleless drabness of these places, and indeed of virtually everything in the village – the red brick schools, the box-like, brick bus shelters – as the very familiarity of these things. Although I had never lived anywhere remotely like a pit village, I felt I was somehow back in the world as it had been, or as I had sensed it to be in my early childhood.

We passed the allotments. From a distance, the pigeon crees, picked out by their brilliantly painted doors and palings among the disorder of sheds and battered caravans, made the place look like a devastated gypsy encampment. High fences of corrugated iron, old doors and scrap wood shielded the small plots, blocking out any view of the crops, though as far as I could tell many were used only for dumping scrap and old furniture.

On a bare piece of land above the seaward side of the allotments stood three new factory units. This was where the coke ovens had been. And this, I was surprised to learn, was where my grandfather had worked. I'd always thought he'd been a miner. 'No, he was a cokeman. He was one of the founders of the Cokemen's Union branch in Horden.' I tried momentarily to imagine what coke ovens would be like. Fred said that when the wind was blowing in the wrong direction, the smoke and sparks used to blast all over the houses that lay only yards away on the other side of the allotments, and over the allotments themselves. What about the vegetables that were grown there? 'They had to wash them well,' said Fred with a rueful laugh.

On a kind of promontory overlooking the sea, adjacent to the road that led back into the main shopping street of the village, was the place where the pit head had been. The whole area was grassed over. A single pulley wheel had been set in a brick plinth, benches arranged facing it, among beds of brittle, thornlike shrubs, as though around a very bleak war memorial. But there was no explanatory plaque, and there was no one else around – only a considerable amount of dog shit, and the wreckage of crisp packets and soft drinks cartons impaled on the shrubs rattling in the wind that sighed and sang over the bare headland. Generally I had been surprised at the extent to which the people of Horden must have thrown their litter down where they stood. I would have expected of their personal habits a native rigour and control, however rudimentary their surroundings.

As we were turning the car round near the Working Men's Club, I noticed a kind of alley bearing the name 'Hudson Street'. I pointed it out to Fred. 'Aye. They named it after your grandfather. There's a Hudson Avenue as well.' I felt considerable pride, and a certain importance, as though the blazoning of our name in this way over the thoroughfares of Horden had given me sudden seigneurial rights over the place. Hudson Street! Hudson Avenue! I'd always known that my grandfather had been active in his trade union, and that like Mollie and Fred he was involved in local politics and the Labour Party. But I hadn't realised he'd been such a significant figure. Before I'd left London, I'd asked my sister what she could remember of him. She said she couldn't really remember anything – she was younger than me – but she had known from an early age that he was committed to the 'raising of the working class'. Of course! The Raising of the Working Class. As far as I was concerned, that was what Horden had always been about.

I can remember my grandfather's shoes on the white maple floor of our house in South Wales. They were big and black and highly polished, their leather soles so thick and hard they looked as though they would dent the delicate wood at their very touch. The house had huge windows overlooking the Bristol Channel; there was a courtyard with rocks from the nearby beach, tropical plants, and on the walls, prints and constructions by my father and his friends. But while some would have sat looking out at the still milk-like sea and the vaporous outline of the Somerset coast, Percy sat with his back to the windows, attending to his pipe, his knees apart, his feet in the big black shoes flat and firm on the blond floor. As I remember it, the tweed of his jacket was of good quality, and he was wearing a cap of the same material – though I can't believe now that he could have been wearing a cap indoors.

I can remember him engaging me in conversation, challenging me, his eyes above the pipe he was lighting the same level as mine, bright, mockingly humorous, and browner and darker than the tobacco he smoked – and yet at the same time uncertain, for he didn't know people like my eight-year-old self any more than I knew people like him. And proud as he might have been that it was *his* son who had called this house into being, there was much in it and what it represented that was incomprehensible to him.

I can remember that I always felt rather awkward, rather intimidated in his presence, his comments, his gentle teasing, seeming in his extraordinary short-vowelled speech almost brutally familiar. Percy – like his clothes and his big, black shoes, his name marked him out as part of the old cruel ugly world, the world of the smoke and the grinding steel of the machines with which he worked. Yet I understood even then that he was himself in some way partly responsible for our release from it.

His hair, as I remember it, was very, very dark. It never got the chance to go grey, because he died the following year.

Over the next few days, I did little but ask Fred questions about my grandfather. He had become for me suddenly a figure of intense interest and curiosity. He was – if one were to go by the ties of blood – the nearest example to me (one could not count my father for he had long since transformed himself into something totally

different) of that traditional figure of awe and revulsion – the dark
and unacknowledged *other* of every middle-class Englishman – the
Working Class Man. He seemed to me then, as I had seen him
seated in his tweed jacket, with his pipe and the cloth cap he had
probably not been wearing, a figure as pregnant with fascination
as the women of the Gambia had once been for me, clothed in
their brilliant turbans and the purple exoticism of their blackness.
Suddenly everything Percy had ever thought or felt or done was of
urgent, overriding importance. If I was to come to a closer and more
profound understanding of Horden, it would be through Percy. It
was Percy, who had lived nearly all his life in Horden, Percy, with
his glorious but vague political achievements, Percy, of whom I had
such a small, but vivid memory, but about whom I knew virtually
nothing, who I now saw as my strongest claim on the place.

'He loved gardening,' said Fred. 'He never had an allotment. He
always had his own garden, because they were always in council
houses. He never showed, never went in for competitions. It was
just vegetables for the table. Mind, I think he always put a few
chrysanths in as well.

'He was a bit suspicious of me at first. Then when he found out
I was planning to buy a greenhouse, he warmed up a bit. He soon
had me helping out the back. But it was really your grandfather who
was responsible for me joining the Labour Party.'

I could still remember the way they used to say the words
'the Labour Party' – the way I used to hear them in my childhood.
They had an almost ritual resonance – like the password to a more
exalted state; redolent of an almost medicinal goodness.

In 1935, Emmanuel Shinwell had taken the local constituency,
Easington, from the 'traitor' Ramsay MacDonald, and he'd held it
till he retired in 1970. It was he who had coined the much quoted
phrase that in that part of the world they didn't bother to count
the votes, they just weighed them. I'd always felt that the Labour
Party had been these people's lives. Fred had been Shinwell's constituency agent. And whenever I went into a polling booth, I could
feel the presence of Percy, Fred and the others, as though they were
physically standing over me.

'He saw what I'd done with the scouts and the youth club in
Thornley, organising sports days and raffles. He said if I could
do all that for the scouts, I should be in the Labour Party. So I
joined.

'He'd always wanted your dad to go into politics. He never
could understand what he was doing with his art. He thought he

was wasting his time ... Mind, he sharp changed his mind when he saw your dad was getting somewhere with it.'

How about Jane? I asked Fred. What was she like?

He looked blank.

Percy's wife.

'You mean your grandmother!'

Of course, my grandmother. It still came as a surprise to me that I had such close and definite links with these people, whom I saw through a kind of anthropological lens as representatives of a fascinating but alien mode of existence.

'Jenny!' said Fred. 'Her name was Jane, but she was always called Jenny.'

I could just remember her. A warm, white-haired presence, her features vague, wreathed in a silvery haze.

'She was tiny,' said Fred. 'But she was very quick tempered. She could fly off the handle at anything. At first I was a bit disconcerted by it. But I soon got used to it, because as soon as it had happened it was over.'

What had she got annoyed about?

'Little things. Untidiness. People just throwing things down when they came in the house – like your dad did. But she was always very welcoming. Whenever your dad came back from the army or from college, he'd always have someone with him, and she'd always be pleased to see them. She'd have a party for anyone, your grandmother – bacon cooking, the lot.'

Before I left London, I'd asked my mother what she could remember of Percy. He had, she said, been a great talker. What about? Politics, trade unions, anything. But then, they'd all been good talkers. Mollie, with her lean, strong featured face, had always been a great raconteur – and my father of course. That's how she remembered them. All talking. All having their say. Putting the world to rights. Saying what *should* and *shouldn't* be done. Percy, the father, was the one who held the floor, but the mother would still have her say.

As I sat in the Galilee Chapel of Durham Cathedral, I reflected for the first time since I'd decided to come North, that my separateness from that world, from Horden and all that it represented, was at least partly self-created. As I sat sheltering from the rain, shivering in a corner of the bare and draughty chamber, its rows of serrated arches not so much adorning as bitten out of the grey stone – the hard Northern light filling it, scouring it, so it seemed, of all mysticism, all romanticism, all soft, comfortable beauty, leaving only this hull of flintlike, accusatory hardness – it occurred to me that as a child, the Northern world had seemed as harsh and unyielding as the cold, hard surfaces of the chapel. It wasn't just the unrelenting physical ugliness – for in those days, what was now rolling farmland had been riven by a pit heap round every corner, and the colliery winding gear and belching chimneys stood over every hamlet – but the very brightness and hardness of the people themselves – my relatives – people who in the blunt forcefulness of their speech, the strident communality of their way of life, seemed to live wholly outside and not inside themselves. It was a world and a way of living that seemed to mock, to negate anything soft, anything lovely, anything that was beautiful for its own sake – all the little psychological comforts with which one attempted to pad one's childhood existence. That world had always represented something from which I longed to escape. And my father, as the primary representative of that world in my life, though he had in a sense created me more than anyone else, had always been an alien and obtrusive presence.

As I turned the corner by Safeway, and felt the full force of the March wind off the North Sea, I suddenly realised why I felt so exposed, so out of place in Peterlee (and I had seen people pointing at me quite openly as I passed across the broad forecourt of the precinct). Everyone was in fluorescent tracksuits, stone-washed jeans and trainers, bum freezing cotton blousons exposing T-shirted chests, shirts open at pink throats, hair cropped short at the back and sides prickling, bristling in the wind like the brushes that appeared to have scoured the raw bare legs of the girls. Everyone seemed to be smoking. I remembered somewhere back in my childhood, at a time I had almost forgotten – that age when one seemed to be per-manently in the wrong, to be somehow out of tempo with the rest of humanity – hearing my father's scorn for the scarf: the badge of the hypochondriac, the sign of the snuffler, the mollycoddled shirker of honest discomfort who tempted the fates with his greasy muffler. To wear a scarf was to invite ill health, and nobody in Peterlee was wearing a scarf – except me.

   Later, an even older, but gentler memory came to me, a memory I held not so much as an image or a form of words, but as a dimly recalled physical sensation – that my great-grandfather, Percy's father, had never washed his back. He had left it permanently black, because, like many miners, he had believed that to wash it would not only weaken this most crucial and, to a miner, most vulnerable part of the body, it would diminish him in some critical and essential way.

Seated in his easy chair by the back window, Fred was often quiet and withdrawn, looking out at his garden and the dark pines of Castle Eden Dene, often for hours on end. He seemed abstracted, remote in his grief – an expression of unchanging, placid bemusement on his regular nordic features. But then again, it was difficult to be really sure, as he had always been like that. Although he had been a headmaster, a JP, and the secretary of Easington Labour Party, he seldom initiated conversation, and spoke in his evenly modulated tones only when he had good reason. Fred, I always felt, never did, said or felt anything unless it had a clear and worthwhile purpose in view. And this had always made me feel slightly awkward with him, for I had devoted my life, as my father had, to things he would no doubt have found pointless.

In the evenings, however, when we talked, I realised that although there were certain things – most of the things I cared about – that could never be discussed, were meaningless in this context, and although he treated me in a sense as much as an alien as I regarded him, he recognised me. In his mind, adrift in the world of Mollie, and the characters, many of them my relatives, who had populated their life together, I and my father and Percy somehow overlapped. He would refer to Percy as 'your father', sometimes correcting himself, but often not noticing he had said it. I felt at such moments that I had a stake, that I had played a part, that I had an identity in an earlier world that I did not yet know about.

This was the world of our conversations, a world, I now realised, I had known virtually nothing about, the world, it was acknowledged, without anything really having been said, that we *should* talk about. It was the world as Percy had known it, the world of my father's childhood and Fred's own childhood. A world, the traces of which were fast disappearing, which had in a sense created Horden and all the mining villages in this area. For while I had assumed that my family had been in Horden from time immemorial, in fact, a hundred years ago, Horden hadn't even existed. Horden was only as old as the century, the bore hole having been sunk on the day Edward VII came to the throne, and the village being brought into being only in the service of the pit. That was the time when the earth and the air sang to the rhythm of work, when the women were as a much a part of the colliery as the men, serving their fathers, brothers, husbands and sons, who under the three-shift system were coming and going every hour of the day and night, constantly needing to be fed and bathed and clothed. When the miners, men like my great-uncle Bob, took it as their right to take a little bit more from the coal owner by poaching on his land. When many of the miners, coming off their shifts at eleven in the morning, would later work a couple of hours on the local farms, slaving in the fields in the summer, mucking out the byres and stables in the winter. When the men, waiting at the crees for the returning pigeons, talked of nothing but mining and the affairs of mining – the owners, the unions, the conditions. 'That was where you got your political training,' said Fred. 'You used to stand there for hours as a boy, just listening. I was at Thornley, and your dad would be doing the same at Horden. That's what gave him his personality, his "social concern", if you like.' Fred's father had been under-manager at Thornley, and people had naturally assumed Fred himself would be a Conservative. But as a child he'd never separated himself from the people around him. He'd gone to the same school as them. He'd played football with the miners' sons; he'd gone out with their daughters. So when the time came, he had stood at the crees with the rest of them. In those days no Protestant child would cross the 'green line' in Thornley, but down the pit they were all one. Down a pit there could be no such thing as a strict division of labour, because another man's life might depend on your immediate assistance. In those days it seemed, men had felt an almost mystical sense of their vocation as miners – fuelled by the blood of those who had 'gone before' – of their destiny bound up in their 'cavill', the lots they drew to see where they would work in the pit, whether in low, dangerous, half-flooded seams, or in warm dry conditions, where the roof was as high as a house and the coal yards thick. Of course, it had been awful. One knew it had been awful. But the awfulness had all been part of the richness, and, dare one even think it, the romance of that world.

During the days I would wander the streets of Horden; looking at the houses of the remaining colliery rows, some derelict, others haphazardly gentrified with pebbledash, carriage lamps and 'Georgian' doors; at the dingy, inadequate shops; and at the people: the teenage mothers with their prams, their features pasty and resigned beneath their outgrown perms, their legs bare to the biting North Sea gusts; the old miners on their way to the betting-shops, taking the broken pavements an inch at a time; the children, their skinhead haircuts echoing unconsciously the heads of the children in the Thirties, shaven against lice; the sea coal men, in their huge tank-like lorries with their closed-in, furtive expressions; at the neglected gardens and broken fences of the council estates. 'Well, Horden always was a rough place, you know,' said Fred. At times it was difficult to imagine that even Percy, let alone my father, had come from a place like this.

2

Queer Lives

IN DURHAM CITY, not far from the magnificent sandstone viaduct that carries the London to Edinburgh trains over the top of the city, behind the row of shops that leads from the Methodist Chapel down to the old Miners' Hall (now a disco) – but out of sight of any of these monuments – is the bus station that serves the outlying villages. Beneath the deep eaves, the twilit murk relieved only by the glow of a neon strip light, the queues of passengers stood in hunched and sodden reverie. Litter spilled from the brimming bins, and in the febrile half light the water trickling from people's raincoats and umbrellas took on a faintly sinister appearance as though it were oozing thick and unhealthy from between the gum-blackened flagstones. When a bus pulled into one of the 'quays', the people waited, then began to move slowly and silently forward, with a curious abject lowering of the head. Even the lads sprawled on the window ledges behind had been reduced to silence.

The quay second from the bottom served the villages to the immediate west of Durham, villages whose names printed on a neon box over the head of the queue resounded for me as potently as any I had come across in more exotic parts of the world – Ushaw Moor, New Brancepeth, Alum Waters, Old Esh. For these were the places from which my grandparents had come originally. My grandfather, Percy Hudson, had been born in Ushaw Moor in 1897. But the person I really associated with that village I had never visited, was my great-grandfather, James Hudson. His features as I had seen them in an old photograph, on the back of which was written simply 'James

Hudson of Ushaw Moor' – hard-bitten above the stiff Edwardian collar, remote in their steely narrow-eyed indifference, softened only by one of the large moustaches typical of the period – were for me burnt irrevocably into the very sound and conception of the name Ushaw Moor (or Usher Mooer or 'Shermower, as they said it).

One afternoon I took a bus up the Deerness Valley. The stream, a tributary of the Wear, ran through a narrow and thinly wooded glade between the broad and draughty bank sides. Ushaw Moor, a grid of dark colliery rows, with its Working Men's Club, its Miners' Hall and its Co-operative Store, all in the style I had come to think of as Colliery Baroque – bits of cheap and nasty classical detailing slapped cursorily on to huge box-like structures in red brick – lay on one side of the valley. On the other was the much smaller village of New Brancepeth, where my grandmother Jenny Turner was born, where her father had managed the Store (Co-op) greengrocer's. In New Brancepeth you could still get a flavour of the old semi-rural life of the mid-Durham pit villages. Ushaw Moor, however, was dominated to the east by a vast post-war housing estate.

In the County Records Office I had found the address where my great-grandparents had been living at the time of my grandfather's birth: No. 6 Water Row. I imagined a line of lean-to hovels, encrusted on to the back of a hardly more stable structure, around which, over which, and occasionally through which, the seasonal torrents would pour. Near the war memorial I saw a woman cleaning the windows of a newsagent's. She looked up at my approach, a smile of alarm spreading over her features.

'I don't know it.'

'It's a street somewhere round here.'

The smile broadened into a grimace. 'I've never heard of it.'

'It's where my great-grandparents lived. A long time ago. Maybe it's one of the old colliery rows that were pulled down.'

She winced as she shook her head. 'I've never heard of it.'

I thought that her husband, who stood at the counter, might be more knowledgeable. I got half a foot over the threshold.

'There never was a one.'

'It's suppo . . .'

'There never was a one.'

'Maybe it was . . .'

'I've lived here all my life, and it's not there because there never was a one.'

As I came out, a group of schoolgirls was approaching along the pavement. One of them, a tall, brawny girl with a shapeless mop of hair, was directly in my path. I caught her intent look. She imagined that finally, from some residual Pavlovian courtesy, I was going to make way for her.

No, you don't, I thought. Not here. Not in this shithole.

At the last moment she leapt aside.

'Queer lives, aren't they?'

'How do you mean?'

'When you look back. Sometimes, I don't remember getting into bed. Then all at once, I open my eyes, and it'll all come back. That I should have done this and I should have done the other. But I wouldn't have my life over again. I definitely wouldn't.'

I had a photograph of Percy Hudson, aged about seventeen, his arms folded, in the uniform of the Royal Navy, for which he had recently volunteered. A big nosed, big eared lad with a short back and sides, his eyes and mouth dark gashes across his lean, raw features, creased in a smirk not so much cocky, as imbued with the natural, apparently indomitable confidence of youth. A likely lad, ready to face whatever life threw at him. Over the next four years he was to take part in the Gallipoli campaign, the Battle of Jutland and the surrender of the German navy at Scapa Flow, and to undergo experiences, now completely unknown to us, that were to make him a lifelong and active socialist. Looking at the photograph one might have thought, 'The face of youth, caught before the horror of the Great War.' The most significant thing for me however was that, the uniform apart, it was the exact image of my younger brother, a poet and designer of neo-classical typefaces in Vancouver.

There was so much about Percy's life that seemed already irrecoverable. He had only died in 1966, at the age of sixty-eight, but the number of people who could remember him, even in Horden, was dauntingly few.

My father, of course, had plenty to say about his parents, about their ever loving relationship, about his mother, Jenny, quick-witted and endlessly competent and resourceful, and his father, the dogged trade unionist, pragmatically idealistic and incorruptible. But I found this retrospective reverence as much an obstacle as an assistance in seeing these people as they really were.

I wanted to see Percy with all his foibles, idiosyncrasies, and even his failings – as his workmates and his colleagues on the Parish Council and Labour Party had seen him. Had he been quiet or talkative in these public arenas? Was he easy going or cantankerous? Did he have ideas of his own, or did he simply follow the prevailing drifts of opinion? Had he been an astute judge of character and situation, who knew when to speak and when to shut up? Or had he been a bit of a bore?

The woman to whom I was talking, Mrs Graham, was one of the very few people left alive who had known my grandparents well. We were in her room in Wilding Lodge, an old people's home in Horden. Outside, at the bottom of the grass slope, the rush hour traffic on the main Sunderland road, the road known as the Top, was still quite thick, but in here, within the walls of Wilding Lodge, the night was already well advanced, for the residents had their tea – their main evening meal – at four-thirty.

She really was tiny, her neat, kitten-like, but exceedingly wizened features seeming even smaller behind a pair of large and very thick glasses. On her feet were a pair of enormous trainers, for her feet were, she said, bad. We sat forward in our chairs by the window, talking in low, conspiratorial tones.

'I don't go down there much,' she gestured in the direction of the dining-room and lounge. 'I've never made friends easily. I've always been the sulky type. I take after my father. But Jenny and me were always very friendly. We lived in with them, you know, when we first came to Horden, because they were here before us. We were with them seven months, till we got our house. Jenny had yer dad, and I had our Lily. My husband Jack was on the same shift with Percy Hudson at the coke ovens. So we all got on very well together.

'But I knew them both a long while before that. When first we moved to New Brancepeth, when I was fifteen, Jenny Turner comes to the house, and she says, "You're Church, aren't you?" I says, "Yes." "And do yer dance?" I says, "Oh, yes." "Well," she says, "let's all join the Girls' Friendly Society at the Mission Hall, and be together." But she wasn't well, you know . . . when she died. She was getting very deaf. But I never saw her in a temper. She was always such a lively little thing. She was tiny, much smaller than me, and she was always rushing around, always making something. Even when she was dancing she was in a hurry. But everybody liked her. And I remember in the war, the First World War, she looked canny in her WACS uniform.'

But what about Percy? What had he been like?

'I met Jack, when I was sixteen, and his sister was knocking about with a lad who lived in Ushaw Moor, next door to Hudsons. So that's how we met Percy. Very quiet he was in those days. He'd make conversation, but he wasn't always laughing and joking the way we were. He was always a bit on the sober side.

'We all went to church together on a Sunday morning. Then we used to go up on to the fells and come down by Brandon Bank. That was our walk, every Sunday, after church.'

Was Percy good looking?

'Oh, he was nice looking when first I knew him. All Hudsons' lads were nice looking. That Hal and Charlie. They were canny. They were the younger ones. Then there was Bob, the eldest, and another one, but I can't remember him, because he and Percy didn't have much to do with each other. Did you know Hudsons' lads?'

The way she said it, they might have been people a year or two older than me at school. To the extent that I'd thought about my grandfather's four brothers, they'd been dim figures, hardly differentiated, around Percy's more sharply edged persona, figures who had about them some of the tragic, wan athléticism of the doomed Adonises of the Great War – though their Passchendaele was not the trenches but the narrow seams. And if one looked closely one could see more clearly their paleness, their gauntness, their faint look of malnourishment. I had heard about their poaching, their putting out lines, their crabbing, and these activities had always seemed to have about them an air of desperation – of real hunger.

Now however, I felt as though I had only just missed them – as though in the great bus queue of time, they had got on the one just before mine.

'I knew them all,' said Mrs Graham. 'Nice lot of people. Very quiet. No bother there. I knew the five lads, and the three lasses. Winnie was the eldest, then Martha, and Annie was the youngest. And I knew the mother, and the father. They only lived along here, you know.' She gestured out of the window along the Top Road.

All these people – first my great-uncles, then my great-grandfather – people I had assumed lost in the obfuscating fog of the generations, and now my great-grandmother, a person to whom I'd never given any thought at all ... This woman was pulling them all from the air. Suddenly their tread along the very pavements outside these windows seemed to have been tantalisingly recent. The other side of the road was Thirteenth Street, the highest of the colliery rows, the doors of the dour flat-fronted houses opening straight on to the main road. A little further along was where my great-grandparents and all the rest of the family had lived when they first came to Horden. I felt that if I looked very, very hard, I'd be able to see my great-grandfather, James Hudson, stocky and poker-faced in his cloth cap, walking doggedly and intently past. What had he really been like? What had my great-grandmother, Isabella Hudson, been like? I felt that if I was to understand Horden, I had to make these people come alive. I had to see and feel and understand their presence in this place.

Had Mrs Graham ever heard, I ventured, that Percy and his father didn't get on?

'It could be,' she said. 'Because the father never came to Percy's house. Jenny used to go up to their house, but Percy never went near.'

In Jesmond, a quiet Victorian suburb of Newcastle, I met Percy's last surviving sibling, his youngest sister, my great-aunt Nan. She stood in the doorway of her house, a tall grey-haired woman in her early-seventies, well-built, with a broad face and dark unflinching eyes set rather close together. 'I'd have known you anywhere,' she said, scrutinising me with a knowing grin. 'He's got the look, hasn't he?' Fred and her companion, a very tall man with gold-framed glasses and twinkly eyes, both laughed. 'I'd have known he was a Hudson anywhere. Come in, pet.'

When I'd settled myself in the comfortable living room, I asked her if she could remember anything about my great-grandfather, James Hudson.

'My father!' she said, with a proprietorial firmness that seemed to obviate anyone else's claims on him. 'Oh, he was lovely!'

Lovely? I'd always imagined my great-grandfather as *hard*. A man from the days before comfort – all bristle and muscle. A life lived through gritted teeth. A life like freezing water down the back of the neck. A man of rigid Victorian principle who had cast his own son and his heavily pregnant wife out into the howling night. *Lovely*?

'He wasn't a big man,' said Nan. 'None of the Hudsons were tall. And he was very quiet. But he was very sure of himself. Oh, he was sure of himself! If he thought something, he knew he was right. He was absolutely right, and that was the end of it. Your father reminds me of him sometimes. When he's sitting in that chair where you're sitting, going on with his opinion about something – so sure he's right – I can almost hear my father talking.'

She produced a small brown book of sepia photographs set in gilt-edged mounts. Stiffly composed Victorian photographs flashed past, as she stood over me, quickly turning the pages. Somebody's father, somebody's uncles, somebody's sister. All too quick for me to take in. There was my great-grandfather's father, or was it his father's father. I was losing track of who was who. A stocky man in a very thick frock coat stiffly buttoned to the neck. Then, a rather handsome woman, her dress elegantly fitting at the breast and arms, artificially composed, with a dreamy child with long Alice-in-Wonderland hair. A succession of smart, but distant-looking young men. The last was a handsome, fair young man with a slip of a moustache and cold, rather disdainful eyes. 'That's my father,' said Nan.

The book was put back in a drawer. What had surprised me most about the pictures as they flashed so briefly before my eyes was the apparent affluence of these people, the quality of their clothes, their look of respectability and glacial complacent confidence – and indeed the fact that they'd had such photographs taken at all. I'd always imagined the generations before my grandfather to have lived in a condition of almost medieval poverty and darkness. But these people didn't even look like miners. I wondered for a moment if I'd been looking at the wrong family by mistake.

They had all, Nan said, come from a place called East Acklam, on the borders of the North and East Ridings of Yorkshire. Their father, Jackson Hudson, my great-great-grandfather, had moved North to the mines of Durham probably in the late 1880s, taking his three youngest sons – Hardy, Hal and James – with him. He had become some sort of high up official at Ushaw Moor Colliery.

Later, I had another look at his photograph. He stood beside his seated wife, and while she, with her set features and down-turned mouth, looked as distant, as remote from emotional recovery as a figure on an Egyptian tomb, the camera had caught a curious light in his eyes, the spurious, transparent emotionalism of a Dickens character.

I had always known the Hudson family had come originally from Yorkshire, that my great-grandfather's conservative attitudes were somehow rooted in the old agrarian world where the master knew best, and to know one's place was an essential part of one's pride and self respect. I'd imagined them generations before, bent to the cold furrows, living out their lives in a condition of wind-harried semi-serfdom. Now I found not only that James Hudson had himself been born into that world, but that the family's position within it had been quite different from what I had imagined. This man with his thick frock coat and his Pecksniffian quiff was no mere labourer. He had worked on Lord Zetland's estate training the great man's lurchers. When he moved to Ushaw Moor, he had ascended, apparently automatically, to a position of senior officialdom.

There was also a photograph of James as a round-faced, rather complacent three year old, seated on a *chaise longue* in a sort of

Highland cap and jacket, with the billowing skirts worn by children in those days, and on his feet a pair of enormous black boots. On the wall behind is what appears to be a kind of *trompe l'oeil* tapestry, and at his feet lies the recumbent form of one of Lord Zetland's lurchers. Are we in a photographer's studio, or in one of the loggias of the noble lord's mansion? Either way, these people clearly had a position of some substance in the lower echelons of the old world. They had a vested interest in its perpetuation. They were trusted, their skills valued by their employer, and they had come to identify with his values.

A whole new dimension of history was opening up for me, and this woman, hardly older than my father, with whom I was sitting, had lived in close, informal proximity to it.

'My father was a very intelligent man, you know,' said Nan. 'He had very beautiful copperplate handwriting, and he had a very good head for figures. He was a teacher at one time, in Doncaster. But by that time, his father was at Ushaw Moor. He wasn't well, and he wanted his sons to be with him. So Father had to give up teaching and go into mining. He always said it was the biggest mistake he ever made.'

By the time Nan was born, just after the First World War, the family had moved to Horden. 'My father was very quiet, and very particular, but he was always very nice to us children. He had a big garden on the other side of the Top Road, and we could help ourselves to anything we wanted. Young carrots, turnips, peas. Those were our sweets.

'We didn't have much, but I had a very happy childhood. I always thought of Horden as a very nice place. Although there were certain people we were told not to talk to.

'You see, in those days the village was divided into two parts – the top and the bottom. We were from the top, and we were told not to play with children from the bottom of the village. All the better people lived at the top of the village, and the poorer, rougher people lived in the lower streets. I went to the Higher Tops school, like your father before he went to the grammar school, and we never had many children there from the bottom of the village. Those that did come never seemed to be able to learn as much. We were told not to talk like them. We weren't allowed to talk pitmatic, and we weren't allowed to bring them to the house.'

Pitmatic – the dialect of the pits – was mostly old Norse words, with bits of dialect from all the different parts of the country from which the miners had come. The pronunciation and even the words varied from pit to pit, so it became a kind of code by which a miner's origins could be ascertained. I'd heard my father using the term 'pitmatic', and assumed he was joking. But it existed. That was the way the people at the bottom of the village had spoken.

'If my father heard us say "gan yem",' said Nan, 'he would make us say it correctly. We had to say "go home", pronouncing it very correctly.'

Until now I'd always attributed my father's small rise from the world of Horden – from the drudgery of manual labour to the professional classes – to a spontaneous burst of energy and intelligence on his part. Now I realised that he'd already been halfway there. His family were from the top of the village. And his grandfather, James, had once been a teacher – a pupil-teacher, no doubt, but a teacher none the less.

But how did Percy's socialism, born as I understood it from poverty, adversity and class solidarity, fit into this world of pettyfogging village distinctions?

'To tell you the truth,' said Nan. 'I never could get on with your grandfather. In fact, to tell you the truth, I couldn't stand him. He was very much older than me. But that wasn't the problem, because I could talk to Bob who was older than him, and I could talk to Jack who was just below him. No, the truth is, he had an argument with my father, he upset him, and I just couldn't forgive him for that.

'You see, up till then, the Hudsons had always been Conservatives. It was only Percy who became a socialist. He seemed to be all right before then. You could talk to him in a normal way. But when he got involved in the Cokeworkers' Union and the Labour Party, he seemed to become all toffee-nosed. He didn't seem to want to know the rest of us.

'I used to call him Lord Durham, because he used to walk round Horden as though he owned the place. I used to say to my mother, "I've just seen Lord Durham in the street." She used to say, "Now, now." But that's what he was like. He became friendly with those people, what was their name?'

'Cuthbertson,' said Fred.

'He was the drapery manager at the Co-op. Maybe Percy thought they were better than us. I don't know. Then when Jenny died, he couldn't wait to marry the Co-op manager's widow. He became a church warden, though whether he was religious, or whether it was just an excuse to wear a bigger and bigger trilby hat, I don't know.

'What caused the problem between your grandfather and my

father, I'm not precisely sure. But I think it must have had something to do with politics. I remember one night hearing a terrible
argument going on. I didn't dare go and see what was happening.
I asked my mother. She just said, "It's your father and our Percy."
But she wouldn't say what it was about. About a week later I was
walking along the street with my father. I would have been about
fourteen at the time. I saw Percy coming towards us. But he didn't
say anything, he just walked straight past. My father was obviously
upset, but he didn't say anything. I said, "What's the matter with our
Percy?" He said, "Something's happened, but I can't explain it."

'The next day I went to Percy's house. Jenny was in the kitchen.
I said, "Is our Percy here?" She said, "Yes. He's in the other room.
You'd better go through." He was sitting there, reading a newspaper.
He didn't look up. I walked over, and I pulled his newspaper down.
I said, "What d'you mean by ignoring your father in the street?" He
looked a bit embarrassed, but he just said, "Whatever's happened,
it's none of your business." After that, we didn't speak to each other.
If I went into a room and he was there, he'd just grunt and lift his
newspaper.'

I was getting confused. In the version I'd heard from my father,
Percy was still living with his parents when the great argument took
place, and James Hudson had put him and the heavily pregnant
Jenny 'on to the streets', only weeks before my father was due to
be born. It had been that unforgivable action that had caused the
rift between them. But if that was true, Nan would have been only
three, not fourteen as she had said.

Fred was sceptical of my father's story. 'As far as I know
Mollie was alive when it happened.'

'It was a long time after that,' said Nan. 'They were living
in that house along from the Co-op by then.

'Your grandfather and my father didn't speak for seven years.
They'd both made their minds up, and neither would back down.
They must have been very similar in a way. They were both absolutely sure they were right, and you couldn't reason with either of
them. But they were both intelligent. Maybe that was the problem.

'But in the end my father had a terrible death, as you know.
I was working the day he died. I was a nurse, you know, dear.
When I got home, he'd already died. I met your grandfather, Percy,
coming out of the sick room. He'd been with him at the last, and
he looked very upset. I said, "How dare you come here! You didn't
speak to him for years, and you have the cheek to come here now!"
He said, "I know. I regret it."

'I only saw Percy a few times after that. The last time he was with Mary, you know, his second wife. It was at a funeral. He invited us back to the house afterwards. He seemed to be making an effort to be friendly. He died shortly afterwards.'

Later, I reflected on the epic struggle of wills between the two men. The father with his obdurate sense of his place in the scheme of things, attempting to wield his dour, patriarchal authority over a son caught up in the dynamic new world of action and change. And the son, his heroic sense of purpose all too easily transmuting itself into a dogged, curmudgeonly sense of his own rightness. And yet for all its destructiveness, for all the misery it had caused them and those around them, there was perhaps something not totally unadmirable about this obstinacy. People in those days did not regard their progeny as an extension of their own egos. These people had not been interested in *relating to each other* as equals and friends as fathers and sons are today. These people had been *men*, in the old fashioned sense of the word. They had *spoken* on a matter of principle, and they were prepared to make almost any sacrifice rather than go back on their word. That was an option that was simply not open to them.

I always used to think I couldn't imagine anything worse than having been on a battleship in the First World War – those terrifying vessels, like towering cities of iron and steel surmounted by their great columns of black smoke, improbably afloat on the heaving oceans. At the age of sixteen, Percy had been a stoker down in the very bowels of one of these ships, stripped virtually naked to shovel coal into the roaring mouths of the great boilers, while all around the freezing immensity of the North Sea pressed against the iron sides. Percy had been down there during the battle of Jutland. The German navy had been prevented from breaking through the North Sea blockade. But six thousand men were killed on the British side alone during the twenty-four-hour engagement.

Shortly afterwards he answered a call for volunteers for the newly established Australian Navy, and was sent down to Portsmouth to join the giant battlecruiser H.M.A.S. *Australia*. On arriving, according to family legend, he went to the mess for refreshment after his long journey. The mess room was deserted, so he wandered into the galley. His proferred mess card was ignored, and a huge Australian cook aimed a cooking vessel at his head. 'Pick it outta that, ya pommie bastard!' The pan crashed off the wall behind him, and Percy leapt at his assailant. The two men were dragged down into the hold, stripped off and hurled at each other like dogs for the entertainment of the stokers. They were all outbackers, big raw men who looked on the war as an entertaining diversion from the rigours of life in the Central Australian wastes, and they bawled and hooted their approbation as the two men, the mountainous Aussie cook and the skinny Durham lad, slugged it out. Percy must have acquitted himself reasonably well, for he always spoke of his time among the Australians with great affection. He could have stayed on and been demobilised in Australia, but Jenny was in England – serving in the WACS, learning the intricacies of Edwardian cuisine in the officers' mess – so he returned to the Royal Navy in time to be present at the surrender of the German fleet at Scapa Flow in the Orkneys. He was on the great dreadnought *Colossus* when the Germans most ungallantly scuttled all their ships.

Percy's formal education had ended at the age of eleven, when the school in Ushaw Moor fell down. Before the war he'd been a butcher's boy at nearby Esh Winning. He'd never been further than Durham City, four miles away. He returned from the war a socialist, and with a commitment, amounting almost to an obsession, that neither he nor any of his children would ever work down the pit. By this time the family had moved, first briefly to Easington, and then to Horden, the great new pit, highly mechanised and capable of massive production, to which it seemed everyone was going. Percy got a job at the newly opened coke ovens, which had been built during the war, partly by a group of massively brawny miners' wives known as 'the navvyesses'. Percy and Jenny married and moved in temporarily with Percy's parents in one of the streets of deputies' houses on the Top Road, known as 'the big houses'. Big they may have been by the standards of ordinary colliery houses, but his adolescent brothers Hal and Charlie were still at home and working at the pit, and there were the three sisters – the youngest Nan still a baby. In these cramped circumstances, Percy soon found himself at variance with his father.

My grandfather had sailed all round Europe, he had been present at some of the key moments of the war, he had met people from a multiplicity of backgrounds in many continents. He had witnessed unspeakable horrors, and like all soldiers, he had experienced in a few short years the terrors of several lifetimes. More than that, he had swum in the waters of the greater world, and felt exultantly their tumultuous swelling against the ice of the old world. As far as my great-grandfather was concerned, however, nothing had changed.

He had moved his family from Ushaw Moor to Horden. But on the calendar of his existence, marked only by the changing shifts in the dark underworld, a world without holidays, the seasons registering only in the changing labour in his garden, the boomings and bangings of the wider world were heard but faintly if at all. His third son Jack had gone into the army. But now he too had returned, and things could go back to the way they had always been.

There had been two short strikes since the war, but as far as James Hudson was concerned they had been vain, futile endeavours which, like all strikes, had led to nothing but debt. And now here was this stripling Percy, this overgrown youth who had married a shopkeeper's daughter – and shopkeepers were, in the hierarchies of the collieries, equivalent to senior officials if not to the managers themselves – here he was, not only laying down the law to his father, but centrally involved in the nascent Cokemen's Union branch in Horden.

One night in 1922, so I had always heard it, only two weeks before my father was due to be born, the tension came to a head. The women, who had tactfully withdrawn, heard voices raised in anger. Harsh words, unforgivable words, had been said. Percy and Jenny were turned out 'on to the streets'. Percy did not forgive his father, and the two men did not speak again for fifteen years.

Percy and Jenny went to 'live in', with a Mrs Hall, in one room upstairs in old Fifth Street, where my father was born. Then they got their council house in Oak Terrace, where Mollie was born five years later.

The Thirties were hard times for everyone in the colliery villages. Children went unshod, their heads shaven against lice. Some hardly had a decent meal from one week to the next. There was rickets. And as you entered the houses the sweet, sickly smell of bugs. In the Thirties, when the women stood by the doors in the evenings, waiting for the buzzer to sound from the pit, to let them know which seams would be operating, and whether their men would be working the following day, Percy would often work only three shifts a week and then be on the dole for the following two – twenty-eight shillings for three shifts, thirty-two shillings on the dole. But Jenny was an excellent manager, and could make a piece of meat costing sixpence last a good three days. The house was always spotless. Like all the traditional colliery wives, Jenny did all the decorating herself, making all the floor coverings – not the basic 'clippy mats', but the superior proggy mats, where the clippings are knotted through into the hessian. She baked all the bread and cakes, and Percy grew most of the vegetables in the garden at the back.

One year, however, things were so difficult they had to apply to the British Legion for assistance with my father's school uniform. But the garments, when they finally arrived the day before the start of the new term, were not the sleek blue and grey uniform of Henry Smith's Grammar School, with its black and amber tie and badge, but a rough and hairy suit of a bizarre hue that could only be described as 'purple'. My father was never to forget the walk to the station, waiting till the last minute to go on to the platform, sure that all eyes were upon him in his 'suit of shame'. That night, blinking back the tears, he told his mother he'd rather go in rags than 'that suit'. Jenny, resourceful as ever, decided to have it dyed a less noticeable colour.

But one way or another, they managed to keep the two children at grammar school. Indeed, when Jenny's uncle who had been president of the Brandon and Byshottles Co-operative Society, died leaving her £250, they were even able to send my father on the school trip to Belgium.

Sometimes, on the nights when Percy wasn't working, they'd roll back the mats and dance as they had done at the Mission Hall in New Brancepeth, the children joining in too.

Percy was secretary of the Horden Cokemen's Lodge, and went on to represent them at Area and National level. Since he had had little formal education, he always said that it was necessary for him to know the plant better than the manager, and to read the market prices, since it was no good asking for what could not be reasonably achieved. He always said that if you had to take the men out on strike, you'd failed – as a negotiator and as a tactician. Because it was impossible with a strike of even modest duration to make up the wages lost.

Although they were a 'Church' family, James Hudson had never gone to church. Percy, however, went every Sunday evening. And he liked to listen to the services on the radio, particularly the sermons of the Revd Jack Shepherd of St Martin-in-the-Fields, whom he admired for his socialistic, egalitarian attitudes.

At the age of eight, my father had stood in front of the altar in St Mary's in Horden, and denied the existence of God, while his friends waited for him to be struck down by lightning. But such was the importance of the church in the social fabric of the village, he remained in the Church Lads' Brigade till the age of eighteen, engaging in Highland dancing, Cumberland lift wrestling and many other civilised pursuits, while Jenny was in the Mothers' Union, and Mollie the Girls' Friendly Society. But if Jenny and Percy considered themselves religious, they never talked about their beliefs. That would have been considered most odd, and most embarrassing.

Percy had to travel as far afield as London for trade union conferences. But the serious business was carried out in Newcastle, at the Coal Trade Offices, where the Owners' chairman, Lord Barnard of Raby Castle, would be lined up with his legal and professional advisers against the workers' representatives. As Percy often commented, on one side of the table would be Eton, Harrow, Oxford and Cambridge, and on the other, the tumbledown school in Ushaw Moor and the hard drinking, semi-literate cokemen's chairman, Micky Driscoll.

On one occasion, during a break from some particularly stiff negotiations, Lord Barnard had come over to Percy and asked him about his family. 'You will no doubt be hoping for better things for your children, Hudson. The company could, under certain circumstances, provide for your children through university.' Percy had replied, a trifle gruffly, that with a socialist county council in power in Durham they could make their own way, and he would himself provide any other support necessary. 'You should have takken it, man,' said Micky Driscoll later, his thick black eyebrows beetling mischievously. 'If they tried to bribe me, I'd takk it – even if it was only five pund. They'd get nowt for it, mind!'

On another occasion, six men at a plant somewhere on the other side of Durham had been sacked and fined for hiding their tools under piles of coke in a storage area. After three tedious visits to the plant, Percy had managed to get them reinstated. They were so delighted they said they didn't mind the high fines they'd had to pay. Percy however was adamant that legally these must be reimbursed to them, and after several more visits he won the case, to the men's jubilation. A few months later he learnt that that branch had not voted for him as their representative to the TUC. But as he always said, you shouldn't be surprised at anything the men did. And you certainly shouldn't expect them to be grateful to you. 'Mind,' as he also said, 'you cannut damn them arl for the few.'

The Hudson's great friends had been the Cuthbertsons, the Co-op drapery manager and his wife who lived round the corner. The two couples often went on holiday together, and through the Cuthbertsons, Jenny and Percy became friendly with the Morrises, the Co-op manager and his wife, Mary.

In 1960, Jenny died aged sixty-five, after a year-long struggle with cancer. Percy continued living in the house on the Crossroads Estate above the north end of Horden where they'd moved after the war, subsisting on fry-ups. 'Something's got to be done,' the doctor told my father. 'He's killing himself.' So, everyone was thankful when, less than a year later, Percy married Mary Morris, whose husband had also died the previous year.

I hadn't seen Mary for at least twenty years, but I had a much clearer picture of her than I had of many of my other Northern relatives. For she had seemed, even then, to be somehow closer to my own world.

She still lived in the 'cottages', the development of two bedroom colliery bungalows on the Top Road, in the same house where they'd been living when Percy died. The very address spoke to me out of the past, though as I walked along the ends of the interminable terraces of drab little houses I had no clear recollection of having been there before.

It was extraordinary now to think that this area had once been in the very shadow of the pit, subject to the screaming and grinding of the belts – the conveyors from which the men and boys picked the stone from the coal – for sixteen hours a day. As technology progressed, and the conveyors became quieter, the lights from the colliery grew brighter, the booming of intercoms more frequent. Now however, beneath the rumble of the Top Road, an ominous quiet hung over the treeless and deserted streets.

Mary sat in her armchair, with her back to the window. She still spoke in the same tone of faintly amused surprise, with the constant confiding appendage, 'yer knoo' – as many women in the North do. She did not seem particularly surprised by my visit, but she was rather flustered, as the girl who normally came to do her hair on a Thursday had not appeared that morning, and she thought she looked a state. She now found it difficult to walk, but managed to get up to the end of the road at least once a week. Apart from that, she said, she felt very well. She'd recently been in to hospital to have a cataract removed, and while it sounded odd to her to say she'd enjoyed going into hospital, well, she had.

She came originally from Sherburn, just east of Durham City, where her father had been a colliery overman. When people were ill or women were in labour, her mother was the one they'd send for. 'She always used to say it was shocking, but some of these people had nothing. She used to say to me, "Always make sure your cupboards are full. Because you can be ill at any time, and that's when people'll find out what you've got."'

Mary herself had won a scholarship to a prestigious girls' grammar school in Durham. She showed me a sepia photograph of herself and some fellow pupils, all in big-collared blouses with loose fitting ties. She had been extremely handsome.

'Yes,' she said, as though that were self evident but irrelevant to this conversation.

But what about Percy? What was his character like?

'Well, I don't know if I really could describe his character . . . I mean, he was very narrow minded.'

Narrow minded? In what way?

'I had to be very careful who I spoke to, particularly before we got married. And I thought, Well, I don't know if I can be doing with this. I said to him, "I've worked with men, you know." Because I'd worked in the Co-operative offices, and the men, they'd joke with you, but they were never nasty. My previous husband had been the Co-operative manager, and all the stretchers and the trestles for laying out the bodies were kept at our house. So if someone had died, men would be coming in the middle of the night to get them, and I'd have to answer the door with only my dressing-gown on, and take the names and addresses of the deceased. But Percy was expecting me not to talk to any man outside the family.

'He and my previous husband were two completely different men. If my first husband ever said anything that wasn't quite right, I'd say, "Now, I want the truth and only the truth, mind!" And he'd laugh. It got to be a game between us. He'd make things up, just to see if I'd catch him out. But Percy? Dear me, no.

'I'd never thought of him as like that. But before he was always with Jenny, and she was such a lovely person. Jenny and my husband died in the same year, and Mary Cuthbertson seemed to want to get us together.

'Then there was a coach trip from the church. Percy asked me if I'd like to go with him, and that was that really. In those days there were coach trips from the church all the time. When we got back, he'd ask me if I'd come back to the house and cook him a meal, or if he could come to the flat for a meal. But he wouldn't sit by me in church, not until after we were married. We'd both be in church, but we wouldn't sit together.

'One day, shortly after we were married, when we were still living in the house up at the Crossroads Estate, he just started shouting at me – for no reason. I said, "Look, nobody's ever shouted at me before, and they're not going to start now!" So he never did it again. But he was that jealous.

'Once we were on a coach trip up to Balmoral, and we'd looked round at everything, and I'd had enough, so I thought I'd just go and sit in the coach. Well, the driver and another man were standing talking beside the coach. As I arrived at the coach, I heard Percy behind me. "Get in!" That's all he said. Just like that. "Get in!" So I sat there in the coach, on my own, with him outside, and I thought, "Oh dear. What have you got involved with here?"

'But he improved as he went along. He liked to go to Evensong, while I liked to go to the eight o'clock Communion. And when I got back I always found my breakfast waiting for me.

'One winter it snowed in, and he said he'd like to dig the path of the woman opposite, but he didn't know what people would think. He was like that, you know. He cared a lot about what people thought. I said, "Never mind what people think. You get over there and dig!"

'He didn't go out much. There was a bench up on the Top Road, by The Bell, and sometimes he used to go and sit there. He didn't like to miss his church, and he went to the Labour Party meetings once a month. But he never discussed politics. If something political came on the television, he'd never talk about it.

'But he was well known. He was on the Parish Council. They got that cemetery built up there, and on the fine nights he used to go and walk round it with his friends, to make sure it was all in order. In fact, I think he'd just been made chairman of the Parish Council when he died.

'He was working at the coke ovens at Murton most of the time we were married. They'd closed down here. He was supposed to retire at sixty-five, but he and Mr Hughes, the union treasurer, were offered a "lump sum" if they carried on working another year. It turned out to be a hundred and twenty pounds. He had two years of retirement. Then he had to have an operation on his ulcers, and he caught pneumonia. They said, "The operation was successful, but the patient died." I don't know how they worked that out. It was a shame really that he died when he did, because we were just getting to know each other's habits.'

3

The Numbered Streets

SIX MONTHS after my initial visit, I was back in Horden, living in a room in a house in Hardwick Street, belonging to a Mrs Hancock, a Kentish woman, whose husband, a Horden man, had brought her 'home' on his retirement. He had died within a couple of years, leaving her virtually stranded, since the returns on a house in Horden didn't yield much in any other part of the country. A modest, easy-going woman in her mid-sixties, she was active in the church and Women's Institute and seemed resigned to her existence.

Hardwick Street was one of the original streets of the village, part of a private development thrown up around the same time as the first colliery houses, and built to a similar plan, from blocks of compacted ash. The fake rusticated surfaces, and the tiny shield of the Burdons, the coal-owning family, over each front door, gave them a spurious baronial appearance that was supposed to mark them out from the 'free' housing of the miners.

Opposite the front door were the back gates of the largest Co-op branch in the village. Now devoted entirely to furniture, it had in the days of independent co-operative societies belonged to the Sherburn Hill Co-op, and was still known as 'the Sherburn Hill Store' by most people in the village. The abattoir had been in the yard, and you could still see the bases of the stalls, the broken ceramic tiles sloping into the channels along which the blood had run away, just inside the gates where the young lads used to hang around hoping to filch a bladder for a football. Further along had been a blacksmith's shop, spitting sparks out on to the pavement, the

wheezing of bellows and the ringing of anvils mixing with the lowing
of the doomed animals at the Co-op. Now the yard was empty,
the blacksmith's had decades ago been boarded-up, and beneath
the rumble of traffic on the nearby Top Road, an atmosphere of
ominous dilapidation prevailed.

The window of the room in which I slept and worked looked
down through net curtains on to the back lane and the high-walled
back yards in which much of the original life of the village had been
lived. But now, apart from a few yelling kids and the odd rogue car
alarm, it was almost too quiet. There were no trees in Hardwick
Street, no leaves to fall. But it was already mid-October, and you
could feel the year dying all around you. Some days it seemed hardly
to get light along the back lane of Hardwick Street.

A friend of mine, a fellow writer, a Yorkshireman, who lived
in London as a kind of cultural refugee from Northernness, had
expressed incredulity at my decision to come to live in Horden.
Such places were, he said, a living death, full of narrow-minded
macho men and tight-lipped suffering women. They all voted Labour,
but when you examined what they believed, most of them were
actually fascists. He himself had decided to go and live in Hong
Kong. This had struck me at the time as defeatist, even perverse.
Now, however, as I passed the bleak, windswept bus stops, and
stood among the other morose shoppers in Presto's supermarket
in Horden, it made perfect sense. There was a society in the throes
of cataclysmic change, poised on the brink of a profound, possibly
tragic destiny, upon which the world's eyes would be riveted. And
I had chosen to come to this place.

It wasn't as though Horden was utterly insignificant. In its
heyday, it was the biggest colliery in Britain. It had the biggest
surface area of any single pit in the world. Nearly five thousand men,
not only miners, but cokemen, electricians, fitters, blacksmiths, tub
menders, horse shoers, enginemen and dozens of other occupations
were employed, while over a thousand ponies walked the subterranean roadways. Records for weekly, monthly and annual production
were broken several times in the century at Horden. But of that
glory, little remained. Even the tumultuous strike of 1984–5, after
which Horden was summarily closed, seemed remote; the passion
and even the bitterness of those events – the pitched battles between
police and pickets, the valiant women talking so powerfully of their
husbands' 'right' to be miners – seemed unimaginable in Horden as
it existed today. Crouching abjectly on its sloping shelf of land,
under the relentless onslaught of the North Sea winds, Horden

seemed bludgeoned, benumbed and cast aside by history.

As I tramped the dismal shut-in streets, it was clear to me that nothing was going to happen in Horden.

A dustbin liner hovered, lolling uncertainly in the sky above Hard-wick Street, before a gust snatched it, pulling it away and out over the sea. The howling of dogs on the allotments and in distant yards was caught up in the sighing and the moaning of the wind around the eaves. I was waiting for a man who was going to show me round the area where the colliery had been.

He was a miner. A retired miner. But a miner none the less. My background reading of the last few months had given me a curious and confused set of perceptions about miners. The word now carries with it a potent and inescapable romanticism. But before the war, when there were over a million of them, miners, cut off from respectable society in their beleaguered villages, were considered almost sub-human. A young woman from Horden who had gone to train as a nurse during the Twenties had found that the attitudes of her fellow students, mostly vicars' daughters who had previously been very nice to her, had changed markedly when they found out she was from the collieries. It was, she said, as though she had been a 'coloured person'. Now, however, well-meaning middle-class people were pleased to know miners, in the same way they were pleased to know black people, and they were for the same reasons not at all sure how to behave towards them. Miners were a species apart, and the more I learnt about them, the more difficult I found it to believe that anyone related to me could actually have been one. Miners were, to take a random sample of the impressions I had formed: unimaginably brave and resilient; small; physically powerful of necessity; capable of handling themselves physically as a matter of course and utterly devoid of sympathy for anyone who could not; incapable of abstract thought; obsessive about their hobbies; incapable of seeing the value of any social activity that did not involve the drinking of beer.

The most disturbing account I had read was by an ex-public school boy who had become a miner as a kind of rite of passage, and been most cruelly abused by his workmates. I had not been to public school. I didn't represent the ruling class in any way. But that didn't matter. Up here, such distinctions were totally academic.

The miner, John, was a slight, wiry man, with lugubrious clown's features, and a shock of hair stained a brilliant yellow by nicotine. His hunched but agile gait made him seem shorter than he was. One hears of people having 'lived-in' faces – this man's looked as though it was *infested*. Every millimetre looked as though a great deal had happened to it. But although he'd survived forty years underground, he didn't seem anything like his seventy years.

He'd started at the pit when he was fourteen, still in short trousers, picking stone from the coal on the conveyor belts. Then at the beginning of the war, he'd been called up before mining was made a reserved occupation, and served six years in the Royal Engineers. So when he came back to Horden, he was automatically made a fitter – a mechanic – servicing the machinery at the coal face. In those days most of the mechanics worked on the surface. There were only two mechanics and two electricians underground on each shift. But as mechanisation progressed, these 'tradesmen' became more numerous and more important.

So were mechanics classed as miners, or did they constitute a separate profession?

'Oh, a separate profession. He wasn't a miner. He was a fitter. If you were working at the face and the deputy – who was responsible for your safety – said you needed a couple of props in there, he'd get a miner to do it for you. You never put your own props and your own timber up. Oh, no. You weren't allowed to. It wasn't done.'

As we walked he talked freely, with little prompting from me. Each of his stories, of which there were many, seemed to end with him being carried out of the pit on a stretcher, at which he would thrust his chin forward, nodding in silent laughter. He impersonated himself in these stories in a mournful nasal drone. And it seemed to suit him to portray himself as one of the world's stooges – a doleful, long suffering character, soldiering stoically on through floods, rockfalls, the excesses of egomaniac officials, the blunders of incompetent managers. A man who prided himself on his lack of illusions, who set a low value on himself, but would go to any lengths to protect that value.

We passed the church and turned up by what used to be the village's main school, now boarded-up, the weeds springing up thickly behind the railings among piles of rubbish uncleared, apparently, for years.

'You'd be in the playground, here,' said John, 'and a couple of miners would come past, pushing a hand cart. On it would be an injured miner, or even a dead miner, covered in a blanket or just a couple of old sacks. We'd all stand and watch, and as it went into one of the streets, all the women would go to the windows to see which house it stopped at. That's all there was, just this hand cart. It was the miners themselves who had the colliery ambulance brought in. They paid for it – so much a week off their pay note.

'If a miner had been killed, the cortège would come along here on its way to the church. The colliery band would be leading, with the drum going, boom ... boom ... boom ... We'd all be in the classroom listening, and the teacher would say, "Shut that window!" Then he'd sort of look at us, yi knar? Because he knew that every boy in that room was going down that pit. There was no way it could be avoided.'

We were now in the network of dark rows – the 'numbered streets' – that formed the heart of the village. Across the tarmac that gleamed indigo in the cold afternoon sun, the shadow of the Miners' Hall loomed towards the entrance of the Big Club, the village's legendary working men's club. A decrepit double-fronted Edwardian building, its grime-encrusted paintwork was flaking away in shards, and those of its windows that were not broken or boarded-up were hung with filthy net curtains. Behind this mean and unpromising facade rose a vast barn-like structure, the huge windows of its upper storey all broken or boarded-up. Ahead of us, between these two buildings was the red brick wall of drear and uncompromising blankness that ran around the Welfare Ground, the huge recreation area that took up most of the centre of Horden. To our right, a gateway led into a promenade of surprising, almost classical graciousness – benches and flower beds at intervals between neatly trimmed laurel hedges. It would have been a pleasant place to stroll were it not for the freezing wind that came funneling through it. Along with the park at the end, with its lovingly maintained bandstand, it was part of the Welfare Ground. There were two rugby pitches, a football field with grandstand, a cricket ground, two play areas with swings and roundabouts. And it had all been paid for by the miners. Sixpence a week was taken off their pay to maintain it.

To our right, past the laurel hedge, was an area of flat grit that had been the tennis courts, and beyond that the bowling green, still up to county standard. To our left, behind a high wooden fence, there had once been an open-air swimming pool. 'All this was paid for by the miners,' said John proudly. And it had all been in the very shadow of the pit.

A path led through on to the roadway by the pulley wheel monument. Beside it, twelve stone steps had once led down into the pit yard. But now there was just an expanse of gritty, grizzled earth, sloping away towards the railway line, and beyond that the sea, a few grey and ragged sheep munching their way desultorily over the thin grass. John sighed in muted wonder. 'When you got browned off at the face, you sometimes used to say, "I wish they'd give the farmer his field back." It was just an expression. You never thought it would happen. Not at Horden . . .'

'Mind,' he said, as we continued on our way, 'I wouldn't have it back. Most of this', he gestured over the expanse, 'was just rubbish. Pit waste – great heaps of it. He bent down and picked a piece of red shale from among the grass. 'That's ash from where the rock spontaneously combusted. There was always somewhere on the spoil heaps that was bursting into flames. When the strikes were on people used to come up here foraging for bits of coal. They had to be careful where they walked.'

A hundred yards or so away towards the railway line was a group of low buildings. Beneath that was the shaft of the Hutton Seam, the lowest of the three original seams. They were still pumping from there, to prevent Easington Colliery, a mile up the coast, from flooding.

We were now well out of the village, in what to all appearances had always been countryside. We went along a lane through an arch under the railway into a field that sloped gently upwards before descending towards the sea. You couldn't deny that someone had done a most effective job of disguising every trace of the pit's existence. This had been the main pit heap. An immense black mountain, it had dominated the foreshore, half filling the beach. Now levelled off and grassed over, it lay back innocent and unnoticeable among the mud ramparts of the headland. From the top, the wind buffeting around our ears, we looked down on to the maelstrom of foam seething and raging on to the black beach. It glowed ominously in the fading light, churning and boiling for miles back out to sea, and all the way down to Hartlepool, and beyond that to where Teesside faded into the darkening spray. Below us, where the tumult was at its fiercest, three dark protrusions and one shorter one stuck up out of the churning froth, disappearing and then reappearing, like sinister black teeth. John said that that had been the base of Horden's aerial flight. When there was no room for any more waste up on the headland, they'd started dumping it down there. For thirty odd years an overhead conveyor of buckets had gone round and round continuously tipping the black muck into the sea. The idea was that the tide would carry it out. It had done. But then it had brought it back in again. At the bottom of the bank, the wheels of numberless sea coal lorries had churned the foreshore into a Somme-like void of mud, beyond which a purplish grey mass of pebbles

sloped down into the foam. Underneath that there were golden
sands. At one time people had come from miles around to disport
themselves on this beach. Postcards had been printed saying, 'Come
to Horden!' 'Who'd come here now?' asked John.

I wondered where the Horden workings had been in relation to
where we were standing now. He pointed out into the darkening
grey mass of the sea, in the direction from which the breakers came
crashing towards us – the North-east. The main Horden road had
gone straight out there for five miles. It was extraordinary to think
of people working out there, six hundred fathoms – one thousand
two hundred feet – beneath the tumult of the sea. But down there,
encased in hundreds of feet of rock, it must have been totally silent.
But had it been warm or cold?

'On a day like today, it would come roaring through the upper
seams. You'd be sweating on the inside, 'cause you were working,
and freezing on the outside from the wind. But by the time the air
reached the lower seams it would be warmed by friction. It was
boiling down there – a real claggy heat.'

And what was it like down there, thinking of the incredible
weight of rock and water overhead?

'You never thought about it. If you did you'd never go down there.'

We made our way back to the road along the North side of
the heap. In the next field, the Coal Board had had a million and
a half tons of coal half buried, in readiness for the last strike. It
had been like that all over the country. Everywhere you went there
were mountains of coal by the railway sidings. 'It was a lost cause
before they started,' said John. 'All that about there being no hit list
for pits. They'd put out to tender for the break-up of this pit before
the strike even started.'

As we slithered through the mud, he continued with his fund of
stories, and I listened. Up here in the North-east, people would talk
to you, or at you, for hours. But if you attempted to express some
opinion of your own, or particularly, if you attempted to introduce
some subject that was not directly related to them or to the area,
they just looked at you blankly, as though they didn't know who
you were.

Suddenly, however, John's tone became more confiding. 'I was
going to be a teacher, yi knar. When I came out of the army after
the war, they were offering us the opportunity to do different types
of training. I'd always fancied being a teacher, so I applied. There
was this great flight of steps going up to the place where they were
having the interviews. I got up as far as the last step but one. Then

I thought, No . . . no. I turned round, came back here, and went straight down the pit.' He gave his grim chuckle again, shaded this time by just the faintest tinge of regret.

No matter how able, no matter how talented he might have been, at the last moment he had not been able to make the leap from being one of the acted upon to one of the actors of the world's stage. He had been unprepared to relinquish his protective self-image of the hardy, ironic underdog.

It was almost dark by the time we re-entered the village. John pointed out where the Empress, the most famous of Horden's three cinemas, had been. It had long ago burnt down, and the site was now the car park of Barclay's Bank. I was suddenly struck by a sense of the pathos, not only of the cinema's departure, but of my own position in searching for significance on the site of what had no doubt been even in its heyday, an uninspiring edifice. Here I was with a little half-bent, unshaven man who seemed unable to communicate except through stories – some of which he had already begun to repeat – looking for resonance along these dismal terraces. For him and for countless others, the idea of the Empress evoked poignant memories. But what was that to me? I felt suddenly overwhelmed by the meanness and the drabness of Horden and everything in it. My previous visits had all been extremely brief. I had always been on the verge of returning to my familar environment in London. Now, however, I was stuck here, with no clear means of escape in view. I felt suddenly desperate to be somewhere where everything was not hang-dog, tarnished, used.

That night, however, as I looked up into the sky above Hardwick Street, the brown acrid smell of the coal fires blurring the edge of the raw starless blackness, I felt with a keenness I had never felt during the day-time that this was the place where my father had grown up – my own father, the person to whom I felt closer, in some ways, than anyone else in the world, who had had a greater influence on my life than probably anyone else, but from whom, although he was alive, I felt, had felt for many years, in some way already irrevocably parted. The ordinary little council house in which he had grown up, so mundane in appearance it was difficult to believe it could be seventy years old, lay less than a hundred yards away, down the bank on the other side of the Co-op. These were the pavements along which he had played, the very flagstones along which he had walked. I could see him – as though if I went to Oak Terrace now, he would be standing there by the gate in the darkness, as he was aged eight, in the striped pullover he seemed to be wearing in all his childhood photographs.

As a child, my father's childhood self had haunted me – a satyrlike, but benevolent mentor. In his early childhood, the houses of Horden had ended one row above Oak Terrace, and within minutes, he and his friends – whose names now escaped me, but who had once lived for me as vividly, more vividly, than the Outlaws in the William books – could slip down into the Dene, the wooded gorge that ran from the sea along the southern edge of Horden. In those days it was still the private property of the Burdons, the coal owning family. But for the people of Horden, for the solitary poacher like my great-uncle Bob, for whole families of bramble pickers, its flora and fauna were fair game. For my father and the other lads of the village it was a magical domain, a private landscape for real and imaginary battles, for bows and arrows, for tree houses – which were, according to my father, far superior to any of those illustrated or described in books – of secret labyrinths of tunnels and whole rooms cut from the dense brush in the height of summer. In all of this, as in everything else he had ever done, he had been the leader, the one with more ideas, more intelligence, more physical daring, who could if necessary sort the others out – physically; like a proletarian William Brown, but leaner, more narrow eyed, more purposeful. As a child, the Dene he described had been archetypal. It had become the woods in which I myself had played.

Now, however, I saw this all-purpose forest of the childhood mind as an actual place, the Dene, which lay not far away, just beyond the limit of Horden's street lights, down the scrambling banks in the plunging darkness. And while its new-found physical existence, like the independent existence of Horden itself, seemed to repudiate everything I had ever felt these places to be – seemed to repudiate even my own familial connections with them – I now knew that it was only through these familial connections that I could make Horden as it existed today mean anything to me. Without these connections my time in Horden would be simply a matter of lonely endurance in another place with problems.

Later that night, I went to the Big Club. In the brightly lit extension on the corner, youngish men could be seen, absorbed and intent over the snooker tables. But beyond that, the rest of the vast edifice lay in total darkness. I stumbled along a pathway down the side of the building, and there, through the glass doors, was a dimly lit cubby hole, a book of tickets showing that this was where the doorman sat. I waited for a few moments. Ahead was a gloomy passageway with notices for forthcoming dances and sporting fixtures. So this was the Big Club, the great Working Men's Club of Horden, of which old and young still spoke in tones of affectionate reverence. It was well known that the huge upstairs concert hall had not been used for years, that generally the place was a shadow of what it had once been. But I had still not been prepared for this sad and muggy decrepitude. The dim strip-lights and ingrained nicotined grime gave the place the air of queasy desolation normally found only in all night mini-cab offices.

The doorman came rushing through a door on the right, his brow conscientiously knitted. 'Sign the book, sign the book.' I wanted to become a member of the Club, but he said I should wait till January and join for the whole year. It would be cheaper – though the annual subscription was only £1.30.

As I turned towards the bar doorway, he blurted something at me. 'Sorry?'

'Ten pence. You've got to pay ten pence.' He stared at me, wide eyed and intent. From his tone, it might have been £50 I'd owed him personally for years. He meant to have it.

I walked the last few yards to the bar doorway. People had told me that if I was to write a book about the North-east, I would have to spend a lot of time in working men's clubs. I had not been at all keen on the idea. But here I was at last.

It was a huge square box of a room, brightly lit with strip lights, and apart from a few lozenge-shaped panels along the front of the bar, totally devoid of decoration. The two barmaids watched as I made my way across the great floor. Even ten years before, the Big Club would have been packed at this time on a Saturday night. You'd have had to fight your way to the bar. Tonight it was practically deserted.

I settled myself on the red plastic banquette and felt my eyes closing. After the darkness and the crashing wind, the warmth, and the nicotined glow of the bare walls, the low jangling of the gambling machines, the dull crack of the snooker balls was soothing and somehow reassuring. I could have fallen asleep where I sat.

Through an archway I could see the snooker players, while at a table nearer to me a man in late middle age with a face of extraordinary blunt plasticity, the sort of face that seems made to have a cloth cap perched above it, was telling a story with all the remonstrative force typical of the region. 'Noo-ah!' he had said to someone. 'Noo-ah!' He would pause, pulling his rubbery face into a grin of rhetorical incredulity, before repeating the word again. His listener, who had his back to me, leant forward, intent, caught within the grip of the narrative, pulled and held by the bulging eyes and elastic grimacing of the storyteller, like a small animal toyed with in the talons of a bird of prey.

On the other side of the room, a group of old men sat around a table in a glazed and silent stupor. One, wearing a suit of some dark purple material, with yellow waxen features and lips the same colour as his suit, stared upward through his thick glasses as though at some invisible but immense range of mountains beyond the bar, while his mate, who had a huge and bulbous red nose, stared always at the floor.

Those are the sort of people who would have known my grandfather, I thought. They'd have been only a few years younger than him. I should have just gone over, sat down and got chatting with them. I doubt if they'd have minded. They'd probably have welcomed it as a diversion. But at that point I could no more have approached them in their hermetic stupefaction than I could representatives of some strange and irremediably alien culture. But of course it was I who was the alien – who had slipped unnoticed into that place, and would now slip from it, without engaging with it, without taking anything from it, and without leaving the slightest imprint upon it.

At the bottom of Hardwick Street, a lane ran steeply down between the gable ends of the parallel rows, giving, through the thin skeins of domestic smoke, a sudden and surprising view of the sea. These streets, built a couple of years after the first streets, were still known – in descending order as one went down the bank – as New Seventh Street, New Sixth Street, New Fifth Street. They had originally been earmarked for the 'tradesmen' at the pit – the mechanics, electricians and blacksmiths – but they were built to exactly the same design as all the other colliery rows. The same flat fronts of bruised, liverish coloured brick, lines of pale yellow brick, and a lintel moulded with a kind of gothic curlicue over every door; the back lanes paved with blue flint cobbles that reflected the marbling of the sky and the domestic smoke, all sloping towards a central drainage channel.

Between the bottom of Hardwick Street and the back of New Seventh Street, a lane led through on to the broad, bare slope of the Parish Council Park, with the box-like bulk of Horden's neo-gothic church at the bottom. Cutting down, and heading up the steep street at the side of the church, one found oneself coming on to the level of Eighth Street, a boarded-up shop looming blackened and monolithic from the far corner, to the left, the gable ends of the numbered streets diminishing in size as they stretched away towards the Top Road, a faint haze of smoke muting their blue-black outlines.

There were parts of Horden – council developments of all periods, from the Twenties to the Seventies, private rows, crouching po-faced behind their front hedges – that could have been anywhere in Britain. When you were in the numbered streets, however, no matter how grim, no matter how inadequate you might have thought them as a social environment, you were at least aware that you were in a place with a clearly defined historical identity, that had been created by social and economic forces that were unique – that you were at least somewhere.

It had come as a surprise to no one that I was interested in finding out about Horden. And in general people were happy to point me in the direction of people who were, they felt, qualified to talk about 'Horden'. For by Horden they did not mean the whole of the village as it existed today. They meant life as it had been lived in the numbered streets earlier in the century.

The first dwellings in Horden had been the wooden shacks of the sinkers, the men who had dug the pit's three shafts. But the first proper houses were East and West View, two short rows facing each other immediately in front of the pit gates. And since in those days it was considered a privilege to live as close as possible to the place of work, these were reserved for the senior officials – the manager, the engineer, the colliery vet. Behind West View were more houses, large by the standards of the collieries – Grant Street, Thorpe Street – for the overmen and deputies. Behind East View, beside the back of the colliery offices, a street of more large houses, Sea View, was built for the hewers and their huge families who were arriving daily from all parts of the country. It is said that in the early days of Horden, the contractor Henry Bell was completing a house a day, the *gallowas* – the pit ponies – dragging tubs of bricks and sand through the mud, along the same rails that were used to transport the coals underground. For none of the streets was made up. The whole place was a huge building site, the doughty pit wives stagger-ing to and from the standpipes with their buckets over the uneven ground.

Sea View kept on extending till it hit the lane down to the station. Then they squeezed another street between it and the sidings that ran up to the pit. They called that First Street. Sea View became Second Street, and they carried on building parallel rows up the sloping shelf of land till they reached Thirteenth Street, only one side of which was built, facing the track known as 'the Top', which became the main Sunderland Road.

They came from the colliery villages of mid-Durham, from Tyneside, from traditional mining areas like Staffordshire and Derbyshire, from the mill towns of Lancashire, from Cornwall, Wales and Scotland. Some came by cart, with their possessions piled on the back, others came with nothing – without even a plate to eat off. But their neighbours made them welcome, giving them a meal – 'of the sort that was found in colliery homes in those days'. And so everyone got to know everyone else very quickly. After the opening of the Coast Railway in 1904, most came by train, dragging their tin trunks up from the station, across the bridge over the Blackthorn Gill, the dene that then ran through the middle of Horden.

If a man had five or six sons (as was quite common in those days), he would get a job and a house immediately. Because those lads would all go down the pit at fourteen, and the colliery needed the guarantee of a workforce for the future. But if a man only had daughters, he might be turned away – even if he was wearing a collar and tie.

'They were all there,' one old man told me, 'and they were all speaking in their different accents and dialects – very strongly!' His parents had spoken Welsh in the house, and when they first came to Horden, his elder brother couldn't speak English. 'But it was wild,' he said. 'You've got to admit it was wild.'

The first streets had no yards. The netty – the toilet that served six houses – and the communal tap stood apart on waste ground behind. There were no pubs or clubs, but every pay day, which was fortnightly, a cart would come round selling beer. In Middle Seventh Street, there lived three or four women who were known for their drinking. 'They'd get drunk,' a woman told me. 'The men and the women. They'd sing and dance in the street. Then they'd fall out and start fighting, throwing bottles at each other. Every fortnight it was the same. Us children used to stand on the corner and watch, because these women did things we'd never seen or heard of before.

'The only school was in the church hall. There was only one master, and the mistress was his wife. There was a green curtain down the middle of the room, with the infants on one side, and the juniors from Standard One to Standard Five on the other. When you were trying to concentrate, you could hear these children endlessly chanting their twice times table on the other side of the curtain. Some of these children had been left to run wild. The master was a nice man, but he couldn't cope. It drove him mad in the end.'

To extend Second, Third and Fourth Streets, it was necessary to fill in part of the Blackthorn Gill. The upper part of this dene remained, a deep dell, thick with silver birches, in the centre of the village. Beside it, Colonel Burdon, the local landowner and principal shareholder in Horden Collieries Limited, had built a large and impressive neo-gothic church, with a broad and distinctive square tower surmounted by a low pyramidal cap. Its rusticated surfaces green beneath their encrustation of grime, it still brooded impressively over the centre of the village – by far the most splendid church in the colliery villages of East Durham. It had become known as the 'Pitmen's Cathedral', the legend having developed that it was the miners themselves who had paid for its construction. It was taken as a symbol of the permanence of the community growing up around what was soon to be the biggest single colliery in the world.

Blackthorn Gill was filled in for allotments during the First World War, eventually becoming the Parish Council Park. The back lanes of the village were paved with cobbles shortly afterwards. The senior officials moved from the colliery gates to a more salubrious development above the Top Road. For the manager, a large mansion was built, high on the bank above Horden, from which he could look down on the smoke streaming like rippling water over the rooftops of the village, and beyond that the fields, and the grey remorseless immensity of the sea.

Walking round Horden, you could still see by each front door a curious blank rectangle. In most cases it had been covered with an ornamental house number or simply cemented over, but in some streets you could still see the pieces of slate embedded an inch into the wall. Before he went to bed, each man would chalk on it the time of his shift the following day. Then, at two in the morning, the 'carler' or 'knocker-upper' would come round with his long pole, knocking on the upstairs window of those in First Shift. He was employed by the Union to make sure no man missed a shift by sleeping in.

But the front doors themselves were hardly ever used. To this day, some were painted over so they wouldn't open. It was in the back lanes that the real life of the village took place. In the outer wall of each back yard there were two patches of newer bricks, where the 'let-ins' of the coal houses and the steel plates of the *netties* – the earth closets – had been filled in. People put their ashes into the netties, and some people even threw in a kind of powder like

Vim to keep the smell down. But you still couldn't stop some of it from seeping under the steel plates at the back, and attracting insects and vermin. Every two days the midden man came round with his cart – a huge iron container, with sliding lids into which the mixture of ordure and cinders was shovelled. If you happened to be sitting on the netty at the time, it was just too bad.

The carts were emptied into the remaining section of Blackthorn Gill on the other side of the railway tracks – a black and fetid bog, its surface permanently smoking from spontaneous combustion. One day one of the cart horses slipped down the bank into it, a great dray horse, dragging the great iron cart in on top of it. It proved impossible to rescue, and had to be shot.

Every week the colliery coal carts came along the lanes dumping fifteen hundredweight of coal at every coal house door. It was not 'clean' coal, but mixed with stone, duff and other waste. People who were not able or willing to hold down any other kind of job eked out a living, putting it in at a tanner a time, or small boys came round – 'Put yer coal in fu yer, missus?' – leaving the stone and waste in heaps in the lanes.

Even in winter, most of the washing was done in the back lanes, and in those days, before the pit-head baths, when the men came home black, as many as nine per household, what washing there was to be done! The younger children would be put to 'dodding' – beating the pit clothes against a wall to get the dust out. Then the women would use 'poss sticks' – a long stick with a flat circle of wood at the end with flanges – to pound the clothes in a wooden tub. Lasses would put their tubs together, get up on stools and 'double poss' – pounding alternately to build up a rhythm. On a Monday morning you'd hear the double possers thundering like African drums all over Horden. When they'd finished, they'd throw the youngest children into the tubs to wash them.

On a Monday, you just hoped the wind wouldn't be blowing from the colliery, because the back lanes would be hung thick with washing. Then the coal cart or the midden man or the Storeman and his dray would want to come through. That's what they loved to talk about in Horden, about the arguments between the women and the cartmen on washing days.

Friday was pay day, and when they'd cashed their husband's paynotes, they'd head down to the piece of waste ground at the bottom of Third Street for a gathering known as 'Paddy's Market', since many of the costermongers were Irish. But every shop in Horden had a stall down there on a Friday. People went to get cheap produce, to avail themselves of the services of – or merely to observe – characters like the black dentist who removed teeth without anaesthetic, the whole place lit up on winters' afternoons with huge and terrifying naphthalene flares.

That was the kind of thing people liked to tell you about. The Horden of Paddy's Market, of vanished practices and pastimes. Of the illegal gambling: pitch 'n toss on the beach banks on a Sunday morning, from which many a man came back in just his shirtsleeves! Quoits behind the Big Club. And the Handball Alley. Handball could be played against any gable end, but in Horden there was a specially created alley. And all the stars were from Horden: Trapper Charlton, Pauly Tennant, Jacky Cook, Trapper Harkness, and of course the two Mordue Brothers, who were said to be the handball champions of the world.

A faint veneer of cosiness had accrued even to the most notorious and extraordinary event in the village's history: the burning of the Big Club. I had heard this event alluded to many times, but I finally read the details early one black, wet evening, sitting in the tiny public library on the Top Road.

The event had taken place in the winter of 1910, when the miners of Horden were 'locked out' by the owners for two months following a dispute over the number of hours in the shift. The winter was the worst in living memory – the earth like iron under a thin covering of snow – and the miners were on the verge of starvation. A general election was imminent, and all over the country feelings were running high over the Lloyd George budget.

The two candidates in the South-east Durham constituency were Mr Evan Hayward (Liberal) and the Hon. F. W. Lambton (Unionist). In those days the Durham miners supported the Liberal Party, but the steward and stewardess of the village's main social centre, the recently opened Colliery Club, were Unionists. The Club, a huge and grand edifice, had been built by the colliery company, and although it was patronised by the majority of the workforce, it was controlled by the officials.

The trouble began when the stewardess put up a Unionist poster. Children began throwing stones and snowballs at the building, jeering and singing ribald songs. She responded by calling them 'blue pigs', which must have been considered an unimaginable insult, for soon a crowd of adults had gathered outside the Unionist election headquarters. Stones were thrown. The crowd got bigger, and soon several hundred men were marching on the colliery.

The colliery compensation doctor, arriving inadvertently at the scene, was dragged from his car and thrown over the embankment by the coal depot. (It was assumed in those days that doctors were bribed by the companies to record judgements unfavourable to the men.) Offices were wrecked. Tubs of coal thrown down the shafts. Then the mob headed towards the Club. A squad of police had arrived at the scene, but they were powerless before the huge crowd. Indeed, the sight of the blue uniforms only seemed to incense the crowd still more. Trade union officials and the headmaster of the village school remonstrated with the crowd, but to no avail.

Furniture was thrown from the Club windows; fittings torn from the walls. In the cellars hogsheads were smashed open, and men and women linked arms to dance in the frothing flood. Housewives did their best to carry the beer away in pans and basins. Drunken children staggered about in it. One woman nearly drowned in it. The police arrived in force, but not before the Club's concert grand had been tipped through an upstairs window and smashed to pieces on the railings below.

There was a sudden crash, as though something had hit the front of the library with great force.

'What was that?' asked a little girl, startled.

'Just some boys being silly,' said the librarian, quietly, but through gritted teeth.

I went back to my reading, slightly shaken. I had, to tell the truth, been rather horrified by what I had been reading. The weird festivity of the destruction of the Big Club, the delirious drunken gusto with which all signs of culture and refinement were smashed, were disconcerting to read about, even eighty odd years later – particularly when one was sitting only a few hundred yards from where these events had taken place, in a community where manifestations of 'high culture' were still few and far between.

That summer – 1991 – the whole of the country had been shocked by the riots on housing estates around Newcastle, at the readiness of certain sections of the community to destroy the few amenities that had been provided for them. Afterwards, young children from the area were asked by journalists what facilities would improve the area from their point of view. A playground, they said, and a city farm. They'd had these things before, but the big kids had smashed them up.

Just as the country had been divided on whether this was an inevitable outcome of social and economic deprivation, or simply criminally inspired vandalism, so it was difficult to ascertain whether the Horden Riot had been the legitimate protest of ill-used men or a gross orgy of destruction for its own sake. And if the latter, did a propensity for such things remain latent in the people among whom I was living?

While Elswick and Meadowell burned, there had been portents of similar events in Peterlee. Crowds had gathered on one of the 'worst' estates. A firebomb was thrown at the old Horden manager's house, now a community centre. But in the end, it all just fizzled out.

Meanwhile, back in Horden, 1910, the police had called for volunteers to try to persuade the remaining revellers to come out of the Club cellar, but before anyone had a chance to step forward, flames were seen leaping from an upstairs window. The police soon doused the flames, but it was a foretaste of what was to come.

The next day, more than a thousand miners, many armed with pickaxes and pick handles, marched on Hardwick Hall, a manor house near Blackhall, a mile or two to the south, home of J. J. Prest JP, agent of the Horden Colliery Company – the man in charge of Horden, Shotton and Blackhall pits. They found only two policemen blocking their way. But Prest, having locked his family in a back room, appeared at an upstairs window armed with a shotgun. The miners tried to rush the policemen, but Prest fired over their heads. They rushed again, and a young boy named Joseph Raine was hit by gunshot in the legs and hip. Shocked, the miners fell back, and asked if they could speak to Prest. Still armed, he met a deputation of three miners in the hallway. They pulled the gun from him and ran back to their fellows. More police arrived from Horden, and a pitched battle began. One policeman's life was saved by the presence of his notebook in his breast pocket, when he was hit full in the chest with a pickaxe. The miners retreated, and after tipping Mr Prest's carriage over a cliff into Castle Eden Dene, set off back to Horden.

With so many police away at Hardwick Hall, another crowd had congregated around the Club. Some got through the police cordon, and shortly after 7.30 pm on the 27th January 1910, fire broke out in the Club. Jimmy Rammage, a twenty-three-year-old coal hewer, saw the flames from the beach banks where he was walking with friends. They ran back to the village to find crowds laughing and singing in the light from the flames that lit up the whole village as if it was day. 'It was a grand fire,' he said, 'and everyone enjoyed it.'

A little girl who lived a few doors away in Seventh Street looked through the front door, past her mother, at the street lit a gaudy orange, and she heard a sudden and enormous crash as the glass awning at the front of the Club exploded.

The next day a blizzard swept over Horden, but thousands of people still came out to see what was left of the Horden Colliery Social Club. It had been virtually razed to the ground. Nothing further happened. A detachment of troops that had been sent by train to restore order was turned back. Of the dozens who were arrested, five men were sentenced to five years' imprisonment each.

I wondered how Horden had been transformed in less than fifteen years, from the raw half-formed township of the Horden Riot, to the Appollonian society, stable to the point of placidity, in which my father grew up – everyone stoically getting through the Depression with their community spirit and their hobbies, their gardens and pigeons, brass band and amateur dramatics.

Now it was convenient to view the Horden Riot, not so much as a political or social event, but as a kind of bacchanalian festival, a piece of folklore, which according to the local history pamphlet in which I was reading about it, was 'handed down from father to son'. In my father's childhood, however, it was almost never mentioned – certainly not through personal recollection – even though those involved must still have formed the bulk of the population.

4

The Matriarch

I HAD BEEN TOLD that Mrs Davies, who lived in the house in Oak Terrace where my father had grown up, and where my grandparents had lived till 1949, would have no objection to my paying a visit. The red brick, semi-detached dwelling had been built in 1923, but was of such austere utilitarian plainness, so totally lacking in decorative elements – so close in fact to one's archetypal conception of a 'council house' – it would have been very difficult to estimate its age by appearance alone. I was pleased to see, that while it had been redecorated inside many times since my grandparents' time, it remained relatively bare and spartan – though there was a large stereo in the living room, and of course a video (I had never seen so many satellite dishes as I had in Horden; though I was told that this was because people had taken them on approval, never paid the first instalment, and when the company came to reclaim them, the people were never in).

Mrs Davies, a short, homely person, showed me where the range would have been – the kitchen stove heated from the living-room fire on the other side of the wall. She said it kept the kitchen nice and warm in winter. I reflected that it must have made the place devilishly hot in summer if they had to light the living-room fire every time they wanted to cook. I didn't realise then that it was the custom in miners' homes to keep a fire burning round the clock, winter and summer, because of all the men and boys who'd be coming in from the pit needing baths at all times of the day and night.

Mrs Davies had been born in the house directly opposite, where her mother still lived, in the row called Elm Terrace, the first council houses to be built in Horden.

'It's funny,' said Mrs Davies, 'but I can always remember that even when I was very small, I always thought that this would be a nice house to live in. All the ones on this side of the road were a little bit more modern than ours. They had inside toilets, but ours were outside. But it wasn't just that, because it was always this particular one I liked. I don't know why. The Hudsons always seemed such nice people. Mollie was the same age as my elder sister, and they used to play together. Tom was a bit older, but I can remember that he was always very artistic. Mrs Hudson was very nice. Mr Hudson was a bit more reserved. I couldn't tell you much about him. But he always dressed very smartly – always wore a collar and tie.

'Then, about fifteen years ago, the house became vacant, so we moved in.'

According to George Orwell's *The Road to Wigan Pier*, people used to the 'frowzy huddle of the slum' did not fare well in council houses. They felt alienated by the relative distance from their neighbours, by the houses' damp and chilly newness, and often neglected their gardens. Those who were able to make good use of the new dwellings tended to be 'of superior type'. We must have been of superior type, I reflected.

But I was surprised at first to hear that these houses had not only always had inside toilets, but proper bathrooms with hot running water – facilities that were not installed in Horden's colliery houses till the 1970s. My father, although his parents had 'lived in' in one room at the time of his birth, had actually grown up in a house that was ultra-modern by the standards of the time. He had enjoyed levels of comfort and hygiene similar to those I had myself grown up with. His contact with the world of the old colliery houses, that he described so vividly in his stories, came entirely from his time spent at his grandparents' house, people who had for him 'already taken their place in history'.

'It's funny,' said Mrs Davies, 'but when we were decorating two years ago, we stripped the wallpaper in this room, and we found that each wall was painted a different colour. And I remembered that your father had done it like that. He'd have one wall here, say, grey, and another one there orange. Like modern art, see. When I saw it, I could remember him doing it just after the war, when he came out of the army. It brought it all back.'

They lived, my father's grandparents – Percy's parents – in Cowell Street, one of the streets of deputies' houses, still known as 'the big houses', between the Top Road and the upper edge of the Welfare Ground. While at a glance they looked no different from any other colliery houses, they were slightly more capacious, the very high walls giving a fortified, almost medieval appearance to the back yards. The Hudsons lived at number 28, only one off the Top Road, though in those days, the road petered out into fields less than fifty yards away, and the plot opposite where the Catholic church was to be built was all gardens.

From the yard, the back door led into the tiny back kitchen with the one tap in the house, and a fire and a boiler for washing clothes. That led into the large kitchen-cum-living room where all the cooking and eating and talking took place. By the window was a scrubbed table around which people ate. At the other end of the room was another table covered in a green baize cloth, on which were placed several framed family photographs. Two more large framed photographs of my great-grandmother's parents hung on either side of the 'press', a tall dresser of dark mahogany, its glass cabinet hung inside with lace curtains. But the dominating feature of the room was a huge black-leaded range, with a large boiler beside the fire which was kept burning day and night. The zinc bath which was kept, proverbially, hanging on the back door, was filled on the red tiles in front of the fire. Then the girls and Hal and Charlie, the lads still living at home, would be shooed from the room, and my father, small and unnoticed in the corner, would watch as the patriarch, having eaten his meal black, sat upright in the tub, as though afloat on a red tile sea, moored amid the polished fire irons, with the boiler breathing hot and hard, and the quartz veined coal spitting in the grate, the warm sponge revealing the white sinew, marked with bruise-like weals, where the flesh had healed translucent over the blue dust. Then the grandmother would be called in to wipe carefully round the jet rectangle of his back. In houses less refined than this one, that part of the body was never touched at all. 'Dinnut wash that,' a mother would warn her children. 'That's thi fattha's strength.' But James Hudson would usually leave it only about ten days before allowing it to be scrubbed clean.

Then he'd take the beautifully laundered, immaculately ironed white shirt that his wife had laid out for him, and put it on over his still black back, before sitting back with his pipe and the *Daily Mail*, while his wife returned to her tasks.

My great-grandmother! If my great-grandfather James Hudson was a historically remote figure, how much dimmer a presence was my great-grandmother. In all the stories about my grandfather and my great-grandfather, there was only the supposition that a mother and a wife must have been there – a spectral fulfiller of functions in the houses they had inhabited, who must have been there since nobody had said that she was not. For in those days, the women did everything in the houses, and made most of the decisions about what happened in them. A man behaving properly, according to the mores of the time, handed over his entire pay packet to his wife, and she gave him pocket money. He might be the lord and master, but he was essentially a stranger, an honoured guest in his own house. The women ruled there, and any woman who had achieved the position of grandmother was among the chiefs of women.

In Africa I came across women, particularly old women, who had lived all their lives in a condition of extreme poverty and in a position of submission to their menfolk equivalent to slavery, yet who none the less had about them a formidable gravitas and personal dignity. They were, in the society of women, the arbiters and uphold-ers of the law, and their universe had for them a completeness in which everything was so self-evidently what it was that the asking of questions was a superfluous, even an irrational activity. And I in my role as questioner had put myself in a position of inferiority. I imagine that my great-grandmother had something in common with these people. I say this despite the fact that I know virtually nothing about her.

Shortly after my return to Horden I was shown a photograph of a big woman dressed in black, tall, and broad in brow and chin and breast; grey hair pulled severely back in a bun, she squinted back at the viewer through oval wire-framed glasses. Her features were rather small in her broad face, but there was something in the firm, almost masculine set of the jaw, that suggests, not defiance – certainly not defiance – not even confidence or determination, but certainty. Something in the way the left-hand side of her mouth twists very slightly downwards suggests she would not tolerate any nonsense whatsoever. And nonsense, as far as she was concerned, would, I imagined, be virtually anything that did not come within the sphere of her domestic concerns.

She stands, appearing to teeter slightly in the high-buttoned shoes of the time, against the grim prison-like walls of a colliery back yard, next to her younger brother Jack Wilson, a master bricklayer at the pit, who stands slightly forward of her, but still perceptibly shorter, poker-faced and stiff limbed in his best suit, a short back and sides accentuating his huge jug ears.

The Wilsons were old Durham people, colliery officials who moved through the coalfield as their employment dictated. Isabella was born, as far as I could gather, at East Rainton, near Houghton-le-Spring, in 1876. But her family moved to Ushaw Moor, where her father became Master Shifter, when she was very young.

The Master Shifter was the overman of the Stone Shift. If a seam of coal was eighteen inches deep, the workings would be two and a half or at the most three and a half feet deep. As the hewers dug into the coal, crawling into the seam to cut around themselves in a semi-circle, they left behind a ledge of stone that had to removed before the face could move forward. This was called the canch, and every night, at ten o'clock when the last shift of hewers was coming out, the Stonemen went in to 'shoot the canches' – blowing them down with gunpowder where the layers of strata didn't 'drop' of their own accord. Where the 'bottom', the rock floor, was buckling it had to be hacked up with pick points. Then the roof, the rock overhead, was secured with 'packs', great walls of broken stone.

A drift mine – a system of tunnels whereby the men simply walked into the workings – had been established at Ushaw Moor in 1858, and a shaft was sunk to the Busty Seam in 1881. Later that year a strike began over the owner's attempts to suppress the union, during which scores of strikers and their families were evicted from their homes and forced to camp out on the moors in makeshift shelters. By that time, my paternal great-great-grandfather, Jackson Hudson, was also employed at the colliery as Master's Weighman, weighing the tubs of coal as they came to bank on behalf of the owner. But how any of my forebears, either the Wilsons or the Hudsons, behaved during this bitter dispute, which dragged on for two years and was by far the most momentous event in the history of Ushaw Moor, or what they thought of it and how their lives were affected by it, there is no evidence whatsoever. They were, apparently, all 'very Church'. 'Church' was the Anglican faith, and in mid-Durham, where Methodism still predominated among the miners, it was identified as the religion of the bosses. Both families had their names carved on their pews in the parish church. Both fathers were church wardens, and Old Hudson was even a lay reader. But for all their smattering of learning, their self-perceived propriety and superiority, these people were, when all was said and done, miners, and there is even today, for all the computerisation and high technology, an inescapable brutality and primitivism in the act of coal mining.

Bella's older sister Mary became a teacher, and married Matthew Hettles, a solicitor who owned a considerable amount of property in and around Durham City. Bella, however, was kept at home to help with the domestic labour, and she remained there till she married James Hudson at the age of eighteen. We can imagine the satisfaction of the heads of two of the most illustrious pit families in Ushaw Moor, at the marriage of their respective offspring on 14th July 1894.

James was twenty-two, and studying at night classes for his colliery manager's certificate. (He had been famous at school for the beauty of his copperplate handwriting.) He had been a pupil-teacher in Doncaster, when at the age of nineteen, his father, already in ill health, had summoned him and the two other younger sons Harold and Hardy to work beside him. And since in those days it was the duty of a son to do whatever his father asked without question, he had naturally complied. Old Hudson, who was apparently a pomp-ous, autocratic character, insisted that his sons all study for their manager's certificate. When Bella's father, Robert Wilson, became Foreshift Overman at Ushaw Moor, Harold Hudson became Mas-ter Shifter, and he later became manager of Kimblesworth colliery. James's other brother Hardy became Heap Keeper, in charge of the surface operations, at Ushaw Moor. It was said in the family that the old man would not allow Hardy and James to leave and get collieries of their own, as he wanted them near him to help him with his work.

Bella's first child Robert, born within five months of their mar-riage, died, but was immediately followed by another Robert, then Percy, Jack, Hal and Charlie. Then came the girls: Winnie, Martha and Nan. When we next catch sight of the Hudson family, towards the end of the First World War, they are in Horden. Jackson Hudson, James's father, has, presumably, died, and Harold and Hardy, the other brothers and all their offspring have totally disappeared from view. James has become 'the Old Man', and Bella, her youngest daughter just born, is soon to be a grandmother. I had been told that the problem with her eyesight had been caused by a feather boa being accidentally flicked in her face while dancing. And the first Robert, the one who had died, had been born only five months into marriage. Had he been born prematurely, or had he been conceived out of wedlock? Whatever the rather muddy circumstances under which such an event might have occurred in Ushaw Moor in the early 1890s, of these putative earlier selves, nothing now remained. Bella had taken on the appearance, the persona and the name by which she was to be known for the rest of her life – Grandma 'Oodson.

It has become proverbial that grandparents are the ones who are likely to indulge a child. Emotionally, because they are not primarily responsible for the child's behaviour, and financially, because they probably long ago finished paying for their house, and have all kinds of pensions and investments coming to fruition. In the early days of Horden however, grandparents remained distant and often austere figures in the chain of familial authority.

So my aunt Mollie had been able to pass on through Fred only the information that her grandmother had been strict. Others could say only that she was 'big' or 'upstanding'.

'She always held herself very well,' said Mrs Graham, who had known the family before they came to Horden. 'But I don't suppose she had much of a life with all those lads, because they all worked at the pit, you know, and they all had to be fed and bathed and their clothes washed. She must have had a hard life. She had bad legs you know. And she had a funny eye. Sometimes when you went past the house, you'd see her standing there in the doorway, in a long white apron, like they did in those days.'

It was as though there was nothing one could say about a woman of those times but recite the calendar of activities that constituted her existence year in, year out. It was as though Grandma Hudson had existed entirely in terms of what she knew: the knowledge and skills that it was her responsibility to inculcate into the next generations of the family.

Monday, washing day. Each of the daughters had her own particular task. Winnie ironed the table cloths and serviettes, Martha the pillow-cases and Nan the towels and handkerchiefs. Grandma, of course, doing the shirts herself. Tuesday and Wednesday, the bedrooms were cleaned. Thursday, the parlour, the best room at the front of the house that was hardly ever used. Then there was the cooking – and baking twice a week – and every evening the sewing and darning and altering, the girls taking their part in the struggle to keep everyone looking reasonably respectable. On Friday, as in every house in Horden, the yard was swilled out, the living-room floor was scrubbed. The black range was scrubbed and polished, the steel handles rubbed with emery paper until they shone. All the grates came out. The inside of the oven was white-washed, the fire irons cleaned and polished, and laid at the back of the green baize table covered in a cloth. Then on Saturday morning, everything was put back, sparkling like new.

Every Sunday, except Christmas, there was roast beef, with the Yorkshire pudding eaten first, as they still do in the North – not small 'individual' ones, but great puffy wads of batter, cooked in loaf tins or in pie tins, ten inches across, smothered in onion gravy. The men and boys would have a whole one, or even two each, to cut their appetite before they started on the meat. In summer, Grandma would make them all start with a plate of what she called 'summer medicine' – shredded lettuce and onions sprinkled with vinegar and sugar. When they'd had that and their Yorkshire pudding, they went on to the meat and vegetables – Grandfather always served first and most. The girls didn't get any of the lean meat, only the fat. Dessert would be bread pudding or rice pudding. The food was plain. Their clothes were plain. Everything was plain. If anyone was late for Sunday dinner, they got nothing. As Grandfather said, 'Your mother's taken the trouble to cook it, you can be here in time to eat it.'

Shortly after the dinner had been cleared away, preparations began for the Sunday tea, an event as sacred as the church service. The scrubbed table would be covered with a gleaming white cloth, the usual motley collection of old mugs and chipped cups put away, and the best china got out. The three-tiered cake stand – an heirloom – was piled with different kinds of cake. All home made. Grandfather wouldn't have anything bought. The meal ended with fruit, usually tinned cherries, Grandfather's favourite.

My great-grandmother's life *was* my great-grandfather. His meals were always on time. The shirt, always perfectly folded, there after the bath. His shoes, highly polished, stood ready in the usual place. A broad and stocky man, he'd played scrum half for Durham City when young. He rarely raised his voice in the home, not so much because he was even tempered, but because he didn't need to. In fact he didn't need to *do* anything. His wife and daughters were there to serve him, and in those days, if a boy misbehaved, his mother would say only, 'I'll tell thi fattha' and that would be the end of it. Once Bob, the eldest son, was punished at school for stealing. When he got home his father tied him to the iron bedstead and thrashed him till his arm ached. That was the expected thing in those days, and James Hudson desired only to do what was expected of him.

In those days, it was said that men *had* to drink, because on a Friday night the women took their baths, and the men went out to preserve their modesty. But there was many a man who, while he brutalised and bullied the home, felt permanently forced out, felt driven to the Club by his sense of inadequacy and alienation at his own hearth. James Hudson, however, sitting in his chair by the fire, remote behind his thick Edwardian moustache, assiduously studying the Tory *Daily Mail* through his half-moon reading glasses, was comfortably indifferent among his women. He was known as an intelligent, well-lettered man with a head for figures. But this intelligence remained largely latent, a matter of mildly awed repute. For he was no great conversationalist in the home. And he didn't go out much. To his garden, or to the pub for a pint. When he came in from work or from a walk, he'd say, 'All right, Bell?' and that would be that.

And although he came from a family of officials, he appeared to have remarkably little ambition for his own sons. For all that he was educated, he never encouraged them to read or study or seek to better themselves. So, with the exception of Percy, they all gravitated to the pit as soon as was legally permissible.

This mysterious indifference stemmed perhaps from a kind of inverted compassion. Just as there was no point upsetting yourself about things you could do nothing about, so there was a level a man would naturally reach, and there was no point fostering futile aspirations beyond that. He himself had been a teacher and his father had forced him to abandon this path in favour of mining. And although he had, at his father's insistence, obtained his manager's certificate, he had never risen above the position of deputy – the first rank among the non-commissioned officers of the pits, and not even an 'official' in the proper sense of the word at all.

In those days, women relatively seldom 'went out'. They certainly never went to pubs or clubs, and their groceries were delivered by the Store drays up the back lanes. But if women were not much seen on the 'front' streets, they were constantly in and out of each other's houses along the back.

If a woman had a mat on the harn (hessian – usually an old sack), the children would be put to cutting clippings from old clothes, which might be dyed to make particular patterns, and on the day of the mat-making, she'd make toffee. In the evening, every woman in the street would come to the house, and the woman would do nothing but make tea, while they ate the toffee, and the mat would be completed in an evening, everyone talking and laughing the whole time. On Sunday evening there was Mothers' Union for the 'Church' women, where patchwork-quilt making provided another opportunity for a good natter.

'There was a family lived next door, in the top house,' said Nan. 'The father had been killed at the pit. There was only the eldest son working, so the mother had to take in washing and go out wallpapering just to keep them going. My mother had us girls forever handing food over the wall to them. There was another woman at the bottom of the street, who never seemed to get out of bed. I suppose looking back on it, she must have been depressive. Mother would say, "Go and make her a cup of tea. She's not well." If someone else wasn't well, we'd be sent to cook or clean. Or if their man wasn't working, we'd be sent over with food. We were lent out! But if we were given threppence, we were sent straight back with it. You weren't allowed to take money for doing favours.'

On baking days, my father would watch Grandma standing at the scrubbed table, her powerful arms white with flour working the dough in the large earthenware crock – loaves in tins standing in line on the steel fender in front of the fire, waiting for the dough to rise, the golden crusts of others, freshly baked, cooling at the other end of the table. To my father, she was a person constantly absorbed in activity, too busy with the management of that factory of domesticity, too preoccupied with the ordering of the female world – the actions of the daughters, the son's wives, and ultimately the granddaughters – to have much time for idle chatter, or even for overt affection. But there was something about her unsmiling, phlegmatic presence, the way physically she never seemed to change, with fashion, or even with age – the grey hair always drawn back in a bun, the slightly sallow complexion, and always dressed in black – that was reassuring, even soothing. And once she had told my father of the most extraordinary event of her life. It had happened when she was eighteen. The doctors had been frightened for her sight, and she had had to have an operation. She was strapped down. Then her eyeballs were removed from their sockets without anaesthetic, and laid on her cheeks where the operation took place. She said it felt as though they were being scraped. This operation had left her severely cross-eyed, and she always avoided having her photograph taken.

On Saturday mornings, the uncles would go crabbing. Bob, the eldest, was the most practised and the most cunning at teasing the crabs from their crevices under the rocks. By midday, the back yard would be full of the mad creatures, climbing over each other in their desperation to find shelter around the blank walls and the doors of the coal house and the netty. Hal and Charlie, the two uncles who still lived at home, would hang my father out of the window by his ankles, and he'd scream with terror as the crabs sidled around him through the coal dust and the pools of stale washing water, their huge claws raised. They were served for Sunday tea, in the traditional way, a mound of the dark meat surrounded by the white. 'No one can do crab like Grandma Hudson,' everyone used to say.

My father, I now learned, had as a child lived for a time with his grandparents, and he was a frequent visitor to the house. I wondered if he hadn't been rather spoilt, surrounded by all these women – the grandmother and the three aunts.

'Spoilt?' said Nan, the youngest of the aunts, and the only living representative of that world. 'They ruined him! I never paid much attention to him, there not being much difference in our ages. But the others had to take him wherever they went. They had no choice. Mother used to send us out on errands, and she'd say, "Take Tom with you." Martha used to get fed up, trailing him round. She used to say, "Do I have to?" But Winnie was always very devoted to yer dad, and so was my mother.

'My father wasn't a talkative man, but he was always very fond of your father. All the grandchildren used to come to the house after church on a Sunday morning. The others all used to leave as soon as they could, but your father liked to stay. He always seemed to take an interest in what was going on. And my father used to take an interest in him. He used to tell him things – things he can't have told anyone else in the family. Because I can't remember him ever telling anybody anything very much – and you weren't allowed to ask questions. Maybe it was just because your father was more intelligent than the others. Maybe that's what it was – and my father knew it.'

As a young man, James Hudson had been a keen fisherman on the Deerness, the stream that ran along the bottom of the valley below Ushaw Moor. He had made all his own flies and all his own rods. When my father was thirteen, he had given the boy a greenheart trout rod of superb elegance and precision. Into the making of these things he had put a tenderness that had otherwise lain fallow all his life, but traces of which clung on in his dessicated heart to the very last.

The more I learned of the tight, integrated world of Horden – the impregnable nexus of the pit and the Big Club – the less it seemed to have to do with me. Percy, for example, had never been a great one for the Big Club. The cokemen had held their meetings at The Bell Hotel, not at the Miners' Hall like the other unions. Once my father went to the grammar school, he had, it seemed, been orientated socially towards Hartlepool rather than Horden. He once took my stepmother, a Wiltshire woman, into the Big Club – the massive upstairs hall packed for the turns – and she hadn't been able to understand a word that was said. I now realised that far from showing her *his* world, it was only about the second time he had been in there.

Now I learned from Nan that instead of suffering in the narrow seams, Percy's two younger brothers Hal and Charlie had not been miners at all. Charlie had had some kind of low level clerical job, while Hal had worked at the pit briefly, but never underground. My connections with the old pit world of Horden seemed to be dwindling by the day.

One afternoon, however, at the house of Joyce Spark (my father's cousin, and my last surviving relative in Horden), I came across a photograph of two miners from earlier in the century. No crash helmets or fluorescent overalls for them. Cloth caps, old jackets and waistcoats, and a muffler at the neck, long metal lamps dangling from the middle fingers of their left hands. Characters straight out of folklore – 'two owld pitmen'. The tall one on the left with the walrus moustache looked like a saturnine and slightly demented version of Kitchener. But the one on the right, the stocky one with his hand on his belt, equally moustachioed, but with a keener, colder gaze through his mask of black grit, looked strangely familiar.

There he was, my great-grandfather, James Hudson, in his knee-length breeches and thick woollen socks, his big boots more mud and encrustation than actual leather – the real thing: a miner. You couldn't get more authentic than that. Looking closely at the lamp he was carrying, I could see that at the time this photograph was taken, he was no longer a deputy. Although he looked vigorous enough, he must already have been in decline.

There were twelve steps that led up out of the pit yard. And one day, at the age of about sixty, James Hudson slipped on the top one, fell and hit his head. He got up, and he didn't mention it to anyone. That was just like him. He never told anyone anything. Then he started to have terrible headaches. His wife told him to see the doctor. But he refused. Oh, no. There was nothing wrong with *him*.

Finally he admitted he'd had a fall, and Nan arranged for him to see the doctor. He lost the power of speech. At the time he was believed to have cancer of the throat. But Nan, who had been a nurse, now believed he had had creeping paralysis of the throat, caused by a compressed fracture of the skull.

'He gradually lost the ability to swallow,' she said. 'So he couldn't eat or drink. Nowadays they drip-feed people, but in those days they couldn't do anything for them. He was unable to eat, so he just wasted away. He starved to death, actually. It took four years. We all had to watch, and there was nothing we could do. He was sixteen stone to begin with, and he was less than five by the end. I could carry him round the house in my arms.'

He was put on light work at the pit, first 'back-bye' – maintaining the roadways – then a storeman at bank.

As each of the sons got married and left home, it left another of the daughters free to go into service – to 'place' as they called it – as was the inescapable fate of any daughter whose presence had become superfluous in the home. That was the pattern of those times. There was no point having a girl sitting about with no work to do, and still needing to be fed. So, one by one, girls were sent away to do the most menial tasks in the big houses – sometimes nearby, but often at the other end of the country. At fourteen, Winnie and Martha were working from six in the morning till ten at night, Winnie as a maid in Manchester, Martha in the workers' accommodation department of a department store in London. They had Sunday afternoons off and two free evenings, and earned five shillings a week. Some girls got work in their own villages, working for pit families with several sons and no daughters. But this was generally agreed to be even greater 'slavery' than going away.

They would remain at 'place' until they came home to get married – though many of course never did return. It meant that there was always a dearth of young women in the colliery villages. One of the saddest sights of the interwar years was seeing groups of young men on a Sunday evening slowly wandering the roads between the colliery villages. Boys from Easington walking to Horden. Horden lads on their way to Blackhall – kicking stones, whittling sticks, skylarking around – but just wandering, aimlessly and despondently.

Soon there was only Nan left, and they were moved from the big house in Cowell Street to one of 'the cottages', the bungalows on the Top Road. Then Nan went to 'place' at Seaton Carew, and they were alone.

My father was the only one of the grandchildren to pay regular visits. The others had always felt uncomfortable in the Hudsons' strict, old-fashioned regime. Now they avoided the house of death as much as possible. But my father was at one time going there almost every day.

By this time the old man could not talk at all. The only way he could communicate was by writing, gripping a pen in his shaking fist as he formed words effortfully on a pad. Then he was unable to handle paper and had to use a child's writing slate and chalk. Finally he was reduced to rubbing marks in the chalk dust with his fingers, looking waterily up at my father to see if they evoked any resonance. What were they, these indecipherable marks, these runes? They were things about the family. Things he'd never told anybody, which needed to be passed on. All his life he'd held back. And since in his world it had been considered bad manners to ask questions, his children had not been encouraged to feel any curiosity in such matters. Now however he wanted to communicate. He wanted to get it off his chest. But it was too late.

'It was tragic really,' said Nan. 'Because he'd always had such beautiful handwriting.'

After he died, Grandma Hudson went to live with Martha at Cotsford Park at the bottom of Horden. She had suffered for decades from pernicious anaemia and migraines. But she never talked about it. She never complained. The ulcers on her legs got worse. She had to have them bathed and bound every day. One Sunday evening they got home from church and found her lying dead on the bathroom floor.

It was dark, but at Fred's, the curtains were not yet closed, so at either end of the long lounge-dining room there was a gaping expanse of night. Betty had come as she did every Sunday evening to do the ironing. We sat, Fred, myself and Betty's husband Jack, in a semi-circle round one side of the dining table, and watched her. There was no sound save for the occasional thud of the iron on to the ironing-board.

'How's yer dad?' asked Betty at length.

'Not so bad.'

There was a long pause while Betty completed the shirt she was on.

'Is he coming over this year?'

'I think so.'

'He's not been over for a couple of years now, has he?'

'No.'

'I didn't think he had.' She looked up from the ironing. 'Ee, I remember when he cooked the meal on New Year's Eve. I don't know when that would be. Must be forty, forty-five years ago. He cooked pheasant. I'd never had it before. I've never had it since, come to that. Anyway, it was beautiful.' She went back to the ironing; the same smooth even strokes over the cloth. 'Mind, you should have seen the washing up afterwards. He must have used every pot and pan in the place.' Jack and Fred chuckled. 'I don't suppose he's done any washing up in his life, yer dad, has he?'

'Not a lot.'

'I didn't think he had.'

The last time I could remember seeing Jack and Betty was on a New Year's Eve more than twenty years before. Jack had taken me 'fust footing'. A man had come staggering towards us out of the darkness. Jack said the man was drunk, and I'd been very excited as I'd never seen a drunken man before. In those days, Jack's hair had been absolutely black. It was now steel grey. He had an extraordinarily broad face, his very wide mouth set always in an expression of slightly watchful placidity.

'What number you living at in Hardwick Street?' asked Betty.

I told her.

She paused, stared into space for a few moments, then told me the house's exact position in the street. She chuckled to herself and carried on ironing. 'I know me streets, don't I? Me mam used to make me deliver the parish magazine. I must know every house in Horden.'

Jack and Betty had been Mollie and Fred's best friends. Mollie and Betty knew each other through the church – the Girls' Friendly Society. As children they'd virtually lived in each other's houses. Jack and Betty had become almost part of the family with the same rights and obligations as the children themselves. They'd go off on their own and stay with our relatives, like Aunt Ethel, my grandmother's sister in Barnard Castle. Betty would help out in the kitchen, and if Percy needed anything doing in the house or in the garden, Jack would have to do it in the same way Fred would. 'And if he told you to do something,' Jack said, 'you had to do it.' Jack and Betty had no children, so when Mollie's and Fred's two, came on the scene, it was as though they had two sets of parents.

When my sister and I went to stay with Mollie and Fred, we always wondered who they were, these strange people, who of all the people who came and went apparently uninvited in and out of the kitchen door, were even more omnipresent than the others – and seemed more part of the family than we were. But of course they weren't strange. It was us who were strange. They were part of the world of 'our so-and-so' and 'our so-and-so' from which we were necessarily excluded. We knew that we would never be 'our Mark' or 'our Katie' to anyone.

To us there was always a slight feeling of discomfort in that house, as though you could never be quite warm enough. Not that it was actually cold, but it had about it a kind of spiritual draughtiness, cooled by the hectoring cadences of all those people in the – to our eyes – bare, spartan rooms, who talked all the time of people unknown to us, as though we must know them, or certainly never questioning whether we knew them or not.

My sister told me years later that she had never felt able to relax in that environment, because she felt constantly that she was about to overstep some invisible cultural boundary, infringe some unknown custom, for which she would be told off. She never was of course. But Mollie was always forthright. In that house she had always held the floor, because Fred preferred to do rather than to talk. And like many people in that part of the world, it was as though she had a tone of rising indignation built into her speech. It didn't mean anything. It was just the way she spoke.

'She's a Hudson!' Fred had said about Nan. And like Nan, Mollie always said exactly what she thought. It meant they had sometimes had to be careful. But also, like Nan, she had had this habit of taking people on. Nan had had an old couple living next door to her in Jesmond. They were well off and could easily have afforded paid help. But Nan could see they were the kind of people who wouldn't bother to look after themselves, so she was always taking hot meals round to them. Mollie was the same. Nan had just been copying her mother, Grandma Hudson. Mollie was just copying her mother, Jenny. But unlike the women of those earlier generations, Mollie had had a job. She was a teacher – of what are now called 'children with special needs' – and she was active in the Labour Party. At Mollie's funeral the church had been packed. You couldn't get in the door.

I hadn't even been aware of Mollie's death till after the funeral had taken place. Now I felt I had missed Mollie totally. It was sad.

5

A Hammer called Monday

I WAS INVITED to visit by Joan and Denis Reardon, who I'd met them at the church, where I'd gone in the hope of coming across people who had known my grandparents. They were slightly younger than my father, but could both remember him. They'd invited me to their house to meet a neighbour who would be able to tell me about Horden in the old days.

Before being apprenticed at the pit as an electrician, Denis had gone to work in the garage at the bottom of the road which now led up to Peterlee. In those days it had belonged to the father of my father's friend Fat Wrathall. He wasn't particularly large, but had assumed this nickname as his real name, Aubrey, had seemed embarrassingly posh. Denis could remember my father going there frequently to chat to the lads. With his corduroy jacket and his cravat, he had seemed an 'arty type'.

Joan had grown up a couple of streets down the bank from my father, and had just been starting at Henry Smith's Grammar School in Hartlepool when he was in the sixth form. She had had intentions of going to London to become a nurse, but her mother had needed her assistance at home, so she had never gone anywhere.

'Didn't Tommy Hudson go out with Norma Lindoe?' asked Denis.

'I was just going to say,' said Joan, 'Tommy Hudson and Norma Lindoe rings a bell. She was a lovely girl, mind.'

'Very pretty,' said Denis.

'She had long dark hair and beautiful dark eyes.'

My father's cousin Joyce had shown me a photograph of my father, looking alarmingly young and fresh-faced, sitting in the middle of what looked like a flower bed with a very beautiful dark girl who stared into the camera with a look of gracious and indulgent benevolence. On the back it said 'Tom and Moira'. Moira was my mother, and this certainly wasn't my mother. I'd known for a long time that my father had had a girlfriend, a rather shadowy figure, to whom he'd been engaged before going into the army. While he was lying in a hospital bed after the Battle of Kohima, recovering from a shrapnel wound, he had received a letter saying she was about to marry someone else. He had always maintained that since a hundred and forty-six men of his company had gone into Kohima, and only eighteen had come out, he was so relieved to be alive he had found this news only mildly annoying. As to who this woman was, however, and what she was actually like, he had always been exceedingly vague.

'What happened to Norma Lindoe?' asked Joan. 'I haven't heard of her for years.'

'I think she died, didn't she?' said Denis, sipping his tea.

'I don't know,' said Joan. 'She lived, I think, Hamilton Street ... or was it Hanley. One of those streets along there, what they call the Big Houses. I think her father was a deputy at the pit or something. I used to sit in the same compartment with her on the way to school every morning. To try and keep order on the train they used to make you go in the compartments in groups with a prefect in charge – boys in some, girls in another. Norma Lindoe used to be one of the two prefects in the compartment I was in. Some mornings I used to hear her and her friend talking about what she'd been getting up to with Tommy Hudson.'

What sort of things *had* they got up to?

'Oh, I can't remember. But it was well known. Tommy Hudson and Norma Lindoe.'

'That's right,' said Denis.

I wondered what my father had been like in those days.

'I thought he was wonderful,' said Joan. 'I thought all the big lads were wonderful. You do when you're a young girl. They all seemed so handsome and athletic.'

The doorbell rang.

A man came in, took off his coat and cap, and almost immediately began talking, counting off lists of names on his fingers – names of the children in certain families, and the names of the children of the families who had lived next door to them. Lists of the shops that had been along Blackhills Road, the main shopping street of Horden, in the 1930s – and all in the correct order. The names of the five women teachers at Horden Elementary School. The names of all the doctors that had worked in Horden, in chronological order. Although he had obviously come for my benefit, he paid no attention to me, but seemed to address himself to the world in general. He was only a few years older than Joan and Denis, but had the resigned tone of a much older man – though the way he wrestled with his slight stammer as he grasped the finger on to which he was counting, made it seem as though he was bursting to get his information out. Yet all the time his grey eyes remained expressionless in his smooth, pink face.

'Now,' he said. 'T-T-Tommy Hudson. They lived Seventh Street, Hudsons. There was Tommy and the three lasses.' He gripped his digits again. 'There was Mavis, Audrey . . .'

Joan turned to me. 'I think your dad just had the one sister, didn't he?'

'Yes,' I said.

'I think this is a different Tommy Hudson you're talking about, Alec.'

But the man insisted on telling us about these people anyway, as though to admit the irrelevance of this information would diminish him personally. It reminded me of the way some older people reacted to questions in my childhood – shrugging them off, as though to mention subjects of which they were ignorant were a critical affront. It was an attitude I was to come across many times in Horden. The man told us all about this other Tommy Hudson and his sisters, and threw in a list of their cousins for good measure.

'You used to go to Reeford's Farm at the top of the bank for the Sunday School treat. You used to think that was the day of all days, the Sunday School treat. The prize would be maybes a pennith o' sweets, something like that, or six Dirty Dinahs or, what did they call them toffees you used to get in Walter Willson's?'

'Horner's toffees?' suggested Joan.

'Aye. And six o' them. And they used to give you a drink. You used to think it was wonderful. Aye, they talk about things were hard up then, but we used to go to the Deluxe for two jam jars. The Big Club had a cinema upstairs called the Deluxe. You'd go along, hand over your jam jar and you'd get in. And they used to have talent shows on there. I remember, there was a lad called Riley, Fatty Foster – his fattha was the policeman – Speg Gibson and me, and we went up on stage and sang, 'We four p-poor Italianos from fair I-ta-ly!' We won first prize!' I got the impression that for him life could have held no glory greater than winning the talent competition in the Deluxe Cinema in Horden in – when would it be? – 1930-something. I could see him up there with his three pals, putting his heart and soul into the inane ditty. With his fresh face, and his grey hair neatly parted at the side, I imagined he hardly looked much different now than he had then.

'Aye, it's nice to look back. Because they were far better days than what they are now.'

'Were they?' asked Joan.

'Every Friday you used to see the people swill the yards. They used to scrub the steps and put some stone on. All the fireplaces used to come out, and they polished the black leading. They whitewashed underneath. Every day was a day for something in them days. Some days you walked along and you could smell the bread they'd baked. I've seen the stottie cakes, lying, all wrapped in white tea towels waiting on the steps to cool. Nobody shut their doors then. The doors was open all the time. You used to go round on a New Year's Eve, and just call at anybody's house. Now you dursn't go out at all.

'It's sad growing old ... But I've had some good times in Horden. Oh aye, I've enjoyed Horden. They'll say, what is there about Horden? Well, I would far rather live in Horden than Easington.'

'Unless you've lived in both, you cannut really judge, mind,' said Joan.

'You'd go to the first show at the Empress. Then you came out and there was the pork shop and you could have a penny dip – a bread bun dipped in gravy with a piece of fat on top. Or you could have a saveloy or a pork sandwich. It was that thick with meat, then they'd put the stuffing and the crackling on top. Then the fish shop was only round the corner. Fish and a pennith was threppence. Then you could go up to the Picture House, and catch the second show there. So you could have your whole evening's entertainment for sixpence.'

'Sixpence was a lot of money in those days,' said Joan. 'A lot of people didn't have sixpence. Your father was a deputy, so maybe you could afford it.'

But he went on, oblivious, in a waking dream of women making their own toffee, of clippy mattings and double possing, and how he'd spent his honeymoon upstairs in the double seats at the Empress.

'My mother never saw my father's paynote,' said Joan. 'He used to give her two pound a week, housekeeping. When I went to the grammar school, she heard that poor people could get assistance with school uniforms from the council. But when she applied, they said, "Oh no. This is for poor people." She found out he'd been earning up to £7 a week. We were well off, but he was drinking it all. Even so, she couldn't do anything about it. But we were happy. I mean, he never mistreated us.'

Behind the driver of the 'hoppa' bus, a canvas blind swung with the bouncing motion of the vehicle. Beside it, a woman sat sprawled, talking through the gap between the blind and the window, as though to the unseen figure of a priest in a confessional, but with a constant animated insistence. Above her, a sign in letters rendered minute by the No Smoking sign above them, asked passengers not to distract the driver's attention while the bus was in motion. This woman was not only engaging the driver in a narrative of intense and all-absorbing interest as we went careering along the byways of East Durham, she was sucking on a cigarette which in the light of its flagrant flouting of the above injunction, appeared enlarged to grotesque dildo-like proportions. It would have seemed outrageous if everyone else on the bus, with the exception of myself, had not also been smoking. The couple behind me, both over sixty and sitting directly beneath a No Smoking sign, were heedlessly blasting clouds of grey toxic matter all over me. Had we been anywhere else in the country, I would have drawn their attention politely to the sign. But we were in East Durham, the web of pit villages around the new town of Peterlee, of which Horden was the largest – and in East Durham, where Durham City with its cathedral, university and olde worlde tea shops seemed almost as far away as London, such things as No Smoking signs seemed the mark of a remote and irrelevant authority.

Through the smoke and the grime on the window, I could see out on to the grey rain-lashed fields before the bus plunged into a dip in the land, and then climbed the hill towards Easington Colliery. The woman was now standing beside the driver, swaying and teetering with the wild lurching of the bus, clinging desperately to her cigarette, as though it rather than the hand rail were supporting her, and without once letting up in the headlong velocity of her narrative.

At night, taking the bus from Durham after a brief visit to London, my spirits would sink lower and lower the further east we went. At Sherburn Hill, the road ascended on to the high clay plateau of East Durham, the bare fields invisible in the darkness, the former pit villages apparently deserted except for small groups of shell-suited kids, looking up through the black drizzle in forlorn expectancy. Beyond the lights of the small council estates, one could see the lights of further villages, spun out like undulating webs in the darkness, indicating that the landscape through which we were travelling was a kind of false countryside, densely populated, and that much of the life it supported was highly urban in character.

Suddenly the words 'Ave Maria' appeared written on the darkness, the figures of the Virgin and Child illuminated high in the darkness above them – a reminder that this was a part of the country that retained a high proportion of Roman Catholics.

From Shotton, the villages became larger, the detours round their estates longer and more circuitous. One looked out into living rooms, the net curtains looped or rouched coquettishly back to reveal neat interiors of Co-op furniture. There was dad settling down to his evening's telly. There were the first arrivals in the snooker rooms of the Working Men's Clubs. People queuing in the fish and chip shop, the pizzeria, the Chinese take-away. And in the lounges of the vast old people's homes the games of housey would be well under way.

Very rough-looking people would start to get on the bus. Drawn pale adults heading straight for the rear seats; grimy children not dressed up for the cold.

When you arrived in East Durham, you realised immediately where you stood in relation to class. If you had wondered if terms like 'middle class' and 'working class' still had any meaning, or if such a thing as 'working-class culture' could still be said to exist, you were immediately disabused of your illusions. The moment you arrived in East Durham, you were *in it* – up to your neck. In East Durham, it often seemed that there *was* nothing else. And if you found it unattractive, if it made you feel uneasy, if you couldn't wait to get away from it, that meant you were middle class.

Until the beginning of the nineteenth century, it was assumed that the coal seams must deteriorate or 'nip out' altogether as they disappeared under the water-bearing limestone of the East Durham plateau. So while the collieries proliferated on Tyneside and Wearside, and around Durham City, the coastal area between Sunderland and Hartlepool remained scarcely inhabited well into the last century – an area of bleak, infertile clay, its meagre vegetation blasted by the relentless North Sea winds into gnarled and twisted formations.

In the early 1800s, however, it was discovered that the Hutton

Seam continued under the limestone at Hetton, in the north-west of the area. Hetton colliery opened in 1822, and was quickly followed by South Hetton, Haswell, Seaton, Thornley and Wingate. The financial costs involved in sinking shafts through the limestone were massive and 'unprecedented in mining'. The water, which bore down through the permian from the west of the county, created underground streams capable of delivering several thousand gallons a minute, which could only be stemmed or pumped out at great expense. The sinking of the pit at Murton by the South Hetton Colliery Company, which began in 1838, was at the time the most difficult and expensive in the history of British mining. The three-shift system, the continuous production of coal, twenty-four hours a day, was introduced for the first time at Murton to try to recover some of the enormous costs involved. It soon became the normal method of working throughout the country.

The coastal collieries between Seaham and Hartlepool – Dawdon, Easington, Horden and Blackhall – were the last and the biggest in the coalfield – the *ultima thule* of the Durham coal industry. Compared to the semi-rural pit villages of mid-Durham, from which much of their populations had come, the communities that grew up around them were thriving metropoli. In those inland areas, it had been common for men to move every few years in search of better pay and conditions. Every pit's life was limited by the relatively small areas of land available for extraction. But these coastal collieries had the whole of the North Sea under which to mine. They could surely keep working, virtually for ever. The size and grandeur of structures like St Mary's Church in Horden testified to this sense of permanence.

So 'East Durham' had been created by mining – a densely populated area, in which according to a survey of 1929, 89 per cent of the working population was employed in the pits, while the representation of the professional classes was virtually negligible. While this was no longer true, it was a well known fact that the majority of professionals – doctors, teachers, policemen, social workers – who served the area, preferred to live outside it. And many attested to an almost missionary sense of purpose. Not that these people were all necessarily fired by a personal improving zeal, but the resonance of the whole 'concept' of East Durham in the demonology of the social service world of the North-east, made such an attitude inevitable. East Durham had become synonymous in such circles with economic, social and cultural deprivation.

One afternoon in a pub in Durham, I met a genial ex-policemen, who I was told had worked for several years in East Durham.

'Fucking awful place! Where did you say you were living? *Horden*?' He winced. 'Fucking *awful* place! They ought to put a fence round that whole area, chip it away and push it into the fucking North Sea. It's got the highest crime rate in the county, and the lowest level of public co-operation with the police. In Peterlee, if they see someone breaking into their neighbour's house, they don't phone the police, they just look the other way.

'They're *hard* people over there! Have you seen the sea-coalies? Standing up to their knees in the North Sea in January, to dig a ton o' coal? Fucking *awful* place!'

I wondered if he'd lived in the area while he was working there.

'Did I *fuck*? Very few policemen who work in that area live there. The few that do, come from there. Nothing against them, mind. It's their life, and it's what they know. But there's no way I would live there. We used to call the police station in Peterlee "Fort Apache". Policemen from other districts coming through the waiting area, see-ing the state of the people sitting there, used to wonder, "What the fuck place is this?"'

One often heard that because Peterlee was a new town and housing was relatively freely available, it had attracted the dregs of the rest of the country, which had brought the rest of the area down.

He looked sceptical. 'Why, you do hear a few odd accents. But most of these people are of local origin. They're from mining families . . . Don't get me wrong, mind. I'm from a mining family myself.'

As I walked through Peterlee town centre, I wondered why my meeting with the Reardons had made me feel so angry.

From the beginning, Peterlee had been intended to be a special place. It was conceived of during the last war, in response to the chronic overcrowding in the colliery villages. In Horden alone, hun-dreds of houses were double tenanted – one family living upstairs, another downstairs – or whole families 'lived in', in one room, at a rent higher than they would have paid in a council house. People who had lost their jobs through accident or illness, and families where the father had been killed, lost their entitlement to colliery houses, and were forced to live in caravans or in sheds at the allotments or on the beach banks. In the older colliery villages like Haswell and Thornley, people were hanging on in crumbling lean-tos that had been sub-standard in the nineteenth century, while a mile down the coast, at Blackhall Rocks, there were families living in caves.

The existing colliery villages being deemed inadequate for social development, it was decided that housing development in the post-war period would take place at a centralised site; with playing fields, open spaces, shops, tree planting and social and cultural facilities integrated into the overall design. Berthold Lubetkin, modernist architect of the Penguin Walk at London Zoo and the High Point flats in Highgate, was approached with the brief of creating the 'Miners' Capital of the World'. Having gleaned that because of the nature of their work miners were used to travelling in lifts, he proposed a succession of vast Corbusieresque tower blocks with panoramic views over the North Sea – and this on an area already undermined, in the minds of the local people, to a condition of spongelike insubstantiality. Later, the artist Victor Pasmore was employed as consultant on the South Western housing development. The resultant 'cubistic' designs were conceded by all as revolutionary, but they had since been so heavily refurbished because of design faults that they were virtually unrecognisable.

It was originally imagined that the old colliery villages would gradually disappear through slum clearance. In the original planning document, 'Farewell Squalor', Middle Seventh Street in Horden was illustrated along with the worst hovels of Shotton and Wingate as evidence of the conditions that needed to be escaped. But while many found contentment in the 'clean air' of Peterlee, in houses with private gardens, hot water and indoor lavatories, others, used to the 'free' housing of the collieries, resented the relatively high rents of Peterlee. People for whom leaving their villages even for a day was a major event, who had worked every day of their lives with their former school fellows and close relatives, found living next door to 'strangers' – even people from neighbouring pit villages – alarming. By the Seventies, people had started moving back to the villages. The demolition of the old colliery rows was arrested. And while it was proverbial that because of the gimcrack building methods of the 1960s there was not a single house in Peterlee that had not been at least partially rebuilt, and whole developments had already been demolished, Middle Seventh Street in Horden was still standing.

Not that Peterlee was declining. It was expanding. Not with houses for workers in the industries that were supposed to replace the pits, but developments of 'Heritage Homes' for the young and modestly mobile. The idea of Peterlee as the future of the colliery villages, or indeed the 'future' of anything, no longer obtained.

'The Future'. What had happened to that gleaming prospect? A man or woman 'conscious' in the 1930s, for all that they suffered in their daily life, could feel the distant warmth, the oncoming brilliance of the egalitarian dawn. As a child, in our sun-filled house in Wales, with its clean modernist lines, its vast open vistas of the sky and sea, I felt myself to be already living in the age towards which these people had been working. When I had visited that house earlier that year, however, I found that like the Pasmore developments in Peterlee, it had not only been largely rebuilt because of the shoddiness of the original construction methods, but its elegantly simple proportions, supposedly representative of the functional rationalism of the modern age, had disappeared under a blandly traditional superstructure and an encumbrance of anachronistic ornamentation.

That world, the post-war period, with its absurd hopes and pathetic *folies de grandeur*, its failures and betrayals, was a historical moment so discredited, so universally derided, it had achieved almost a kind of quaintness. And the very conception of Peterlee had in the mind of many of its inhabitants acquired a sense of bathos, even a faint disgrace. The much vaunted Science and Technology Park, that would not only bring much needed employment to the area, but 'add immeasurably to the influence of Britain in Europe', and the long promised arts centre, a brick of neither of which was ever laid; the trial and imprisonment for corruption of the town's Development Corporation chairman T. Dan Smith (on charges that had nothing to do with Peterlee); the Stamford and Levaggio murder, a gangland killing connected with the installation of one-armed bandits; the decision to get an artist to erect flat-roofed houses under the onslaught of the North Sea wind and rain: all these things somehow cohered in the minds of many of the inhabitants to taint the idea of Peterlee.

Among middle-class people living in places like Durham City or Newcastle, the fact that one was living in or near Peterlee elicited a groan of sympathy. Beleaguered down there on its windswept area of coast, among the grimly ossifying remains of a dying industry, Peterlee lacked even the high drama of the inner city. For such people the very name of Peterlee had a derisory ring.

Yet it continued doggedly to exist. It could be considered, on many levels, a success. But the idea that it represented a stage in the transcendence of a class was laughable.

'The Raising of the Working Class'. How hollow those words seemed as I walked through Peterlee shopping centre. There was no theatre, no bookshop in Peterlee, or in the whole of East Durham. But it was not the absence of middle-class cultural pursuits that I objected to about Peterlee. It wasn't even the drab mundanity of its architecture. It was that even by the light of its own modest ambitions it was an extremely *bad* shopping centre. Anything bought in Peterlee was, I found, not only of poor quality, but more expensive than could be found elsewhere. Like the products one is forced to buy at inflated prices in corner shops after everything else has closed, they tended to have some critical design fault that rendered them useless. I bought, for example, an adaptor so that I could plug my Walkman into the mains. Having forced it into the socket, I found it virtually impossible to unplug without half demolishing the wall. Peterlee seemed a shopping centre entirely given over to such products. The shop assistants, when not actively surly, were listless and bored, while the functionaries in places like public libraries – one hesitates to call them librarians – positively bristled with hostility.

In such an environment, the branches of the two principal chain stores, Safeway and Boots, which were exactly the same as those to be found anywhere else in the country, seemed representative of almost exalted levels of refinement.

But the most depressing thing about the place was the abjectness with which the population appeared to accept this mediocrity and third rateness.

'Peterlee was the death of Horden,' one heard the older people saying, lamenting the decline of the old ways. But it seemed to me that Peterlee was the spiritual successor to Horden. It wasn't just that Horden was now an administrative appendage of Peterlee. Peterlee was what 'Horden' had become.

It was easy, too easy, to see a kind of beauty in the back lanes of Horden and the life that was lived there. To detect an appealing symmetry in the way its every detail was shaped by the demands of work – to perceive a dignity and a nobility not only in the stoicism with which it was endured, but in its very rigidity, its very hardness. But for all the energy and enterprise the people had put into that way of life, what had the 'culture' of Horden led to? What had 'Horden' created?

After my conversation with the old man at the Reardons, I had felt angry with my forebears, not only for having left so little of themselves in that place for me, but because the life they had lived had been so easily reduced to nothing more than an old man's memories of snacks. The world of Grandma Hudson had not only a completeness, but, so it seemed to me, a self satisfaction in its own utter demise. And this world had left behind nothing but the capacity to accept Peterlee – a world in which Safeway and Boots seemed the apogee of sophistication.

The proud old ways of resistance and communal enterprise had gone leaving only a slavish aquiescence at the lowest level of consumerism.

To me, Horden was not so much associated with socialism, it *was* socialism. But I had been living in the place for over a month, and I hadn't heard the word once. And now I began to find the word suspect even in connection with my grandfather.

Percy's socialism – was it a matter of strategies and ideas that could actually be discussed? Or was it simply a blank assertion of the rightness of whatever the Labour Party did? According to Fred, Percy had rarely discussed politics in the home, as Jenny didn't like it. Percy had described himself, according to my father, as an old-fashioned Christian socialist with little formal education, but long practical experience of his industry and a certain amount of native cunning. When my father was fourteen, Percy had given him a copy of Marx's *Wage, Labour and Capital* to read. Or so my father said. It wasn't that I didn't believe him. But where were they today, these Christian socialists who read Marx? Where was their legacy? From what I gathered, the people in Horden didn't read much, even in the way of Jeffrey Archer and Danielle Steele, let alone dense tomes of political theory.

Generally, my search for Percy had been an uphill struggle. Biographers manage to put together remarkably full accounts of people who lived hundreds of years ago. Percy had died only twenty-five years ago, but so far I had managed to learn extraordinarily little about him. He had left £300 in his will, but otherwise, like his father before him, he had left nothing behind him but a few grainy photographs. No furniture, no heirlooms, no books, no letters of recommendation, not one single document to attest to forty years of active trade unionism. And although he had been a prominent figure in a tightly-knit village community, very few people could remember him. Most of his generation had hardly lived longer than he had. And the few slightly younger men who could remember him from the coke ovens, the parish council and the Labour Party could say only that he was a 'nice feller' or a 'grand chap' – and I felt they would probably have said that about anyone.

One day, however, I met the old park keeper, sitting in the tiny shed at the top of the Parish Council Park, a pipe clenched firmly between his gums. 'Percy Hudson? I should remember him. His brother married my sister.'

'Who was that, Hal?'

'Aye, 'Al 'Oodson. Went to work in a fact'ry down Rugby. Died . . . oh, a canny while agan now.'

But what about Percy? What had Percy been like?

'Percy Hudson? Why, he was a bit of a swanky feller to tell you the truth. Liked to dress up and hang about with the big nobs.'

Who?

'The big nobs. The top people in the union. Mind, he was on the Parish Council. And if you were on the Parish Council you were some bugger in them days.'

'I remember him,' said a woman, related to my father's cousin Joyce, who had so far been able to say nothing about anybody, other than that they were 'nice'. 'He was a bit of a dandy, wasn't he?' A gleam came into her eye. 'He always seemed a bit different from the others, a bit more of a gentleman.' She became suddenly apologetic. 'I wouldn't say anything against him, but he always seemed to keep himself a bit more to himself. Now his younger brothers, Charlie and them, they were more like the rest of us.'

What was that like?

'Oh, free and easy! Just enjoying ourselves, you know.'

One thing you *did* hear about Percy was that he often wore a collar and tie. In those days, that was the sign of someone who was marking himself out, not as better than his fellows, but as someone of worth, a leader – someone who was aspiring.

Before the coming of the collieries, East Durham's most notable feature was the denes, the magnesian limestone glens – the beds of ancient rivers that had cut through the high boulder clay and the permian as they ran towards the sea. The biggest and most famous was the Castle Eden Dene, which ran for five miles along the southern edge of Peterlee and Horden, two hundred feet below the level of the surrounding fields, narrowing at its westerly reaches into a sheer and spectacular chasm, through which the burn tumbled on to massive boulders said to have been deposited by the devil. For two and a half centuries, the place had been the private property of the Burdon family, the local landowners and principle shareholders in the Horden Colliery Company, who lived in 'the Castle', a neo-gothic mansion, obscured by trees, high on one of the southern bluffs.

The steep wooded sides both fended off and tunnelled the blasting winds, creating extremes of temperature, humidity and light – pockets of air where it was said to be warm even in the middle of winter, others that were gardens of ice from autumn to spring. Thus the Dene supported innumerable forms of unusual life; strange orchids, some of the rarest butterflies in Britain; there were a hundred and fifty different kinds of moss and liverwort on the humid valley floor; roe deer flourished in the most thickly forested areas, but were seen only occasionally by walkers in the early dawn.

The hanging groves of sycamore, ash and beech were studded with ornamental pines, and in the higher reaches, rhododendrons. But from almost any point in the Dene, one species could be seen, the yew, its evergreen foliage, like clusters of dark candles, slightly sagging, giving a curious aspect of melancholy to the darker north-facing slopes. In the early nineteenth century, with the passion for the 'picturesque', well-to-do people came long distances in their carriages to enjoy the eerie beauty of the Dene – the limestone cliffs overhanging the pathways in great grottoes, festooned with dripping ferns, or hidden from the light by curtains of ivy; others standing iron-bright to the day like slabs of crumbling Wensleydale. Now the estates of Peterlee lay only yards from the northern ramparts of the Dene. The Blunts Gill, an offshoot of the Dene, its one side a precipitous wooded slope, the other a huge cliff of red earth, ran right up into the town centre. Incorporating this famous beauty spot into the design of Peterlee had been one of the aims of the original planners. And although it was invisible from most parts of the new town, once you knew of its existence, you were always aware, up there on the windswept estates – if not always consciously – of the darkness, the relative stillness, and above all the otherness of the fecund hollow below.

I say 'otherness', because although people often referred to the beauties of the Dene, especially when standing up for their area, it seemed to me that few of them ever went into it. One could walk the length of the Dene several times over without meeting a soul; a group of ramblers perhaps, from further afield, a couple of furtive kids in shell-suits. Otherwise its atmosphere of desertedness was one of its chief attributes. In the past it had belonged to the nobs. Before the building of the first club in Horden, men used to walk through to the pub at Hesledon, south of the Dene. They'd get drunk, lose their way back and fall asleep on the Dene floor. Otherwise, only poachers, illicit bramble pickers and gangs of marauding kids went in there.

Nowadays, the place belonged to the Nature Conservancy Council, on behalf of the public. But you didn't know who you might meet there. And in this day and age, persons unknown were a threat. There were stories of people being beaten up in the Dene, of strange people lurking there. One afternoon, two women were about to mount the steps that led up to Peterlee, when they saw a dark figure bearing down on them through the trees. It was Batman, in his black cloak and mask, but with a square of material cut away around his private parts. They screamed for help, but he disappeared as quickly as he had come.

Entering the Dene from the Horden end, the only sign of human habitation, apart from the well-tended pathways, was a Safeway trolley stuck in the middle of the burn. All along the four miles of paths, I could hear the jangling of an ice-cream van, now nearer, now further away, sometimes dying out altogether, as it made its way round the estates of the upper world. Sometimes I would hear children's laughter, a little further up the slopes, or just around the next bend. But when I got there, no one was ever there.

For a long time, Horden was virtually self sufficient as a community. Water from the Five Quarter Main of the pit mixed with local streams dammed into a reservoir provided its domestic uses. Electricity came from the pit's own power station. At first it was free, but when they found that people left their lights on round the clock, the colliery company put meters into the houses. The company owned three farms adjacent to the village, which supplied the shops with milk, eggs and other produce.

At the pit itself, the cages – the lifts in the shafts – and the underground haulage and excavating machinery ran on compressed air, powered by five huge coal-fired boilers. The exhaust from the boilers drove the power station, which provided the electricity for the pit and village. Nothing was wasted. The dust from the coal that had been 'washed' to purify it was burnt in the boiler furnaces, the dust from the unwashed coal at the coke ovens. When it was burnt, it was sent back down the pit as stone dust for the roadways.

One afternoon, when I was walking in the Dene, near a pile of massive moss-covered boulders, I met a tiny yellow-skinned man, bright eyed, his black hair Brylcreemed back over his diminutive pate. It was said that everyone who had worked at the coke ovens had this sallow look, their skin stained by the tarry, sulphurous emissions of the ovens.

He was, he told me, Welsh. Or at least his parents were. He had been born at Bishop Auckland, but his family had moved to Horden in 1910, when he was three years old.

'Horden colliery was producing thirty thousand tons of coal a week, and it was all hand work. I served my time at the pit as a blacksmith, and there were no power tools. No acetylene welding or cutting. It was unknown. If you were cutting a big sheet of steel that wouldn't go in the shears, you did it outside on the wagon rails, with a cold set and a ten-pound hammer, cutting across it — steel, a quarter inch thick — till you could snap it.

'There was one huge hammer that was called "Monday" — I don't know why. Its head was five inches wide, by about ten inches high. It weighed two stone. A terrific hammer! And it was often used. They'd say, "Fetch Monday!" And we'd use it to bend the square rails for the wagon way down the pit — bending a piece of iron, an inch and a half thick, over a hollow block. You had to hit it in the middle with Monday so the ends came off. As you can see, I'm not big. I could hardly lift it.

'There were ten blacksmiths on the day shift, two in the afternoon shift and two in the night shift. There was the cage smith, who was also a blacksmith, and some other blacksmiths who weren't up to the standard of the others — the tub menders. We made all our own tools — hammers, tongs — everything except the sledgehammers. And everything was reused. Any piece of machinery that wore out was beaten down to make new parts.

'The blacksmiths, like all the mechanics except the electricians — all the fitters, joiners, horse shoers, tub menders — were under the authority of the Colliery Engineer. And they were tyrants some of these people. There was one Engineer called Walter Johnson, used to stand over you. And if you paused for a moment, say, while you were waiting for a piece of metal to cool, he'd be on to you. "What the bloody hell are you doing? Get your bloody self back to that anvil!" Once he was in his office, and he looked up and saw some of the casual labourers playing football during their dinner hour. He sacked them.

'In 1927, I was sent to the coke ovens, "on loan" from the colliery. I was there till they closed in 1959. Your grandfather, Percy Hudson, was the union secretary, and it was a very important job, 'cause there were two hundred and twenty men working at the plant. Many of them were ex-shipyard workers who came every day from Hartlepool, and it was quite common for the manager to set twenty-five men on in the morning and tell them they were finished

in the evening. Any misdemeanour meant the sack. If they caught
you somewhere on the plant where you weren't supposed to be, or
caught you dodging work, you were finished completely. If the coke
was slightly too saturated . . . As the coke came out of the ovens, a
man used to stand over it with a hogger – a huge hose, about four
inches in diameter and with a very high pressure – playing it over
the hot coke. If the coke was slightly too saturated, or it hadn't been
quenched enough, so that it flared up again in the railway wagons,
that man was in serious trouble.

'I used to make the guide the coke came through. It was about
six feet long, eight feet high and two feet wide, with flat steel bars
along each side, about an inch apart. The red hot coke was shoved
through this cage until it was over the sloping bench. There was a
water pipe running over the top, with holes in it, so it sprayed down
on to the coke. And there was the man with the hose, spraying it
at the same time. Then the fillers loaded it into the waiting railway
wagons. That was a job that only the very strongest men took. And
as soon as their health went at all they had to come off.

'They put eleven tons of coal in each oven and got about seven
and a half tons of coke out. That meant 990 tons of coal a day,
seven days a week. That's getting on for 7,000 tons a week, and
roughly three quarters of that came out as coke.

'It was heated indirectly, by gas burning in flues in the walls of
the oven chambers. There was no air, or the coal would just have
burnt to nothing. First it turned into a gluey substance, semi-liquid.
Then gradually, all the excesses were burnt off. Sulphur! No carbon,
because there's no air to burn it. The coke came out hard, and when
it was quenched it was shiny like china, and silver in colour.

'From the ovens, the excess gases went up pipes into the gas
main, that took them to the Exhauster House to be converted into
tar, benzene and sulphate of ammonia. Most of the remaining gas
went to fire the ovens. There was 142,000 cubic feet of gas used
every hour on each of the two batteries. What was left went to a
small power station beside the coke ovens that supplied electricity
to the coke works, the colliery and some of the village housing. But
even so, they still had to burn some of it off with flares from time
to time, because there was just too much gas.'

A lot of people blamed the coke ovens not only for the tarry
sulphurous smell, but for most of the filth and grime and smoke
that hung over the village. But when the ovens finally closed, it
didn't make a great deal of difference to the place. Because the pit
was still powered by the five huge boilers. The dust blew up with

the smoke and settled on top of the chimneys. Sometimes the people would wake up and find the entire village covered in a thick carpet of grey dust – big feathery flakes of it – where the boiler chimneys had blasted it up during the night.

But there was always dust. Black! If you cleaned your outside window sills, within half an hour they'd be covered again. Even if you had your windows closed, a fine layer of black grit would accrue on the inside sills. It meant that the women were forever washing the curtains.

'If you walked through the village wearing light-coloured clothes, by the time you got from one end of the village to the other, you'd be covered in black and grey spots.

'For a long time I was the only blacksmith at the coke ovens. And I had a lot of work – far too much for one man. I used to make the fittings for the pumps, the valve levers. I did all the steel work, plating the hoppers, repairing the hoppers, looking after the screens.

'The manager, McQuillan, was a notoriously difficult character. But he was always very nice to me, because as the only blacksmith, I was indispensable. Even so, you couldn't refuse to work. The ovens were functioning twenty-four hours a day, every day of the year. And I used to get knocked up at all hours. They'd come round in the middle of the night, and knock on the bedroom window with a long pole.

'The manager was a staunch Roman Catholic, and he'd have me up at the Catholic Church or the Catholic youth club, mending the gates or the boiler, while I was being paid to work at the coke ovens. But that's what it was like in those days. You didn't question anything they asked you to do. I worked seventy-two hours a week, and sometimes much more, for most of my life. There were no weekends. You worked seven days a week, even Christmas Day. And there were no holidays. They didn't come in till the war.'

As you entered the pit yard, you passed a gatehouse, beside which the ground sloped down to the right towards the South Pit Engine House. Straight ahead of you, however, one structure dominated the forest of chimneys, cooling towers and pit winding gear blotting out the smoke-laden skyline. A huge windowless edifice on a towering steel structure, the great bunker of the coke ovens – into which two covered elevators carried skips of coal from the pit head, continually, day and night, three hundred and sixty-five days a year. For the coke ovens never stopped working. If the walls of silica brick were once allowed to cool, they'd immediately start to crack and then to collapse.

The ovens were laid out beyond the bunker in two parallel batteries of sixty ovens each. A 'charger', a tram-like car, powered from an overhead rail, ran the length of each battery, filling the ovens with coal from the great bunker. For as long as anyone could remember, Percy Hudson had been the 'chargerman' on the Number One Battery. With his team of two, the chargerman would move the car, its three hoppers full of coal, into position over one of the ovens. Then, using iron bars, they'd remove the three oven lids. Percy pulled a lever on the charger, and the coal poured down, giving a great roar as it hit the heat of the oven, sparks and great clouds of sulphurous yellow smoke blasting up and billowing away over the oven tops. The cast-iron plates were so hot under foot the battery men had to wear wooden-soled clogs with a quarter-inch layer of steel nailed on to the bottom. Even so, up there on the battery, exposed day and night to the blasting North Sea winds, the rain, the sleet and the snow, they were wet through and freezing from their ankles upwards for much of the year. It was hardly surprising that in his thirties and forties, Percy had suffered very severely from rheumatism.

If the coal was dry, it poured down easily, but if it was wet, they had to stick their iron bars up into the hoppers to try to 'poke it down', while all the time the toxic fumes poured up into their faces. The middle was the hottest of the three holes, so they put the youngest, nimblest lad there, who could more easily dodge the flames licking up as the gases issuing from the oven chamber ignited.

In Thirteenth Street, I met Davey Hucknell, at sixty-four a wiry agile man, with an eager nervous smile, his skin, like that of the tiny man in the Dene, of an unnatural tan. He had been 'middle-hole lad' on the Number One Battery just after the war.

'Sometimes you'd slip, and get a leg down the hole. You'd feel the heat from the oven, but you'd use your hands to lift yourself and you'd be out in no time. The holes weren't big enough to get two legs down. If you had you'd have been burnt.

'We used to wear pieces of old conveyor belting on our hands with finger holes cut in them – called "hand rags" – because when we went to pick up the bars to put the caps – the lids – back on, they'd been lying on the oven tops and they were that hot you could hardly pick them up.'

So the charger moved back and forth over the ovens, charging every third oven. As soon as the whole battery had been charged, the process began again automatically. Fifteen ovens were charged on each battery every shift. Ninety ovens were charged and ninety ovens emptied on the two batteries every twenty-four hours.

When the coal had been in the oven for twenty-three and a half hours, the doors at the ends would be opened, and a great mechanical ram came through 'shoving' the red hot coke out on to a huge sloping 'bench', where it was quenched – sprayed with water from the great hogger – and allowed to cool before being shovelled into the waiting railway wagons. The men who did this were called 'fillers'. They used a gripe – a great bowl-shaped fork – which weighed nearly a stone empty, and held two stone of coke. They were the best paid of all the workers on the plant, but they had to 'fill' twenty tons, three ovens worth of coke per shift, to get the minimum wage. Whatever they filled on top of that was extra. The railway track ran down a slight slope beside the ovens, so the man nearer the battery head had to lift his gripe more than a foot higher than the man further along. It was a source of constant complaint, but due to the construction of the ovens it was not possible to do anything about it. Not that many could stand such work for very long. It was said that the men who chose to stay on coke filling for twenty years ended up bent from the waist upwards.

'It was considered a good job then,' said Davey. 'You got more for your basic than the miners. So it was hard to get a job at the coke ovens. But it was an unhealthy job in the long run. Because you were breathing in the gases all the time, particularly if you were up there on the battery where your grandfather was. It was all right if you had a steady south wind. You just stood to the side and it blew past. But if you had a real gusty wind, blowing all over the place, it would be coming up into your face, and you'd be coughing . . . I dare say they'd all have lived a bit longer if they hadn't worked there.

'You were working continuously, the three shifts. Six in the morning till two in the afternoon. Two till ten at night. Ten till six in the morning. Saturdays, Sundays, Christmas Day. There were big lights shining down, and when you took the lids off there were flames coming out, so it was always bright enough.

'Before the war, when things were a bit tight, they used to pay double time on Christmas Day and Boxing Day. But later on, when times weren't so hard, people would say, "No, I'm not going in on Christmas night." They were offering triple time with days off in lieu. Anything to get the men in. And they always managed it somehow or other.

'I've done every job on the ovens. I started as a dauber, sealing the oven doors with clay – filling it in where the bricks had burnt away. You had quite a bit of time to spare, so you'd ask the quencherman if you could quench an oven. 'Cause you'd think it was great standing there with this great big hogger.

'That was the hottest part of the ovens – on the bench where the coke came out. The steam came belting off where it hit the red hot coke. Even in the middle of winter, you just worked in your shirt sleeves. If it was raining it was worse still, 'cause you were hot and wet. You used to come off work into the freezing cold, still wringing wet and sweating. You'd go up into the bait cabin, to have your snack, and it was freezing up there too, and you didn't have anything to change into. You were in your wet clothes all the time.

'I drove the charger once or twice. It was considered one of the top jobs. The quencherman, the chargerman and the ram-man. You had to have been there at least twenty years to get a job like that, like your grandad had. But there was nothing to it. You just pulled a couple of levers. Anybody could have done it.'

The ovens were rebuilt twice, in 1935 and 1951. But they weren't modernised, they were just rebuilt as they had been in 1919. It was the hand-filling that finished Horden ovens – the laborious process of shifting the coke into the railway wagons, 'off the shoulder'. By the end it was the only plant still working in that way. At the great new plant at Murton, where Percy went to work when Horden closed, the coke was quenched and conveyed into the wagons automatically. But even that didn't last very long. The blast furnaces of Teesside that took most of Horden's coke began building their own ovens, on-site. Then they devised new methods of steel production that didn't require so much coke.

'I was at the ovens till they closed in 1959,' said Davey. 'I worked at the plant at Fishburn for a while, then I went into the factories. I didn't miss it. As I said, it was a bad job. They were a good bunch of lads. Close knit. Like a family. We made the most of it, laughing and joking. That was the only thing that kept you going.'

Could he remember much about Percy?

'Not a great lot. He was the union man. He was a quietish sort of feller. He never got involved in arguments. He would just stand back. For example, the charger on Number Two Battery wouldn't be able to get back in the bunker if the Number One Charger was ahead of them – 'cause they couldn't overtake. So if they were rushing to get away for a drink at the end of a shift, they'd be shouting, "Howay! Get a move on!" You had to put so much coal into an oven. But they'd be saying, "You've got enough in there. Howay!" But Percy wouldn't pay any attention. He just carried on in his own time, puffing away on his pipe.'

He smoked a pipe up there – among all the smoke and fumes?

'Oh aye. Nearly all the battery men smoked pipes, I think.'

6

An Ordinary Man

M EN! I THOUGHT as I entered Horden Rugby Football Sup-
porters' Club.

I'd walked through the heavy drizzling blackness along the
interminable rows of two-bedroomed bungalows known as 'the
cottages', where, in different houses, my grandfather and my great-
grandfather had both ended their days, and where Percy's second
wife Mary still lived. Suddenly I saw ahead of me a brilliantly lit
interior of Men. Men who didn't so much inhabit as wear their
bodies. Men who hung predatory over the snooker tables, as inef-
fably potent in their stillness as an African shepherd leaning on his
staff in the vastness of the savannah. Men who rationed out their
flint-like gazes – who knew where they should rest, and didn't bother
with owt else. Men who stood with their backs to the bar and their
loins foursquare to the world, throwing out their harsh laughter like
a challenge.

I walked mechanically up the couple of steps out of the drizzle
into a meagre corridor. Ahead was a board announcing fixtures.
There was no mistake; this was it. I walked into the room whose
window I had passed. It was large and low ceilinged with hard chairs
and formica-topped tables – a plastic banquette and a pall of nicotine
the only concessions to comfort. To my right was a table full of old
men. The nearest, a tiny individual, sat looking up at me, his neck
craning from his jacket collar, like a tortoise's from its shell, his grey
eyes bright with hostility.

'Whadyerwant?'

'I'm supposed to be meeting Denis Reardon,' I said, taking a step forward.

'Sign the book!'

I signed.

'Ten pence!' The fierceness with which they demanded this piffling amount of money still took me aback.

Alec Thompson, the 'old' man I'd met at the Reardons', appeared looking rather dashing in an olive green suit. He was taller than I remembered him, and impressively upright. 'They're not here,' he said. I assumed he meant Denis. They were supposed to be introducing me to a very old man who could tell me more about Horden. I asked him if he wanted a drink. 'Just get yerself one,' he said.

I advanced towards the bar in a manner that was supposed to look nonchalant and unconcernedly self-contained but was in fact a strange mixture of a jerk, a shuffle and a lope. Why did I feel so painfully awkward in these Northern clubs? It wasn't as though there weren't such places in London, but they seemed to exist in a peripheral dimension of urban life that was beyond my concern let alone my comprehension. I would certainly never think of going into one. Here, however, they were part of the bedrock of mainstream society, and if you wanted to learn anything about that society, you had to put some time in. Yet I felt physically incapable of looking into the main body of the room – as though some forcefield were preventing my eyes from fixing on any person or object in it. There was just a blur of jeans and T-shirts and muscle and a great wreathing of cigarette smoke, through which I felt as though I was wading, as absurdly overdressed in my denim jacket and oilskin coat as if I had been wearing a full-length mink.

I settled myself at a table near the door. The area in the middle of the room, around the bar and the snooker tables, was occupied by the younger men, and apart from the lad with his Aran sweater tucked into his jeans, none of them was wearing anything thicker than a T-shirt. But for all the self-conscious meanness of their postures, the overbearing masculinity of the stylelessness of their manner of dress, I had nothing to fear from any of these people. They were what would be described as 'good lads'. I began to relax. This was the *rugby club* after all.

Alec Thompson returned and led me to a table on the far side of the room where Denis and a group of other men of the same age were playing dominoes. They seemed to be engaged in a kind of tournament, everyone moving in rotation along the tables by the banquette. I sat back to watch, though it struck me as an exceedingly uninteresting game. Immediately beside me was a man in a tweed jacket, who kept apologising, rather gallantly, for having his back to me. Waiting his turn to play was a thickset man in a dark blue suit, who sat stolidly back, puffing on his pipe, his eyes occasionally meeting mine with an expression of dark disapproval. He must have been well over seventy, but he looked as though he and his chair would be very difficult to tip over. Near him, on the opposite corner of the table was a grey-haired man in glasses. He drew at intervals on a small cigar, wincing – drawing back the corners of his mouth, and sucking at the air – as he peered at his hand. I couldn't tell if this was evidence of extreme intellectual effort or a mere involuntary facial mannerism connected with his smoking. He was dressed, like most of the older men, casually, but with a tweedy repectability. Yet although with his cigar and his steel-framed glasses he looked one of the most affluent and urbane of the men, he also seemed the most remote, the most absorbed in the stupor of the club – as though if I spoke to him he would not understand me, would not even be able to hear me. How many Friday nights for how many years had he and the others been coming there, and taking part in exactly the same pursuits – in snooker as the young men were now, in cards and dominoes, losing themselves in the beer and the nicotined fug in which time seemed to stand still? In which a Friday night could be any Friday night, in any year and in any decade. (I didn't realise then that this was one of Horden's newest clubs. But before then they would have gone to the Big Club, still then not too far past its prime.)

Denis, though he was friendly enough, seemed slightly embarrassed by my presence, as though I were something of an encumbrance. And I could understand why. Men, traditionally, like to carry only what is necessary. Men, the hunters of the world, need to be light on their feet. Denis was a kind man, but in that context I was a burden to him.

I was suddenly struck by the fundamental passivity of manhood. It seemed for a moment as though all the atrocities of men – all the wars, the invasions, the beatings and the rapes – had been but a hiccup in the vast somnambulism of manhood.

Alec Thompson moved proprietorially round the room, a cigarette poised between his fingers. He took his turn at the domino tables, but he seemed less involved in the game than the others. Not that he was not giving it his full concentration, but there was an element of performance – as there was in the wearing of his suit

– even about that concentration. Games of dominoes were what happened in clubs, and it was necessary for him to participate to his fullest ability, in the same way that it was necessary for him to wear his suit to maintain the standards of the club. If he didn't do these things, the world would fall apart. I began to warm to him.

He told me that one of the worst things about the area was that you could no longer buy a suit. Thirty years ago there were at least two places in Horden where you could get a suit made to measure. I asked him, during a pause between games, what job he'd had. He said that like Denis he'd been an electrician at the pit. I couldn't imagine him, with his choirboy's complexion and his cared-for fastidiousness, crawling around down there in the blackness and the water and the filth. But then he told me that during the war he'd been in the Western Desert, and I could picture that even less. When not playing, he was constantly going in and out of the room, to see if the old man had arrived yet. Finally he gestured me through. The lounge was smaller and quieter. There was even a woman present. At one of the tables sat a very small old man, in thick glasses, smartly dressed in a black jacket, with a collar and tie, and a pair of neatly pressed grey flannel trousers. Alec said he would leave us to talk, and went back to the dominoes.

The old man had been a blacksmith at the colliery and had done some work at the coke ovens. He said he could remember my grandfather. I wondered what he could tell me about him. 'Nothing. I can just remember that he was there, and that his name was Percy Hudson. But I couldn't tell you anything else about him.' He really was tiny, and with his dark hair slicked back, he looked like a little shrew. 'I'm happy to tell you anything I know. But you'll have to ask questions. Otherwise, I won't know what it is you want to know, like.'

The Thirties. What was it like in the Thirties? How bad was it?

'Why ... Now let's see. The Thirties ... You're talking about before the war now, mind. Well ... they had the buzzer. At the pit. If it sounded once, the Low Main was off. If it sounded twice, the Main Coal was off. These are the different seams at the pit I'm talking about now. If it went three times, the Hutton Seam was off. If it went four times, the Low Main and the Hutton Seam was off. If it went five times, the Hutton Seam and the Main Coal was off. And if it gave one long blast, the whole lot was off. Now is there anything else you wanted to know?'

My head was whirling with all these permutations. How on

earth was I going to remember all of this? Meanwhile, I had to keep him talking. 'The buzzer . . . when did it go off? Was it every day, or every week or what?'

'Every day, at six o'clock.'

He had enjoyed telling me about the buzzer, putting the information forward with a purposeful, emphatic exactness. Now, however, we were back on the uncertain, shifting sands of him not knowing what I wanted to know. I was putting him on the spot, and no one liked that. He returned to his tight-lipped former self. He stared straight ahead, hoping this excruciating audience would soon be at an end. Like a crab which had retreated into its crevice I would have to prise him out again with my questions. But I could not think of any that were not feebly vague and general. Another man joined us, a slightly younger mild-mannered man, with bushy grey hair, and the old man seemed to relax slightly.

'How bad was it in the Thirties?' I asked. 'I mean the conditions and that?'

'Turrible.' He spoke to the world in general. 'I'm not joking, man, when I say that a man aged fifty today doesn't know what hard times are.'

'He wouldn't,' said his friend contentedly.

This was more like it – what I had expected to hear, and therefore what I wanted to hear. The rhetorical rehearsing of the wrongs of the past. The use of the word 'man' for forceful emphasis. The way the cadence of the sentence kept on rising towards that final 'are'. And yet . . . I listened as they continued talking among themselves about how things had got better for the miners during the war with the drive for increased production – and then there had been the Labour government – before they went on to talk about other things. And yet it was all too piecemeal, and at the same time there was not enough detail. I was weary of having to drag things out of people. I wanted the Big Picture and the detail all put in place for me. I wanted to be taken in hand and put in the picture. I wanted someone to tell me what was what. That, I had imagined, was what Horden was all about. I tried to imagine how Percy would have reacted, if I'd come to him in this way. Would he have sat me down in a chair opposite him in his rather bare living room, and lectured me commandingly for a couple of hours, without me being able, without me needing, to get a word in edgeways? Or would he have been as diffident and uncertain as this man?

As I rushed through the streets from the club, the heavens heaved over the village. You could see the water bucketing through the air

around the streetlamps. Within seconds I was soaked to the skin. By
The Trust, the wine bar in Horden most popular with young people,
close by where the road from Peterlee met the Sunderland road,
vast crowds were spilling from the street corners, their Friday-best
sodden, the huge raindrops spinning endlessly through the glare of
the street lights like millions of tumbling coins, bouncing off the
heads of the lads, who stood proudly, triumphantly oblivious in
their baseball shirts, baggy jeans and short back and sides, and the
girls, their drenched clothes clinging satin-like to their bodies,
sodden manes matted over their faces. There were huge queues at
the pizzeria, the chip shop and the Chinese take-away, and all
along the torrential gutters, the lads and lasses, their clothes
plastered to their bodies, stood languorously plying their mouths
with fried rice, chips and gravy and great slithering chunks of
pizza. Taxis veered queasily among the dripping multitude, who
milled unconcernedly back and forth over the main road, indifferent
to the skidding traffic. In the brick box bus stop at the bottom of the
Peterlee Road, dozens of couples could be seen groping in the glare
of the car headlights. What world were they in, these young people?
What did the preoccupation with Horden's past mean to them? It
was because of these children – and hardly anyone in the thronging
masses was over eighteen, let alone twenty – that the older people
of Horden were afraid to go out. The local newspapers were full of
stories of old women murdered by thirteen-year-olds, arson attacks
on old people's homes. It sometimes seemed, talking to the older
people in Horden, as though the younger generation had declared
war on the old. They were said to be bent only on violence and
destruction. They were the ones who were ruining everything with
their vandalism, joy riding and ram raiding. It was difficult to find
anyone among the older generation with a good word to say about
the young. More than that, they seemed not to recognise themselves
at all in the young. They spoke of them as though they were of a
species fundamentally different from themselves. The sense of a
generation inevitably becoming what the one before had been,
seemed to have been lost, to have been broken in Horden.

The streets around the wine bars were said to be places to be
avoided on Friday and Saturday nights. But I walked, as though
invisible through the sodden throng, through the lads bawling at
each other through the downpour, as apparently oblivious to any
concerns outside their own as the old people locked in their memories
and dreams of the past.

'Billy Bradley!' someone at the Rugby Club had said. 'Gan and see Billy Bradley! He served his time at the coke ovens.'

The hour had gone back the previous weekend. It was not yet five, but as I approached the old people's home where Billy lived, it might already have been the middle of the night. I felt a certain trepidation. I wanted to see Billy, but would Billy want to see me? Old people were said to be always glad of company, but I had no introduction. He might be having his tea, and the rugby international would only just have finished on the television.

The home turned out to be a block of purpose-built flats set among gardens in the middle of what had once been Old Fifth, Sixth and Seventh Streets – the most densely populated part of the village. Everywhere signs warned the inhabitants to beware of suspicious callers. I caught sight of myself reflected dully in the glass doors. I looked highly suspicious. I walked straight in. A short, square woman like a box on legs pointed me towards Billy's door, just around the corner. The institutional lighting sent a metallic and faintly sinister glow over the bare corridor. The jamb of each door had recently been replaced on the lock side, but remained unpainted, giving the impression that the place had been subject to a large scale break-in. I stopped in front of Billy's door. Around the letter-box was a flurry of large black fingerprints, as though, during a struggle, someone had been desperately trying to grab hold of it. I could hear a television blaring on the other side of the door. I knocked. But would anybody be able to hear me over the din? I knocked again. I thought I could hear a voice calling over the sound of the television, but I couldn't be sure. 'Hello,' I called tentatively.

A woman emerged from a door on the other side of the corridor. Here I was: a suspicious caller. 'I'm looking for Billy Bradley . . .'

'Just go in.'

'But . . .' The door swung open.

Billy supported himself on sticks, his black hair cut in a short back and sides and Brylcreemed in the way that was the norm forty years ago. He was wearing a black-and-white dogstooth sports jacket that would once have been very smart. His very dark eyes bore the expression of someone who only ever has to deal with callers rather than welcome them. 'I understand you used to work at the coke ovens,' I fumbled. 'I'm trying to find out about my grandfather.'

Billy was already gasping for breath. 'Howay in.' I followed him. 'Wh – what was his name, like?'

'Percy Hudson.'

'Aye. I remember him. Wasn't he in the Australian Navy or summat? Whenever he got up to speak at the y-y-union meeting, he always y-used to start off by saying' – he affected a gruffly pompous tone – ' "Wh-when I was in the Australian Navy . . ." Every bloody time.' Billy sank into the chair in which he always sat. 'Sit down, lad.'

My first thought on entering that room was how short a period of time I could spend in it before making my excuses and leaving. Not that it was dirty or smelled. It was reasonably clean and well-ordered – but there was altogether too much of Billy in it. Billy's entire existence took place in it, and everything Billy needed to live – his clothes, his food, his beer, his bed – the sheet folded neatly back – was arranged around him easy to hand. And it all reflected Billy too physically, too intimately. I felt that just by being there I was already too close to Billy.

'I was ten year at the coke ovens. A l-l-lead burner.' Before I had the chance to ask what a lead burner was, he'd gone on. 'We used to hold the union meetings in a room at The B-bell Hotel. And every time Percy Hudson got up to m-make a s-speech he'd say, "When I was in the Australian Navy". We'd be thinking, "Oh God, not again."' He laughed, a high sardonic, droning sound, his dark eyes, in his pink smoothly shaven cheeks, shining brilliantly, before he lapsed back into a lugubrious detachment, his chin lolling on to his chest. His trousers were unfastened around his capacious girth, around which he clasped his hand like a child clutching a beach ball. His legs, however, were not those of a fat person.

On one of them, on the area of very pink calf between his sock and his brown trouser turn-up, was what looked like a running sore. While on his head, through his slicked hair, I could see a cut – quite a fresh one. I tried not to look at these things.

'How did you find out I was at the c-c-coke ovens?'

I told him, and he mused on it briefly.

'How did you know I was here?'

I told him.

He gave again the curious droning laugh. 'He-e-e! Yer bugger! Every time he got up to make a speech . . .' He trilled merrily at the thought of it. Then his eyes, suddenly suspicious, flashed up at me. 'Didn't he have a daughter? What was her name?'

'Mollie?'

'Aye. Mollie, and his son Tommy.'

A game show was in progress on the large television. On the walls were two paintings. They looked like real oil paintings, but it didn't seem right to ask about them.

'That's my father,' I said.

'You Tommy Hudson's son?' he asked, incredulous. He gave again the high-pitched cooing laugh.

A woman came in. A big woman, aged about thirty, in a matron's housecoat, a cigarette in hand. She had an odd insinuating smile, and on seeing me looked faintly embarrassed. 'I've just come for the paper.' She picked up one of those free advertising rags. 'I won't stop,' she simpered, 'seeing as you've got company.'

'Have you got many relatives?' I asked, sensing visits were rare.

'I've no relatives,' he said with lugubrious defensiveness. 'I've a brother, but we quarrelled. My parents had that shop above Kings Farm.' Kings Farm was a huddle of ancient barns beside the road to the beach. I could picture the shop. 'I used to live in the flat over it. But I had a break-in. Kids! I couldn't sleep after that so I came in here.

'Tommy Hudson's son!' he mused again on the extraordinariness of it. 'I remember Tommy Hudson. He was older than me, but I remember him.'

I had to check myself for a moment. Billy was *younger* than my father! Of course he was. It was obvious when you thought about it. But the injustice of it made me feel for a moment quite sick. And I wasn't sure why. Billy wasn't exactly living in squalor, and some people might say my father was not in such great shape. But he was at least living in the 1990s. Billy seemed stranded in some drab, ahistorical hinterland. Here he was in the world of his room, totally unknown to my father, and no doubt totally unknown to my father even when he was living in Horden, probably unknown to Mollie and Fred too, yet knowing all about them.

'He'd be sixty-nine now. He was four years older than me. And Mollie was a year younger. What's he doing now? He's in *Canada*? Wh- What's he doing there, like?'

He clenched his teeth and began rubbing his calf. 'I've had problems with my legs.' He pulled his right trouser leg up to reveal a mass of scarred flesh, and two purple blotches. 'That's where they removed the nerves.'

I hummed politely, wishing he'd cover it up again, but he continued pulling it up further and further, revealing the white flesh with a great band of scarring running up towards his trunk. He began pulling the other trouser leg up. 'I had a bypass operation. My veins were playing up, so they took them out . . . See!'

'Yes,' I murmured, trying not to look.

'You cannut see from there. Come round here.'

The meeting had suddenly taken a turn on which I was not at all keen, but I felt powerless to disobey. I put one leg forward, and launched myself hands first on to the floor. 'Careful,' said Billy, his eyes narrowing at my clumsiness.

I stood over him as he began unfastening his already unbuttoned trousers. 'It went right up here,' he puffed, pulling aside his shirt tails to reveal rolls of hairy white flesh. Oh God! I thought, in a nightmarish rush of realisation. So that's why he's on his own! He's a nasty evil old man! But I'd no sooner seen the great white scars, two inches wide, than he began fastening himself up again. He rubbed his leg. 'Hurts like hell,' he said, wincing.

I sat back, feeling exhausted but curiously relaxed. Billy pointed to two metal objects on top of the television. 'Fetch them over here,' he said, in a tone that suggested that after my ordeal I deserved some kind of treat. One was a pair of brass scissors with a kind of box moulded on to one of the blades. 'Bet you can't guess what this is.'

'It's for putting candles out,' I said.

'How did you know that?' he asked, his annoyance tinged with suspicion, as though to know the answer I must have broken into the room in the middle of the night and had a go with it.

'I just guessed.'

He put it down, still eyeing me darkly, and raised the other object, certain of triumph. 'You'll never guess what this is – not in a million years.'

It was a decorative tweezer-like contraption, with a ragged cord attached. I had no idea what it was, but I wouldn't have said, even if I had known.

'Women used to put this round the bottom of their skirts,' he said, fitting the two rounded prongs to the bottom of his trouser leg. Then he pulled the string to clasp them together. 'So they could pull them up when they were riding a bike.' He mimed the motion. 'Hundred year old, that,' he added confidentially. I put them back on the television, and he sat back, cackling almost gleefully. 'Why, yer booger! You Tommy Hudson's son?'

I said I was.

He laughed again, shaking his head and staring up at the corner of the ceiling. Then he turned to me suddenly. 'Didn't he go out with a girl from Cowell Street, Hamilton Street, one of them streets up there? Wasn't it . . . Olive Foster or summat?'

He'd got the wrong name, but the right part of town. 'Norma,' I said.

'Aye, Norma, that was her. Norma Lindoe.' His eyes narrowed. 'She your mother, Norma Lindoe?'

'No, she was years before my mother.'

He nodded, then shook his head again, tittering gently to himself. 'He-e-e! Tommy Hudson, yer booger!' Then he turned to me, suddenly serious. 'Didn't he go out with a girl called Norma?'

'Aye,' I said. This was my chance. 'What was she like, this Norma?'

'Just a medium sort of girl. Dark. I fancied her! She was older than me, but I fancied her.' He chuckled with admiration at his former daring. 'Aye, I've often thought about Tommy Hudson . . . I liked him.' Then he became serious. 'But I cannut tell you much about your grandfather. He was just an ordinary man, like . . . Except when he got up to make his speech in the union: "When I was in the Australian Navy." Bah! You'd be thinking, "Siddown Percy, man. You weren't in no Australian Navy." He'd go on for hours, and always the same thing.'

'What was that?'

'Nowt . . . Well, it was a load of bloody shite actually.'

I was feeling more and more relaxed, but I could tell that Billy was becoming restless. I decided it was time to go.

He ushered me to the door. I now realised that had he been able to raise himself to his full height, he would have been well over six feet. To his great credit he had not been the least bit grateful for my visit.

Meeting Walter Laidlaw was a much simpler matter. I simply looked him up in the phone book. 'When d'you want to come?'

'Whenever's convenient for you.'

'How about now?'

After taking a hoppa bus on an intricate serpentine route round the satellite estates of Horden and Peterlee, I found myself in Walter's sitting room. It was plainly furnished, plainly lit. Pictures of the Pope and St Peter's Square, notices of forthcoming events at the Catholic church and the Catholic social club. A very ordinary Roman Catholic sitting room in Peterlee. Walter composed his long body in his customary easy chair, and folded his long legs. He spoke in an imperious gasp, at times barely audible over the roaring of the fan heater. He was well over eighty, but his voice seemed unconnected with his age. It was part of his mystique. It was intended to draw you in, so that you were always craning forward to catch what he was saying.

'I really don't know where Percy came from. There was such a rush for jobs, with so many out of work after the '21 strike. There was a great boom in coke at the time. There were about twelve coke plants in the county, but Horden was the biggest. The coal came direct from the colliery, straight over the line, up the elevator and into the storage. Down below, the chargermen took control. Percy was one of these chargermen, and he was secretary of the union. There were three of them, a feller called Micky Driscoll, who was chairman, and Tommy Hughes, treasurer. And they were very lax. I shouldn't say that, should I? But they were very lax.'

Lax? What did he mean, lax?

'Nowt bad. But they didn't bother to keep accounts, and I don't know ... It was the attitude that was prevalent at the time. This Driscoll and Hughes used to collect the union subs in The Bell Hotel, and the men used to wonder, Why, how do we know how the union funds are standing? And coke being something of a seasonable trade, there were certain men laid off, who some people felt should have been kept on. Well, there were ructions in the union. I never used to the bother with the union, because I was on the by-products side, working on the tar and benzyl in the Exhauster House. But when it came to election time, somebody nominated me, and before I knew where I was I'd been elected secretary. Well, we decided to totally reorganise. We got the men proper union cards, balance sheets and so on. Percy took an interest in other things. He went into local politics and was on the Parish Council. But that wasn't convenient for him either, because council meetings were always at six or seven, and if a man was on two till ten shift he couldn't get there, and if he was going to work at ten, he hadn't time. So I think he only lasted about five or six years on Horden Parish Council. But Mollie, his daughter, she married a lad called Freddy Alderson, who was a teacher at Murton Colliery, and he eventually became a magistrate. But they were all staunch Labour people, mind. All very staunch ... Well, I think that's Percy, really.'

Walter looked at me, urbanely impassive, his eyes pale in his gaunt but still elegant features, his glasses perched on his narrow pate. He rested his elbows on the arms of his easy chair, the tips of his long ascetic's fingers touching together. There was something about the husky, Mandarin expansiveness with which he conceded Percy's 'staunchness' that softened the blow of this brief dismissal of everything my grandfather had ever been. But what was he saying, that Percy had been corrupt?

'Why, they weren't corrupt. But there were so many lads lived away – Hartlepool, Durham, Hutton Henry, and them places there

– that wouldn't come up for a meeting. So Percy and them could just tell the men what was happening when they were on the job. They'd tell them what was going to happen, and they just accepted it.

'Percy had these two friends, and they ran the union for themselves, not for the men. I mean they'd call a union meeting, and the men would turn up, and there was no meeting on. They'd just say, Ah, to hell with it. We'll not bother tonight. That attitude! So lax! Well, the friction started because of these laxadaisical methods they had. They'd just put a notice up the night before, and there was only half a dozen would turn up for the meeting, and they'd make decisions affecting the whole membership. That was the sort of thing went on.

'His character was great, mind. I always thought a great deal of him. I mean he was stubborn. If he had a bee in his bonnet, he'd go to the limit with it as far as he possibly could. I never knew him do no harm to anyone. But I used to think many a time, Why, Percy, you daft softy, man. See, he was always just on the battery. Never no place else but the battery. He wasn't concerned with the labouring side or the by-products side. Well it got to be later on, the by-products side and the maintenance side extended, till they had a bigger say in the union than what the battery had.

'There was a job on the battery, working the middle hole on top of the ovens. We used to call it the Middle Hole Lad, because it was only a boy's job. It was the worst job of the lot, the dirtiest and the worst paid. That was something Percy slipped up on. He should have seen that lad was getting the same pay he was getting himself.'

'Maybe he had low pay himself when he was young, and he was doing that job,' I suggested.

'That was it! There was altogether too much of saying, "We used to hafta dee this, we used to hafta dee that." But that wasn't how it should have been. There was no need to do it like that now. But they never thought. . . A man, once he got to be a gas regulator, or a chargerman, he had to prove he was more important than the rest.'

I'd wanted someone to give me the big picture. Walter was doing that all right. But this wasn't quite what I'd been planning on hearing. Percy as a kind of caricature 'union man' – the stodgy, parochial nay-sayer of Tory folklore, who fails his members not through ill-will or corruptness, but through sheer lack of imagination. A man, not stupid exactly, just a bit limited. But if he had been like that, it was,

I reflected, hardly surprising. He'd left school at the age of eleven, and spent almost his entire working life in one place. But while I could not help but be impressed by Walter's evident intelligence, his formidable urbane self-confidence, why should I trust him? He was a total stranger, and this was after all my grandfather he was talking about. And anyway, Percy had represented the cokemen at the TUC, and in negotiations with the coal owners and their representatives as far away as York, Newcastle, and even London. Hadn't he?

'No,' said Walter. 'He never got anywhere on a national level. He was on the Easington District Federation Board, which represented all the different classes of workmen round the area, and he'd get his expenses for going. Say the meeting was at Easington, the bus fare might be thruppence.'

Three pence? But they'd named an avenue in Horden after him.

'No, that wasn't him. That was a feller called George Hudson, who built them houses. Different person altogether. Not Percy.'

Hudson Avenue had, I reflected, never been much more than a glorified driveway anyway. As for Hudson Street, I'd never been able to find it again. I must have imagined it.

'During the war, it was a risky job. The colliery was bombed twice, you know. When they shoved an oven, there'd be thirteen, fourteen ton of coal coming down on to the bench – bright, bright, red hot. Why, it used to light up the whole sky over Horden. So they put this great big hood – sort of a huge canopy – over the whole of the ovens, to hide it from the German planes. The quenchermen had to open the ovens and stand over the coke to quench it. Why, when they put this hood over that, the way these quenchermen suffered, it was cruel, man. But Percy and them never thought to ask for extra for the lads that were working in them conditions. Whether they put it down to patriotism, or whether it was just because it didn't affect them, I don't know.

'Now, in the Salter House, they used to produce sulphate of ammonia, about twelve ton a day. They put it into twelve-hundred-weight bags, and when we had the order, we'd fetch the wagons in and put two men on to load them. They used to have to run up a ramp into the box wagon, carrying these bags. By! It was hard work. And they only got a ha'penny a bag. But men would do anything for money in them days. Well, I got them one and six a ton. They were over the moon. See, that was another thing Percy slipped up on. He hadn't thought of that. He was a battery man, as I say.

'You could see the sulphur coming off the ovens. It was yellow. But most of the men, it didn't do them any harm. In fact, they thrived on it. Mothers used to bring children in and hold them over the tar wells, and make them breathe in the fumes as a cure for asthma and whooping cough. And it worked! You'd get men working sixteen years without having a day off. There was no holidays in them days. You'd get men working there twenty, thirty, forty years, great big strong men. And as soon as they retired and got out into the fresh air, they died. It often seemed to be the way.

'But coke filling – loading the coke into wagons – that was heavy work. I did some of that. The plant was on short time, and I was only getting eight and fivepence a shift in the Exhauster House. I'd just had another little girl, my second daughter. So I had a word with the manager and he put us on filling, which was about a pound a shift. The coke was heavy with water, because it had just been quenched. You used to see men getting old before their time doing work like that. But it was desperation and need got the likes of us to do work like that.

'But Percy, he seemed to give in too much to the management. They were things that maybe didn't make much difference at the time, but in years to come did make a big difference. Percy's attitude was, "Why, we've arlwus done it that weh." I used to say to him, "They only paid ninepence to the union before, but they're paying half a dollar now." "That's got nowt to dee wi' it." But, taken as a whole he wasn't a bad sort.'

But what had Percy been like, as a person? Was he quiet or talkative?

'He was quiet, but once you got him started, oh hell, you couldn't stop him – he'd be pacing backwards and forwards, still talking. That type! Took some getting away, then once he started . . .

'He wasn't a great mixer. He had his own colleagues around him, and he used to stick with them. He'd take a drink, but he wasn't a boozer. He'd go out with his mates now and again. But he'd go out with his wife more than anything else. He was a home lover, Percy.' He thought for a moment. 'He was a *man*, if you know what I mean by that.'

I didn't.

'Why, he was a man's man. He did what a man should do. He said what he thought. Opened his mouth when he should. Helped his wife. He thought a lot of her! Looked after his family. Was a good citizen. You cannut expect any more of a man than that. Oh, I *liked* Percy!'

I looked around again, at the small pictures of Pope John Paul and St Peter's Square, the notices of coming events at the local Roman Catholic church, the cross of palm leaves. That was it. That was the source of his formidable, urbane self confidence. He was someone of consequence in the Roman Catholic world of East Durham.

He'd been made foreman. And he had, he told me, been on Horden Parish Council and later Peterlee Town Council. I wondered if he'd ever thought of trying to get in on the management side. After all, it wasn't as though he hadn't had the ability.

'No . . .' He breathed dryly. His features seemed to tighten, and for the first time in our conversation I thought I saw a look of something approaching uncertainty pass across them. 'I was always on the men's side.'

'Have you got a title yet, for your book?' he asked, as I was leaving. 'How about "History through Percy"? You've got to have something with popular appeal, you know.'

One evening, a few days later, I phoned the headquarters of the Cokemen's Union — or what was left of it — in Barnsley. The general secretary told me he had no records relating to the Horden plant, but gave me the number of a man on South Tyneside who had been centrally involved in the Durham Cokemen's Area. He, while cheerfully amiable, turned out not to know anything, but he gave me the name of another man, who had been the union agent in the period in question. He answered the phone, cautiously masticating.

'Aye, I do remember Percy Hudson. He was the secretary at Horden. I used to give him and Micky Driscoll, the chairman, a lift through to the Area Executive meetings in Durham.

'He was a grand old chap, as far as I remember. Of course, I knew Micky better, because he got on the National Executive, and then he became an industrial relations adviser for the Coal Board.

'But Percy, I don't think he ever got anywhere nationally. He was always just at Horden. As far as I remember he always was the secretary there. But I couldn't tell you anything else about him. I mean I couldn't say there was anything remarkable about him. He was just one of the lads.'

How about Walter Laidlaw? Did he remember him?

'No. That name doesn't mean anything to me at all. Now, if you'll excuse me, I'm eating me tea.'

7

Under the North Sea

I WOKE in the middle of the night squirming between the sheets to relieve the sense of pressure against my back. I had rarely experienced feelings of claustrophobia, but already I could feel the entombing weight of the rock between my shoulder blades. Eighteen inches! I tried to measure it with my hands against the darkness. Not even the width of a man's body. I had talked to men who had worked for ten years at a time in such seams. But none had been able to convey much sense of what it was actually like. I had read that these seams sometimes narrowed to only nine or ten inches, and that sometimes the rock would shift minutely against a miner's back and he would be trapped. What would happen under such circumstances? Would they hack him out? Or would they simply leave him there to die?

The pit! That was the central defining experience of this area, the conditions of which I had a duty to experience as minutely as possible, the experience beside which everything else I had so far undertaken was mere prevarication. My application to go underground at Easington Colliery, a mile up the coast, had at last met with a positive response, and I was only waiting for confirmation of the time and the day. Now, however, I decided that I was not going to go. From having felt that because my ancestors had gone down there it was an experience I had a duty to undergo, I now felt an atavistic sense of revulsion against it. Those people had been worn down, crushed and broken by the pit, had their life and breath drained from them aforetime. Percy and my father had managed to get away from it. I had a duty in fact *not* to go there.

Before I went back to sleep, I resolved that I would go down, but if I did not like it I would turn round no matter where I was and come straight back out.

By a quarter to eight in the morning I was sitting in the blue velvet and mahogany – and the almost tropical heat – of the boardroom at Easington Colliery, still thickly buttoned against the freezing winds outside. After some time an office boy came and led me along a corridor, down a flight of steps, and left me at the door of a small changing-room, totally empty except for a set of pit clothes. From the thick grey underwear to the plastic helmet with its huge Mickey Mouse ear clamps, they hung clean and mysteriously ready like garments left by fairies in a children's story. A young miner with the narrow eyes and flat hammer face of an English bull terrier stuck his head round the door and told me to get changed. I donned the grey smalls, the fluorescent orange shirt, undershirt and trousers, and the long thick socks. When you went down the pit you left everything of the surface world behind, even your underpants. Finally I put on a pair of pit boots stiff with someone else's use. I noticed that one was a size 8 and the other a 9.

The young miner led me out across the yard. He handed me a pair of knee-pads, and said that when the time came I should fasten them 'canny tight' at the bottom, and leave them slack at the top, to prevent them cutting into the backs of my knees. Since I had heard that walking in a crouched position for prolonged periods causes agony anyway, I heeded this advice well.

In a kind of store room I was introduced to the two men who would take me down. One, tall, wiry with a mousy moustache and loquacious eyes, greeted me with an enthusiastic handshake. He was the Chief Safety Officer. The other, stocky, dark, Welsh-looking, was talking on the phone. He was the Press Officer.

I was led outside, up a staircase and into the draughty area of the Lamp Cabin, where I was hauled up to the counter like a side of bacon, had my waist measured and an extra notch banged into a belt for my benefit. Then two heavy metal objects were threaded on to it: the power pack of my helmet-lamp, the flex of which was threaded round my back and an unmarked tin canister. Everything was done quickly, eagerly and with a great deal of barked banter and discussion. I was told to carry my lamp in my hand till I needed to use it. All around was a disorientation of noise: the howling of the wind blasting through the open doors, the grinding of boots on concrete, the slamming of metal doors, the ostentatious hawking of the miners. I had so much to do getting used to the weight of the helmet, the battery and other objects on my belt, and trying not to trip over in the stiff boots, I hardly had the chance to take in my surroundings, let alone wonder whether I felt nervous about my imminent descent into blackness.

The miners pushed under the mesh, into the cage and I was packed cursorily in with them. The wire door was slammed shut and we were plunging downwards. In the light from the landings of the upper seams I picked out momentarily the impassive faces of the men around me, mostly looking down, as though trying to extend the night's rest, if only by a few seconds. I waited for the sickening sensation of plummeting into endless space, but it never came.

The cage door ground open again and the miners surged forward into the brilliant neon-lit roadway. One imagines that being taken deep into the rock under the sea will arouse certain sensations. But in fact, the knowledge of being in an unfamiliar work place, whose mores must on no account be offended against, and where everyone has a clearly defined purpose except you, plus the need to stay upright on the uneven ground in a hard pair of someone else's boots, while trying to pay attention to everything you are being told, override more high flown considerations. 'So you're writing a book about Horden,' said Colin, the Press Officer. He had a broad, pasty face, as flat and expressionless as his voice.

'Aye,' I said.

'I reckon a leaflet should do it,' he said.

The upper part of the white-washed tunnel was clogged by a chaos of huge pipes and blackened cables like a great mass of arteries and veins running away under the sea. All around were huge pieces of machinery, but I had no time to look at anything as the miners strode forward, I shepherded between Davey and Colin, desperately trying to keep up without tripping over. Soon we were squeezing into the darkness between the tunnel wall and a series of flat-topped trucks that came to about the height of my chest. I glanced into one of them, and was disconcerted to see that it was crammed with helmeted men, hunched and blank faced in the dimness. Davey gestured me in through one of the T-shaped portholes, and I clambered on to a bench on which there was just enough room to sit upright. Then the Man Riding Set trundled away into the darkness. Above the noise Davey told me that when we returned to bank

I should have my photograph taken in front of the pit winding gear with my face black and my pit-claes still on. This was exactly what I had been hoping to do, and I eagerly concurred. In the half light I could just make out Colin smirking enigmatically at my enthusiasm.

After walking a short distance we made our way through a plastic door which each man held open for the man behind against the wind blowing from the rear. I was not quick enough. The door snapped shut, and it took a considerable effort by Colin to get it open again. I don't know where the other men went, but soon we were walking alone in the darkness, our helmet lamps on. On our left was the stationary conveyor belt, and under our feet a set of narrow, closely spaced tracks. The amount of water, mud, dust and other matter, and the relative height of the ground were constantly changing, so I had to pay continual attention to where I was treading. White stone dust had been thrown on to the ground, but this had been largely trodden into the mud and grit, giving a strange impression, given the relative warmth this side of the plastic door, of walking through snow and its residual slush. The beams overhead were piled with the stuff. In the event of an explosion, the beams would drop and the dust would fall, neutralising the inflammable coal dust.

All the time Davey complained – while telling me how pleased they were to have me there – about the lack of notice they had been given for my visit. He had been telephoned only the night before to come in specially and they had only been aware of my presence at the pit five minutes before I walked into their store room. Davey was the kind of person who takes a constant, eager, excitable interest in the workings of the system, who knows – or thinks he knows – exactly who should be doing what, where, when and with whom, and will fret endlessly and with delighted self-righteousness if any detail is overlooked by anybody other than himself. Colin was the inevitable complementary type, who sits placidly back in the knowledge that all systems are inherently corrupt. Their main concern was to get me back on bank as quickly as they could and while they genuinely wanted to help me I was unable to persuade them that I actually wanted to stay down there as long as possible.

Davey assured me that had I been 'a piece of fanny', not only would the under-manager himself have brought me down, but I would have been 'straight in and straight out'. They told me that the manager was also making a visit underground, and we should try to avoid him at all costs, as he would want to know why it was taking two of them to take me round.

Colin, who seemed to be paying more attention to the practical considerations of my visit, said that on our next mode of conveyance I should lie down with my head up, and get off with my right foot first. Before I had had time to wonder what on earth this could consist of, or to notice that the conveyor on our left was now moving, Davey had stepped on to it, and lying down face forward, was swept away along the undulating tunnel. 'OK,' said Colin. 'Step on with your left foot first, and follow with your right or you'll be knocked off balance. Then drop to your knees, and then down.' The belt was moving alarmingly rapidly. I felt sure I'd be spun straight off and would go crashing into the wall and then do myself some horrendous injury on the wires and bits of plant that surrounded the belt. A few feet ahead a sign hung low over the belt. If I didn't get down quickly enough, I'd be sure to hit it.

By now Davey must have been miles ahead. Colin said patiently that we didn't have to use the belt, though it was rather a long walk. No, no, I said. I jumped on to the belt, fell on to my backside and lay back to avoid the looming sign.

'Sirrup!' hissed Colin, already immediately behind me. 'Get on to your front.' I did so. The belt was barely the thickness of lino, and ran swinging along the undulating tunnels, over steel rollers that jolted constantly against one's hip bones. Overall the effect was not unpleasant; like a very low-key fairground ride – except that my mind was consumed by one thought. How the hell was I going to get off? I would not be able to, and would be sent hurtling onwards into the impaling jaws of some fiendish piece of machinery.

'If you don't get off,' called Colin, 'I'll pull this wire, and it'll stop automatically. But you'll see the signs.' Ahead red letters, picked out by my helmet-lamp, were shooting towards me: 'Forty-five metres'. Then more: 'Fifteen metres'. Then the platform – like a tiny railway station picked out against an endless black oblivion. 'Your right foot,' Colin was saying. I was up, put my right foot out, and was thrown against the platform rail, to which I clung, shaking.

The tunnel was now much smaller. The bricks had long since given way to arch girders and dense metal meshwork. At a junction in the roadway, we came upon a miner sitting, completely black, biting into a pristine white sandwich. Ahead, in the tunnel to the right, others stood and sat. 'You'll want to put them on,' said one, referring to my knee pads. To our left, the wall was completely covered by a dense mass of cables running horizontal to the ground. Davey had disappeared. Colin and I put on our pads. Then Colin bent down, as though to point to something at the base of the wall, but instead he climbed in under the wires, and I knew immediately that this, a point unnoticeable to an outsider, was the entrance to the coal face.

We were kneeling in a kind of forest of pit props about three feet high, the nearest shining dully in the light from our lamps. Between them, to the left, I could make out the workings, every-thing stationary for the moment, and to the right, between a dense mass of beams and wire mesh, the grey splintering rock. Until now, although Davey and Colin had told me we were about two miles out under the North Sea, I hadn't had time to reflect on our exact physical position, any more than on the London Underground one bothers to try to visualise the streets overhead. Now, however, a kind of chill passed through me as I saw the rock, and sensed its immeasurable imprisoning force above us. Meanwhile Colin was pulling ahead. I headed after him, making each knee stride as long as I could, clambering over the concrete bars set into the black grit and mud. Once we were able to rise to half height to splash our way though a puddle. Then we were on our knees again. I paused for a moment to further slacken the upper strap of my knee-pad, but Colin told me it would hurt at first no matter what I did. If I pointed my lamp beam to the left, I could see the face itself – the solid wall of coal, glittering blue-black – and I was surprised most of all by how beautiful it was. Everything was stationary – the coal-cutting machine, the conveyor that took the coal to the main gate (the tunnel at the other end of the face) and the big con-veyor that took it towards the shaft bottom. Nothing could move unless everything was moving. Ahead of us, a group of men lay in the grit, apparently just waiting for something to happen. They greeted us, 'Areet,' as we clambered over them. Then as I passed, a gruff voice boomed out.

'Why, he's gor odd fucking byuts on!'

'Whassa?'

'Odd byuts, man. An eight and a fuckin' nine!'

'If he gans to Newcastle on a Sarradeh, he'll gerra gyem!'

They all roared with laughter. Then they called after us, asking if we'd like to see the machine in operation. We were now about level with it, but it lay invisible beneath a heap of coal. There was a great grinding roar, and I caught a glimpse of shining whirling steel before the heap of coal came pouring suddenly towards us, like a great mass of dusty jewels that threatened to engulf us. Then it ground quickly to a halt. We thanked the men, and moved on.

As we crawled gratefully out into the main gate, a moustached man threw something at me. I put my hand out and felt a cylindrical object three or four inches long. 'Dynamite,' he said, and the men around all laughed as I jumped. They were deputies, preparing the next face, a few yards back out-bye. The dynamite was used to blast the rock away and was apparently quite safe without a detonator.

We walked back towards the main road, Davey – who had rejoined us at the main gate – and Colin speculating constantly on whether we'd get to the shaft bottom in time to catch the next cage back up. I had wedged my glasses' case into the back of my belt to stop it falling out of my breast pocket, and I now noticed I no longer had it. Still, it was a small price to pay for such an experience. It would soon be ground into the grit of the face, and, who knew, in a couple of million years, it might end up as a lump of coal.

I wondered at the purpose of the heavy tin canister on my belt. Davey and Colin looked at each other in horror. Then they looked back at me.

'Did nobody tell you about that?' asked Davey. 'That's your personal rescuer.' They both sighed long and hard. 'If you as much as smell fire, there's a mask in there. You grip it between your teeth and you walk towards the shaft bottom. You dinnut run! And if you see any cunt on the ground, you leave him there! If he's got his mask in, you can help him. But you dinnut share! If you take that mask out for four seconds, you'll be dead!

'You have to keep in front of the fire. You have to go round, ahead of it, no matter how far it takes you. Your rescuer'll keep you going for ninety minutes. So if the fire was ahead of us, we'd go back through the face, come down the tail-gate – the roadway at the other end – till we were in front of the fire. Because the fresh air is always going out through the tail gate. If you ever get lost in here, keep the wind behind you. It may take fifty yards, it may take five miles, but eventually it'll lead you out of the pit.'

It was at Easington, on the 28th May 1951, that the last great disaster in British coal mining occurred. Eighty-one miners and two rescue workers were killed after an explosion in a district of the pit known as 'the Duckbill'.

According to the subsequent inquiry, sparks caused by a coal cutter hitting pyrite, the brassy strata in the coal, had ignited gas accumulated in cavities beside the long wall face.

In that area, the dust lay on the ground a foot deep. It was like the 'bloody Sahara Desert'. Coal dust is, of course, highly inflammable. If you throw a handful of it on the fire, it flares up like paraffin. The explosion threw all the dust in the air. Suddenly it was black. You couldn't see an inch. Then the fire came tearing through in a great ball. Afterwards they could see by the blasting of the walls where it had bounced and ricocheted along these tunnels. They found tubs wrapped round girders, two foot thick girders tied in knots. It would have gone through the entire pit, coming up the shaft and blasting the pulley wheels off the top, except it came to a corner in the roadway that it hit with such force, that it bounced back the way it had come.

It had, however, pushed the gas ahead of it. Many of the men were found without a mark on them – sitting with a jam sandwich in one hand and a tea bottle in the other. Others had huge lumps of rock embedded in them, or small neat holes in their foreheads and the whole of the back blasted away, or were completely encrusted with coal dust.

Relatives stood at the pit head for weeks, hoping for news of survivors. Only one was found, his glove still smouldering. He died on the way to hospital. The pit started work again with some of the men still buried. But they got all the bodies out in the end. All except the gallowas, the pit ponies; they poured quick lime over them.

A year later, almost to the day, there was a similar explosion at Horden. The entire village gathered at the pit head to await news of casualties. But in the intervening months, appropriate safety measures had been taken, and only one man was killed. It was always said that Easington had saved Horden.

We reached a junction where four roads met and waited by a great battery of telephones and intercoms. I wondered how much of a future they thought the pit had.

'The manager's trying his hardest. He's coming up with forecasts of this and forecasts of that. But the men know – because they're down here every day – that it's just too slow and too expensive to get the coal out. They can see it happening with their own eyes. Morale's at rock bottom, and there's nothing anybody can do to raise it.

'It's affecting management too. That's why there was no preparation for your visit. Everything's that lackadaisical now. By 1993 all the Durham pits'll be gone. There'll be only Wearmouth, and maybe Westoe.

'See, it's very difficult to check up on things down here. If the men at the face say something's wrong, say a pipe's burst, so they can't work, it's impossible to tell from bank whether it's true or not. So if they don't feel like working, or they just want to kill time, they don't bother. Because it doesn't matter now.'

I wondered if the strike of '84–85 had achieved anything.

'Nothing,' said Davey, with a rueful laugh.

'The Coal Board got everything they wanted,' said Colin. 'They saved millions in wages, and they got rid of the stocks of coal they'd been building up. We each lost thousands.'

'I lost the extension I was going to build on my house,' said Davey. 'Many lost their whole houses. Many's still paying back the debts they got into. Everybody lost their savings. Say you'd saved six thousand over the years. How're you going to get that again?'

'Mind, the man that started it,' said Colin. 'Everything he said was true.'

'Even if his methods stank,' said Davey.

'He said there was a hit list for pits, and every closure he predicted has happened – and more.'

Suddenly one of the telephones rang. Davey answered it and turned to me.

'Have you lost a glasses' case?'

A tiny locomotive arrived, and we went screaming back towards the shaft bottom. The little train made such an appalling din I had to put my helmet clamps over my ears. We got off into an icy blasting wind, and took shelter in a tiny cubby hole with some other miners. Colin leaned towards me, his eyes glinting confidentially. 'This book you're writing about Horden, is it going to be an epic? Or is it going to be more of a leaflet? I reckon a leaflet should do Horden.' He sat back, chuckling with satisfaction before repeating the remark to his fellows.

As I walked back to Horden, along the top of the fields that ran down towards the sea, the wet road shining like a ribbon of blue metal under the Northern sky, I felt as though I were commanding the whole of the coast. Beyond Hartlepool, Teesside dissolved into an indeterminate mass of smoke and lights, but above that I could see the hazy outline of the North Yorkshire coast. It was said that on a clear day you could see Scarborough from Easington. I had seen a postcard taken from a 1930s travel poster advertising the charms of Scarborough. It showed a group of gleaming white ships lit up at night off the quayside. 'The tunny fleet' it said, but the pristine vessels and the glamorous glow of their lights were more suggestive of the pleasure craft of Antibes. In my bleakest moments in Horden I had longed for the time when I would leave this mean little corner of the world and head down into the confident, relatively sophisticated world of Yorkshire. Somewhere along the line, however, my original intention to move south from Horden had been lost sight of. Now I faced what I had in my heart of hearts known all along, that my English journey would take me no further than Horden.

When I got home, I sat down on my bed and fell asleep almost at once. I woke shortly to find that such were the jolting unaccustomed contrasts of the day – between sticky warmth and howling cold, silence and screeching noise – I was unable to get warm, even with the electric-fire full on. I crawled under the blankets and succumbed immediately to the blackness.

Frank Johnson lived on an estate right up at the other end of Peterlee. As I headed up the bank from Horden, the wind threatened to lift me from the ground, the rain driving like nails into my face. The flap with a large press-fastener that was meant to fasten the top of my coat slapped me in the face several times, very hard, before I managed to do it up.

From the saucer-shaped area of land in which Peterlee town centre lay, the various estates atop their bare and rain driven swards looked like beleaguered Italian hill towns. I asked several times and took several wrong turnings before I found the cul-de-sac where Frank lived. It lay off an immensely long road of new and characterless detached houses, which seemed to snake back half the way I'd already come, but which was not approachable by any other route. It wasn't somewhere I'd have chosen to live myself, but this was one of the most desirable parts of Peterlee.

It was completely dark as I approached the house, a bare modern bungalow. I walked round the side of the house, but I could see through the living-room window that the place was utterly deserted. Another wasted journey, I thought. I rang the bell on the house opposite. The woman said that was indeed Frank Johnson's house, but they were out. She'd invite me in to wait, but her husband had told her never to let strangers in the house when he wasn't there.

I was about to give up and go home, when a car swung round the corner and up into the Johnsons' drive. A middle-aged couple got out and began removing their shopping from the back. The man was short and stocky and wore a tweed hat. They froze at my approach.

'My name's Hudson,' I said. 'I think you knew my grandfather.'

Frank peered at me through the darkness. 'You'd better come in,' he said.

'Tommy Hudson,' said Frank, his arms resting easily on the table in the gleaming white kitchen, his large and very forceful head ringed by grey curls, his eyes narrowing in recollection. Like many of the better educated people in that part of the world, who had to an extent lost their accents, his voice retained a hard metallic twang, a nasal fierceness, as though he were biting his words out of the air; the way my father himself spoke.

'They lived just along the street from us in Oak Terrace. Your father was about a year older than me, and he was very athletic. That's the thing I remember most about him. At that time the church was one of the main social centres of the village, and we were both in the Church Lads' Brigade. Your father used to organise what they called an "agility group" – leaping over horses and all kinds of physical jerks. He used to train us and devise our various activities. We used to call it, "Strength Through Joy with Tommy Hudson".' He laughed.

'His second great love was the artistic thing. I don't mean it disparagingly, but he used to wear things, like a certain type of sandal, that other people in Horden wouldn't wear. But people knew him. They knew he was Tommy Hudson, and they accepted it.

'Now your grandfather I can remember very well. I can picture him now, as if he was standing here.' He gestured towards the corner of the bright new room. 'Carrying his can of tea, on his way to work. In his clogs. They all wore clogs, because it was that hot on top of the ovens. And always with his pipe. Our house faced along Sixth Street, and I used to see him every day, going to and from work. He'd been in the navy, I think, and he had a very distinctive walk, with a kind of seaman's roll. Then, he was just Tommy Hudson's dad. But later on I went to work at the coke ovens myself, and I got to know him in quite a different way.

'I'd been quite good at physics and chemistry at school, and I had an idea I'd like to be involved in the coke and by-products side of the coal industry. So I made an application to the coke ovens, and I was identified as potential management material. Well in those days, even if you were destined eventually to be a manager, you had to start at the bottom. You started by doing every single job on the plant, and you began with the lowest, same as any other lad who went to work there.

'Your grandfather was the chargerman, and he was known.

It was known who Percy Hudson was, and he was known as a character. For example, when you went to work with him and his team on the charger, he'd tell you how he wanted the work done, and it didn't matter what you thought, it had to be done his way. He wasn't a foreman or anything. It was just accepted that he had a kind of senior position.

'He was a very considerate man – and I'm not just saying this because he was your grandfather – and a very conscientious man. He took the work seriously. He could talk. If it was something that concerned him, he could talk endlessly. And he had the kind of sense of humour where something was only funny if he said it was. For example, he might make a disparaging remark about somebody. But if you said something like that, he'd say, "You shouldn't say things like that." And if you reminded him of what he'd said, he'd say, "Oh, that's different."

'It was just accepted by the men on his shift that what he said went. For example, if he said that every man should put in a shilling a week so they could all go and see Sunderland play, or go to Pontefract for the races, they would. He seemed to believe there should be a social side to the work.

'He was never a foreman. I don't know why. Perhaps because he wanted to carry on with his union work. If you got made foreman, you had to drop your union activities immediately. A man who was active in the union was seen as a troublemaker, and if they were able they were often promoted just to shut them up. That never happened in your grandfather's case. Whether he was never asked or whether he refused, I don't know.

'He was one of the old type of trade unionist, who weren't in it for the glory or to make a political statement, but because they genuinely wanted to make things better for their fellow workers. The things your grandfather was working towards: better pay, shorter working hours, better working conditions, protective clothing – goggles, masks, gloves. All these things eventually came in. But not in his time.

'They were struggling for these things under very difficult circumstances, because in those days the managers had an incredible amount of power, and the manager at Horden coke ovens was a very difficult man called McQuillan. He was anti-workers, anti-unions, anti-everything. His son had been the first lad in Horden to be killed in the war, and it was said that that was what had made him that cantankerous.

'He was a Roman Catholic, and it was very difficult to get

a job there unless you were a Catholic. I don't know how your grandfather managed to get in there, let alone get a position in the union. On pay day, the Roman Catholic priest would be standing there in his wide black hat, waiting for a donation from each of the workers. It got so they would dock the donation to the church automatically off the Roman Catholic workers' paynotes.

'There were three of them who ran the union. Tommy Hughes, the treasurer, who was of a similar temperament to your grandfather – fundamentally serious. But the chairman, Micky Driscoll, he didn't let anything bother him. He never worried about tomorrow – not him! He was in the union totally for himself. But everybody knew it, so you couldn't dislike him for it. He had a laugh and a joke for everybody, so he was popular with everyone. He was a Catholic, of course. Broad Durham, but his family had only come over from Ireland a generation before.

'He was a rough diamond, but he had his pretensions. He liked to dress up, and he'd always had aspirations to mix with people better educated than himself. And he managed to do this with some success when he went to represent the area on the union's National Executive, and later when he got a job with the Coal Board as an industrial liaison officer. But really, he knew nothing. We used to call him the "hairy-arsed gas regulator". He worked in the Salter House where they made the sulphate of ammonia. Every thirty minutes he had to half turn a wheel, but he had no idea why. He didn't know what gas was. If it went bang he had no idea why. I don't mean any disrespect to your grandfather by saying that he wasn't very well educated either. But he never pretended to know more than he did.

'You used to hear funny things about the coke ovens, and when you went to work there, you found out they were true. For example Micky Driscoll used to cut the hair of virtually everybody at the ovens. He used to do it in his little shed. He didn't do it particularly well, but he was happy to do it. He was generous. That was why he was popular.

'And they used to kill pigs there. In those days, the allotments came right up to the edge of the ovens. During the war and after, when rationing was on, they'd lead a pig they'd been keeping there illegally through into the Salter House and kill it. Then they'd boil it up in a great cauldron, cut it up and sell the meat. They never had any problem finding buyers.

'There was a granary beside the coke ovens, where they used to keep the feed for the gallowas, the ponies from the pit. Some of the grain would be, shall we say, appropriated, and little trails would be left through the allotments to try to tempt out the ducks and geese that were kept there. If you followed these trails, they all led to Micky Driscoll's shed, and at Christmastime you'd see plenty of duck and goose feathers mixed with the hair clippings on the shed floor.

'Walter Laidlaw was another notable character at the ovens. If you see him now, he looks like an old man – and an old man that's not well. But if you could have seen him in his heyday. What a fine upstanding figure of a man! Your grandfather always held himself very well, but Walter Laidlaw? No muffler for him. He *always* wore a collar and tie. He was on the union committee for a time as well, then he was made foreman. Before he got on the union, he was always complaining that Percy and the others weren't doing enough, that they were letting the management get away with murder. Then as soon as he got made foreman it was, "This is what the management wants, and that's the end of it." He became very unpopular, and was virtually sent to Coventry by the men, who regarded him as a traitor. Then he lost his job very suddenly. No one was quite sure why. But there were lots of stories as you can imagine.

'He was typical of a certain type of Catholic you got working at the coke ovens. Several of his family were on the council or had been on the council, and he was on the council himself for a time. It was a great blow to him when he lost his job like that. You had to feel sorry for him in a way. The ironic thing was that afterwards he went to work for ICI on Teesside as a security guard.

'But they were all characters at the coke ovens. You had to be a bit of a character to stand it. And it was very close knit. It was like a kind of brotherhood in a way. But it had to be, because you had men working there twenty, thirty, forty years, without a break, and really it was an awful job. Up there on the battery like your grandfather, with the smoke and the sparks and the flames and the toxic gases belching out of the ovens. Or filling the trucks. That was the best paid job. But it was slavery. Slavery, man! I did it for eight months, and I'll never know how I stuck it. You had a kind of fork called a gripe, wide as this table. Lower down the bench, you were lifting it two feet off the ground to get the coke into the wagons. But higher up you'd have to half turn round and sling it over your shoulder. You had to shift twenty tons a shift before you were even paid. Imagine doing that, with gas coming up through the grille underneath, in the middle of the night in the pouring rain. Most of the men who chose to stick at that for twenty years ended up as cripples. Aye, cripples. In wheelchairs some of them . . .

'But they were completely different in their characters, the father and the son – Percy and Tom. I never felt that Percy had much of a life. But Tom – he was full of it. He was boiling over with it!

'He used to go out with this girl called Norma Lindoe, who was definitely one of *the* girls to go out with at the school. She was dark and pretty. Very pretty. I mean she was a cracker! She went out with various people. Jackie Carpenter was one. And your father for a time. But not me. I never got to go with her to the Christmas Party, I'm sorry to say. But there were many that were tipping their caps to go out with Norma Lindoe. She was the belle of the ball, and no mistake . . . I don't know what happened to her.

'My father was the manager of the Deluxe, the cinema above the Big Club. Where we lived in Oak Terrace was considered one of the more desirable places to live in Horden, believe it or not. Further down it got a bit rougher. Our house faced the end of Sixth Street, and we were absolutely forbidden by my father to go beyond Fifth Street. The very bottom, First, Second and Third Streets were known as China Town. That was where the really rough families, the real hard men, lived. In the Thirties, it was terrible for some people. You can't deny it. I remember when I was at junior school, there was one family called Luke – and it breaks my heart to think about it, even now. They used to come to school in winter with no shoes on, or in plimsolls with no soles. There was a teacher called Wilkinson, who I greatly admired, who seemed to me at the time to be an example of everything a human being ought to be. He used to cycle to school from Wingate. And every day he used to bring apples and bread for these kids. Because the story was that at dinnertime they'd go home, walk twice round the kitchen table and come back, because there was no food.

'But it was at least partially self-inflicted. Because they drank, a lot of these people. In those days the Big Club was *the* thing. When they got in the Big Club that was it. Many of these men, their lives revolved completely around the Big Club.'

8

The Ninepenny Rabbit

ANYONE who wants to say they have *seen* Durham Cathedral, should see it not only in summer, the three great towers rising hazy and visionlike through the balm of the great cloud of foliage, its interior bathed in golden light, the majestic columns dappled with the reflected hues of its stained glass, but also in the very dead of the year, when the last leaves have departed the elms that cling to the great rock, its gaunt winter face peering down through soot encrusted eyelets into the black dank water of the Wear, when the light seems hardly to penetrate much of the interior, and the broad blank expanses of stone between the rows of upper and lower arches rising from the submarine dimness towards the feeble light from the upper windows, have about them the clammy, irremediable chill of river mud.

In the south aisle is a large and elaborate piece of seventeenth-century woodcarving that has been turned into a memorial to the miners of the county, and beside it, in a glass case, a book with the names of all those killed in the county's pits since 1945. Around the corner, in the south transept, opposite the blasted banners and battle-torn standards of the Durham Light Infantry chapel, is a possibly even more poignant and more significant memento. High on the great bare wall is the huge banner of the Haswell Lodge of the Durham Miners' Association. At Haswell, a village on the road between Durham and the coast, in 1844, ninety-five pitmen and boys were killed in an explosion, causing an unprecedented outcry over mining conditions. From this sombre relic – its expanses of charcoal, maroon and olive green fading to an appearance of sparse monumental flatness – three august figures in black Sunday suits look blankly off to the left: Alex Macdonald, the miners' National President, William Crawford, secretary of the DMA and standing beside them in his stovepipe hat and Old Testament beard, Tommy Ramsey, the 'owld crakeman'. He is holding the crake, an instrument like a huge football rattle, which up until the last war was still used to summon men to union meetings in the pit villages. After the collapse of the United Colliers' Union in 1832, Ramsey had walked from village to village, sounding the crake, and instructing the men not to forget the self-evident nature of their 'rights'.

Beneath these figures were the words: 'They being dead yet speak'.

Every year, on the second Saturday in July, the greater part of the population of that part of the world – up to a million people – would crowd up to the walls of the great cathedral, cramming the aisles so that it was impossible to move, for the service of the Durham Miners' Gala – the so-called Big Meeting. The bands of the three collieries at which most men had been killed during the course of the year would play as they marched into the cathedral – the booming of the bass drum, pounding with a funereal slowness, heard first in the distance, becoming louder and louder, then as it entered the cathedral, the droning and the grinding of the brass, swelling and filling the cavernous interior. Then the banners, draped in black, were carried up the aisle and placed on the high altar.

Up to the 1960s, Durham Big Meeting was bigger than Christmas. On that day, the most hardened capitalist could breathe the atmosphere of socialism, could become giddy, drinking it from the very air. Early, early in the morning, the people of the city could hear a faint wheezing and a sighing carried on the still air of a high summer's morning – the sound of the bands marching towards Durham – not plaintive and heartfelt, as they played into the cathedral, but booming and crashing, triumphant and majestic along the country lanes. Then, all of a sudden, they were descending along their different routes into the centre of the city, and the air would be filled with the delirious cacophony of two hundred bands, each playing a different tune. The shops would all be boarded-up against the crushing and the pressing of the hundreds of thousands of onlookers crowded along the route. Down they marched towards the racecourse where the speeches would be held, past the County Hotel where the speakers – the most eminent socialist politicians of the day – and the union leaders, stood watching from the balcony, everyone smiling and waving in the great, reverberating bowl of sound. And over their heads swayed the great banners of the lodges, with their messages of hope: 'Unity is strength', 'All men are brethren', 'The Future is in your hands!' – the lodge officials marching solemnly before the banners, behind them the work-hardened faces of the miners in their cloth caps and blue serge suits, evincing a flinty-eyed pride on their annual day of glory.

Now, however, there were only four mines left working in the whole of the old Durham Area. And although men still died in them, and the banners were still draped in black and the bands still played into the cathedral, only a few thousand people now turned out for the Durham Big Meeting.

I could hear the booming of the brass while I was shaving, and I ran out through the back lane to see the Horden Band, in their short jackets of midnight blue with the bright orange lapels, marching down past the blackened rockery of the Parish Council Park, towards the church. I had attended one of their rehearsals at the Miners' Hall, and had felt curiously detached from the proceedings. This however was the way to see a brass band: not sitting down trying to analyse the music but with the drum thudding beneath, blasting indefatigably into the bitter morning air – the peppery grinding of the cornets and trombones, the blistering oomph of the euphonia and bass horns surging thrillingly and seeming to warm one from the inside. It was Remembrance Sunday, but the procession they were leading was pathetically small. After the Cadet Corps, with a surprising number of lasses, their poodle manes stuffed up into their berets, it petered out into a small huddle of a nurse with a standard, a few kids and only three ex-servicemen.

I was surprised at the smallness of the turn-out, as people in that part of the world were unusually susceptible to appeals to patriotism and nationhood. For all that they had developed a culture tangential to the established currents of British society, for all the bitterness they had felt towards the ruling class as represented by the coal owners, they were probably the most royalist people in Britain.

Yes, I thought, as the band laid down their instruments and filtered meekly into the church, that was the kind of music you would expect to hear in Horden – bracing, convivial, unreflective. You wouldn't expect, I thought with more than a touch of regret, to hear the lone voice raised in anguish or yearning. You would expect the rhythms of Horden to be strident and foursquare, not sultrily swaying or syncopated. There was, as far as I could see,

nothing seductive or smooth or silkily sinuous in or about Horden.
I sometimes wondered how people managed to make love in Horden.

Horden was less than a mile by road from the sea, and much less
as the crow flies, only a steep field of clay separating the allotments
on the east side from the top of the low earth cliffs. Yet although you
could see the sea from most places in Horden, and you could hardly
ignore the relentless hammering of the winds off it, you were in most
senses unaware of it. For most of the year, the sombre indifferent
backdrop was simply there, signifying nothing. Although there were
a few individuals who liked nothing better than to stand for hours by
their trembling rods, staring into the oncoming breakers, the pulling
of the grey-brown foam, and there were of course the sea-coalies,
who made their living from it, Horden in general ignored the sea.
The feeling of space and freedom associated with the presence of the
sea, the sense of empathy with the lonely inhabitants of distance – the
seagulls, the stars, the far ships – were simply absent. One always felt
cramped and shut in in Horden.

The beach road led down past a scrap-yard, through a gulley
filled with rubbish to a small car park with four huge blocks
of concrete intended to stop the sea-coal lorries from getting on
to the beach. These vehicles had ridden the upper beach into a
formless mud morass, from which tiers of black and violet-grey
sand and grit led down to the water's edge where a finer blackness
suffused the lapping foam like squid's ink. Horden's golden sands
had once been famous, and after the First World War it had been
a kind of afternoon resort for the villages of East Durham; people
sitting up on the bank sides, all in their Sunday best. At Dene Holm,
the mouth of Castle Eden Dene, there had been a beautiful meadow
with a bridge over the stream and a tea hut. Hawkers came from
all over the area to sell to the day trippers, and there'd be dozens
of games of football.

Now Dene Holm was an area of hostile marshy scrub where
teenagers tested unlicensed motorcycles, the beach was five or six
feet higher than it should have been, and few people from Horden or
anywhere else bothered to go down there, except for the sea-coalies.
For no matter what precautions were taken by the Council and other
authorities, their lorries, a blackened camouflage green, always found
a way down.

There had always been coal on these shores. In medieval times,
monks used to collect the precious nuggets worn away from where
the tops of the coal seams touched the sea floor. But when Horden,
Blackhall and Easington began tipping on to the beach, a lucrative

and highly organised trade had developed. Twenty years ago, it was booming. There were pitched battles between rival gangs of sea-coalies, their lorries churning the beach into an El Alamein of black grit as they tried to, literally, drive each other off the beach. The godfathers of the trade became rich. It was said that every night-club in Hartlepool had been opened with sea-coal money.

Now, although Easington's aerial flight was still in operation, leisurely tipping bucket after bucket of black waste on to the blackened moonscape, twenty-four hours a day, the pickings were relatively meagre. But one still saw the sea-coalies, grim faced in their combat jackets, up to their knees at the water's edge even in the middle of winter. And many an unemployed man still went down to fill a bag for his own domestic use.

The air was filled with a grey miasmic drizzle, the cliffs reduced to a dark numb presence. I kept to the sea's edge. It was always marginally less cold by the water, and the lowest tier of the black turd-like pebbles provided a tiny amount of shelter. I walked southwards mindlessly towards Blackhall, enjoying the relentless rhythmical motion of the waves as the drizzle grew thicker and darker. A few feet in from the lapping waves was a tidemark of used sanitary towels. Further up the beach, a group of youths were taking it in turns to ride back and forth on a motorcycle at breakneck speeds. Once, when I strayed from the water's edge, one, though he had almost the whole of the beach at his disposal, rode the little machine within about three feet of where I was walking – his face as he flashed past, helmetless, drawn by the wind into a mask of impassive determination.

'The handbarl alley?' asked Harry Sugden. 'I was barn on it.' He sat back, relaxed but erect in his armchair, a faint lisp lending a slight whimsical quality to his short-vowelled speech. 'You know where the Big Club is? Well, the handbarl alley was behind there.

'What they used to call Old Sixth Street used to run along the side of the Club yard. The first eight houses, the ones beside the Club, had yards, but the ones after that had none. Ours was the first of the houses without yards. The toilets – they used to call them netties – and the coalhouse used to stand apart from the houses. There was nay warl, so when it rained, all the water used to pour down from the cricket field, through the handbarl ally, and flood us out. There was a big sink outside the door, next to the coalhouse, and when they tipped the coal cart, nine times out of ten they'd blog it up, and we'd be flooded out again. There was nay taps in the houses.

There was a communal tap with a big sink, where people used to gan and fill their pails with watter. That's if they wanted it!'

He chuckled. 'Them was the olden times!

'I was barn in Harden in 1912, in that same house. Old Sixth Street. They pulled it down years ago, and built new houses. But when I go down there, I always knar exactly where I was barn, because you can still see where the handbarl alley was. There was a woman looking out the door the other day when I went past. I said, "I was barn here, missus."

'She said, "Yer warn't. We were the first in 'ere."

'I said, "I was barn here."

'She said, "How could you be barn 'ere, when yer've nivver lived 'ere?"

'I said, "I lived here. Where this house is now, I lived here."

'The bookie used to hide in our netty. In them days there was nay betting shops. The bookies' runners used to stand on the corner by the Miners' Hall. If he saw a policeman coming, he'd run along and hide in our netty. He had a brick in the wall he used to pull out. He'd stuff the bets in there, and put the brick back. But the police got wise to it. They used to say, "We know you're taking bets. We'll come for you, half-past one, maybes Tuesday." They'd take him in, fine him five pound. Then he'd go back and carry on. It was regular that.

'That house was right on the handbarl alley. The men who couldn't afford to gan in used to climb up on to our netty top to watch. My father used to look after the handbarl alley, and he was a member of the Club.

'The alley was a wall about forty feet high. It was the only bit left of the original Club that was burnt down. In front of it was like a court, fifteen yards long, with lines running all the way round, and the men used to crowd in to watch, right the way round that line. There was an eight-yard line, and you stotted your ball inside there, and hit the alley – braying it out as hard as you could against the other man's left hand, because a man's left hand is always his weakest.

'The Mordue Brothers were from Horden, and they were known as the handbarl champions of the world. When they were playing, the crowds were huge. You could hear the noise all over Horden. They were supposed to be world champions. Tucker and Billy. They came from a good footballing family. Their grandfather Jackie played for Newcastle, and Tucker went on to play for Newcastle. But handbarl was really their game. They'be playing for fifty pund a side, and there'd be side bets.

'There was a net on top of the alley to stop the barl going over. Because I've seen a feller bray a barl right over, halfway down Seventh Street to the church. It was bigger than a tennis barl, but it had a thick skin. They used to call it the "wind barl". Before they played they used to soak their hands in "apple dill dock" to make them hard. But you'd see them split their hands right down the palm. I've seen my father come in, his hand split down to the wrist. Do you know what they used to do? They used to fill it with cobbler's wax. Red. They'd heat it with a candle and pour it into the crack. Then they'd go back out and carry on playing. It never bled.

'I've seen them start playing at two o'clock, and still be playing at half-past eight. I've seen my dad come into the house, and my mother's had to pull his shirt off him, he's sweat that much playing handbarl. Then he'd go to the pit and work a full shift.

'Now I used to love the game, but I wasn't a member of the Club, because I wasn't old enough. I used to climb over the wall to watch, but the doorman of the Club used to keep coming over. "Hey, yer booger, get on wi' yer!" And we used to hop like hell, back over the wall. Then, when I was nine or ten, if my father was playing, he'd say, "Meg, make a pot of tea and send our Harry over with it." There was a chair at each corner, and at the end of every chalk the players would sit down, and one man would play the civvy and he'd be massaging their knees. Then they'd say right, and they'd carry on playing. I used to take the tea in at halftime. It cost a tanner to get in, but I'd get in for nowt.

'As I got taller I used to go in with the men, because they used to have a pint, come out and have a game. And I used to get bit game wi' them. I was nearly eighteen year old. I still couldn't join the Club, but there was one feller used to play regular in the handicaps. They called him Brumwell. And these two fellers cracked him out. He said, "I haven't got a marra, man." They said, "Here, play with Harry Sugden." That was on the Saturday afternoon. We played two games off the belt. Eleven up each time. It lasted from one o'clock till half-past seven.

'It was summer, red hot. My father and mother had gone to Sunderland that day. Very rare my father used to gan with my mother, but they'd been to Sunderland. And when they came back I was lying on the settee, blood red from the sun. "What the hell's tha been deein'?" "Playin' handbarl." "Where at?" "The Alley." "Tha's not allowed in." "I've been playing there." "Who's tha been playing with?" "Freddy Brumwell." "Freddy Brumwell?" I said,

"Aye." "Who's tha been playin'?" "Sammy Alderson and Jackie Harrison." Jackie Harrison was not long out of the army. Strong lad. Played to me all the time, because I was the youngest. But I was running by then. I was doing foot handicaps for money. I was fit. I didn't drink. I didn't smoke. I could play all day. They tried all ways to knock us down, but we won both games, me and Freddy. I won four bob. I was ower the moon. Freddy won two pund, and he didn't give them a shillun.

'There was an old feller, always wore a bowler hat and a gold watch chain. One day he sees us and he says, "Come here, son. I want tha." I said, "Oh no, I'm not coming over there. Tha's ganna report us, tha knars." He said, "Come here, man. I'm not ganna touch tha . . . What do they call tha?" I said, "Sugden." "Is Billy thi fattha?" I said, "Aye." He said, "Thou's the next champion of the world. Tha's that fast and that cute." Oh aye, they all said that.

'I'll tell you something else. Have you heard of the ninepenny rabbit?'

I hadn't.

'Well, do you know where the "cottages" are? All where them houses are was just a big cornfield. And that's where they used to hold the whippet races. My father and his marras used to get together to buy the rabbits. They used to come in boxes, two dozen to a box – sixty altogether. People had to pay so much to put a dog in, and that's how they made their money back. They used to call it a "Rabbits Week" and they held it on a Saturday afternoon. One dog would beat another, and they'd go to a final. People used to come from all over. They used to put the dog on a bench, and one of the men – it was my father actually – would measure them from the back toe to the top of the hip, and if a dog was an inch higher than another it had so many yards start. Them little dogs was nippy, see. They could turn quicker than the others.

'As soon as they'd killed the rabbit, I used to run after them and pull it off them. I was only about nine or ten. I used to have a stick. I used to pick the rabbit up by the back legs, and I used to hit it on the back of the neck to make sure it was dead. Then I used to skin it straightaway and sell it for ninepence. That was the ninepenny rabbit. Your Sunday meal for ninepence! There was a firm that bought the skins. They used to make gloves out of them and all sorts.'

Not for the first time since I came to Horden, I thought of the meaning of the phrase, 'The Raising of the Working Class.' It had a fine-sounding ring, but what did it actually mean? It implied that the working class should somehow transform and transcend itself. But from what, and to what? Till now I had naturally assumed it simply meant getting away from the ugliness and limitation of Horden and the whole East Durham world. According to my grandfather's vision, as I understood it, the working class should 'raise' itself through education. He had made every effort to ensure that my father had the best education available, and my father, like many of his more able fellows, had lost no time in leaving the area and discarding as many as possible of those attitudes and ways of behaving that had made them working class. So was that what was meant by 'the Raising of the Working Class'? That they should simply become middle class.

Here, however, represented by Harry, was a culture not so much at variance with, but simply indifferent to this self-improving ethos – a culture enterprising, virtually self-sufficient and resolutely apolitical, that had no aspiration to be anything other than what it was. I had asked Harry what he had thought about the last miners' strike. 'I didn't think owt about it. They should have closed that pit forty years since, and we'd all have lived a lot langer.' Here was a man, thoughtful and imaginative, whose considerateness and cheerful stoicism seemed expressive of an innate gallantry, who actually liked many of the aspects of Horden – the betting shop, the Big Club, and doubtless the bingo hall too – that I felt so bitterly that people should want to be raised from.

'This is your hobby,' said Harry, referring to our conversation. 'Now I'll show you mine.' He led me through into the back kitchen, and took a large polythene package from beside the fridge. Inside were a number of pieces of hardboard and a few stretched canvases. His paintings.

He'd always loved sketching. When his first son was born, he used to let 'her' go out on a Sunday night, and he'd stay in and copy the picture of the film star from the front of *Woman's Own* in pencil. Later a neighbour had shown him how to 'clart out wi' paints', and in 1965, he had won the first prize in the NUM National Art Competition. Many of his paintings were of eighteenth-century naval battles. Others were of woodland glades. Some were obviously copied from photographs, others, like two colliery village scenes came from imaginative memory. He'd sold many pictures, and had been commissioned by a local businessman to paint his country mansion. He showed me a photo of the finished work, and the photo from which it had been copied. Then he led me into the bedroom. Over the bed was a large seascape – the setting sun sending livid patterns of orange and purple among the dark rocks. 'I copied that off a chocolate box,' said Harry. He reflected for a moment. 'It's kept us busy, yi knar.

'I was asked to go way for trials to play football. But my father wouldn't let us gan. Why, they only got three or four pound a week footballers, then. He said, "Thou's the eldest in the family, the next breadwinner to me. Tha'll stop here." I started the pit after the 1926 strike. I left school in September, and the strike ended the back end of November. My mother said, "You needn't start the pit till the New Year, when everything's properly put back." Well, the strike ended, and I was mad to get a start. I went down the colliery to get meself set on. When I got to the office door, he said, "What does tha want, son?" I said, "I want to start work." "What do they call tha?" I said, "Sugden." "Is Billy thi fattha?" I said, "Aye." He says, "Why, he'll have to sign tha on. I cannut. Thy parents must sign tha on, or some relation." I said, "Why, me dad's in back shift. He cannut get down." "Ah why," he says. "Tha'd better come back next week." When I came out, me Uncle Tommy was gannin' past. I said, "Uncle Tommy, will tha come and sign us on?" He said, "Tha da'll have to dee that." I said, "Me da's in back shift, Uncle Tommy." He said, "Howay then."

'I started on fore shift, three o'clock in the morning. I got a job trappin'. They had trap doors down there, to make the wind go round the pit. I had me lamp, and all I had to do, when I heard the putter coming, was open the door. As soon as he'd come through, I had to shut it again. The putters used to take empty tubs into the working places, and bring the full ones out. Their lamps used to keep gannin' out, so they'd pinch mine, and I'd be sitting there in the dark for hours. I got me first pay at Christmas. I got eleven and threppence one week, and twelve and fourpence the other – alternate weeks. I got one and sixpence pocket money. I bought mother a bar of chocolate. She was ower the moon. I was still in short trousers then.

'I used to see the lads driving the ponies, fetching tubs in. They had bigger ponies than what the putters used. Gannin' about with five or six tubs from one flat to the other. And I liked that! I said to the Wagon Wayman, "Will you set me on driving?" By the time I was fifteen and a half, I was getting datal putting [paid by the day rather than by production; the lowest level of payment in the pit]. I was lying in my bed on my sixteenth birthday, and Mother comes up and she says, "What've you been doing? There's a man here wants you to go to the office." I went down and saw Bob Raiment, the Foreshift

Overman. He said, "Harry, it's tha borthdeh, isn't it? Sixteen, aren't yer? Many happy returns. Yer datal putting's finished. Now you're a putter." See, when you were datal putting, you got your datal wage and whatever you put on top of that – a few shillings extra. But they stopped that, and I was a putter.

'Rough times! Aye, I've sat down in that pit and I've cried me eyes out many a time, and I'm not ashamed of it. You're *putting* off men, and they'll say, 'Put us twenty-four out, and I'll give you a token.' That meant if you got twenty-four tubs out for them, they'd let you fill one of your own. They put a token on every tub that went out, see, to show who'd filled it. Why, that tub was worth two and odds to you then, because if a putter managed to get a tub filled, he got more for it than the hewers. I've seen us stickin' and scrapin' and heavin' the tubs round, and maybes on the last tub, the twenty-fourth, going in for your token, you can't get past a tub a shade bigger, catching the side. You couldn't get it out. The hewers would gan out, and just laugh, 'cause I hadn't got any tubs filled.

'Me and our Bill, the one a year younger than me, we were both putting together, on the same shift – night shift. We'd come in, half past two in the morning, and mother would have the big pan on full of boiling water, and the tin bath there. We used to sit and get our meals first. "It's thy turn to get washed first." "It's not. It's thy turn. I got washed first yesterday." I've seen her come down in the morning to get the bairns to school, and we'd both be lying fast asleep on the mat, black, tired out. There'd be hell on!

'They did away with the handpicks. Brought in the pneumatic drills. They ran on compressed air, and all the time it was blasting on to your chest. Your chest was bare and you were sweating like hell. It was pouring down yer. That's why miners, they never lived very long, man. But anyone who kept hisself on datal work, who didn't work on the faces – they were the ones who lived the longest. I was down that pit forty-nine and a half year. And I was lucky. I got hurt! In 1953 I had to go on light work. But the accident happened a long way before that.

'A tub o' coal is supposed to be ten hundredweight, but some of them get to be twelve hundredweight. The two coal hewers put the metal plates in – like rails for the tubs to run on – the tub drops over, and they fill it up. If you're the putter, you turn your pony round, you put it on to the tub, and you gan, "Geeup!" and it pulls away. Why, this day, when it pulled away, the two plates on one side slipped out. The wheels was on the plates that was nailed down.

I was ganna lift it back on. The two hewers was standing there, "Little bit higher, son, little bit higher." I lifted it up, put my foot on the plate to jerk it, and I slipped and went down with the full weight of the tub on my back.

'I slipped three discs, but I didn't know that at the time. I was only eighteen. I used to play football with it. Then all of a sudden it used to gan off. There's many a time I've been in bed there, and I've had to rock meself backwards and forwards before I could get up. Once I'd got warmed up it used to be a lot better, then as soon as I got cold, it used to gan off again. I came back from the football match. She said, "Your tea's in the kitchen." I said, "Righto." I reached out for the tea-pot, and it went. I was in bed sixteen weeks. Another time I was in the back yard. There was a pail of coals out there. She said, "Fetch them coals in." I said, "Righto." Down I went, coals and all. In bed another fourteen weeks. They had masseurs, osteopaths, all sorts working on it. But as I said, I didn't go on to light work till 1953.

'Now, if I have the telly on how I like it, she says the whole street can hear it. Cause you know how you've got them pneumatic drills out in the road. It was like that all the time down there, and we had nay earplugs in. You'd have two next to each other gannin' at once, and you got the drill on your shoulder. Ngrrrrrr! Gannin' like that all the time. Shakin' yer. Right by yer ear. When I went on light work, they put us on the engines. Why, the dynamo's gannin', Mmmmmmmm . . . all the time, and then the engine starts, and that gets away. It's all noise, man.'

9

True, that

'EVERY MORNING we'd stand to attention in the classroom and sing, "God save the King". There was the map of the world. India was red. Africa was red. Canada was red. Australia was red. The British Empire had taken over the world. There were fifty-six children in the class, and none of them had nay byuts! If a lad had byuts, you knew his dad was in bed, and he'd come wearing his dad's byuts.' He sat back on the red banquette, laughing soundlessly to himself. I was having to lean forward to hear what he was saying anyway, amid the hubbub of the club. He was tiny, his chin hardly coming over the edge of the table; a little dandified man, with neatly combed black hair, a suavely clipped moustache on his polished vermilion face. He wore a rakish dogstooth jacket, with a suede waistcoat underneath.

'I never had nay byuts,' said Jackie Hudspith. 'When I joined the football club here, they gave us a pair of byuts. That was the first pair I had.' Jackie was seventy-five, two years younger than the small man, with red ham-like fists and a red ham-like face. A fall of stone in the pit had half closed one of his eyes. He wore an old grey suit, a muffler, and had his cap on the table beside him. One summer's day in 1944, during the 'Stay-at-home holidays' – a programme of events organised to enliven the pit's third annual holiday – he had fought Micky Cundy of Shotton for the Pitman's Boxing Championship. 'Yi knar Maurice Cundy?' he would ask any-one who cared to listen, referring to a minor champion who, I have to confess, I had never heard of. 'That's his son.' Jackie had broken Micky's jaw in the second round, and what with the war and one thing and another, he had never had cause to defend the title. He was still Pitman's Champion of Northumberland and Durham. Two nights before, I had gone to the Comrades' Club to interview him. I could hardly understand a word he said. Now I could understand about a third of it, and he was showing me round the various clubs of Horden. We were now in the Catholic Club, where much of the Big Club's natural clientele now went on a Thursday night.

Jackie tilted his head towards the tiny man. 'He's a bookie, him. He was a bookie before he had byuts. He used to run a book at school.'

'Do you know what Churchill said?' asked the erstwhile bookie, apropos of nothing.

'No.'

'Turn the guns on the bloody miners!' he squeaked indignantly. 'Everybody says Churchill was the best leader this country ever had. He was the *warst*! We didn't win the war. The Americans didn't win the war. The *Rooshans* won the war, because their women were better soldiers than their men!' This was more like it. This was the kind of pugnacious anti-establishment rhetoric I had expected to hear in Horden. I wondered if this man might have known Percy.

'My grandfather worked at Horden coke ovens . . .' I began.

'I was barn in Harden!' he snapped with renewed vigour, as though this fact obviated any claims I might have on the place. 'In Second Street.'

'They used to call it China Town, First and Second Street,' said Jackie. 'I was born at 85 Second Street.'

First and Second Street had been the very bottom of the village – the rough end of town.

'They never closed the doors down there,' said the small man. 'The dogs used to walk in the front door and gan straight out the back.'

'Why, they never went to bed down there,' said Jackie.

I imagined it: the big families, the uncontrollable rabble of barefoot kids running round the streets at all times of day and night. The men carousing into the small hours. The winds blasting through the open front doors. Pigs kept in the pantries – as I'd heard in more than one account – ferrets in the back yard. Hard-faced boys ganging together to confront strangers. Nice people didn't go down there. Any lad who didn't belong was guaranteed a hiding in China Town. The Police Station, now the Comrades' Club, had been built at the end of Third Street, with the intention of bringing the hand of authority into the heart of this area. But it was well known that they had started their beat in Fifth Street. But they weren't bad people down there, everyone said. They were just rough. Hearts o' gold, some o' them.

'I've played on every football field in Durham,' said Jackie. 'I used to come out the pit on a Saturday afternoon, get changed in the Big Club, and play for Horden – still black!' He chuckled merrily. 'True, that!

'The army used to take us away in the cattle trucks to box. In the war. Used to make out I was a sowldier. Took us down to Wales.'

'Whereabouts?'

'Oh . . . I din't knar. Knocked their champion out in the first round. Feller called Taylor. Died two year since. *Nice* blark! Always sent us a Christmas card.'

Horden Colliery had closed in 1986, but the Union Committee still met every Wednesday night in the Miners' Hall to process the death benefit and compensation claims. The Horden Miners' Hall and Literary Institute was a dour, red brick building on the corner opposite the Big Club, built in 1911 to provide a centre for social and improving activities, and it had quickly become associated with the union. In the late-Sixties, a large extension had been added, and it had been reopened as the Social Welfare Centre. But to most people it was still the Miners' Arl. This was the very heart of Horden – the social centre of the village on one side of the street, and the political centre on the other.

The Meeting Room was closed for repainting, so the little knot of men clustered round the ill-lit counter of the cloakroom at the bottom of the stairs. The ladies, making their way upstairs for the sequence dancing, eyed the group of men a trifle nervously, but each was given a rousing greeting, '*Areet!*' At which they would flit even more quickly up the stairs. The union secretary and chairman were present, Johnny Fairclough, a committee member, Frankie Skinner, the hall caretaker, naturally a former miner, and, of course, Jackie, in his cap and muffler, on the way to the Club. They grunted at my approach.

'Areet, young 'un?' said Jackie. 'Still 'ere?'

'Aye.'

'Ow long's tha bidin', like?'

My original intention had been to move on after the New Year.

'Oh.' He leant forward conspiratorially, and gestured at the floor. 'Frida' night, this was arl covered in miners! Playin' brag! Arl jit black!' Everyone chuckled partly at the recollection, and partly at Jackie's enthusiasm for recounting it. 'True, that!' he said.

Joe Summers, the secretary, was a big, grey-haired man in his fifties, with a low and deceptively flat voice. The chairman, Jimmy, who also functioned as the treasurer and had the smart leather briefcase full of union documents, was younger, a small, dark, curly haired man whom Joe referred to as 'my little meht'.

Given my grandfather's connections, I'd always regarded the union as a natural source of support in this alien environment, but they seemed to regard me with a certain amount of circumspection, to say the least. I was not the first person to come looking for facts and figures. There had been academics researching theses, and at the time of the closure, journalists, TV producers and all sorts. It came as no surprise to them that people should want to know about Horden. It had been the biggest pit in Durham – never mind the world. But I sensed they were weary of the ill-informed questions of outsiders. And I was the youngest and scruffiest incumbent yet. I hadn't come to them through union headquarters, and I didn't have the backing of the BBC or a university. Who the hell was I?

'What was it you wanted to know?' asked Joe, regarding me sceptically from his considerable height.

What did I want to know? Everything. I wanted to know every-thing about the union in Horden.

'Well, I don't know,' said Joe, doubtfully. 'You'll have to ask specific questions, like.'

How about the '84–85 strike? That had been the most crucial event of recent times.

'Horden has always been a moderate pit,' Joe Summers said later when we were standing at the bar in the Big Club. 'We were one of only two pits in Durham that didn't vote for Arthur Scargill for the National Presidency in 1982. When he was doing his campaigning, I got a call from Redhills, the union headquarters in Durham. They said he was going to speak at the Miners' Hall here, and would I gan and meet him. I said, "Arthur Scargill? I din't knar Arthur Scargill. I din't want to takk to 'im." I didn't gan, but apparently he got crucified in there. They wouldn't let him speak. At some of the pits the militants were very strong. But not here!

'They've destroyed this union. It used to be the most powerful union in the country, and now it's a laughing stock. But whether you like the man or not, everything he said was true. Everything he predicted – the closure of all these pits – has happened. But naybody believed him. He should look in the mirror and ask himself what it was about him that made people not believe him.'

'He's a funny feller,' said Jimmy, the treasurer. 'Mind, I don't think he wanted a strike – not then anyway. At the Big Meeting, a year before, this lad from Wearmouth got up and called for a strike. Scargill nearly fell off his chair.'

'We were on the overtime ban by then,' said Joe. 'He wanted to stick to that, use up the reserves of coal they'd built up, and wear them down slowly. But the militants wouldn't listen, and in the end he couldn't control them.'

'Like you say,' said Jimmy. 'He's a quaer feller. He's not sociable. He couldn't stand here and chat like this.'

'He'd be sitting in a corner fidgeting with a half,' said Joe. 'He'll have his entourage around with him, but he'll be looking through some documents. He never stops. It's all politics with him.'

'When you went on these courses,' said Jimmy, 'if he was there speaking, he'd never come and talk to you. Say you're having a drink in the evening. He'd be sitting there, but he wouldn't talk to anyone. Peter Heathfield, the General Secretary, he's a leftie, but he's all right. He'd come round the different groups, like, "Where yer from? What d'you think of it so far?" But not Scargill. He'd just ignore you.

'But as for that money they say he had, he never touched a penny of it. He's too honest. His principles is too strong. He wouldn't compromise them for anything.'

'That's his tragedy,' said Joe. 'He said, "I will not prostitute my principles." He won't sit down with the strikebreakers – the UDM – so nobody's talking to him. He's not doing anything. He's finished.

'He never would sit down with the Coal Board, even before the strike. In fact he never has negotiated a single pay rise for the union. People used to say that Joe Gormley was too close to Ezra, gannin' round drinking with him and that. But he would always get something for it. People like Gormley might not get everything, but they'd at least come away with something. We were on strike for a year, and we got absolutely nowt for it.

'We went out for Little Herrington. They were going to be the first pit to close in Durham if Macgregor got his way. And if we didn't come out for them, who would come out for us when our turn came? But we went out, like the rest of the county, on the understanding, and with the expectation, that there would be a National Ballot – which, as you know, there never was.

'Mind, once we were out we were solid. We had a few fellers

went back – maybe four or five – but that wasn't until right at the end. I said to them, "What you going back for now?' You've been on strike for a year. We'll all be going back in a fortnight's time. You're stupid! You're going back for a few days' pay, and you'll be castigated for it for the rest of your life." And they have been. There's one feller goes in the Catholic Club. Sits there. Nobody talks to him – and they never will.'

The Big Club had been built in 1912, by Henry Bell, the contractor who built most of the houses in Horden, on the site of the old Social Club, burnt down during the riot, keeping the design as close as possible to the original. A year later, the Club was bought by its members for £9,000 and since nearly every man in Horden worked at the pit, and it went without saying that every man who worked at the pit was a member of the Big Club, the place was effectively the property of the people of Horden.

It was always said that being on the Committee of the Big Club was the equivalent of having a son in work. Because there was the fee for duties as a member – ten shillings. Then, on a Sunday morning, you inspected the cellar – another ten shillings. There were fees for being on one of the special committees, say the finance committee – ten bob; fees for things like emptying the drum from which the draws were taken – ten bob. So when you considered that at the height of the Club's membership – which would be after ladies were admitted, but before the pit's workforce began seriously to decline, say the mid-fifties – a miner was only earning £6 to £8 a week, being on the Club Committee would be a significant source of income. Come the half year, there was an agreed sum for duties over and above the duties of a Committee man, another £7 or £8. And at Christmas, of course, you got your gifts. So in those days, it was necessary to get at least three hundred votes before you even stood a chance of getting on the Committee. And you had to be off for two years before you could stand again. Nowadays, of course, the latter rule didn't apply. Now, it was difficult to get people to be on the Committee at all.

The amount of alcohol consumed in the Big Club was legendary. It had been, as one man put it, 'a fountain'. At the height of the Club's fortunes, more beer was given away than they sold today. In the year 1957–8, £3,500 had been spent on free drink. With beer sold at 6d a pint, that would be 140,000 free pints from the bar. But in fact that was the amount the *Club* had spent buying the drink wholesale, so the amount consumed would actually be far greater.

Every Christmas Eve, there would be a great queue of members up the stairs, waiting for their free bottle of whisky. And at various points during the year they would each receive vouchers entitling them to so many free pints. Any son of Horden who went into the armed forces would drink free in the Big Club when he was on leave. Then there were the beer tokens called the 'brass cheques'. There was a lending library in the Big Club, and the librarian was paid in brass cheques. If the piano needed shifting from one bar to the other, anyone who helped got a brass cheque for their trouble. And of course the committee men and their cronies utilised the brass cheques.

The Club was a shareholder in the Federation, the Co-operative Brewery that served the working men's clubs of the North-east. There was a dividend on every barrel sold and every £1,000 kept in the brewery entitled the Club to a vote in elections for the Federation's board. Horden Big Club had twice as many votes as any other comparable club in the area.

The early-Sixties saw the beginning of the depletion of the Club's resources and the steady decline in its fortunes that had continued to the present day. There were many reasons put forward to explain this, and hints at corruption and dark dealings in the background. What was certain was that in 1974, the Club had accepted an interest-free loan from Whitbread for renovations to the premises, in return for trading exclusively with the brewery. The upstairs concert hall was completely redecorated and the snooker extension was put in. The old No. 2 End, the singing end with the piano, and all the little committee rooms, where men could meet in the old days for a quiet game of cards, and the old library, along the corridor from the main bar, were knocked through into one carpeted lounge. At first it was packed, but after a while people stopped going. They said the heart and the atmosphere had gone out of the place. The piano had been replaced by background music. But if you had background music, you wanted something sweet and soothing, not 'Top of the Pops'. Now the lounge was usually deserted and the huge concert hall upstairs had been closed for years.

It was said by some that this was a kind of punishment, poetic justice for having deserted the working man's brewery in favour of one of the biggest donors to the Conservative Party. Years afterwards, however, when the loan had long since been paid off, the Club had tried going back fifty-fifty, with Whitbread and the Federation. But the members had shown so little interest in the Federation beer that the scheme had had to be abandoned.

Still, on a Friday night you would still get enough people to create a frowsty hubbub in the main bar – the old men round the edges of the room, the young men in their baseball shirts and short back and sides playing cards and pool in the middle, as was usually the case in clubs. 'Them's all gannin' to Sunderland and Hartlepool,' said Jackie. 'On the bus. To the clubs, yi knar.' He seemed proud that someone was doing something to maintain the social standards of the village. Horden people knew how to get about!

He'd been filling me in on Horden's history, mostly descriptions of eminent football and snooker players, each of which ended with the exclamation, '*Nice* blark!'

He was sitting at the side of the room, his back to the snooker end, in the seat where he always sat, with his mate Frankie Suppitarl, the Club's chairman. Frank was some years younger than Jackie, but it was difficult to say how many, as in comparison with him, Jackie was a picture of vigour and freshness. Frank had a full head of hair, but his eyes bulged alarmingly from his devastated purple visage. He'd got his name from the fact that whenever the under-manager had said, 'Can I have a sip of your coffee, Frank?' he'd said, 'Gan on, sup it arl!' He'd thus got a job as a gearman, carrying the under-manager's equipment into the pit or simply sitting round his office all day answering the phone. There was no earning potential in such work, but it was cushy, and you might at least live a bit longer. However, Frankie had since more than made up for such benefits through his social habits. He and Jackie only drank halves, but the glasses were soon piling up on the table like pillars of foam-spattered crystal.

When they'd started at the pit in the old piecework days, the hewers worked in teams of *marras* – six men all on one paynote. 'Frida'' said Frankie, 'they'd come in here and share their pay out. Why, nine times out o' ten, they'd lose it all at cards and dominoes!' He let out a filthy yobbo's laugh, the sort of laugh one hears echoing along pedestrian underpasses at two in the morning.

What did the wives think? What did they feed the children on? How did they get through to the next pay day?

'Why . . .' He paused, indicating that this was just too bad. 'They'd gan to the shops and get credit. Mind, there was so many people deein' that, the shops was arlwus gannin' bust!' he laughed again – the ostentatiously murky guffaw of a fifteen year old hearing a dirty joke in the school lavatories.

'He's from Second Street,' said Jackie earnestly. Yes, I could believe it. 'They used to have the big families down there.'

'See, people was more sociable in them days,' said Frankie. 'If you were ill, you didn't call the doctor, you went next door.' This was what you heard, that in every street there was a woman who knew about such things, another who was a midwife and another who knew how to lay out bodies. 'If your mother was ill, the woman next door used to send a bucket of broth round.'

But wasn't it hard in those days, getting enough to eat?

'Why, they had the broth in them days. Arl vegetables an' arl! And the stotty cakes. You'd get a stotty cake – still hot, mind – cut it up the middle, put jam on it.' He leered lasciviously. 'Lovely, that!'

'There was nay vilence in them days. If two men had a disagreement in here, they'd go outside, get their coats off and fight it out. Then they'd come back in here and carry on drinking. Nowadays a group of lads'll get another young 'un on the floor and kick his ribs in. Not in them days. They fought fairly then.'

Frankie felt in his pocket and handed me a card. 'Have you seen this?' On it was a drawing of a large naked woman, sticking her backside out towards a man sitting in a chair. The man was tiny, but with a huge erect penis. What was disconcerting was not so much the subject matter of the printed card as the amazing crudeness of the execution. 'Turn it ower,' said Frankie. On the back was a curious view of the same scene a few moments later. The little man had entered the woman, and from the rear we saw him, chair and all, flattened against the woman's back – virtually disappearing into her vast girth. Frankie took the card, his nose wrinkling with delight, his shoulders shaking as he rocked with mirth.

Meanwhile, on the other side of the street, upstairs in the Miners' Hall, the Mechanics' Social Club was in full swing. They took the lounge over every Friday night, but anyone was welcome to attend, provided they signed the book. The room had just been decorated in a pastel green, and had an atmosphere of still, anonymous comfort, like an upmarket airport lounge. After the battered warmth of the Big Club, the atmosphere was decorous, even exclusive. At the long table near the bar, a group of friends, many of them associated with the union, sat engaged in one of those epic games of dominoes, where everyone takes it in turns to play everyone else, over an entire evening.

'Pull up a chair,' said Jimmy, the union treasurer, when I'd bought myself a drink. I sat down feeling excruciatingly awkward. For some reason, I had far less idea of how I should behave with them than I had with Jackie and Frankie. They were closer to my own age – though many of them were grandfathers – and I could actually understand everything they said. Yet I felt my presence to be an embarrassment and an intrusion. What were the bonds that had brought them together, always on this particular night over a period of decades? Not just the school, the pit, the neighbouring houses in the neighbouring streets – though they were all with one exception from the Bottom of the village – or even the union or the strike, for these factors alone could have brought quite a different group of people here. But factors far more subtle, things which they themselves might have had difficulty in naming, but which were none the less of great importance. And here was I, a total stranger, a whippersnapper, just walking in and sitting down with them.

Soon, however, the stories of old Horden were flowing – any anecdote or vignette or observation I might find useful. They began asking each other if they might have known any of my relatives. They began calling on the attention of a big white-haired man in the centre of the group, deeply absorbed in the dominoes, who they all said was three hundred years old. 'Mollie Hudson . . .' he said abstractedly.

'That's my aunt. My father was called Tom.'

'Tommy Hudson!' he said, with a gleam of roguish triumph. 'Good-looking lad? Dark?'

'Could be.'

'I know exactly who you're talking about now. Tommy Hudson! He was always a bit, how shall we say . . . *snappy*! He was a ladies man I'll tell yer *that*!'

At the end of the table sat Mel Hudspith, Jackie's son, who had been union treasurer, taking over from his uncle Micky just before the last strike. When the pit at Horden closed, he had gone to work at Selby in Yorkshire, 'with the biggest scabs in the world', commuting each day on a special train laid on by British Coal, with changing rooms and showers on board. He'd lost so much weight, however, he'd taken redundancy, and now ran a general store on the Top Road. He was a broad bear-like man with a deep husky voice and the same ready amiability as his father, but he dressed in a way – smooth beige V-knecked pullover, beige knitted tie – that suggested he had long since outgrown his father's world. He raised his eyes at the mention of the old feller, in a way that suggested pride, as well as mild embarrassment and a certain amount of annoyance – the normal reaction of sons to their fathers.

'There were no babysitters in those days,' he said. 'If mi fattha wanted to take mi muttha out for a drink, he'd give me thruppence

and put me on a bus that went right round the area. By the time it
had gone round three times, he'd be ready to go home.' He told the
story with amusement, but a certain amount of mild aggrievedness.
As though it was all very well for us to laugh, but what had it done
to him – but at the same time confident that he had himself risen
above it. 'Once we were at a union meeting in Durham. He hadn't
known what to do with me, so he took me along. They all went for
a drink afterwards, so he put me in that cinema by the bus station.
When he got back to Horden, about midnight, he realised he'd left
me there.'

I'd been told I should go and see Mr Salter, the former manager
of Horden Colliery. Not the very last one, but the one before that,
who had started as deputy manager in 1961, and held the position
of General Manager till just before the last strike.

He was, I understood, one of the old school of colliery managers,
who had a deep understanding of the traditional ways of the industry,
who had no illusions about the nature of their relationship with the
miners, but had a hard won and deeply ingrained sympathy and
respect for them. He lived in a rather imposing house on the Top
Road, that had been built for the manager of the coke ovens. His
wife answered the door and told me to call back in the afternoon
when it would be more convenient.

I had assumed that he would be expecting me, but he just
stood there, looking up at me, over his glasses, his lower lip thrust
dourly upwards – the practised look of someone who has spent his
life answering to inane interruptions. He was in his late-sixties, a
little pale man, his dark hair still thick, but his moustache somehow
unconvincing – as though he had grown it as a statement during
puberty, and never got round to shaving it off.

'I suppose you'd better come in,' he said at length, with a studied
reluctance that was supposed to pre-empt any nonsense from me. I
tried to remind myself that I was not intending any nonsense.

He led me into the large sitting room, decorated with a pseudo-
Georgian frilliness, with a fire burning in the grate. It was obviously
his wife's taste but he seemed quite comfortable in it. He sat down
on a large sofa, from which his feet hardly touched the floor. I
sat on the other side of the broad fireplace. He seemed miles
away – hardly ideal circumstances for an intimate interview. He
regarded me suspiciously over the distance, his eyes half closed.
I'd spent the morning trying to think up intelligent questions and
had hardly come up with any. Since I could think of nothing

more appropriate, I asked him how the last strike had affected him.

'Didn't affect me at all. I'd retired a few months before it started. A new man came in as manager. I didn't want to be on his tracks. I wanted him to be able to start with a clean slate. So the day I retired, I resigned my chairmanship of the rugby club, the cricket club and the operatic society. The wife and I kept out of the village. We did our shopping elsewhere. So I can't tell you anything about the strike or the effects of the strike.'

He had one of those droning Northern voices, not so much flat as concave, that can sound almost camp. It was another weapon in his arsenal, designed to give the impression he was weaker than he was, and lull one into a false sense of security.

He lapsed into indifference, then he added, 'I first came here in 1945, when I was doing my training, and in all that time nobody's ever said anything discourteous to me or my wife. They've always been very nice to us – even during the strikes.'

How had he become a manager?

'My father worked for the miners' union as a clerical officer at the Redhills office in Durham City. We didn't live the pit life – not at all. But I grew up reading agreements, and I just fancied being a colliery manager. I don't know why. I wouldn't recommend it. I wouldn't say it was a good way to make a living, not even for someone who's grown up as a miner. Going down there, lying about in water, getting drenched, then cold, then hot.'

It was difficult to imagine this little domesticated man going down there, doing all those things. But that was the way it was in those days. Managers had to undergo every aspect of the work at first hand, as part of their training.

'I did my training at Bearpark. That was a terrible pit. They used to work the Mothergate system. All these tiny roadways, just high enough to get the tubs along, leading off the main roadway to the coal face. It was all hand putting. There were no ponies in that part of the county. They had these small tubs – held about eight hundredweight, and the men had to shove them along the best they could. The putters used to get these terrible scabs along their backs where they grazed them on the roof, and they never had the chance to heal up.'

Didn't they call them 'buttons'?

'Aye, "a card of buttons". You've heard about that, have you? Well, that was a very old-fashioned way of working even then. But I didn't know anything else, so I thought it was normal.' He almost smiled at his former naivety. 'They had the narrow seams there. The Victoria Seam was only twenty inches at Bearpark. Then I came to Horden and I saw the roadways in the Hutton Seam. They were as high as this room.'

So there weren't any narrow seams at Horden?

'The narrowest seam at Horden was about two and a half to three feet, which is narrow enough. But they didn't have the really narrow seams, no. No one ever lay down to hew at Horden. Not to my knowledge anyway.'

Another image from my ancestral mythology was casually shattered.

As he'd talked about the 'card of buttons', he'd become almost enthusiastic, now however, he was once again dour, closed off. Normally I would have hesitated before calling anyone in that part of the world dour. The ethos of the area was too hedonistic. The Irish influence was too strong. But this man, under his soft, puppyish exterior, was as dried out and as tough as one of the thick slates crunching below. I sensed again a resistance towards having anything to do with this conversation. His sympathy for the miner was derived not from some vague liberalism, but from the realities of life down there – the harsh, unforgiving realities of stone and water and coal – where every man's life depended on the man next to him, be he manager or datal lad. He'd lived it. The people who'd lived that understood it. They didn't need to talk about it.

He retreated into his former expressionlessness. I was there on sufferance and might at any moment be ejected. I had to keep him talking, but I could think of nothing to say that was not hideously banal.

'How did you find the relations between men and management at Horden?'

'Very good. I always thought it was a happy pit, Horden.'

One often heard that in the period leading up to the '84–85 strike, there had been an attempt from above to break down the traditional relationships between management and unions at the individual pits, by imposing a more authoritarian management style.

'I'm not talking about that,' he snapped. 'I was employed all my life by the Coal Board. My loyalties have been to the Coal Board, and that's where they're staying.'

'I'm not trying to . . .' I fumbled.

'No, and there's no fear of you getting me to!'

He sat back. 'I'll tell you the kind of men they are at Horden. Before the strike they were on an overtime ban – as they always were before a strike. And a lot of them didn't like it, because they were losing money. They did do overtime on pumping work though, which they'd been instructed not to do by the Area Union. The lodge was fined £500 by the union. But they did it. Not just out of loyalty to the pit, but because, let's face it, they knew that if they didn't do it, the pit would have to close. And that work was shared out fairly by the union among all the men.

'They'd have an overtime ban before a strike to wear down the reserves of coal. So that when the strike came the Coal Board would be desperate. And they'd start it in the autumn, when the need for coal was at its greatest. That's why I couldn't believe it when they started this last strike. It was almost summer!'

Why had they started it then?

'It's my belief they were pushed into it.'

Who by?

'Macgregor, the government and the rest.'

And how had they done that?

'By refusing everything they asked. By just saying no, until they were forced to strike. If you just refuse everything – systematically – you leave people with no alternative.'

But why should they want to push them into a strike?

'To pay them back for 1972 and '74.' He thought for a moment. 'I've always been for the union. I've always believed that every man should be in the union. It's much easier for the management to deal with men through a union. It creates many more problems if you've got some that are in the union and some that aren't. And anyway, those that aren't in it are going to get the benefits the union fights for, so why shouldn't they pay their subscriptions the same as the others?'

10

You're in Horden Now!

I WAS TOLD by Joe Summers and Jimmy, the union treasurer, that if I wanted to find out about the union in the old days, I should try to talk to Bill Hodges – though I'd be wasting my time, as Bill Hodges didn't talk to anyone these days.

I'd heard about Bill Hodges since I first arrived in Horden. Bill Hodges, the notorious communist Lodge Chairman, for whom a 'neck-tie party' had been planned in the Big Club, but who had none the less managed to dominate the union in Horden for decades. I had assumed him a figure remoter in history than Percy. It had never occurred to me he might still be alive. This was the man I had to talk to – not only a socialist in the true and definitive sense of the word, but a man who had had the vision and courage to stand outside the pragmatic mainstream.

'He must be pushing eighty now,' said Joe. 'But he'll not see yer.'

'He does everything by the book, Bill Hodges,' said Jimmy. 'He's like Scargill in that respect.'

'If you saw him in the street,' said Joe, 'and you went to ask him about anything connected with the union, he'd just say, "Seven o'clock, Thursday, Miners' Hall," and carry on walking. He wouldn't even look at you. Then, when you got there on the Thursday, if it was something he considered of a financial nature, he'd say, "That's a matter for the Finance Meeting. Come back on Wednesday." It might be something that couldn't wait a week, or you might be on a shift where you couldn't get there next Wednesday. But that was too bad. You had to wait.'

Joe pointed to a door in a small ante-chamber beside the Parish Clerk's office. 'They used to hold the committee meetings in there. The young lads who'd never been before used to be terrified. They didn't know what to say. The committee members would be sitting up either side of the table, and old Billy would be sitting up at the end glowering. They didn't like to make it easy for them.'

'I went to school with his son,' said Jimmy, 'at Horden Modern. He always had polished shoes, a tie and a blazer with a badge on it.'

'Aye, you always had a few like that,' said Joe.

'Didn't you all have to wear school uniform?' I asked.

'We didn't have it,' said Jimmy. 'We just had one suit of clothes, like. But he had the whole lot. He wasn't allowed to play football, in case he scuffed his shoes.' They continued for some time, discussing Bill Hodges' son and his school uniform in tones of wonder.

'He stood that many times to become Agent,' said Joe. The agents were the three paid officials of the Durham Area NUM. To be elected Agent was the dreamed of summit of every lodge official's career. 'No one from Horden had ever become an Agent,' said Joe. 'Billy stood that many times, but he never got it. He'd left the Communist Party in 1956, over the Hungarian uprising. But he couldn't shake the image off. Then Archie Dodds went for it, and he got it first time.' Archie Dodds was the determinedly apolitical secretary of the Horden Lodge, who had become Financial Secretary of the Durham Area in 1967. 'The irony of it was that of the two, Hodges had by far the greater ability.'

'Go and talk to Bill Hodges,' said Jimmy. 'He may entertain you or he may not. He may be right friendly, or he may just ignore you.'

'How do I find him?'

'He'll be in the Victory Club. He always gets in the Victory on a Thursday, for the housey. He likes a game of housey, Bill Hodges. But don't leave it too late. He goes home early.'

I had my doubts about accosting so notoriously difficult a character in a public place, but I set out there and then. Because in County Durham a club is the place where you can and should meet a man. The home is the woman's place. You would no more expect to meet a man in his living room than you would in his lavatory. His club was the place where he would feel most comfortable and at home. But I couldn't help feeling certain misgivings at this course of action. Whatever he had been, Bill Hodges was now old and vulnerable, and the ease and speed of finding him added curiously to the sense of violation.

The narrow 1960s facade of the Victory Club, more commonly known as the Deputies', stuck out like a prow at the junction of two of Horden's main shopping streets. Its windows with their scenes of nicotined bonhomie glowed garishly out of the darkness like magic-lantern slides. For some reason, I'd never much cared for the look of the place. But now, my sense of propriety overrun by an urgent, intemperate curiosity, I hurried up the steps to the door.

The doorman was unusually polite and friendly. He didn't even want my ten pence. 'Oh, yes,' he said. 'He's over there.' And there he was, seated, slightly hunched in the middle of the crowded room. The idea of a communist trade union leader had invoked in my mind an image of a wild-eyed Trotskyite, his fist raised in defiance. With his shiny pink pate and his tweed jacket Bill Hodges might have been a retired archdeacon. As he looked up and caught my eye, however, there was a look not only of thorn-like hostility, but of dread and a curious kind of recognition – as though he'd been expecting my visit for a long time, and without pleasure. The doorman pointed to the column where it said, 'Introduced by . . .' 'Just put Bill Hodges,' he said genially.

'I've never met him before,' I said.

'Oh, I see,' he said, somewhat taken aback.

As I crossed the brightly lit room, its every surface bathed in a warm nicotine glow, I felt the wrongness, the utter inappropriateness of my action. The low tables with their padded stools were crowded closely together. I felt as though I were blundering uninvited through a stranger's living room. People were turning round to look. Who was this person going to talk to Bill Hodges? He was sitting with three women younger than himself, and they all looked down as I approached. Bill Hodges looked away. 'Are you Mr Hodges?'

'I am.'

'Can I sit here?'

'You can sit where you like.'

I told him I was trying to find out about my grandfather, and someone had told me he might have known him.

'Who?'

'Someone I met at the Miners' Hall.'

'What was their name?'

'I don't know.'

'I built the extension to that place, when I was on the District Council.'

One of the women asked me my name, and soon all three were gleefully trying to ascertain if they'd known any of my relatives. None of them had, but they enjoyed themselves trying to work out if anyone they knew had lived next door to my grandparents.

A stocky young man with a mop of fair curls sat down at the organ beside the low stage, and began playing tunes of a queasy oozing sentimentality – the kind of thing 'cultured people' can't bear to think about. When I hear music like that, I realise I must be a 'cultured person'. The young man played with great intensity, however, every change in the surging chord progression registering on his broad smooth features.

'He's blind,' said Bill Hodges. 'He comes here every week from Hartlepool. He's rather good, don't you think?'

'Aye,' I said.

'Yes,' said Bill Hodges, correcting me in a deliberately bland flat tone.

He began talking about people he'd known at the coke ovens. The only problem was that I could barely hear above the surging of the organ – and I felt he knew it. In fact, I thought he might be talking deliberately quietly.

'I'm afraid I could hardly hear a word you were saying,' I said, when the number had come to an end.

'I didn't think you could.'

'To tell you the truth, I'm writing a book about Horden.'

'I thought you were.'

He went to get himself a drink. I offered to buy him one, but he said he preferred to buy his own drinks. When he stood up, I realised he was not as small as he had appeared when sitting down. He was actually quite a broad, thick-set man.

'I've had any number of people coming to me for information. College professors and all. They'd phone, or just come to the house, or even come up to me here in the club – as you have done. The wife wasn't well, so in the end I said to myself, "Billy, it's got to stop."'

There was a pause for a game of housey, then the organ continued with a sprightly up tempo number. Bill told me about how when he was trying to sell the *Daily Worker* outside the Miners' Hall, a woman had attacked him – whether physically or merely verbally, I couldn't hear. 'The bookie said to me, "Billy, if you need a witness you know where to come!"' He spoke as though he'd been the subject of intense persecution, of how his sick wife couldn't stand all the banging on the door – though whether it was the college professors who were doing the banging, or urchins ragging him for his communism, I couldn't tell over the swelling of the organ.

'My family originally came from North Yorkshire,' he said.

'So did mine,' I said with ready enthusiasm.

'Did they?'

'Aye.'

'Yes,' he said, in the bland correcting tone. He'd been born in New Brancepeth, the same village from which my grandmother came, and by the time he was twenty-two he was lodge secretary at the colliery. 'Have it in mind that I've always been able to talk.'

'I believe it.'

'You do, of course.'

He asked me where I was living, and told me that it was a man named Booth, who had lived near Hardwick Street, who had got him to join the Communist Party. This was all fascinating, but I wanted to be able to hear it properly, without the surging of the organ and the constant interruptions of the housey. I wasn't going to have any problems with this man. He enjoyed talking too much. He wouldn't be able to resist it.

'Will we be able to have a longer chat?' I asked.

'Maybe we will, maybe we won't. These ladies come here every Wednesday, to hear the blind lad play. When my wife died, two years ago, they told me I should sit with them. Now, as it happens, on this occasion no offence has been taken, but it might have been very different.'

The three women sent me warmly into the night. But Bill Hodges just looked away. 'I talk too much,' he said to the women, with a twisted smile.

I'd always been impressed by the depth of my uncle Fred's knowledge of coal mining. At first I'd thought that this must simply be the innate knowledge that anybody from that part of the world must have – and of course, his father had spent the greater part of his life down the pit, as under-manager. But after a time, I realised that his talk suggested an intimacy and a familiarity with the old ways of the industry that went beyond mere general knowledge. I was none the less surprised when Joyce told me she was sure Fred had once been a miner.

He shrugged his shoulders with mild embarrassment when I broached the subject, as though I'd at last caught him out. It was true that when he left grammar school he was apprenticed as an electrician at Thornley, his father's colliery. His own father had begun as a miner, cycling the twelves miles from Pelton Fell in North Durham to Newcastle, on top of a full shift, to attend night classes at Rutherford College. So Fred had reckoned that what was good enough for his father was good enough for him. As soon as the war broke out, however, he had taken the first opportunity to join the RAF. But while he was at the pit, he had met men, among the older miners, who had impressed him greatly, and whose attitudes had influenced him for the rest of his life. They had been miners, but they had had a 'philosophical' attitude towards life – towards the future, and what the future might be.

'They were the men who had led the union during the 1926 strike, and who had lost their jobs and been blacklisted afterwards. But after two or three years, they'd been able to drift back to the pits.

'To meet them you'd never have thought they were miners at all. You could hold a rational discussion with them. They'd lost the "why, aye" thing, through meeting different kinds of people through their involvement with the union. One of them had the biggest collection of classical records I've ever seen – and he could talk about it!'

Were these the kind of men one heard about, but now never seemed to come across – the kind who had educated themselves, through reading?

'Very much so.'

And were they Methodists?

'Some of them.'

These were men of the same breed as those whose grave, but benign visages looked down from the miners' banners – the self-educated men of vision who had created the union. Men like John Wilson, the first Durham miner to become a member of parliament, and Peter Lee, after whom the town had been named. Men who had raised themselves through their own heroic intellectual efforts, and brought about tangible and significant change on behalf of their class. The existence of such men was, of course, all bound up with the influence of Methodism. Many of them had been lay preachers. Indeed, it was said, proverbially, that that was what had given them the confidence to become political leaders and orators.

These men had devoted their lives to things like trade union law and the provision of running water and improved sanitation. But autodidacts are famously omnivorous in their interests and their reading, and these men must, I reflected, have had a real breadth and intellectual curiosity. They did not look at the mechanical concerns of the everyday world in isolation. While I got the impression that in the post-nationalisation years the union had become preoccupied with dotting the i's and crossing the t's of legislation, these old leaders had sought nothing less than the heroic transcendence not only of their class, but of all mankind – through learning and knowledge.

But what had happened to the spirit and the vision of these men? Peter Lee's Lenin-like profile could still be seen high on the tower of his memorial church in the town that bore his name. Indeed, it was often said, rather glibly, that the place represented his vision of the ideal society. But although he had only died in 1935 – within a decade of the town's inception – it was not only difficult to detect the spirit of the visionary autodidact in this agglomeration of bleak housing estates, it was difficult even to find out anything about him. For most of those citizens who were even aware that the town had been named after an actual person, he was simply a local lad whose death had warranted an obituary in *The Times*. And that was enough.

But what about those slightly younger men, whom Fred had known? Were any of them left alive?

Fred's placid features took on that slightly pained look they always had when trying to dredge things up from the very distant past.

'I don't think so. You're talking about people who were mature men, who had positions in the union in 1926. There was one died a couple of years ago. But he would have been the last one.'

What about my grandfather? Had he been in that mould at all?

'To an extent. But he was maybe less philosophical than some of them. Some might say he was more down to earth. But he'd been moulded towards socialism by his experiences in the navy, by coming across different types of people there. These men I'm talking about were really created solely by the pit and the miners' union.'

What about Bill Hodges? Did he fit in with this type?

'Very much so. He joined the Communist Party. That was his road to self-improvement. At that time the Communist Party was very keen to take up people like that – men who could speak, and who were prepared to. And their involvement with the Communist Party gave them a broader perspective than the people around them. They were aware there was more going on in the world than parochial issues.'

Bill Hodges. He was the crucial link – the man who stood between what I perceived of as the heroic, visionary world of the old union leaders, and the more pragmatic, technological concerns of the post-war era, between the bleak exploitation of the hand-hewing days of my great-grandfather's time and the solid union-dominated practices of post-nationalisation. I imagined him, a union official, hardly out of his teens, marshalling the men in the freezing cold of New Brancepeth pit head. And later in life, as chairman of Horden Lodge and a district councillor, one of the Labour grandees of East Durham. This man could fill in many of the gaps in my comprehension about the transition between the two worlds, because he had not only witnessed the transition, he had lived it – he represented it in his very person. He *was* that history. I could not under any circumstances afford to alienate him.

Sunday evening. Fred, Jack and I were once again watching Betty doing the ironing, and I was asking about Bill Hodges. 'He was a great big bloke. Massive, powerful.'

'He's not so big now,' I said.

'Why, he's getting on a bit. Mind, I'm surprised he said he didn't want to talk to you. I've never known him mind talking.'

'He'll talk to anyone, Bill Hodges,' said Jack.

'Well, if he's declining . . .' said Fred.

'You can't tell,' said Jack. 'He was an awkward bugger in his heyday.'

'You're related to him,' interjected Betty from the ironing-board. 'I can't remember whether it's him or his wife. But one of them is related to you.'

'Aye, I'd forgotten about that,' said Fred. 'I remember Mollie saying that either him or his wife was a kind of cousin to your grandmother. I think it might have been his wife . . . but I can't be sure.'

It was late on one of those days around the turn of the year when it never really gets fully light, that I decided the time had finally come to call on Bill Hodges. His phone number wasn't in the book. I'd thought of writing, but wasn't sure of his house number. Anyway, it was nearly Christmas. If I didn't get a move on, I'd be stuck in this place for ever. I phoned a friend of my landlady's who lived in that part of Horden. 'I know who you mean. Wasn't he once a member of the Communist Party?'

'That's right.'

'They built a row of bungalows by the football pitch at the Crossroads Estate. Twelve ordinary ones and four beautiful ones.

He was offered one of the ordinary ones, but he turned it down, and insisted on having one of the beautiful ones.'

I said I thought he might object to my visit.

'Who, Bill Hodges? He'll talk to anyone. Go round there. He'll be pleased to see you.'

The bare lines of the small red brick bungalows stood out starkly at the edge of the football pitch. None of them could exactly be described as beautiful, but they were neat and tidy enough.

It was nearly four and as I approached through the gathering gloom, I saw a stocky middle-aged man unloading furniture from a van and carrying it into the corner bungalow. When he came out a second time, I called over. 'Excuse me. Do you know which one Bill Hodges lives in?'

The man stopped in his tracks. I was already anticipating the mixture of hostility and weary indifference with which I was often met in Horden. One would have thought people would be pleased at the prospect of a book about their community, that someone was taking an interest in their reminiscences. Apparently not. Now, even before I approached I could see myself, all too easily, as they saw me, a gaunt, tense stranger, a scraggy Levi jacket bursting out of the front of my oilskin raincoat.

'I'm his son,' said the man. 'Who wants him?'

A rail ran down from the porch, dividing the meagre garden from the rubbish-strewn verge of the Coast Road. I made my way across this latter piece of ground so that he could better hear what I was saying.

'I'm writing a book,' I said, 'about Horden, and I wanted to talk to your father about the old days of the union.' Come on, I thought, sell yourself. 'I thought it was important to have someone involved who was a socialist in the true sense of the word, whose memories go back, who knows what Horden's really about.'

The man look down at me blankly.

'Do you realise you're standing in dog's mess?' he asked.

I looked down at the vermilion mass glowing out of the darkness around my foot. 'Shit!'

'Exactly.' He gestured round. 'Third house on the left.' Then, as I headed off, 'I'll be along in five minutes, mind!'

The starkness of the bungalow's appearance was enhanced by venetian blinds, through which, as I approached, I glimpsed for a split-second the dark outline of a human form – standing only inches from the glass; a figure that must have been just standing there in the twilight gloom, staring out at the empty street. But even in that split second, I detected, or thought I detected, a tremor of displeasure pass across it. Then I saw the pink features of a face composing themselves behind the frosted glass door, and I knew instinctively that this visit had not been a good idea.

He opened the door only a few inches. He was wearing glasses, his face, gaunter than I remembered it, pale with annoyance and something approaching fear. There was a tone of recrimination in his voice, as though I'd done him an appalling wrong.

'What does tha want?'

I stood there cringing with guilt. 'I thought, after I saw you in the club the other night, maybe we could have a longer chat.'

He looked back bristling with hostility. 'I've got nothing to say to tha.'

'But . . .'

'I said at the time . . .'

I became almost querulous. 'I was going to phone but I couldn't find the nu . . .'

'It's not in the book.'

'Maybe I should have written a letter.'

'It'd do you no good. I said quite enough to you the other night.'

'I could hardly hear it because of the organ.'

'Well, that's not my fault, is it?' He winced, almost as though he was going to laugh.

I decided to play my trump card. 'I've found out I'm related to you.' His eyes narrowed. 'Or to your wife . . .' Oh no, I thought, now it sounds like I'm insulting his wife. 'Years back . . .' I became pathetic. 'Distantly . . .'

'I'd not know them then.'

My sense of hurt and disappointment must have been evident. 'I wish you well, but I can't . . . I don't want to talk to you.'

I met his son coming along the pavement towards me. 'How d'yer get on?'

'Not too well.'

'No. He's become very wary of people he doesn't know. But I reckon you should talk to him. Like you say, he must know more about Horden than anyone.' The son seemed quite reasonable, a no nonsense person, but well spoken. I wondered if he was the one with the blazer and the shiny shoes. 'Look, he normally comes round for his tea on a Wednesday. I'll see if I can talk him round. I normally can. But I'm making no promises, mind.'

As I walked away, I felt completely demoralised. Not because

I couldn't understand the old man's hostility, but because I could understand it only too well. 'If he's declining, he won't want to talk to you,' Fred had said. 'He may feel he can't control what he says, that he'll ramble, or say things that he doesn't want to say.'

I'd been able to anticipate every one of Bill's answers before it came. And I'd felt as I looked into the old man's frightened, bitter eyes that my own fate was staring back at me. I came from a family of talkers, and ever since I could remember I'd been bursting to share what I knew. It terrified me to think that one day I too, like Bill Hodges, might not have the physical confidence to do so.

What had he been doing, standing there in the darkness? Was he lost in twilit reverie of better times, or on guard for malefactors, real or imaginary? Maybe he'd been standing there waiting to repel me, through the week since I met him in his club. Or perhaps he was just lost in a vague numbness. In his mind, life had done something to him. I didn't know what it was. But maybe I, like him, would find myself alone in a dark house, living out my sentence in bitterness.

After returning to London for a much-needed Christmas break, I rushed back to Horden for the famous North-eastern New Year celebrations. They were the non-event of the century. I could have had more fun in Esher. Having failed through bribery, flattery or intimidation to get a ticket for the Grand Party in the Miners' Hall, I spent the evening in the Big Club with Jackie Hudspith and Frankie Suppitarl. Two young men with electric guitars and matching red polo shirts treated the meagre throng to singalong hits of the Fifties, Sixties and Seventies. The only point of interest came when a hefty woman did the funky chicken to 'Born to be Wild', without getting out of her chair.

A few days later I met Ernie Wilding who had been the secretary of the Miners' Lodge through the 1970s and early-80s. He was a tall, well-built, very upright man in his early sixties, with pale skin and very clear cold blue eyes – his manner a curious mixture of Northern bluntness and a natural austerity and reserve. He had gone to Henry Smith's, the grammar school in Hartlepool that was for many the route to a professional or at least a clerical career. At the age of fifteen, however, his father had taken him out of the school and signed him on at the pit. Later in life he had gone on courses sponsored by the union and become something of an expert in union law. Then when he gave up his position he went on to the Parish Council, 'to give us a bit interest'. He was a figure of respect in Horden, and among many of the older miners, regarded almost with reverence. He had already had an old people's home named after him.

We sat in the newly decorated committee room in the Miners' Hall, where for decades the union meetings had been held, and he talked for some time with a steady if slightly mannered fluency that had obviously been one of his stocks in trade as a union official, about the problems of converting Horden into a smokeless zone. Afterwards however, at the mention of the name Bill Hodges, he became warmer and more expansive. 'He was chairman of this Lodge for twenty-two years, from 1952 to 1974. And in all of that time he was unopposed – whether out of respect, or because people were afraid to get beat by him, I couldn't say.

'He had this little black pocket book, and if anyone dared disagree with him, he'd throw it down on the table – "Standing rules of the NUM!" And no one dared contradict him – partly because they were afraid of him, and partly because no one had the faintest idea what the standing rules of the NUM were. When I became secretary in 1972, I read them. They were completely out-of-date. They'd been out-of-date for years, but Bill hadn't realised it.

'Well, I sent off to headquarters for a copy of the standing rules. When they finally arrived they were a massive volume, about a foot thick. The next meeting, I took issue with him. He threw his book down. Then I got my book out. His eyes nearly popped out of his head. "What's that?" he said. I said, "That's the standing rules of the NUM. You're behind the times, man!" He hung on for another couple of years as chairman, but that was the beginning of the end for him.

'We used to hold the General Meetings in the hall upstairs, and he was used to standing up on the stage and lecturing the membership. As far as he was concerned it wasn't necessary for anyone else to speak, and no one dared try. That year at the AGM, I signalled to him that I wanted to speak. He said, very sarcastically, "We've got a *secretary* here who thinks he's got something to say." When I'd finished I got a great round of applause, but Bill just sat there glowering, giving me a slow handclap.

'He was a communist because he genuinely believed that was the best thing for humanity. Even after he left the Party, he had *Soviet Weekly* delivered to the reading room here. I put a stop to that. I put a stop to a few other things as well.

'But he had his good points. When they held the statutory consultative meetings here between management and union, to discuss matters relating to the future of the pit, the top union people would come over from Redhills and there'd be a delegation from the NCB. They'd all be chatting away, asking each other how they were. Bill would just be sitting there tight-lipped, with his cap on the table in front of him. Then when they came to discuss the agenda, he'd slam his hand down on the table, "You're in Harden now! Aa'll decide what we're ganna takk about!" Oh aye. He had his good points. "You're in Harden now!" ' He chuckled at the memory.

I still hadn't heard from Bill Hodges' son who had promised to let me know how he got on in his attempts to get his father to talk to me. So the next day, I phoned him. He didn't waste any time on pleasantries. 'No luck. That's why I didn't bother to get back to you. He's not interested.'

'Maybe I should write a letter, explaining politely and in detail what I'm trying to do.'

'You can try, but you'll be wasting your time. Once he's made his mind up about something, nothing and nobody will shift him. I've known him all my life, and that's what he's like. I'm sorry.'

He put the phone down.

The wind blasted up through the gulley that led on to the beach. The air was filled with a bitter brilliance, the sun on the breakers, rising in great tiers miles out to sea, dazzling like light on newly forged steel. At the water's edge, it was as always slightly warmer, but the wind still felt as though it were clawing at my exposed cheeks. I stood there before the inexorable force of the North Sea, feeling the withering power of its winds. I thought of Bill Hodges and his rigid immovability. I thought of the dour indifference of the old pit manager. I thought of James Hudson, and even Percy, with their resolute, unchanging and immovable courses of action. They'd made their minds up. They'd said what they'd said on a matter of principle. And that was that. To change their minds, to try to undo what had been done was not a course of action that was open to them.

Bill Hodges' family had come from Yorkshire; James Hudson had come from Yorkshire. That other country, that began only a few miles down the coast, where I had myself been born, was in the mind of the country at large inextricably associated with this kind of arrogance, if one wanted to call it that, this bloody-minded, immovable stubbornness. And if there was a lot of Irish, there was also a lot of Yorkshire in Durham. It was the dour underside of the loquacious, hedonistic pitmatic world. It didn't matter that these people had been mere labourers – regarded by the more privileged of the time as members of an almost sub-human species. They were *men*. They'd said what they'd said, and that was that. It was on one level admirable. But it was also, in some way, very, very stupid.

'You're in Harden now! I'll decide what we're ganna takk about!'

Huh, I thought.

11

Kirving the Jud

'I 'VE SEEN a young man banging an old man's head against a tub down the pit,' said Norman Hawkins. 'I said to him, "Would you do that to your own father?" He said, no, and he stopped. But that was what it was like with piecework. You were working marras, see, and if your partner was older, and he couldn't keep up with you, he was lossing you money. It was frustration drove men to that kind of thing.'

In the old 'bord and pillar' system of coal extraction pairs of hewers drove roadways into the coal, fifteen feet wide. Every twenty yards, new roadways were struck off to the left and right, creating a grid-like network of tunnels, with *stooks* – pillars of coal twenty yards square – holding up the immeasurable tonnage of rock overhead. This was called *coming yehl*.

When they'd reached the furthest extent of a district – and there might be twenty pairs of hewers working in a district on each of the three shifts – they'd start to work back towards the shaft bottom. Where there were areas of habitation, roads or particularly churches on the land above, the stooks were left in place. Otherwise they went for total extraction. They began moving – 'coming back' – towards the shaft bottom, slicing out the pillars of coal as they went. And the 'roof', the incalculable weight of rock, was allowed to collapse in behind them, 'as it liked'. This was called *coming back brockens*.

The idea was that as you moved the face gradually back towards the shaft bottom, the last few yards of rock would always crumble

gently in behind your *chocks* – your last row of props. Often, however, the roof held for dozens, even hundreds of yards. And that was
when it became dangerous, because you didn't know how long it
was going to hold. It might last ten years, or it might come down
any minute. And once a hundred yards of rock began to crack, you
didn't know where it would stop. At the very least, you'd lose your
coal face. You'd hear a cracking and a rumbling, like the sound of
thunder – but as though the thunder were actually inside your house.
Then you had to decide whether to stay where you were, or get out.
That was where your skill as a miner came in.

In the days of piecework – not so long ago – when the men
were paid according to the weight of coal they produced, a pair
of hewers might slave to the end of a shift to get to the good coal,
and then have to leave it to the men on the next shift. So to prevent
one man reaping the benefits of another's labour, the three pairs of
hewers who worked the three shifts in a particular place all used the
same token to identify their tubs when they arrived for weighing at
bank. And at the end of the week they received one pay packet,
which they divided equally between them.

Thus all the hewers were divided into teams of six. And they
were not appointed by the management. The men chose their own
'marras'.

The positions in which they worked were called *cavills*. One team
might have a warm dry cavill where the coal was soft and yielded
easily to the pick, and a man could almost stand at his full height,
while others would be crouching in a tunnel of icy wind with water
pouring on to them, hardly able to 'beat the mini' – earn the minimum
wage and get on to piecework rates. So every three months, the cavills
changed. Under the supervision of the union, lots were drawn in the
Miners' Hall for where each of the teams would work for the next
quarter.

That was when the 'poofler', the leading hand of the team, got
rid of the dead wood. Any man who had not pulled his weight,
or had not been able to keep up with his marras – for whatever
reason – during the previous quarter would be told, 'Sorry, you're
out.' Sometimes men would work extra hard to cover for a friend
or relative, maybe an older man, who was struggling to keep up.
But eventually it would become obvious, and that man would have
to move down.

So the hewers found their own level, from the Big Six – hellish
workers who were capable of making money anywhere – and the

Even Bigger Six, to the Easy Six – lads who weren't bothered. Sometimes if one of the slacker teams got a really good cavill, they'd sell it to one of the more ambitious teams; only perhaps for a tenner – but it was all money.

Every day, the marras would meet at the *kist*, the deputy's chest, where he kept his axe and saw, which marked the entrance to the district. As one set of marras was coming out-bye, they'd pause and talk to their marras who were going in, tell them how the coal was standing and how many tubs they'd filled. If the fore-shift had filled twenty-two, the back shift made it a point of honour to try to fill twenty-three, and so it went on.

Each pair of hewers was served by a *putter*, who brought the *chumins*, the empty tubs, to the face and took the full 'uns up to the landing – the loading bay from which the pony drivers took them to the main haulage. In the inland collieries, where the seams were narrow, and the tubs smaller – ten hundredweight – the putters used their shoulders and even their heads to push the tubs along the narrow roadways, which were often hardly higher than the tubs. At the coastal collieries, where the tubs held fifteen to sixteen hundred-weight of coal, they had ponies to pull the tubs. But they still had to use their shoulders to guide the tubs round awkward corners in the roadway.

The putters liked to sit on the limmers, the wooden shafts of the gallowas' harness, crouching down in the cramped roadways, their shoulders against the horses' backsides, the tails draped over their backs. It was always worse after the weekend, when the hosskeepers would 'physic' the beasts.

The putters were paid by the score of tubs they 'put'. Like the hewers, they were cavilled to a district for a quarter, but they changed their particular place of work every day. If the hewer off whom he was putting was working a long way from the landing, a putter might be struggling to shift as many tubs as a man who was working near the landing off two sets of hewers. Or he might be stuck with hewers who were hardly managing to fill any tubs at all. So every day, at the beginning of the shift, the putters 'put their rubs in'. The deputy chalked the names of the 'gannins' – the different routes the putters took – on the blade of his saw, numbering them in a random order. Then he turned the saw over, and put six strokes on the other side that corresponded to these numbers. The putters would then each rub out one of these strokes to find out which of the gannins they'd be working in that shift.

While there were some men who remained putters almost all

their working lives, they were mostly young, agile lads, itching to get a start hewing at the youngest permissible age – twenty-one. (Traditionally a man did not marry until he became a hewer.) And because of their relative youth, they were usually the most rebellious element in the workforce. If they fancied a drink on a Friday night, they'd stand by the lamp cabin and hoy their tokens (the identifying piece of metal each man had to hand in as he left the pit) in the air. If they came down, they said, they'd go to work; if not, they'd go home. They'd hoy them straight on to the cabin roof and walk out *en masse*.

Norman Hawkins was married to Hazel, the granddaughter of Percy's younger brother Jack. He was in his early sixties, with narrow pointed features, which made him appear slight. His neck and forearms, however, were extraordinarily thick and muscular, giving the impression of an undertow, a backlog of power. As though, if you went for him, you'd go headlong into a wall of muscle; a physique created by several decades of hard manual labour.

He'd worked his way from datal lad to deputy. When he left the pit, he'd worked in various factories and as a security guard, and he'd discovered there was a world of daylight up there that he'd been missing. He said often how glad he was to be away from the pit, but when he talked about it, a kind of glow came over him. In a factory, a man could stand by the same machine for ten, twenty, thirty years. But in a mine, even though his work might be basically the same, the place where he was working and the conditions were constantly changing. As a deputy, his life had been full of new and varied activity.

He'd started the pit at the earliest possible age, as his father and grandfather had done, and as it had been fore-ordained he would. And it was evident that for him the pit was the true, the appropriate life for a man to lead. He now lived in a small village just west of Durham City, and in his work in the surface world, he'd been all over the county. But he was from Horden. And as far as the pit was concerned he had only ever worked at Horden. For him the pit *was* Horden.

'When I started the pit, the different seams were like three separate villages. The cavills – the different working places in the different districts – changed every thirteen week. But unless something out of the ordinary happened a man worked in the same seam all his working life. And it was pure chance which one you ended up in. If when you went to the pit, there was a vacancy for a lad in the Main Coal, you could be there for the next fifty years. So you never saw a lot of the people from the other seams. When they walked in the Big Club, you thought they must be from Hartlepool or somewhere.

'I started in the Hutton seam, the deepest of the three seams, where my father worked. I was on datal work – just doing whatever was needed from day to day. One day you'd be answering the intercoms. The next you'd be shifting gear or driving – taking the chumins, the empty tubs, in-bye for the putters. This day, I was at the kist, the entrance to a district, when this lad my age – about fourteen – came out, and he was crying. He'd been driving, but he couldn't get the tubs in quick enough and the putters were all shouting at him – "Howay, yer lazy booger!" – 'cause he was lossing them money. The overman was there, and in them days the overmen still dressed smart – in a leather cap and breeches that fastened just below the knee. He turned round and he saw me. I stood to attention. "What do they call thou?" he says. I stuck my little pigeon chest out and I says, "Hawkins." "Micky Hawkins's son?" I stick my chest out further and I says, "Aye." "Why," he says, "I bet Micky Hawkins's son could do that job." My chest's getting bigger and bigger and I'm glowing with pride.

'I went in there, ran the tubs over the points the wrong way, they all came off the rails and I got kicked from one end of the landing to the other. When I came out of the pit that day, I went to my father and I said, "I don't like it down there. Can tha get wa out?" Why, to tell you the truth, my father had never been that keen on me going down the pit in the first place. So he went to see the Father – 'cause we're staunch Roman Catholics – and he got us an apprenticeship at the steelworks in Hartlepool. I was over the moon. But when my father went to see the pit manager, he says, "If your Norman leaves this colliery, Mr Hawkins, you'll be seeking alternative accommodation" – meaning we'd lose our colliery house. There was no question about it. I couldn't go. Then the manager says he's moving me to the Low Main. My father wasn't too pleased. He was getting on a bit by then, and if I'm at the pit at all, he wanted me down there in the Hutton Seam where I could help him. He said he didn't want me to go to the Low Main. "Fair enough," says the manager. "Norman can go on the belts." Why, the belts was the worst place in the whole pit. Picking stone off the conveyors all day, and half the people there weren't the full shillun. He knew if I went there, within a week I'd be begging to go to the Low Main. I lasted two days.

'I went to the Low Main on datal work. Then when I was sixteen, my father died, and we lost our colliery house. Me and me mother moved into a council house, and we didn't get any coals. In those days, coals were half-meat, because you cooked with coals, you heated your house and the water to bathe yourself and wash your clothes with coal. So I went to the colliery office. The under-manager, feller called Brown, says, "Tha cannut get thi coals on datal work, lad." Because you weren't entitled to any free coals before the age of twenty-one, unless you were on piecework. So, just before my seventeenth birthday, I became a putter.

'There were some who took to putting like falling off a log. But I was never very good at it. If that tub came off the rail, you had to lift it on yourself, and fifteen hundredweight of coal took some lifting. Some would pull it from the front with their hands, but all the putters had like a little apron at the back of their belt. Called them arse flappers. You'd get under the tub and heave it on to the rails with your backside. You had that arse flapper to protect your hoggers. Without it they wouldn't have lasted a day. Some had leather, but most just used bits of rubber off old conveyor belts.

'But the dust! If you were in a place where they were coming back brockens the dust had been lying for however long. It was inches deep, and your horse was ploughing back through it, churning it up. You'd be black as the ace of spades, the sweat pouring off you, in just a vest and a little pair o' hoggers.

'Some of the gallowas ... Why, they weren't bad, they just objected to being down the pit. They would always be going the wrong way, 'cause they didn't want to do it. It was hard work, see. There was a lad called Geordie Miller killed two gallowas on a morning. He had one up an incline with a tub. He put another tub on, horse went straight down into the trap, broke its neck. Hosskeeper came down and killed it, put it in a tub and sent it to bank. Later that day, the same thing happened. Two in a day. There was a horse called Victors, somebody put its eye out with a lamp. There was another lad got taken to court for knocking nails into a horse's behind. See, they vex you! Because you're so pent up. You want to make money, and when the horse does something wrong ... Really it's the man that's to blame, but he takes it out on the horse.

'There were hundreds of gallowas. Hundreds! But I used to hate hosskeepers. They would give you a pony, see. And that man never set foot beyond the stables, which were at the shaft bottom. He'd say, "Take Duke." You'd say, "But he's nay good, man. He cannut pull!" "Ah, but he can, tha knars!" "He cannut!" So he'd send for the overman, see. "What's the matter?" "Why, that gallowa'll not pull, man." But you'd have to take it, and that gallowa was lossing you money. Mind, a good pony came out at half-past eleven in the morning, and if they were a gallowa short, that poor horse has been turned round and sent straight back in again. Oh, they were definitely beasts of burden down the pit! All this bullshit about a bloke taking in an apple and a sweet for the horse! Whoever did that wasn't on piecework. When he's "waiting on" – when there's no chumins at the landing – that's when a man used to get his bait, because he didn't stop before. Then, if he had a crust, he might give the horse half. But I've never seen anyone take anything down specifically for the pony. Unless maybe he's a driver, one of the lads who took the tubs from the landing to the haulage, because they had the same horse every time.

'If a putter could get a tub filled, he'd get more for it than a hewer. So he'd try to get a tub filled for himself wherever he could. Possibly at the end of a shift, the hewers would say, "We've knocked two tubs out for you there lads." They'd leave the coal there for you to fill. It was like a reward for working well for them. They would go steady out-bye, and you'd sweat your lugs off to fill them two tubs. Then, you weren't supposed to, but if you could get on that gallowa's back you'd ride out-bye to get to the shaft as the last cage was gannin' up. Or you might get in before the men at the beginning of the shift to fill a tub. It was illegal to coal-hew before you were twenty-one, but if it was questioned at bank, the hewer would say he'd filled it for you. But it was rare anything was said. Because in those days, under private enterprise, as long as the coal was getting to bank, the management weren't bothered how. If a putter was killed at the face filling a tub, they'd just say it was his fault for doing something illegal.

'Safety was that slack. Men would leave it to the last minute to put their timber in. They'd be working under unsupported rock, just so they could fill another tub. Or they'd fill "off the sides" – make the roadway wider than it should have been. But under private enterprise nobody bothered. If a man wanted to risk his life for the price of a tub – which was ninepence – that was his affair.

'As soon as I was twenty-one I put my name down to go on face work – hewing or filling. Hewing, it's solid coal, you use a hand pick or a nig-nog – a "windy pick", a pneumatic drill. Filling, you're shovelling loose coal on a long wall face, maybe a hundred, two hundred yards long. They have a machine that cuts under the coal, which pulls what they call the "kirvings" out. That space is called the kirvings – because you can't fire solid coal. The pressure of the blast would bring everything down. When they've done that, a man comes along, drills maybe six or eight holes, depending how big the seam is. Then a shot-firer plugs them with dynamite and fires it. That's loose coal. That's filling. Two hewers working together – that's what they call a short wall face. Then they started the "long walls". You'd have twelve men filling: kneeling to shovel coal on to a conveyor. It would go into tubs, and them tubs were divided among the twelve men. They got paid that way.

'As soon as that coal was cleared off, you'd get some men come in. They'd move the conveyor forward, and you'd start again the next day. You didn't get as much for filling loose coal as you did for knocking the coal down, but obviously you could fill more tubs. There was nay conveyors when I started. It was all gallowas and tubs, and it produced more tonnage at times, because there was no stopping to move conveyors. It was just tubs going in and out all the time. When the conveyors went forward, the props holding up the roof behind had to come forward and that was another set of men.

'Nowadays when they finish a face or a seam, they leave thousands of pounds worth o' gear in there. But in those days, every piece of wood, every nail came out. The chock drawers could tell how much weight a prop was supporting by the sound it made. They'd tap it with their ayxe-head, and listen to the way it rang. They'd leave in the props "with the wyte" – as they used to say – while they took everything else out. There was always one prop they'd leave till last. They'd leave it cut halfway through, and they could tell from the way it was creaking how long the roof was going to hold. There was a little feller called Mousey Molyneaux, and he could always tell, to the second, when the roof was going to come down. He could touch a prop with a hair and know how long it was going to hold. He'd have a sylvester, which was like a chain, on his last prop, and he'd be saying, "Not yet . . . Not yet . . ." You'd hear a crackling noise, like wood burning on a fire, then a roaring and a rumbling. Mousey'd say, "All right, lads. Get back." We'd all get back behind the chocks, Mousey'd pull his prop out, and the whole lot would come down. They were craftsmen people like that. But they weren't acknowledged as craftsmen and they weren't paid a craftsman's wages. Mind, they never worked on anything else. They were never putters or hewers. They were just chock drawers all their lives.

'But all the good workers, the big hewers, are dead – of pneumoconiosis or crippled. See a lot of men weren't fussed to push themselves. Once they'd got themselves a bit on top of the "mini", they were satisfied. They'd get their watch out towards the end of the shift (they all wore watches on chains in them days), they'd see there was three quarters of an hour to go, and they'd say to the putters, "All right, lads. Fill yourselves a couple o' tubs." Then they'd walk slowly out-bye, maybe stopping for a rest on the way. And they'd do the same thing on their way in at the beginning of the shift. They weren't lazy. They maybes had other jobs – as a window cleaner or a bookie's runner – and they didn't want to exhaust themselves. Or they just didn't see why they should kill themselves over it. They were a different breed o' men in them days. They never asked themselves, "Where shall I take the wife on holiday?" They never went to the supermarket with their wives. They had their way of life. They knew how much money they needed so they could give something to the wife and have a bit over for a couple of pints and a bit baccy. And they knew exactly how much work they had to do to get that.

'But these hellish hewers, they didn't believe in the mini. Say they were at the headings, the beginning of a district, where the coal was really hard, where most men'd be struggling to fill five tubs, they could maybes fill twenty, because they knew how to work the coal. They'd get in the cage just as the door was shutting, and the sweat'd be pouring off them. They wanted the money. But also they wanted to be able to stick their chests out when they walked in Horden Big Club, so everyone'd say, "Them's the Big Hewers – the lads that filled fifty tubs a shift." But as I say, they didn't live long. That's why when I was twenty-five I put in for my deputy's ticket.'

You can't fire solid coal. Space has to be cut at the top or bottom of the face to absorb the impact of the blast. The first coal-cutting machines cut these spaces – the juds – at the bottom of the face, slicing straight in, five or six feet under the coal, a young lad following behind, pulling out the loose coal with a long flat shovel. In the old hand-hewing days, however, they found it easier to 'kirve the jud' at the top. A hewer would cut an area eighteen inches wide from the top of the face, to give himself sufficient room as he got deeper into the coal. He'd start with a small head on his pick, working up to a bigger and bigger head the deeper he got. Right up to nationalisation the men had to buy their own picks. The picks came in-bye on the set at the beginning of the shift, and every hewer had his initials on his own picks. In the old days, before they had the detachable heads, a hewer's son would carry his picks in for him. He'd follow his dad in-bye, with a great big arm full o' picks.

The hewers sat down to kirve the jud, on a three-legged stool called a cracket. In the joiner's shop at Horden Colliery, a lad was employed full time making crackets. In the very narrow seams where the men lay down to hew, the legs were cut off at an angle so they could use the cracket to brace their backs against the rock.

The door into the hillside was of corrugated-iron, but set in a brick arch, lovingly crafted, and of a Roman elegance and simplicity. Inside, the brickwork continued in the lower portions of the tunnel. Peter, the deputy, a stocky, self deprecating man with a black beard, who rolled his r's in the back of his throat in the manner of West Northumberland, pointed to the elegant ledges, the arched refuge recesses fashioned with the same care and attention to detail as the arch outside. That was the way they'd done things a hundred years ago, he said, with a kind of rueful wonder.

But even then, these quasi-classical details must have been there purely for effect, for a few feet further on, the brick work gave way to naked rock. At Easington there was such a density of girder, mesh and concrete that one had to go miles into the earth before one came face to face with any real rock. Here, however, it was visible only yards from the door. Huge splintering boulders, apparently bursting from the walls, jammed into position with arch girders, random scraps of wood and metal and, so it seemed, anything else that was to hand. Here they didn't have the resources or the manpower to worry too much about appearances. If it held, it held.

We were in a small private mine a few miles west of Durham, one of quite a number still left in the county, some employing as few as three people. Norman, who occasionally drank with the owner, had arranged for me to go down this Saturday morning, when the repair work was being done. The mine was a tiny part of the old Brancepeth workings, what was called a 'drift', so shallow that the hewers were able to simply walk in-bye. Most of the pits to the west of Durham had begun as drifts, before the search for fresh reserves had necessitated the sinking of shafts. I'd been keen to come here, to see the kind of pit where my great-grandfather had worked – that all the miners had worked in before they moved east to the deep mines of the coast. With me was Kevin, Hazel's younger brother, who had worked at Horden. After putting in time on various building sites, he was now unemployed, and had come along to see if he fancied the idea of trying to get a job here. So far, he didn't seem at all keen. 'We're going back in bloody time here,' I heard him mutter behind me.

We half-walked, half-slid down the steeply sloping roadway, within minutes up to our knees in thick elastic mud, its surface swilling with water. Ahead of us, a huge rock bulged into our pathway. The road turned to the right to pass it. Peter thumped it as we passed. 'A British Coal inspector would never allow that,' he said. 'But a miner knows that that is solid. A miner knows what will hold and what won't . . . generally.'

'A roof may hold for a hundred years without support,' Kevin was saying behind me. 'Or it may only last a few seconds. Then the floor may start to buckle. It may start coming up towards you at a foot a second. That's when you drop everything and run.'

The ground levelled out and we were walking along railway tracks beside the conveyor, stationary on a Saturday morning. Soon we were at the face. Three avenues of wooden props, about two and a half feet high, stretching away beyond the beam of our lamps, the black grit of the floor soon disappearing into inches of water. To our left, the face – the coal itself – stretched for about two hundred yards. Adjoining this drift were the untold miles of the old Brancepeth roadways, sealed off, but into which the water from this pit could be drained. I wondered how they had got rid of the water before the introduction of mechanical pumps. Peter said they'd probably have had a boy working a hand pump, day and night. 'But the need wasn't as great,' he said. 'They probably wouldn't have bothered with faces like this one. Because they had the pick of the coal then. And they knew where to find it. They weren't stupid. They were monks, weren't they, the first people to dig coal in this county. They followed the lie of the land. They looked at the structure of the land, and they could see where the coal would be.'

We headed back the way we had come, turned left and arrived at the *kist*, the central meeting point. There were panels of inscrutable buttons, some glowing, and some incongruously domestic-looking clothes' hooks. We went through the trap-door into the tailgate – the return airway – and my coat soon hung uncomfortably heavy in the warm dust-laden air.

In a mine it was easy to lose track of time, and virtually impossible to gauge distances. It was the absence of detail in the relative darkness, the regularity of the sleepers underfoot, the arched girders overhead, having to pay constant attention to where you were putting your feet. You walked without seeming to move. Then suddenly you were somewhere.

We passed a group of miners trying to repair a piece of equipment. Two of them were larking around, grappling with each other playfully in the dimness. They all looked like you'd expect miners, particularly miners in this kind of mine, to look. Their features, beneath the black blotches and their straggly moustaches, having a mud-like pallidity and a hungry whippet-like eagerness. Here there was none of the butch well-fed complacency of the NCB days. These men, it seemed, were still living in – or had returned to – the era of abuse.

The previous night, in the local pub with Hazel and Norman, I had seen some old photos over the bar, of miners working. The landlord, an Irishman, had no idea when or where they were taken. But I was particularly struck by one of a hewer, taken in profile, sitting bare-headed and virtually naked on his cracket, his features, behind a large drooping moustache, gaunt and totally impassive, his pick raised, poised at the shoulder to kirve the jud. There was nothing desperate, nothing hurried in the motion – it was steady, even. He was a man of my great-grandfather's time. And there was something faintly shocking about that image. It was the contrast between the near nakedness and the air of Victorian propriety lent by the moustache. The embarrassing primitivism, a kind of inexplicable degradation, of working down there sitting on a three-legged stool. The non-expression of the face – a kind of stoicism born of fatalism, the knowledge that there was nothing to be done.

The behaviour of the miners now before me seemed symptomatic of something I had heard about, but never encountered before: the recklessness, the contemptuous devil-may-care of men whose lives are in permanent jeopardy. These were the kind of miners I had often heard about – the ones who didn't care.

At this pit, the workers got £200 a week flat wage. There was no weekend coal production. Overtime was for repairs only. There was no union. 'We're going back in time here,' repeated Kevin, as if it needed saying.

We had to crawl under the conveyor to get into the face. There was just room. We lay in the black grit, as Peter demonstrated a 'windy pick' – a pneumatic drill. It was a spike, about two feet in length. You thrust it into the face so that the rear part ignited the front, and off you went, driving the bit sideways into the 'cleats', the facets formed by the natural breaks in the coal. There was a tremendous amount of noise and dust. But Peter handled the machine with an effortless, thoughtless ease. After a few seconds, he stuck it back into the earth, turning it off with the same thrust with which he had started it. Really, he said, they should have been getting the coal out now. Because they didn't work weekends, it would be standing till Monday, which would give it time to harden, and become more difficult to work. That was the way it was, however. The pit just couldn't afford to have them working at weekends.

The seam we were now in was called the Harvey. I had always ignorantly assumed that each pit had its own self-contained reserves of coal. But these seams ran for hundreds of square miles under the whole of the county. The Harvey seam here, was the same as had been mined at Blackhall, a mile or so down the coast from Horden, until the early-Eighties. But the seams sloped steeply downwards towards the east of the county, and then down under the sea. So that Hedley Hope, far in the west of Durham, where they'd mined the Ballarat, had been a fresh-air pit, where the fillers smoked at the face, and the under-manager wandered in-bye with his pipe. By the time it reached Horden, however, the Ballarat was so deep under the earth it was impossible to reach. But new seams emerged as you went further east, that had in their day been massively rich, like the Main Coal and the famous Hutton Seam.

I had often wondered how they got their wonderful names, the seams. At this pit there were the Harvey, the Tilly and the Busty. The Hutton Seam, for example, was named after the geologist who discovered it in the early nineteenth century. Maybe, like some of the pits themselves – the Emma, the Anna and the Maria – seams like the Tilly and the Victoria were named after the wives and daughters of the old owners. It lent a bizarre air of eroticism to the whole enterprise – the idea of naming the black orifice, into which your employees daily descended, after your own conjugal flesh; though if this was the case, who, I wondered, were Harvey and Busty?

Peter admitted with a rueful shrug that he had no idea of the answers to any of these questions. He'd been out of the pits for some time. He'd worked in a factory, then started his own business, an off-licence. It had been quite successful, but he'd got fed up with it, because he could never get away from it. He'd come here for the relative steadiness and certainty of working for someone else.

'Not everyone can be a miner,' he said. 'Not everyone can stand it, or would want to stand it. It helps if you come from a mining family, because you grow up with the expectation of what it will be like, from a very early age.' He came from a mining family, he admitted, a trifle ruefully, as though because he could stand it, he thus had a moral obligation to do it.

We walked back out-bye, our throats thick with the dust that hung static in the warm stale air. As we splashed through the grey milk-like water, our helmet lamps reflecting the rippling on to the arched roof, the movement of the water seemed to hang in the dustladen air, like distant sunlight caught in a thick and dirty amber. Imagine having to work in this miasmic stickiness for forty years, I thought.

At times we had to walk bent double. But most of the time we were able to walk along the centre of the arch girders, our heads just cocked slightly to the side. Every so often, however, my attention would lapse, and I'd knock my plastic helmet – thankfully cushioned by its inner framework – with a jolting crack against one of the girders. Norman had told me that when he started at the pit, there were no helmets. The men just wore their caps, and underneath his hair, his head was covered in scars.

12

The Belts

E VERY WEDNESDAY night, shortly before seven o'clock, I'd cut
   through the back lane at the bottom of Hardwick Street, cross
the bare slope of the Parish Council park – taking care not to slip on
the frosty pathway or skid in dog shit as I slithered down over the
wet grass – cross Blackhills Terrace by the church, and head up into
Eighth Street. I always felt as I entered that network of dark streets
behind the Miners' Hall – the frost already forming on the blackened
terraces, everything still and largely silent save for the blaring of a
television as a door swung and then slammed abruptly shut – that
I was entering the very ethos, the essentiality of Horden. And as I
went into the Miners' Hall, through the tiny cubby-hole of a corridor
by the Parish Clerk's office, into the Meeting Room itself, and settled
myself at the table around which those bodies that had controlled the
social and political organism of Horden had met down the decades, it
would occur to me that I was as close as it was possible to be to the
centre of a community.

   Sitting there in the warm glow, out of the freezing darkness,
I felt ensconced at the very heart of the nexus of Labour Party
and unions that had controlled, indeed virtually owned Horden
for so long. All those bodies: the Federation Board, the Welfare
Committee, the Parish Council – the membership of which had in
many cases comprised the same people for decades. Sitting there
at the very table at which my grandfather and auntie had sat, I
felt oddly privileged, like a child tolerated in the company of adults
long after his usual bedtime.

There we would sit, the few members of the Lodge committee who still turned up, week after week, together with the odd ex-miner or ex-miner's widow with an enquiry about benefits or compensation, and perhaps an older member of the committee, who gravitated there occasionally at that particular time, almost involuntarily, out of a sense of – what was it? – habit, nostalgia, continuity? And, of course, there was Jackie.

'Still 'ere?'

'Aye.'

'Aa thought tha said tha was gannin' after New Year?'

'I'm just staying a bit longer.'

'That's what tha said last week.'

'It'll be "after New Year" for a canny while yet,' said Johnny Fairclough, a stocky man in his fifties.

'By!' said Jackie, darkly. ''E's a bugger, 'im.'

The room was long and high ceilinged, with a large arched window at the far end, that looked out on to the caretaker's back yard, now of course in darkness. The room was freshly decorated and everyone who entered commented on the new colour scheme. Broad stripes of floral pattern in various shades of beige and pink, leading up to a dado rail, picked out in white gloss, beneath walls and ceiling of a deep Indian red. Most people didn't like it, thought it made the room too dark.

'They should maybe have gone for something a bit more pinky,' boomed Joe Summers, the secretary, as he entered the room. He pointed to the stripes beneath the dado rail. 'Maybe brought out one of these colours here.' He looked around the room. 'They've made it a bit stark.'

Joe was always the last to arrive at the meetings, and he'd always start his opening line before he entered the room. You'd hear his low flat voice booming in the passage outside and then he'd be there. That was his way of commanding the attention of the meeting, of creating a sense of excitement around his arrival. But it was hardly necessary since everyone was always waiting for him anyway. He'd been the boss of Horden Lodge – the last boss. And he knew that as far as these meetings and quite a bit else was concerned, he still was the boss.

He was a big man – not particularly tall or broad, but like a stocky man greatly enlarged. It gave him considerable frontal presence, to which he was fond of referring. ('When I was a lad – and I was big even then.' 'You were Joe, you were.' 'Well, I was.') And unlike the older type of union leaders, who had dragged themselves head and shoulders above their fellows with their hard-won self education, marking themselves out with their collars and ties and their tweed jackets, unlike even Ernie Wilding – the previous Lodge secretary, under whose wing Joe had achieved prominence in the union – with his famous knowledge of union law, Joe's stock in trade was that he was 'one of the lads'. He was a grandfather who dressed like most of the grandfathers on the committee in the ageless leisure wear of our time. Sitting there among his committee members, effortlessly dominating the room with his great size, cajoling with his bullish drollness, his droning boom an insistent undertow to everything that went on, he seemed like the Chief Lad. It was said that he had held the community together during the 1984–5 strike through force of personality alone, and that it was only through regard for him that many of the men had not gone back long before its end.

He had started work in 1949, 'on the belts', the conveyors from which the stone was picked from the coal before it was loaded into railway wagons and taken to the docks at Hartlepool. The noise on the belts, the juddering and grinding of the shakers – the chutes which shook the coal and stone down on to the belts – the 'screaming' of the steel screens, the belts themselves, a constant metallic tearing at the air, was so great that speech was impossible.

'You had deaf and dumb people working there,' said Joe. 'You had people who'd lost fingers and hands down the pit. Old men who were too weak for any other kind of work. Then you had subnormal people, criminals, child molestors, very ugly people, outcasts – the sort of people who couldn't get a job anywhere else. You'd be standing there black, freezing, surrounded by these people. You were fourteen, and you wondered what you'd done to deserve it.

'When the belts started up at five in the morning you could hear them all over Horden. I'd get home at three in the afternoon. I used to crawl into bed and just lie there, the screaming of the belts still ringing in my ears.'

'You used to speak in sign language,' said Micky Douglas, a small cheerfully garrulous man. 'You learnt it off the deaf and dumb lads. It was the only way you could communicate, 'cause of the noise. Nowadays a lot of the people who worked there would be in special schools or getting special care. But in them days, they just stuck them on the belts. When you first went there, you were frightened of them – people like Chocolate Bott. You were scared to go to the the toilet, 'cause Chocolate Bott, if he got a young lad in there on his own, he might try to feel him up. But after a couple of weeks you weren't bothered by them. *They*'d be getting it from you. You'd say, "Hey, Chocolate Bott. I hear you lost your trousers down Hartlepool at the weekend." A lot of these people, like Freddy Lucas and Chocolate Bott, they didn't mind that kind of work. They hadn't missed a shift in over forty years. But when you look back on it, their lives can't have been worth living.'

'The end belts, 4, 5 and 6, had the best coal,' said Joe. 'From the Low Main. It used to come through in big, clean lumps. The lads on there hardly had to do anything, just pick out the odd lump of stone. But where I was, on 1 and 2, it was the Hutton Seam coal, and at that time, 1949, the seam must have been nearing the end of its life. It was mostly just duff – powdery coal. There was so much dust coming off you could hardly see where you were. After a few weeks you were praying to go down the pit.'

That was one of the main functions of the belts: a harsh initiation into the world of the pit, that could last only a few weeks or go on for years, depending on a person's luck – or lack of it. After that, the most menial of tasks underground – working with 'real men' – would seem a privilege. The threat of having to return to the belts was enough to bring the most obstinate and rebellious of miners to heel.

The story was the primary mode of discourse in County Durham. There was no point that could not be better made by means of some tale or anecdote. Stories that elbowed and jostled each other, each man vying with his fellows in the humour and bravura of his stories. They seemed hardly to listen to each other as they stood, waiting to dive in with their next tale – bursting with their narratives.

This was the kind of talk I'd been brought up on, because this was the way my father had received much of his 'education', standing at the pigeon crees, waiting for the return of the birds, which he liked to fancy were the upward-soaring souls of miners, at last freed from their toil underground. There, he'd hear the stories of the pit, endlessly repeated, embroidered, acted out, fragmented and put back together with ever more graphic and visceral detail.

It was, I had learnt later in life when I had become more absorbed into the world of the southern middle classes, a way of speaking, of expressing one's self, that could be a liability. In the south, where the exchange of views and information depended on an assumption of mutual interest, people didn't want to be assaulted with stories, they didn't want you thrusting yourself on them with your experiences. For in County Durham, a story was put forward with the force of an argument, a challenge – that dared the listener to go one better. And always, at the centre, was the great I, the eternal ego, creating and vindicating himself on the cusp of disbelief. It may not have been 'good manners', but in that society you had to exert yourself as a man. If you waited to be drawn out through polite questioning, you'd wait forever.

So I had learnt from a very young age the habit of seeing every fragment of experience as an element of narrative, of seizing experience through description. That really, had been my education. As a child, my father had bombarded me with stories of his own childhood; of hard times in Horden, of beaten-earth floors and snot on the faces of children who hadn't been taught to help themselves; of fights and bullying on the school train to Hartlepool, of urinating into the bowl-like light fittings – the light filtering dully through the liquid swilling with the movement of the train; of the dens in the Dene, the tree-houses and the bows and arrows. But most of all there had been the apparently inexhaustible fund of experiences from the war in the Far East. Of sea sickness and mutiny on the troop ship out; of the coming of the rain at Gauhati in Assam, the thudding of the great drops on the corrugated-iron roof of the hospital, and how though weakened by malaria, they had run outside to dance in it, rolling naked on the streaming earth; of burying the dead on the tennis court of the beleaguered hill station at Kohima, and how as they were strafed by the Japanese machine-guns they had leapt into the freshly dug graves, pulling the bodies of their dead comrades over them for cover, and how as he lay there with a dead man on top of him and a live man squirming underneath, someone had tossed him a tin of bully beef, and how as he plastered the rank gelatinous meat into his mouth it had occurred to him that things could not get much worse; and of the burnished sky over the Brahmaputra river domed like a great brass bowl. I had been particularly impressed by this latter description. Years later, I came across exactly the same image in a book by Eric Newby that I knew my father had read. But that was the way it was with stories. Each man borrowed and took freely from his fellows, synthesising and elaborating so that the great narrative moved forever forward. For it seemed as I stood there in the Big Club, listening to the stories of the belts, that each of them were simply fragments of a larger story, and, as they echoed and repeated themselves, that their experiences had been to a greater or lesser extent interchangeable.

All the men had, whether at the same time or at different times, gone through this deafening initiation, as had many of their fathers before them; and they had all known and worked with each other's fathers and sons and brothers and cousins at the belts, and in the darkness below. They'd seen each other day in, day out for thirty, forty, fifty years. How could anyone who had not shared in these experiences hope to be accepted by them? And yet always, there was this chiming, remonstrative familiarity in the way they spoke.

It was significant that the people who inhabited the Club around us were known as characters. A 'character', it was said, was someone with a good fund of stories. But more than that, it was someone who wasn't afraid to be himself, who flaunted, even doggedly cultivated, certain idiosyncratic aspects of his personality, a person who created stories around himself. Who not only told stories, but lived them. Someone like Harry Turnbull, a little thickset fellow with a huge deep voice, who every year blacked himself up as a Zulu warrior for the Horden carnival, terrifying the children as he went marauding along the procession route with his shield and spear. Every year he won first prize for the fancy dress – only 7/6d, but going in the Big Club dressed like that, he'd be plied with drink till closing time. Every weekend he went away to a different carnival, and he'd always win something. One Saturday, he'd been to Old Hartlepool, a big carnival, where he'd won 12/6d. He'd gone in the pubs, got all his beer for nowt and missed the last bus home. He started to walk back to Horden, but when he got to the big cemetery in West Hartlepool, he climbed over the wall, and was so exhausted by the drink and walking about all day, that he passed out. He awoke at dawn, frozen, still half naked and blacked up. He reached in his fob for a tab end but he had no matches. He lay there, till he heard footsteps on the other side of the wall. He climbed up, and he saw a pitman on his way to work, with his tea bottle, and his bait tin under his arm. 'Ow!' says Old Harry. 'As tha got a match?' The pitman looked up, took one look at the black face leering down at him from the top of the cemetery wall, dropped his tea bottle and bait tin and offed. The tea bottle landed the right way up, and Harry always used to say that was the best drink of tea he ever had – and them sandwiches were beautiful.

But his wife used to play war with him. 'Tha gans away every weekend,' she said. 'Tha gets rotten drunk, and tha never thinks of fetchin' tha grandbairns nowt.' Why, he wondered, what can I fetch them? The next weekend, he went to the carnival at Middlesborough, got rotten drunk and missed the last bus home. The next morning, he went to the fairground where he met a little dwarf. When he got back to Horden, his wife said, 'There tha is again. Tha's got rotten drunk and tha's fetched tha grandbairns nowt.' 'Ah, but aa hev,' he said, and he told her to go in the other room. There was the little dwarf sitting. He was a bloke, the little dwarf, and on the Monday afternoon Harry took him in the Big Club. They always had turns in the Big Club on a Monday, and Harry and the little dwarf did a ventriloquist act. Everyone would buy them drinks. That little dwarf was in Horden quite a few days, and he enjoyed himself no end.

But while Horden had not disintegrated as a community, the moment the colliery closed, the way people had been afraid it would, it was true that you didn't get the characters – the quaer fellers – the way you used to. 'It's because of television,' someone told me. 'You get your entertainment from television now. You don't need people like that. And television makes everyone behave the same. Why,' he said, 'there's only Jackie left in Horden now.'

One night Jackie had asked me what I was having.

'Oh, I'll have a Ninety-Nine,' I said.

The barmaid looked blank.

'It's kind of orange drink,' I said.

Recognition dawned. 'You want a fifty-five.'

'I'll have a sixty-six,' I said.

The barmaid chortled at this witticism.

'What's that tha's drinking,' asked Jackie, when we were sitting, nodding towards my glass with a look of embarrassed wonder.

'It's kind of orange drink.'

'Have a beer, man! Just have a gill.' He leant forward concernedly. 'That lass was laughing at tha.'

Now whenever I walked into the Big Club he'd shout out, 'There's my marra – *Fifty-five*!' And he'd tell anyone who would listen about how the barmaid had laughed at me for drinking orange juice. 'True, that!' If he saw anyone talking to me, he'd shout out from the side of the club where he always sat, 'That's Fifty-five, that is!'

Arthur Scargill came to the Big Club. ''E came wi' is two boonsahs, yi knar. Great, big fellers. Aa was on the door wi' Aad Mattie. 'E was on that door twenty year, Mattie. 'E's dead now, like.

'Scargill comes in. Walks straight past. Mattie says, "Ey! Where the bloody 'ell does tha think tha's gannin'? Howay, sign the byuk!" Scargill turns round, says, "Doesn't tha know who aa is? Aa'm Arthur Scargill, President of the National Union of Mineworkers." Mattie says, "Aa din't give a bugger who tha is. Tha'll sign that byuk!"

'True, that.'

At Horden Colliery, there were, famously, three shafts: the North
Pit, the South Pit and the East Pit. Then there was the West Pit.
And it was said that it was at the West Pit that the most coals were
drawn, because that was where the most 'pit' was talked. The West
Pit was the Big Club.

Nowadays, if you went in a pub or a club, there was always a
game of housey or a quiz about to start. But in the heyday of the
Big Club there'd been no housey, no quizzes, no karaoke, just crack
– talk. There'd been a few games of dominoes and cards in discreet
corners, before the legalisation of gambling, but mainly people went
to the Big Club to talk.

When they took on a new barmaid, the first thing they did
was issue her with a rubber apron and a pair of wellington boots.
Because in those days, with the hand pumps, they spilled more beer
in the Big Club than they'd sell today. On a Sunday morning, they'd
start pulling pints at eleven o'clock, and the great horseshoe bar,
which was said to be a replica of the one on the *Queen Mary*,
would be completely filled with hundreds of single pints and trays
of pints. When the hatches went up at twelve o' clock, there'd be
crowds of men pressed up against the bar, and within minutes it
would be completely cleared – except that the surface of the bar,
an inch or so lower than the rim round it, would be swilling with
spilt beer.

The marras would all be sitting together, at the tables where
they always sat, week in, decade out. You didn't dare sit in anyone else's seat. And then there were the different communities of
the Club. The Irish Nyuk, at the left hand side of the bar, where
the Catholics sat. The Pigeon End for the pigeon men. And in the
opposite corner, where the dart board now was, Spongers' Corner,
where you got the kind of men who'd do anything for a pint. You
knew who they were. They knew you knew. And nobody minded.

People used to take food to the Club on a Sunday. The Hudspiths,
Jackie and his brothers, used to take in bowls of whelks – big bull
whelks as big as your hand – pigs' trotters, hard-boiled eggs. Anyone
who passed their table would be urged to take one. They had these
as a kind of hors-d'oeuvre, to keep them going while they headed
down to the beach banks for the pitch 'n' toss.

Monday was known as 'slackers' afternoon', a day considered
too 'godly' by many of the men to be worked. The main bar would
be full of men recovering from weekend binges. Men on the stone
shift – the ten o'clock shift – and even the night shift, that went
down at two, three or four in the afternoon depending which seam

they worked in. The Club opened at twelve, and if any of these men were still there at half past, you knew they weren't going to work. It didn't please their wives. It didn't please their families. But in those days, pre-nationalisation, not much would be said at the pit. If a man wanted to lose a shift, it was his business.

The piano would be dragged through from the Number Two End and there'd be a bit of a sing-song. There was a woman in Horden, who every week, out of sheer public spiritedness, made several large rabbit pies for the lads to eat on a Monday afternoon. She made them in big catering tins, which the local baker – a loyal Club member – put in his oven. They were laid out on the tables in the Club, everyone helped themselves, and in minutes they'd be gone.

Vestiges of these culinary practices lingered all over East Durham. One night I was in a pub in Shotton, when the landlady came round putting pots of salt on the tables. I thought she must be setting them for the next day's lunches, but a few minutes later she came back with basins of cold roast potatoes. When I didn't partake, the lads at the next table bellowed over, 'Come on, marra! There's gear 'ere!'

To this day, Jackie carried monkey nuts and liquorice allsorts in his pockets, and during the course of an evening, he'd go round depositing them in little piles in front of people he knew.

Now, on busy nights, the central tables and the pool table were occupied by young men, often hardly out of their teens, while round the nicotined walls were tiny men, their features wizened by work and withering wind or bloated red by ages of drink, always sitting in exactly the same place, inert, empty-eyed, like mummified figures at a Mexican shrine.

Others only in their fifties or sixties approached the bar, a feisty laddish roll in their walk, or bawled out with a fifteen year old's randy laughter. Men crouched over the snooker tables in tweed caps, white haired with gold-rimmed glasses and the faces of meek little old men; then as they rose from their shot, you saw the size of the shoulders on them. And most of the grandfathers I drank with dressed sportily younger than I did. Age could be a deceptive thing in the Big Club.

Jackie's was by far the rowdiest table in the room. As I left he would always shout out, 'All right, Fifty-five! Nice to see yer, young 'un!' And it wasn't just me. It seemed that whenever anyone entered or left the room there was a great barrage of bellowing and hooting, banging on the table and the occasional throwing of nuts. None of the men on this table was under seventy.

'It was purgatory, man,' said Johnny Fairclough, referring to the belts. 'They say young people can get used to anything. But I couldn't get used to that. You couldn't sleep at night, because of the ringing in your ears. It was a drone, like the skirl of a bagpipe . . . a badly played bagpipe. It was with you all the time.

'Mind, some of the people there, it didn't bother them. There was one lad, Jimmy Nichols – he was a mongol. When they finished him, he kept going back every day, still carrying his bait tin. The bosses'd say, 'Gan on yem, Jimmy. Tha's not needed here nay maer.' But he'd just say, 'Ah! Fly ower!' No disrespect to the man. It was what he knew. He'd been working there fifty years and he'd never missed a shift.'

The Heap was not as you would assume the place where the waste from the coal was dumped. That was the Stone Heap or the Spoil Heap. The Pit Heap was the vast covered area between the north and south shafts where the tubs were brought as they came out of the pit. The Hole was the mouth of the pit shaft itself. All of these places, like the different parts of the pit, and the different groups of men with their particular jobs, had a different identity, a particular status, character and ethos in relation to the rest of the pit. The men who maintained the shaft were known for their insane recklessness, for how they travelled up and down the shafts standing on top of the cage with no safety harness. If they were carrying girders, they'd just stand close to the cable with their arms round the girders. The winding enginemen, on the other hand, were obstinate and prone to self-aggrandisement, since no one could get to work and nothing could come in or out of the pit without their co-operation. As for the power loaders, the men who worked the coal-cutting machines on the face itself, they were the descendants of the old hewers – the people who actually produced the coal. Most of the men I knew on the union – Jimmy, the treasurer, Joe Summers, Ernie Wilding, Johnny, Micky Douglas – had been power loaders. They said it with a faint and involuntary sense of pride, but with a note that suggested it must be self-evident, since to be a power loader was to be a man. And to be a man was to be a power loader. Being a power loader was as far as a man could go without trying to put himself above his fellows.

When you started at the pit, if you knew someone with influence, you worked up 'on the Heap', sending the tubs of coal from the different seams through to the tipplers, and then on to the different belts. But if you didn't know anyone – if you didn't have a connection with the management – you were down there on the belts.

'You had dead hosses, miners' shit and all sorts coming down off the shakers,' said Joe Summers. 'The smell was disgusting. The miners were paid by the weight of the tub, so if a hoss died down there, they'd make sure no one was looking, then tip it into a tub. There were no toilets down there. There still aren't. So you'd put your hand out to grab a piece of stone and . . .

'If they put you somewhere quieter for a shift, you'd think it was the best thing that had ever happened. Anything to get away from the noise. On every belt there was a foreman, who got maybe a few pence more each week than the others. The one on Number One belt where I worked was this old feller they called the Dummy. Sometimes if nothing was coming through on our belt, or if they'd stopped the belt for repairs, we'd all get in his little cabin where it was fractionally quieter and a bit warmer – because it was feezing on the belts. And we'd get a game of cards going round the stove. All the lads on the other belts that were still working would be looking at us, dead envious.

'Then, when the belt was working again, this Dummy would go like, "barp" – give this low hoot, like an old fashioned ship's whistle. It wasn't loud, but somehow you could always hear it through all the din of that place. And you were back to work.

'There was a walkway that ran over the top of the belts, and there was an official up there all the time, watching what was happening. They were called "keekers", the officials who ran the surface. They wore a dark uniform and a peaked cap. If you weren't working properly, or if a belt stopped, and you didn't get to work quickly enough when it started, they'd shout down at you to get moving.'

It was always said that the keekers (from an old Northumbrian word meaning to peep) had had shares in the old coal company. But after nationalisation they were kept on. The head keeker, Mr Aylesbury, was known as the Duck, because he had the name of a duck and he looked like a duck, waddling around the pit yard, his great belly before him, his cap skew-whiff on his head. One day, his son, then aged about sixteen, was walking through the village, when he passed a group of lads about his own age, who worked at the pit. 'Why, it's the Duck's son!' said one. Then they gave him a good hiding – just because of who his father was.

'You got to know all the different characters on the belts. There was Archie Legget, with his teeth. If he'd had one white one, he'd have had a billiard set. And there was Tex, who thought he was a cowboy. He was always hitching his trousers up as though he was John Wayne. And he was always growling at you: "Yrrrgh! I'll kill yer! I'll fucking kill yer!" Of course he never did kill anyone. He wasn't capable of it. One day they got him to get his prick out. It was the size of your arm. Someone threw a rock at it. They couldn't miss the bloody thing.'

'They were all good workers, mind,' said Jimmy, the treasurer. 'And they were canny lads. Some of these deaf and dumb lads, they were all right. They wouldn't see you get beat.'

'Then there was Durango Kid,' mused Joe.

What did he do?

'Nothing really. He used to have fits. Some of the lads used to provoke him. Just to see him have one.

'There was a feller named Vinnie Rowlands used to work there. He was a pathetic weedy bloke, with a little stringy moustache. He was a child molester. He belonged Hartlepool. He'd go to prison for three months. Then he'd be back at work for a bit, then he'd go back in for another stretch. He used to interfere with little girls. He was a habitual offender. He couldn't help it.

'Nobody talked to him. Nobody ever asked him any questions. You'd go to pick up a lump of rock off the belt and some of it was just duff – it would crumble to powder in your hand – and you'd throw it at this Vinnie Rowlands. You didn't think about it. You just did it.

'We'd bring our tea bottles in every day, and leave them in this rack to keep warm. He'd open his up at bait time, and there'd be cigarette ash and bits of paper floating in it. Every day he brought his tea bottle in, and every day that happened. He never did get a drink of tea.

'There was a feller used to grease the axles in the coal washery, next door to the belts. He used to do it while they were turning. They were supposed to stop the machinery, but he'd been doing it that way for years, and if he'd stopped it every time, the bosses would have been on at him for slowing everything down. This day, the corner of his coat got caught. It started to rip his clothes off him, then it started to rip him apart. Dragged him right up inside. The stairs to that part of the building were all worn away, so they had to lower his body down the outside on a stretcher. They stopped the belts, and we all went out into the yard to look. You could have heard a pin drop. He must have been still alive, because it was cold, and you could see his breath in the air. Then he turned his head and looked at us and said, 'It's funny the things that happen, isn't it?' Then he lost consciousness. He died the next day.

'When I'd been on the belts for two years, they put me up on the Heap. I was all right there. One day, the under-manager said to me, "Tha'll gan down the pit now." I said, "I don't want to gan down now. I'm all right here." I was terrified of losing fingers and hands, and ending up back on the belts for the rest of my life. So I volunteered for National Service. I spent four years in the army. Then I was back here. And down I went.'

13

Putting out Lines

THERE WAS a village in Horden. The area was, as had often been
noted 'rural in name but highly urban in character'. Even today,
its population depleted by nearly a third, Horden gave the impression
of being a small town rather than a village. Two of its three cinemas
were gone. But one was now a huge and palatial bingo hall, and on
the corner opposite was a large video emporium. The people rode
the hoppa buses between the different villages of East Durham with
remarkable ease and freedom, as though to different parts of a single
city. But into the grimy interstices of the larger township of Horden
was crammed a whole semi-rural community. For every playboy or
sluggard who'd no more have thought of going into the surrounding
fields than if he'd lived in the heart of some heaving metropolis, there
was another who was a peasant at heart. Not the pigeon men, who
idolised the 'great-hearted' birds, cosseting them in the palatial and
lovingly constructed crees, but others, who lived in an older, more
brutal, and more honest relation to the beasts of the land. Men and
women whose parents or grandparents had come direct from the land
or from the semi-rural pit villages of mid-Durham, from Yorkshire,
Cornwall or Wales, who combined pit work with the tastes and habits
of the under-peasantry, the poaching classes, and still lived by the
old calendar of moon and wind, who at the end of a shift would slope
off to scheme in their gardens, or off into the fields and denes to
check their snares.

Whole families would go out to dig the huge allotments. And
when the harvest-time came they'd make a 'hog' – burying maybe

a ton and a half of potatoes under the big sheds they had there, to see them through the winter and longer. Onions would be hung up in the roofs to dry. Leeks could be left in the ground and eaten as needed till spring.

Some people kept as many as six pigs on their allotment. If a woman was going to kill a pig, she'd send her children out to get orders for the meat. One child came back with fifteen orders for legs. 'What do you think I'm killing here?' asked the mother. 'A bloody centipede?' But even if they killed five pigs to sell, they'd always keep one for bacon. They'd force salt and saltpetre under the skin with a steel – like you use for sharpening knives – then leave it in the coal-house to sweat through the winter cutting off slices as they needed them.

Jimmy Griffiths, the union treasurer, was this kind of miner. He could trace his family back no further than Seaham, a few miles up the coast, but he looked very Welsh – small, with black curls receding from a ruddy and crinkly smiling face. He liked anything to do with animals. He'd have liked to have been a gamekeeper, but when he took his redundancy from the pit, he eventually went to work for the council – on the bins.

As a child he'd had to go round the streets every morning with a wheelbarrow collecting potato peelings and other vegetable refuse which people kept for him in buckets. Then he'd take it all down to the allotment where he'd boil it up in a huge set-pot, mixing it up with some grain his father had appropriated from the stables at the pit, and feed it to the pigs. He had to do that every morning before he went to school. But he didn't mind doing it. He enjoyed it. Many a time he'd come home to find a pig – a very big one – hanging in the pantry, all cleaned and gutted. The blood was saved to make black pudding, while the bladder was as close as many lads in Horden ever came to owning a football. Nothing was wasted in those days.

Jimmy sometimes went rabbiting with a bloke from Blackhall called Arnold Stoddart, who had been married to my father's cousin Betty. 'He's a character, him,' said Jimmy. 'Him and his brother Tom, they're both quaer fellers. They're dog mad. Whippets, lurchers. Pigeons. Any kind of animals. He had a collection of wild birds down his garden. He had all the aviaries white-washed, branches dug in for them to perch on. Then they brought the Act in – made it illegal – and he had to let them go. I bought two ferrets off him. They were beauties. Fat. Their coats were shining. You couldn't get your hands round them!

'You find the burrow, see. And you put your nets over the holes. Then you put your ferret in, and you can hear them thumping about under the ground. Then the rabbits come rushing out the holes, and they get caught in the net.

'Some people sell them to the dog men, for the whippet races, but not me. My father kept them for the dog men when I was a bairn, and I saw too much of it. They scream, the rabbits. They cry like children when they're cornered.

'I used to go with Arnold Stoddart to Lord Lambton's estate near Sedgefield. The gamekeeper's a friend of his. Reckons it's helping him.

'Why, some of these burrows only have four or five holes. Others have twenty. You try to cover as many as you can. But they always have a bolt hole, that they cover with grass. This day, every time we put the ferret in, the rabbit gets out the bolt hole, scarpers. Arnold says to us, "Why, tha's a useless cunt, isn't tha?" I says, "Aa'm a useless cunt? What about tha? What did tha dee to stop it?" He agreed with me, and we carried on. By the end of the day we'd got about twenty rabbits. He says, "Aa got a few goals today, didn't aa?" And he had. When he see the rabbit in the net, he dives on top of it. Most people just walk over and take it out. But not Arnold. He doesn't want to see it get away. And he skins them with the head on. Me, I cut the head off before I skin them. But him, he skins the whole thing in one go.

'Another time we were out ferreting, the gamekeeper comes over to see how we were getting on. It was nearly midday, and we'd only got four. He says, "You'll be here all day at that rate. Here's a gun. Shoot the fuckers as they come out!"

'His brother Tom, as I say, he's a character 'n arl. He was a bus conductor when he came out the pit. Except he never used to take any money. He'd just say, "Sit down there, lad. You're all right." Or he'd keep the fares. This old woman gets on, he says, "I'll need a cup o' tea when we get to Hartlepool. Just give us the money for that." How he got caught, was a kid got on when there was another conductor. He says, "What yer chargin' us for? That other bloke never does!" End of his career, like.

'Mind, they dinnut like each other, Tom and Arnold. I was sitting outside a pub in Castle Eden with Arnold, this day, and Tom comes up says how about they try breeding their animals. Arnold says, "Aa wouldn't let your dog kiss my dog, let alone fuck it!"'

You couldn't say the Hudsons were a close-knit family. In Horden, you still heard children talking about our so-and-so or our so-and-so, referring not to their siblings or even their cousins, but to their second or even third cousins. The Hudsons however didn't even know who their second and third cousins were. My father had hardly had anything to do with his paternal cousins, even when they were living only a few hundred yards away. He had uncles he hardly knew.

Uncle Hal was probably the one he knew best. He and Charlie were still at home when my father was living at Grandma Hudson's as a small boy. A couple of boisterous pit adolescents, taking their meals black, knocking everything over as they relived football matches at the scrubbed dining table. Charlie was the liveliest; slender, happy go lucky, a practical joker. Fleet of foot, he ran races for money, and to everyone's surprise, including his own, he once won a very important one. (Most people weren't too pleased either, as they all had their money on the other bloke.) He disappeared to the south, almost as soon as he got married, becoming a railway clerk in Dunstable, and dying of a heart attack in his late thirties.

Hal was of a quieter more 'philosophical' disposition, lapsing later in life into an apparently placid, but faintly bemused quietude. One saw him in photographs, usually on the edge of the group, his pleasant, rather nordic features apparently contented, but often with a faint knitting around the brows. Even when photographed on his own, he seemed abstracted, absorbed in some remote but intense internal speculation, though the cause and subject of this 'philosophy' remained a mystery.

He had lived with his wife Ria in the so-called scheme houses, a development of relatively superior houses on the Top Road, beyond 'the cottages', built by the colliery company for the miners to buy at a small weekly deduction from their pay note. My father had often visited them there, and they were always very nice to him. Just before the war, Hal had gone to work in a factory in Rugby (the factories of the Midlands being, along with the army, the most common route out of Horden in those days). He had died some time in the Fifties, without, as far as I could gather, anything worth remarking on ever having happened to him. But then, in a factory you could stand by the same machine for twenty, thirty or forty years, and Hal probably had.

About the next uncle, Jack, however, my father could tell me nothing. He and his family had, I had learnt from other sources, lived in Old Fifth Street, by the gates of the Welfare Ground, but my father could not recall ever visiting them. He could not remember the name of Jack's wife, and scarcely those of his children. But of the reason for this mysterious separateness, he had no clue. It did not appear to have even occurred to him to question it.

Jack was, according to Bob Naisbett, a 'baggage man', an all purpose trainer and manager for Horden Football Club. An 'all rounder', he also taught the young lads to box. In his spare time, he was caretaker of Saporetti's billiard hall that belonged to one of the two Italian families who owned ice-cream parlours in Horden. He used to take his son Ray down there on a Sunday, and when they'd taken the cloths off the tables, the father would give the son a game. He had a terrible temper. In 1940, his spine was fractured in a rock fall at the pit, and his entire torso had to be set in plaster. One day at the billiard hall, one of the lads on an end table said something he didn't like. Within seconds Jack, his body stiff with the plaster, had him on the floor. They reckon he'd have killed the lad if they hadn't got him off.

After his accident, Jack was put on light work, loco driving at the pit. But he never worked a full week. Unable to bend, even to do up his shoes, he was soon pronounced unfit for work of any kind. He died four years after the accident, aged forty-five, of a heart attack, which his family naturally believed was connected with the strain imposed by the accident. Although his son was already apprenticed at the pit as a blacksmith, he and his mother were turfed out of their colliery house and went to live in a small bungalow near the road towards the beach.

But for all his fieriness, Jack, like Hal and Charlie, was not someone who expected a great deal from life. To get through it with reasonable equanimity, to work and allow one's family to exist while having sufficient time for a few private and unremarked satisfactions, was as much as they felt they could reasonably expect. It was only Percy who had spoken up, who had attempted to exert himself, to impose himself in his small way on the world. But compared to Bob, the eldest of the brothers, even Hal seemed part of life's loquacious mainstream. For Bob was by far the quietest and most fugitive of the five.

One might have thought that having a grandfather who was on the Federation Board, who was chairman of the Parish Council, would have given one certain claims on the place. But in fact the names it was good to drop, that had cachet in Horden, were not necessarily those who had achieved the highest official positions, or counted among its more 'deserving' elements, but those who had remained physically closest to the nexus of the Big Club and the

Miners' Hall, the numbered streets around them, and of course
to the pit, which both literally and metaphorically was beneath
and behind everything. People who had through the unarguable
testament of the collective memory, lived and endured 'Horden' for
better or for worse. And Bob's family were, perhaps through their
very lack of aspiration, the ones who had remained closest to that
world.

They were known as the Seventh Street Hudsons, and they
lived in Middle Seventh Street, opposite the shop that now stood
boarded-up at the back of the Miners' Hall. From their front door,
you could look straight up South Terrace, past the edge of the Welfare
Ground, to the Top Road. Bob himself was, people said, often to be
seen standing in this doorway, gauntly impassive – a fair frame, but
not much meat on him – and always slightly hunched, for he had,
as they said, 'a terrible chest'.

Bob's family were, in the rather cloudy picture I'd always held
of Horden, figures of vague misfortune. I'd always been aware that
there was a part of the family whose house my father had dreaded
visiting, because of its fusty disorder and the sickly smell of ill health
that hung over it – people whose haplessly dingy existence was presented in contrast to the sparkling pristine environment created by his
own mother. Once, when he was describing the smell of the place,
a mixture of old cooking smells lingering in unwashed curtains and
ingrained faeces, a friend of the family of about my father's age had
commented that it was 'because of things like that that you became
a socialist'. But my father just looked away, an uncharacteristic
expression of doubt on his face. There was an element in him
that saw Bob and his wife as not entirely unculpable in their own
situation.

A relative had told me that when you visited Bob's house,
the first thing you saw was coats and clothes flung about the
place, a pot of stale tea standing on the table amid a debris of
dishes and half-eaten meals. To my father, there was something
rather frightening about Bob's wife, always sitting in her corner,
her long black hair hanging lankly over her face – something
witchlike in the dazed smile as she roused herself to greet him. A
small child ran bare-arsed and unattended through the chaos. To
my father's childhood mind there was something almost tropically
unwholesome about this airless disorder. Catching sight of a bottle
of Daddy's Sauce among the jumble on the table, he wondered if
it had the same sickly fetid smell as the rest of the room, and he
was always relieved when, his errand done, he could run from the

place, back to his own home, which, I was given to understand, was always kept in a condition of almost antiseptic brightness. His mother, however, told him to be kind to his aunt, as she had once been 'very attractive and well dressed'.

In the past, when I'd introduced girlfriends to my father, I was always rather shocked that his first consideration was not were they intelligent, entertaining, kind, or even sane, but were they 'attractive' – by which he meant did they dress smartly, in a way that suggested cleanliness and order in their personal habits. As though the former could not be achieved without the latter. At first I was disgusted by the primitive chauvinism of this means of assessment. But as I looked into the past of Horden, into the society from which he'd come, I realised that in that world tidiness was a factor in basic physical survival. Living in overcrowded conditions with inadequate sanitary facilities it was impossible to be clean without being tidy, and in unclean conditions children and even adults stood less chance of surviving. So, when you looked at a woman, the first thing you asked yourself was, would she be clean, would she be tidy in her personal habits – or would she bring you down from the position of order the women of your family had worked so hard to achieve? A woman who was not tidy did the unforgivable, she brought the pity of the community on herself and those around her.

Bob was said to suffer from pneumoconiosis, but whether he was ever formally invalided from the pit with compensation, I never found out, for Bob had worked only intermittently for as long as most people could remember. One gathered from people's tone, that this absenteeism was temperamental, even pathological, in origin, but no one blamed him for this behaviour that might have seemed neglectful in others. Something had happened to Bob, something had shattered in him, and the implication was that this had happened at the pit.

When my father was playing in the Dene, he would sometimes catch sight of Uncle Bob, in his cloth cap and his muffler, with his skinny whippet, a lone figure rapt in his own activity, uninviting of interest or comment – before he slipped away among the trees. Or, from the beach, he'd see Bob's blank silhouette against the sky, simply wandering on the cliff tops. That was where Bob was happiest – alone – taking freely from whatever grew along the hedgerows or darted in the undergrowth. He spoke, if at all, in short, jerky sentences, or preferably monosyllables. At family functions he seemed happy to sit saying nothing, staring into space for hours on end. Sometimes he'd turn up at Percy's house, his ragged jacket wriggling, to Jenny's discomfiture, with a pink-eyed albino ferret, and if times weren't too hard at Oak Terrace, he'd be happy to accept a tanner for a pint.

The squalor of his home life was explained by the fact that his wife suffered from 'sleepy sickness', now known as Parkinson's disease; though according to Nan, it was in fact St Vitus's Dance, and it had only affected her quite late in life. She had, apparently, gone off for two or three months with another man. It had been left to Grandma Hudson to look after the children. The house had been in a terrible state, and Grandma had made her three daughters scrub it out from top to bottom.

There had been five children. Jack, who was a bit older than my father, George, who was the same age, Betty who was a year or two younger, and two other boys. My father had little to do with them, as they rarely visited their grandparents. In later life, Mollie had become reacquainted with Betty after coming across her serving in a baker's in Blackhall. She was by all accounts a very pleasant woman, but she had died a couple of years ago, shortly before Mollie's death. The only other one I had been able to find out about was the second son, George, who according to Nan was still alive, living somewhere in Peterlee. She had no idea where, and he had, she believed, been suffering badly from depression.

'Geordie Hudson?' said Norman Hawkins. 'He had a terrible stammer, Geordie Hudson. He looked just like you, mind. If you had a terrible stammer, I'd swear Geordie Hudson was sitting here now. But I've not seen him for thirty years.'

One evening I mentioned the Seventh Street Hudsons in the Big Club.

'Is it them you're related to?' asked Joe Summers. 'You look just like them, mind. They were all dark.'

'I can just remember the father,' said Micky Douglas. 'A big raw-faced bloke.'

'Aye,' said Joe. 'He had one of those faces they used to get with pneumoconiosis or chronic bronchitis – the way my father looked at that age – all hollow, their cheeks sunken ... I can picture Old Hudson sitting on the doorstep in Seventh Street, aged about sixty, sixty-five, with nay teeth in. Maybe a bit of a tash on his upper lip.'

But what about George Hudson?

'Geordie Hudson,' said Micky. 'I knew naybody better. But it depends which one you mean. There were three or four of them, and they were all called Geordie. The taller one was very quiet. I didn't really know him. He was a bit older than us, see. But the youngest one, I knew him well. Mind, you had to be a bit careful with him. I mean, I knew him, I drank with him. I never had any problem with him. But he could be a bit wild if you know what I mean.'

'You'd be standing drinking with him,' said Joe. 'Everyone friendly, like. Then you'd say something, and he'd just turn. You'd see it in his eyes. In them days, if people wanted to fight, they'd go outside and take their coats off. But this young one, if you said owt he didn't like he'd just go for you. He was *hard*. You couldn't fight him, because you couldn't hurt him. It was like he was made of metal.'

This must have been the little boy who had run round the house bare-arsed and unattended when my father had visited sixty years before. So that was how such people ended up.

'Him and this other lad both went to head the ball at a football match,' said Micky. 'Their heads cracked together, and the other lad got the whole of the side of his face smashed. It was just an accident, like. But people reckoned it said something about him.'

'I got his place in the football team,' said Joe, 'because he was never there. I ended up getting the prize he should have had. But he never went to school at all.'

'His first wife died,' said Ted. 'He got married again, and he seemed to calm down a bit after that. He died about two years ago. He'd been out on the beer one afternoon. He came home, fell down the stairs and broke his neck.'

'Bobby, that was his name,' said Jimmy. 'Bobby Hudson.'

'Aye, that's right,' said Joe. 'The older one was Geordie, the big one. The younger one had a bit of a stammer. But he was the one with the real stammer. People respected him. He never did anything. He was very quiet. But nobody messed with him, because you were never quite sure.'

They were oddly impressed by this connection, the union men. I had come to Horden claiming a link to its worthies and grandees, and I turned out to be related to these faintly notorious people, who, not quite desirable, even by the standards of the village, were none the less unarguably part of Horden's grimy solidarity. Whether you liked them or not, these people had been there beside them at the pit. They were *of* Horden, a hundred per cent. You couldn't take that away from them.

But what did these people have to do with me? How could I

be related to them, these semi-psychotic hard men, these problem people? Yet I was related to them – closely related.

'There was a sister an' all,' said Micky. 'Betty. She was a big woman. Tall. She must have been at least six feet.'

Another of those statuesque Hudson women, I thought. Grandma Hudson, Nan, Hazel, they were all big women.

'Aye, she was smart she was,' said Joe. 'Good looking. She was quite different from the rest of them.'

She'd married this great big bear of a bloke with a birthmark down one side of his face. Nobody could understand what she was doing with him. Eventually however, they'd divorced, and she'd married Arnold Stoddart from Blackhall.

'You ought to gan and talk to him,' said Jimmy. 'He's a quaer feller, mind!'

From Horden, the Coast Road dipped at the neck of Castle Eden Dene. Suddenly the curtain of trees parted at the right to afford a spectacular view down into the bowl of the Dene, the great bluff where the Blunts Gill divided from the main body of the Dene, rearing up ahead, the branches of the bare trees all lilac and silver, wreathed in a gossamer web of mist. Then the trees closed in and the road rose steeply towards Blackhall. At the top of the bank, along a cobbled lane, was the bungalow where Arnold Stoddart lived.

He stood in the kitchen window, a stocky, agile man in a red plaid shirt, a smile of immemorial knowing playing across his broad and ruddy features. He was in his mid-sixties, but could have been ten years younger. Eyes of a cool blue appraised me from beneath his domed forehead. He was talking to me, but making no attempt to raise his voice. He narrowed his eyes, lifting his head in a way that appeared to be beckoning me. But I was deterred from proceeding by the growling and the furious scratching coming from one of the wooden constructions in the blackened yard. Then Arnold appeared in the doorway. 'It's all right,' he said. 'He can't get out.'

The kitchen looked as though nothing had been changed since the 1950s. But it was very clean and bright. On the windowsills were cages with small birds in them.

'Call them mules,' said Arnold. 'They're a cross between a linnet and a canary. You keep them for the singing, see. I used to catch fifty goldfinches a day. I'd pick the two or three best, give maybe another two or three to me mates, and let the rest go.' He looked me all the time full in the face, his blue eyes full of light. 'I'd catch bullfinches, greenfinches, all types o' warblers. I kept them down the garden in special aviaries. I had branches dug in – the lot! I never sold them. Oh, no. I was an expert, see. I used to judge at shows. Till they brought the Act in . . . 1954. I had to give it all up then. The only birds I sell now are the mules.' He nodded towards the windowsill.

He sat back in his easy chair by the window. 'If Betty'd been alive I'd have taken you down the garden. It was a massive garden that. Oh, aye.' He exhaled through the side of his mouth to emphasise the vastness of the place. Then he resumed his intimate knowing smile. 'I've seen me go down there at four o'clock in the morning, and Betty hasn't seen me till nine o'clock at night. I used to really enjoy meself down there. I had five or six goats. I sold the milk. Oh, aye. There's many a child in Blackhall's been reared on goat's milk. I used to get thirteen pints of milk a time from these goats. I was doing all right. I used the money to buy corn for the hens. Then I'd sell the eggs, or give them away. I had ducks, Chinese pheasants, all sorts down there. But since Betty died, I haven't had the heart for it.' He looked momentarily crestfallen. 'The whole place has gone to rack and ruin. But there's no point setting a garden if you're on your own, is there?'

He had a way of phrasing his most significant statements as questions, that flattered one, implying access to the same fund of arcane knowledge that lay behind his blue-eyed smile. A knowledge of the inherent pathos of life – a pathos based, for the purposes of this conversation, on Betty's departure and the subsequent depletion of his existence.

I'd never met Betty, and knew virtually nothing about her – and he knew that. But he addressed me – her relative – as though, like a mystic familiar, I'd been privy to their life and experience, their happiness together. I thought it was rather nice of him.

'Ferrets!' he said, happily. 'That's how I met Betty. I went to buy a couple off Bob, and she answered the door. I thought, I wouldn't mind going out with her for the evening . . . Never thought I'd end up marrying her . . . Good-looking woman, mind!' He blew his lips out, his eyes narrowing for emphasis. 'Best-looking woman I ever went out with.' He leapt to his feet and began rummaging in a drawer. Then he handed me a photograph of him and Betty sitting side by side. Arnold with a full head of hair, in a narrow-lapelled, Sixties jacket and tie, Betty, a coolly pretty woman, each with an infant on their knee, smiling straight at the camera. They looked radiantly happy. Looking at this photograph and the spartan order of Arnold's kitchen, which he was at pains to stress was exactly as Betty had left it, I wondered how this competent, well-adjusted woman had emerged from the squalor and emotional chaos of Middle Seventh Street.

'D'you want a cup of tea?' asked Arnold, suddenly restless. He began busying himself at the sideboard. Then he stood above me, his forearms resting on the sideboard as I drank, but he seemed to find it difficult to keep still. Did I need a saucer with it? Did I want a biscuit? Take a few. You'll need a plate. Eat them all up, mind. He leant back against the sideboard, but the itchy restlessness overcame him again. He took a duster and began polishing the surfaces. You had to keep a place decent, didn't you?

I wondered if he'd been at the pit.

'Puttin'! Gettin' them tubs round with yer shoulder. Down in the Harvey Seam, with the water pourin' onter yer! Turrible! Mind, I was out here, then.' He held his hand several inches from where his biceps now were. 'Oh, aye,' he grimaced. 'I've declined turrible!'

But what about Bob? What could he remember about Bob?

'Bob? Oh, canny bloke, Bob.'

But what was he like?

What was he like? He seemed troubled by the question. Then the blue light came back into his eyes. 'Blackberrying. He loved blackberrying. Blackberrying and gannin' out with the ferret! That's what Bob was like!'

How about Bobby, Betty's youngest brother, hadn't he been a bit wild?

'Bobby? Oh, he wouldn't back down from anyone, Bobby. Never. Mind, it was horrible the way he died. I'll tell you how it happened. You're not squirmish, are yer? The day he was made redundant at the pit, he went out for a drink with some of the lads. When he got home, he fell down the stairs and choked to death on his own vomit. I had to identify the body. His brothers, wouldn't do it. They couldn't take it. But it doesn't bother me, things like that.' His blue eyes were now grave with a butcher's humility.

Was his brother George still alive?

'Oh, aye. Lives up Peterlee.' The gleam came back into his eyes. 'He's another one's never married.'

'Oh, I think he's died, Geordie Hudson,' most people said. But they meant Bobby, the younger brother. George was alive. I had been sure of it. He was in Peterlee. Somewhere up there in the great tangle of estates. But where?

But now that I had the address I had been seeking since before

Christmas, I felt considerably less enthusiastic about rushing to see him. Nan had said that he had suffered from depression. The men at the union had implied that like his younger brother he could be unpredictable. Why had he never married? And to be living alone, in a bedsit, crammed in with one's possessions, in *Peterlee* of all places. To call on him unawares would place him at a disadvantage. To catch him at his most vulnerable was in itself a kind of accusation. It might cause him considerable annoyance. What kind of state would the room be in? And Norman Hawkins had said he had a terrible stammer. It hardly boded well for a pleasant and easy conversation. I imagined a great bear of a man, hemmed in by invisible demons, frustrated by the handicap of his stammer, sitting alone for weeks on end, nursing the soreness at the core of his being.

Finally, one mid-March afternoon, which promised daylight for some hours to come, I found myself in Peterlee with no really good reason why I shouldn't head up to where George lived.

At the Catholic church, I turned left into an area of box-like houses, the clusters of dwellings set well back from the road in intersecting rows. Most had had their original flat roofs pitched and had been clad with what looked like corrugated plastic. Slotted in here and there along the rows were houses that the occupants had bought but could not afford to renovate, their paint peeling, their fancy yellow Sixties' brickwork encrusted with grime and coal dust. I asked a man the way, and he led me into an estate of black brick and white wood, its flat roofs as yet untouched by the process of refurbishment. The rows ran at right angles to each other into a labyrinth of lanes that retained from the colliery villages the habit of back yards, dotted among which were two or three blocks of three or four storeys each. I wondered if it was in one of these that George lived, but the young man pointed me off along a lane between what might have been the fronts or backs of houses.

In Peterlee it was not always easy to tell which were the good and bad areas. A place might seem tranquil enough, but it might just be that people were too frightened to go out. But I sensed from the closed in, put-upon expressions of the few people I passed – the colourless tight-lipped tension of the young couple leaving the house with their pram, that this was not one of the nicer parts. Why, with all the green space in and around Peterlee, was it necessary to coop people into this gardenless warren of lanes?

It was hard to see where one 'close' ended and another began. Eventually I found the rear end of the one in which George lived: a long two-storey block, the lower portion obscured by once white, ranch-style fencing. At the side a staircase led up to numbers 40–44. And here were 46 and 47 on the ground floor. There could be no avoiding it, George was somewhere in this block. But where? The fence of the dwelling on the corner had barbed-wire hanging over it and was fortified with bits of hardboard nailed haphazardly but forcefully to the inside. Peering over the gate I noticed the number, carelessly covered when the frame was last painted. 45. The earth of the tiny garden was freshly dug, but completely bare except for a banana skin that someone had evidently lobbed over the fence. I lingered gingerly by the gate, sure that if I opened it a ferocious dog would materialise from nowhere. Then looking up I saw a blonde woman watching me from an upstairs window. She opened it.

'Does Mr Hudson live here?' I asked.

'*George?*' she said, her face completely blank, but just the faintest tinge of irony in her voice.

'Aye. Does he have a dog?'

'No.'

I opened the gate and rapped on the door. A pale visage appeared momentarily, quite high behind the net curtains. Then the door opened. He was tall and spare, pale, gaunt – but not alarmingly so – with grey hair swept back from a broad forehead. His nose curved hawklike above a thin mouth. Joe Summers had said that Bob, George's father, had had the sucked-in features of a pneumoconiosis sufferer. George himself, however, had these same features. He looked at me, with no expression whatever.

'I'm Mark Hudson,' I said. 'I think I'm related to you.'

'Howay in, Mark,' he said in a light and friendly tone.

He was dressed in colourless clothes of no particular style. The room was tidy, but apart from a few pieces of nondescript furniture, completely bare. It was not a bedsitter. A kitchen and bathroom led off the tiny entrance hall, and from where I sat I could see through into the sleeping area, where George's coat was draped neatly over the bed. Being hemmed in by his possessions was not a problem for George, as he hardly appeared to have any.

At first he thought I was some relative of one of his sisters-in-law, then he realised the connection. 'I haven't seen yer d-d-dad for years. I must be the same age as him, but I never saw much of him. I was only interested in the pit, drinking, football and maybe the odd bit of poaching. And I don't suppose your dad would be too bothered by any of that.' He lifted his chin with amusement.

He had a melodious voice, with a kind of laugh in it, and only a very slight stammer. He sat in his easy chair – the chair he must have sat in for much of the time – his watch hanging from a nail on the wall – at ease, but at the same time somehow awkward, as though he would have been too long and too angular for any chair. When he stood up, he was like a great stork. Not that he was stooped; but it was as though there was too much of his long angularity ever to be really straight; though I realised later, when I stood up at the end of our meeting, that I was actually taller than him.

He had been unaware of Mollie's death, and winced momentarily at the injustice of it. 'I was saying to my mate the other day,' he said, referring to the large number of people he knew that had recently died, 'that it's coming to be a-a hepidemic.' He smiled in triumph at the insight. Death was only one of many aspects of life of which he had not himself partaken.

For pleasant, indeed engaging as his manner was, I felt it was tangential, indeed extraneous to what he really was. Indeed the care with which he spoke was the care of someone speaking a language that is not their own; as though the things that could be expressed through that language could never be central to him. But what was central to him? I learned that he had spent fifteen or twenty years at the pit, and then got a job at a factory in Coventry, because his elder brother Jack was living down there. That appeared to have been the only reason. It was as though his life was nothing to him, as though he existed in his essence beyond such concerns. And this room, in which he'd lived for years – from its appearance, he might have moved in last week. He didn't seem tied to it in any way.

But what his real life was, beyond all this, I did not at that moment have the courage to try to imagine. For although his features were not entirely devoid of the cares of seventy years, his movements were those of a seventeen year old. It was not just that it was impossible to imagine he was the same age as my father, he did not seem to be of any age.

'I was sitting in The Comrades,' he said, 'when someone pointed to a young girl, about twenty-three, and said that's your cousin – Joyce Spark. I couldn't believe it. It didn't seem right that a girl that age should be my cousin.' He shook his head and smiled at the incongruity of it. 'Didn't she have a brother?'

'Jim Spark?'

'That's it. He looked a bit like you. Thick, dark, wavy hair. I was talking to your grandfather at the funeral, and he was saying that Jim was looking for a job.' He's lost it now, I thought. He doesn't mean my grandfather. My grandfather had been dead twenty-five years. 'I was working at the steel works in Hartlepool. I said I could get him set on there. Your grandfather was saying that your dad had been doing some lectures in America. I said, "Oh, well. So long as somebody's doing all right." Didn't your dad do some lectures in America?'

Yes, he had. But the ones my grandfather would have known about were getting on for thirty years ago. 'Which funeral was that?' I asked.

'My mother's funeral.'

He'd been chatting with my grandfather at the funeral ... He'd been sitting in The Comrades when he saw Joyce ... Joyce was now in her mid-fifties. These events had taken place thirty and more years ago. Yet he talked about them as though they had only happened last week.

All the time pop music was rumbling from the radio. Now Elkie Brooks was singing 'We Don't Cry Out Loud.' As our conversation moved circuitously in time, so Radio 2 kept up a suitably random commentary of lesser known hits from the last four decades.

He made me a cup of tea. He said he'd been trying out various herbal teas, and would I like one. This wasn't what I'd been expecting at all. Herbal tea with Geordie Hudson? But then despite all I'd heard about the Seventh Street Hudsons, nobody had ever said they were crude exactly. And there was a refinement, a delicacy even, about Geordie.

He had said that Jim Spark looked a bit like me. All the time I was trying to work out who it was that he reminded me of. Finally I realised. It was me. But what was it about him? Was it his hair? His gauntness? The shape of his head? His overall angularity? Or was it his very gaucheness? Or his aloneness?

The intermittent thudding from upstairs became louder. 'It's all unmarried mothers here,' he said. 'We've got three in this building, and I don't know how many along there. We had a terrible time with this one up here. Banging and swearing and bawling and shouting at all hours of the day and night. She's got a new man in there now, so things have quietened down a bit.

'But we've still got all these kids hanging about out here. I was talking to a bloke over the way, and he said, "It would be all right round here if it wasn't for these bloody *kids*!"' His eyes suddenly flickered black and his teeth clenched. I felt momentarily alarmed, for he seemed for a second incapable of gauging the appropriateness of the intensity of his response in my presence – though he was not for that moment even aware of my presence at all. I suddenly felt much less at ease sitting there with this man I did not know.

'They've got six football pitches and a cricket pitch within walking distance. They've got Castle Eden Dene just up the bank. And all they want to do is hang around out here, or over the road – kicking a football against the garage doors. But you can't say anything to them. The woman up here had a window put out. Next door had a window put in. They did one of mine last year, and this one's been cracked, see? There was two empty houses down the street that have been completely burnt out. That's why I've got the wire. I keep saying to people, "I must be the only person in Peterlee with a fence like a-a First World War barricade."' And he smiled again.

What about the poaching? I asked him later.

'All this land here belonged to Colonel Burdon. From the top of the bank down to Horden, it was all open fields, right through here. He used to organise shooting parties. I used to hide in the bushes with my dad, at the back of where the leisure centre is now, and watch them. You had to be careful, mind. They didn't care where they shot.

'It was mostly rabbiting with nets and snares. My dad would set his snares in the afternoon. He'd take me in the Big Club for a drink. Then when the Club closed, we'd go out and see what was in them.

'There were about six farms round here. If we were going past the gates we might snaffle a hen. It was the farmer's fault if he was too miserable to keep his crees in order. If we were off for the day and we were passing Matty Lamb's farm we'd whistle and take his sheepdog. He loved to come with us. He much preferred our company to the farmer's, because he knew he'd get the attention from us. And he knew exactly where the rabbits were. You'd put him in front of a hole, and if there was nothing there, he'd just turn away. But if there was a rabbit there he'd stand stock still, his tail just wagging from side to side.' He moved his finger like a metronome. 'Then you'd send the ferret in.

'You'd keep some of the rabbits and sell the others to the dog men. When they were dead, they'd give them back to you, and you'd eat them. So you had it all ways. Then sometimes we'd go out with the gun after pheasants.

'When the tide was out, my dad would put lines out from the split rock. You'd put some soft-bellied crabs on the hooks, and wait to see what was on them when the tide went out again. Some people would come home and then get back down just in time for the tide. But we'd always wait down there.

'Crimdon was where I liked to be in those days. That was when Crimdon was good. Before they started putting up signs saying you couldn't do this and you couldn't do that. Everyone was just camping there. The sand was white, and the water was the clearest I've ever seen. You'd stand with the water up to your chest, and you could see your feet perfectly clearly. We'd catch crabs. Coax them out of the rock pools, and sell them to the other holidaymakers for three and a tanner each. That was a lot of money in those days. Some of them didn't know what to do with them. So they'd give them back to us, and we'd clean them and boil them for them.

'We'd live like that for weeks, just fishing and hunting and swimming. At night, no one slept. Everyone would sit up round their fires singing songs into the small hours. It was like that for two years after the war. Perfect. Then the council took it over, and they put up signs saying no spitting, no swearing. We put our tents up on the beach to get away from it. But they said you couldn't do that. They ruined it.'

When I left George it was still light. He said he was glad, as he couldn't stand the long, dark nights. The sky was the thick lilac blue you get in the evenings of early spring. Overhead, huge clouds lay inert over the sky like immense silver fish. The last light of the waning sun glittered on the glass and steel and plastic of Peterlee town centre. Near the white illuminated cross of the Peter Lee Memorial Methodist Church, I could make out the broad box-like outline of the Leisure Centre. I imagined Geordie and his father nestling in the bushes behind where that now was, on the edge of the Dene, watching the shooting parties of the coal owners, cowering as the nobs blasted at anything that moved. And I suddenly saw the scene before me as it would have been fifty or sixty years ago. The open fields sweeping down from the bank that led down to Horden, down into the shallow, saucer-shaped valley, in which Peterlee now lay, towards Shotton in the west. And for the first time, I saw that place with its untidy sprawl of estates as a coherent geographical entity. And here was Geordie, living in the middle of that self-same piece of land, only a hundred yards or so from the Dene where he'd set snares as a boy, a mile or two from the beach where he learned from his father the intimacy of the moon and tides, in a condition of semi-urban alienation from . . . everything.

What did a man like that care about time or property? The rooms where he lived meant nothing to him. They hardly existed. He should have been out there in the woods and the fields still –

at one with the rain and the sun and the bark and the leaves. To his neighbours now he was 'George'. A bit odd, but all right. He should have been Old So-and-so, living in a hut in the woods and living from their fruits.

But perhaps, I reflected, that was not such a good idea.

The full moon rode out from behind one of the clouds, charring its silver edges, and giving a sudden nocturnal aspect to the scene ahead. Behind me, the last rays of the sun continued to retreat slowly.

I called in at Safeway to do some shopping, and when I came out it was fully night. As I reached the top of the bank down to Horden, I could see the clouds over Blackhall lit orange by the glare of the village. To the east I could see the same clouds, now clear of the village, illuminated from above with the blue ethereal glow of the moon. And as the bank pitched I could see the North Sea, a great sheet of glittering whiteness, broken only by the black outlines of the ships.

14

A Consequential Closure

SOMETIMES, as Joe Summers came into the union meeting, he'd open his briefcase, and without even bothering to look in my direction, hurl a book at me. 'I'll want that back, mind.' He had a vast archive in his garage relating to the union in Horden. Stuff no one else was bothered with. But he hung on to it, because there was 'history there'.

His maternal grandfather had been a sawyer at Guisborough in North Yorkshire, but times were hard on the land, so he left his family in a barn and went off in search of work. The barn didn't have a proper roof, and Joe's aunt had told him that at night they'd look up and see the moon. After six months the father returned, having got a job at Wearmouth colliery. On the other side, his family were Irish. His paternal grandmother, a huge woman, was the knockerupper – who went around making sure the men were out of bed for their respective shifts – at Fencehouses in mid-Durham. It was really a man's job, but Grandma Summers was more than up to it. One night, everyone was in a panic, because a murderer was on the loose. Getting up in the night to answer a call of nature, Grandma found him hiding in her netty. She sharp sorted him out.

Joe himself was from Fourth Street, but he had built his house in Peterlee, in Deneside, a row of architect-designed residences overlooking the Dene, the first – and some said, still the only – posh estate in Peterlee. In the demonology of East Durham, the inhabitants of Deneside were the kind of people who joined the golf club and invited each other to dinner parties.

'There was this old feller. He was a Salvationist, and he was always very pleasant to everyone. He was a back-bye man, maintaining the roadways – on light work, just waiting to retire. Every day, at the end of the shift, when he was waiting for the cage to take them up, he would always open the gate, and look up to see if the cage was coming.

'It was one Christmas Eve. We were on an overtime ban, leading up to the 1974 strike. There was a shortage of men to operate the cages, so they'd authorised the fitters to operate them, as and when was necessary. Anyway, they found this old feller, lying at the bottom landing, his top half on the ground out of the shaft, with the cage on top of him. Half his head was missing. We found bits of him all the way up the shaft. No one could work out how he managed to be in that position.

'When we went for compensation, management said he had had an "unfortunate habit" of looking up for the cage. It was true, he did have that habit. But these old people, they'd been doing these things for years. You couldn't stop them. It was part of their routine that kept them going.

'But if that had happened in this instance, how did he come to be in that position? I reckon he must have been getting into the cage. It was called from above by the fitters, and he was dragged through the gap, right up to the top of the shaft and then back down again.

'We'd been asking for a system, where if the gate was opened, a red light would come on at bank and they'd stop the cage. Shortly after this happened, they did bring that system in. But it was too late for this feller.

'We got a thousand pounds for the widder. The compensation secretary says to us, "She's ower the moon." I said, "*Ower the moon!*"' He snorted contemptuously. 'The cart was due to stop at his house with his free coal that day. But management stopped it – the very day he died. There was hell on.

'You always got accidents just before Christmas. In the piecework days, people were desperate to get money for Christmas, so they took risks with safety. Later on they just became slapdash, because they wanted to stop. But I always had to tell the widders, see. For some reason the Lodge Chairman always had to tell the widder. That was the worst thing about it.'

February 14th. Friday night in the Mechanics' Social Club, upstairs in the Miners' Hall, and conversation was peripheral to the tension of the domino tables, the groans and the staccato guffaws that punctuated the snap of plastic on Formica. Exchanges were snatched in the brief pauses as men took their turns in the evening-long drive. Frankie Skinner, the caretaker, stood over the proceedings, organising the playing order. Meanwhile, at the end of the table nearest the bar, Mickey Hutchings was telling me repeatedly, as he had done on several occasions, about a man in Horden who had served in the Royal Marines, compiled a vast dossier on the Second World War, and could maybe give me some hints on the publishing business. Mickey, was a short, wiry man of perhaps sixty, whose complexion became alarmingly florid when in drink. His mouth would start to expand sideways, making it difficult for him to get his words out – though he had, of course, no shortage of energy for the purpose – while his neck seemed to become shorter and stiffer, as though it were trying to retract his head through the slightly too small hole of his Aran sweater. And all the time his face was becoming redder and redder. So while I found his endlessly repetitive monologue mildly tedious, I paid great attention, from a superstitious fear that if I did not, his head might explode. Suddenly, however, I found no difficulty in concentrating.

'It's St Valentine's Day. Bill Hodges' birthday. That's how he got his name, yi knar, William Valentine Hodges!'

The idea of the formidably dour former chairman of the Horden Lodge having such a whimsically romantic middle name appealed to me greatly. Mickey drew his head back in a samurai-like grimace.

'He's a sarcastic bugger him. If you see him in the street he just ignores you. So naybody talks to him. He walks through the village and naybody talks to him. He gans in the Deputies' Club, naybody talks to him.'

But though he might have alienated a good part of Horden society, old Valentine Hodges still exerted a powerful hold over the imaginations of many in the village. Whenever you got men together who'd been connected with Horden Miners' Lodge, they'd talk endlessly about Bill Hodges.

'He's a well-lettered man,' said Mickey.

'Self educated,' said Mel, Jackie's son.

'He was educated by the Communist Party,' said Mickey, with a knowing confidentiality. 'Oh, aye. See . . . all these people in 'ere. They're all Labour. But they haven't got tickets, like . . . party cards. Well, that lot 'ave.' He pointed to the parish councillors in their cabal in the corner. 'And 'im,' he pointed to a man on our table, formerly the shaft men's representative on the union, now a district councillor.

'But Bill Hodges, he had his ticket for the Communist Party.'

'He threw it in in 1956,' said Mel, 'over the Hungarian revolution. The lads at the pit were up in arms about it. They could see what was gannin' on over there. They weren't going to have him telling them it was the land of milk and honey.'

'He threw it in to save his job!' spluttered Mickey. 'He was Lodge Chairman and he was a district councillor. He only worked one shift a week at the pit.'

'He threw it in to save his neck,' said Mel. 'They were going to string him up in the Big Club.'

'He lost heart in communism before 1956,' said Freddy Sapsford, the district councillor, a tall dry-voiced man with a penchant for cigars. 'He could see it was holding him back at Durham.' When they spoke of 'Durham' in this way, they meant Red Hill, the union's Area headquarters, the next level of authority up from the branch lodges. After renouncing communism, Bill Hodges had taken several turns on the Area Executive, and had been a district councillor for many years – which in those days was virtually par for the course for a lodge chairman in East Durham. Opinion was divided over whether since his conversion from communism, he had gone to the other extreme, wholeheartedly embracing the moderate mainstream of the Durham NUM, or whether, as they said all too frequently, 'a leopard never changes its spots'.

The constitution of the National Coal Board had provided for the ever greater involvement of the workforce, as represented by the union, in the running of the industry. At each pit, consultative meetings were held fortnightly to discuss the future exploitation of the colliery's reserves. So, a kind of consensus was developed whereby through a much vaunted process of 'give and take', the interests of the two parties could be balanced for the betterment of the industry – a consensus exemplified by the 'partnership' of the miners' president, Joe Gormley, and the board's chairman, Derek Ezra.

There were always a certain number of miners, however, for whom not only the consensus, but the whole process of nationalisation, had been false. Not only were many of the old coal owners given positions on the Board, they were so generously compensated that the industry failed to make a profit even in the post-war years of boom in demand. Furthermore, the miners themselves had no more say in the running of the industry than they had under the coal owners.

In the Sixties under the Wilson government, with the Board

under the chairmanship of Lord Robens, more pits were closed than at any other time in the history of the industry, the workforce being cut by nearly two thirds. The union, however, 'stood by' the government, accepting the massive rundown of manpower (which was due partly to mechanisation) on the understanding that they would receive increases in pay that would bring them to the top of the manual earnings league. The miners, however, had to go on strike twice under Gormley's leadership, for this bargain to be fulfilled to their satisfaction. First in 1972 – the first national strike in their history (1921 and 1926 had been lock-outs) – and 1974 – when proverbially they 'brought down' the Heath government. It was this latter struggle that not only revived the miners' old mythic status as the vanguard of the working class, but created the aggrandising conception of them as a group so powerfully central to the nation's well being that no government could afford to flout their aspirations.

But at the same time, for the old dissenting 'left' of the union – now known as 'militants' – the Gormley executive had not had the vision or the courage to capitalise on these victories to the miners' full advantage. A Labour government had taken power in the wake of Heath's downfall, and Gormley and his men didn't want to weaken it through further disruption. But by the late-Seventies, the miners' earnings had again dropped in the wages league. And the pits were still closing.

Each of the old regional unions, like the DMA (Durham Miners' Association), had been founded independently and under very different circumstances, and under Rule 41 of the NUM, they each retained the right to act as an independent union. Since the failure of the great strike of 1926, and the hounding of many union leaders from their jobs and homes – and the ensuing sense of bitterness and betrayal – Durham had, it was said, been politically dormant. Under Sammy Watson, the adored general secretary who had held the Area in a grip of iron from the Forties to the mid-Sixties, Durham had become either a bastion of moderation and good sense, or one of the most right-wing areas in the country, depending on your viewpoint.

Within the area, each pit had its own identity and traditions. Easington had a reputation for militancy, but while under private enterprise there'd been more than a few flashes of red about at Horden ('And there'd been every right to be,' as everybody said), in the post-nationalisation era, it had been one of the pits that adhered most closely to the consensual ideal. (It was perhaps significant that Horden had the only banner in the coalfield ever to feature a portrait of Harold Wilson.) Old Bill Hodges, even in his communist days, had never been what you could call an extremist. Far from it.

'When nationalisation came in,' said Joe Summers, 'a lot of the old union secretaries got jobs with the Coal Board as Industrial Relations Advisors. It was now their industry, so why shouldn't they work for it? Before that, most disputes were resolved at the pit, between the lodge officials and the coal company. But after nationalisation, the Lodge could call for a member of the Area Executive or one of the Area Agents to negotiate on their behalf, and the management would bring in one of these advisors. So you'd often find that the people sitting opposite you in negotiations had been union officials themselves.

'The way I looked at it was that, after nationalisation, it was only natural that a man should progress to becoming an official if he wanted to. At that time shot-firers were still part of the NUM, and I seriously considered putting in for my ticket. But then the chairman's job became vacant on the union, so I went down that road instead. But in any case, I don't think I could have stood working under some of these bastard under-managers.'

'See, after nationalisation,' said Micky Douglas, 'the union became that powerful, there was only a certain amount they could do to you. But if you became an official, you were, like, part of them. You were working directly for them, and the way the officials were treated by the management was terrible. They seemed to take a delight in humiliating them in front of the men. The way they saw it the officials were representing them, and if they put a foot wrong, they were letting the management down.

'Once Salter [the old manager] was down there with Tommy Joyce, one of the overmen. Salter passes Tommy his stick – they used to carry these sticks, see, the under-managers and officials. Says, "Clean my stick." No please or thank you. Didn't even look at him. Just, "Clean my stick." If it'd been me I'd have said, "That's not my job. Clean yi arn fuckin' stick." But if you were an official you couldn't do that. So Tommy just says, "Yes, Mr Salter" and cleans his stick.'

'They used to goad them to tears sometimes,' said Joe. 'Mind, if you believe some of these stories you hear, relations were good at Horden.' And that, they all believed, was at least partly due to the personality of Salter – the dour little man I had met before Christmas – who was said to have been more sympathetic to the men than to the officials.

He was, they said, the last of the 'family managers' who lived in the village, did his shopping in the village, went to church in the village. He was involved in various clubs in the village, and his wife was prominent in the WI. His father had worked for the union as a clerical officer, and he had grown up, it was said, in the Red Hill headquarters, in the very bosom of the union.

They had no illusions about him. He was a Boss. But they respected him for his cunning and skill in the arts of manipulation, believing their own leaders – men like Ernie Wilding who had been away on courses in union law – to be at least a match for him.

That old manager had been a person of great ability, who could have worked at national level. The fact that he'd always been passed over for promotion was due, they believed, at least in part, to his unreasonable loyalty to Horden.

When they reached a stalemate in negotiations, Joe Summers would lean over the table and shout at him, 'You bastard! Our fathers' subscriptions paid for your education!' But the manager would just laugh. They'd all laugh. That was the way it was at Horden.

'You started to hear about it in the late-Seventies,' said Joe Summers. 'This thing called the Broad Left. Militants – young lefties – taking over places like Monkwearmouth. It wasn't difficult to do, because a pit like that, in the middle of Sunderland, most of the workforce don't live locally, and they don't go to meetings. But it's easy to take over any pit, because most people don't go to meetings anyway. We had some of the lads here who were very impressed by the militants, gannin' on about Monkwearmouth this, Monkwearmouth that. I just used to laugh, because Monkwearmouth had the worst agreements in the county over things like wet conditions and weekend working. Being a militant pit, you'd think they'd have had really tough agreements, but if you went there, the men were all saying, "We want agreements like they've got at Horden."

'If you had a problem with management, you could get a member of the Area Executive or one of the Agents to help you sort it out. Monkwearmouth always had to have the Agent. At that time it was Archie Dodds, who belonged Horden. When it came to the tea break, they'd always fetch him out o' the meeting. "You're not sitting in there with them!" Archie would be right put out. He was used to his cup of tea and his bit crack with the management. See, at Horden, the union always talked to the management. That's how we were able to get things from them.

'When Scargill and them took over at national level, in the

early-eighties, their first response to any problem with the Coal
Board was to order us to withdraw from the consultative committees
at local level. "Don't sit round a table with them." These committees
were held every fortnight, between the management and all the different unions at the colliery, to discuss the future of the pit. In 1983,
during the overtime ban leading up to the strike, we were ordered to
withdraw from all consultative and safety committees. "Dinnut have
nowt to dee wi' management!" We were off the committees for six
weeks, and in that time they shifted the boundaries underground.
We found that part of Horden's territory had been given over to
Easington, which shortened the life of the pit. Easington's down
there now, getting Horden's coal. Management blamed us for not
being there when it was decided. We might not have been able to
stop it, but we could at least have registered a protest. That's why
I would always talk to management. You can at least object.

'Monkwearmouth were all working during the strike. The leaders
were all militants, but half the men were working. They only had
twenty men out by the end. We had a thousand men out. We're a
moderate pit, but we only ever had eleven men working.

'We came out, like the rest of the county, on the understanding
that there would be a National Ballot – which as you know, there
never was.

'Scargill released these kids, the lefties, and he couldn't control
them. During the strike, Jimmy and me went down to the National
Executive. You had the guy from Kent taunting the leader of the
Yorkshire miners, telling him he was deeing nowt – just tuppenny
ha'penny picketing, while he was blockading the ports and stopping
all these industries. How he had two hundred men in prison in
Lincolnshire. We were killing ourselves. We couldn't believe it. He
kept going on about he had two thousand men out in Kent. We had
over a thousand men out at Horden alone.

'But they were all right down there. They were milking London.
They were out there with the buckets taking millions.

'The bloke just got up and walked out. Scargill's saying, "Siddown,
Billy. Siddown." Feller just ignores him and walks out. Scargill
couldn't control the Executive at all. That's the way we saw it
anyway.

'They wanted us to stop doing safety cover here. See, every
man had the option to work one shift a fortnight on essential
pump work. We were asked by the Area Executive to stop doing
it. I said, "If that happens, I'm gannin' back. I'll not strike to put
myself out of a job. I'll take them back, and the strike'll be over."'

His inference being that such was Horden's significance, if the pit went back, it would deal such a blow to the morale and credibility of the strike it could not have held.

'We had one lad lived Seaham, who was threatening to go back. Said his wife couldn't stand it. They were getting into debt, his washing-machine had broken down, and they couldn't afford another one. I told Jimmy Inskip, the Area Treasurer – brilliant bloke ...'

'Hellish bloke!' said Jimmy.

'He died during the strike. It killed him ... He said, "Tell him he can have my washing-machine. But keep him out!" We told this lad he could get £3 a day on picketing. He was getting a shift a fortnight in on safety cover, and he could have Jimmy Inskip's washing-machine. We told him where he had to be for picketing. He didn't turn up. I phoned him and asked him what the problem was. He said he'd been there, but they hadn't turned up. Next day they turned up for him again, but he wasn't there. I drove up to see him. He wasn't there, but I saw his wife. She said she didn't want him to go back. It was *him*. He was determined to go back. There was this dog lying in front of the fire. One of these long curly-haired types. Pedigree. A beautiful dog. I said, "How much does a one o' them cost?" She said, "Oh, a puppy's £500." I phoned Jimmy Inskip. I said, "Keep your washing-machine, Jimmy. Let the fucker gan back!"'

A hundred and twenty policemen turned up to escort that man to work, against only twelve pickets. But while Easington, a mile to the North had been the scene of some of the most tumultuous events of the strike – massive battles between pickets and hundreds of police, the village becoming an armed camp as the police made it their centre of operations for the area – scenes immortalised by a local photographer in grittily grainy black and white images that were turned into postcards, and sent the length and breadth of the left-wing world, Horden had, everyone agreed, been very quiet during the strike. Every morning, a huge tray of hot, 'dripping' pies was carried over from Craggs' bakery for the pickets gathering at the Miners' Hall. From there the men went all over the country. Orgreave 'scared the shit out of yer,' recollected Jimmy the treasurer. But generally, they'd enjoyed it.

The Women's Support Group provided free meals three days a week at the Miners' Hall. Every shop and business pitched in with provisions and services, while the union kept the Co-op, the one down the street from the Miners' Hall, open, by buying most of the provisions for the food parcels there.

At Christmas, a deal was done with Dewhurst, the butcher's factory up in Peterlee, whereby for £10,000 they received £15,000 worth of vouchers. There were toys for the children, sent over by the French trade unions, and every family got a free turkey.

For many, the real hardship came when the strike was over. They had spent their savings, cashed in their insurance policies, sold their cars. Building societies that had suspended demands on mortgage payments for the duration of the strike, 'put the screws on' as soon as the men went back to work. Many who'd taken redundancy payments before the strike had spent them supporting their striking sons, or daughters who were married to miners. Others who had fallen prey to loan sharks faced court actions for vast amounts of compound interest. There were still people in Horden being evicted over debts incurred during the strike. Many shops had closed because they could not recover the credit they had given. Other people had since taken these premises over, but had not been able to do much with them.

It had come as a surprise to many that the Horden membership had voted unanimously in favour of the strike, while other 'moderate' pits like Dawdon and Vane Tempest further up the coast had had to be picketed out. But something had been discovered only weeks before the strike, that a few months before would have been inconceivable even to the management – that Horden Colliery was earmarked for imminent closure.

After the strike, all 'local' agreements, which the unions at the individual pits had fought so hard to achieve, and of which at Horden they had been so proud, were immediately scrapped without consultation. The miners returned to work, as they put it themselves, 'like a defeated army'. Within two months of the strike ending, 6,500 men in the North-east Area had volunteered for redundancy. Horden, which in the early-Seventies had been declared by Lord Robens the 'flagship of the area', a pit with a life at least till the end of the next century, the site, as late as 1982, of large-scale recruitment, and which had had millions of pounds worth of irrecoverable equipment installed shortly before the strike, was declared a 'manpower reservoir'. Every miner was invited to take redundancy, or transfer to replenish workforces depleted at more 'valuable' collieries. If Horden's workforce fell below a viable level, its closure would be 'consequential'.

The Lodge responded with a vigorous campaign of letters, posters and meetings, urging the men to stand firm and fight for their jobs. The Women's Support Group kept up a picket outside the manager's office, and many baulked at running the gauntlet of the women to claim their redundancy. But although output per man shift had soon reached unprecedented levels, by July following the strike, the workforce had fallen from a pre-strike level of 1,700 to 966. By that time, the representatives of the various unions had already been summoned to the NCB Area HQ, and the closure of Horden Colliery announced.

Seventy-two per cent of the remaining workforce voted to fight the closure through to the review stage. Horden, along with Bates Colliery in Northumberland, was to be the first pit to go through a new review procedure, whereby an independent arbiter was brought in to examine the evidence and make a recommendation to the Board. It was hoped that since this was the first such review, the Board would allow an outcome favourable to the union, to demonstrate the fairness of the procedure.

Horden Lodge brought in the NUM Engineer to assess the pit's reserves, and two professors from Durham University to calculate the economic and social costs of the pit's closure to the surrounding communities.

'We went down to London with the banner and a good group of lads. We handed the material for our case to Peter Heathfield, the General Secretary. He said, "Thanks lads. Well done." Scargill was there. He was the one who was going to be presenting the case. But he just ignored us.

'There's a room at Hobart House, on the second floor, laid out with any kind of food you could want: hot food, cold food, chicken, chops, the lot. You just go in and help yourself. When it came to dinner time, Peter Heathfield says, "You don't want to go in there with that lot. There's a little pub round the corner where a lot of the lads" – he meant the left wingers – "normally go on a lunchtime." I said, "You can go and have a half round the corner. I'm going upstairs, cause it's my labour that's paid for that." We were handing chops and all sorts out to the lads outside with the banner.'

'The feller who was making the decision – the independent reviewer,' said Jimmy, 'was named Shields. He was a QC. I don't know if he'd ever been to Horden, or if he'd even been up here at all. I don't know what his competence was to make such a decision. I don't see why a person like that should be allowed to make a decision that affects so many people's lives when he hasn't even met any of them. But as soon as the Coal Board announced that there would be generous redundancies, I knew we were lost – because he would have no reason not to close the pit.

'Scargill presented our case, and he made a brilliant job of it. He should have been a barrister. His mind's that sharp for facts and figures. But it was a lost cause before he started.

'The independent reviewer recommended that Horden should close and that Bates Colliery should stay open. But in the end, the Coal Board closed Bates as well, because they said the independent body could only recommend. So I don't suppose any of it made a great deal of difference.'

The involvement of the miners' wives through the Women's Support Groups is, in the public mind, one of the most enduring images of the strike – the valiant women, strident beneath their banners, proclaiming their husbands' *right* to be miners in their ancestral communities. It has become proverbial that through the strike countless housewives became politicised, going on to become councillors, media pundits and even MPs. One would have thought there were thousands of women involved in each village. But according to Heather Wood, who co-ordinated the support groups in East Durham, there were only twelve to fifteen women active in most villages, and in some cases, less. Each group sent delegates to an Area Committee, equivalent to the union's Area Committee, but entirely independent of it, which distributed funds that came in from outside. Otherwise, the individual groups were left more or less to their own devices.

The leading light of the Horden Support Group was Ada Williams. I had seen her in a television programme about Horden during the strike, burning with a righteous zeal about how they were *fighting* for their communities. This, I had thought at the time, was a person it was crucial for me to meet. Now, however, the image of the battling pit wife seemed quaintly dated. How people had loved to *fight* or at least to talk about how they were *fighting* for things! It was all such a short time ago, but how little evidence there was of that zeal and passion in Horden to-day. Like the enthusiasm and loyalty many of the men undoubtedly had felt towards Arthur Scargill during the course of the strike, the zeal of the women had all but vanished, even as a memory.

And while everyone had heard of Ada, most people were oddly vague about how she could be contacted. She lived in Eighth Street, but nobody was precisely sure where. I got her phone number from

Heather Wood, but it had been changed. Finally I resorted to walking up and down the street knocking on doors. Every door in the
dark and apparently deserted terrace bore the sign, 'No Hawkers,
Callers, Canvassers' but at the third door they pointed me in the
right direction.

She was a slight woman, narrow eyes glittering out of the
dimness of her hallway. Her house was one of those that had been
turned, as people never tired of saying, into 'a little palace' – walls
of polished pine over the low fireplace of yellow rusticated stone, a
long sheepskin rug in front of the fire on which a large male form
lay luxuriantly recumbent.

'Howay out of here!' shouted Ada. 'I want to talk!'

The form grunted, but made no movement.

Ada looked at me. 'What can you do?'

She'd just got in from the old people's housing on the Top
Road, where she was assistant warden. It was a job that had come
out of her work with the support group. She'd wanted to carry on
working for the community, so she'd done voluntary work with the
elderly until this job came up. She was, however, the only one of the
group who had carried on 'doing things' after the strike.

'All the others went back to what they were doing before.'

'What was that?'

'Nothing.'

'You don't know where that year went,' she said in a voice,
hoarse but warmly confiding. 'It seemed to go in a flash. Everybody
had nothing, and everybody was happy. Yes! It seemed to bring the
whole community together. People you'd seen around for years to
say hello to, you got to know them. Because we were all together.
Everybody was in the same situation. You were exhausted all the
time, but you were happy.

'I was up at six every morning doing my regular job, cleaning
out the infants' school. I'd be at the Miners' Hall at nine to help
start the cooking. Then I was out most nights, collecting round
the clubs. We did the meals Tuesday, Wednesday, Thursday. There
were at least three hundred people there every day. We used to buy
in bulk in warehouses. But everybody gave in whatever way they
could. Pensioners gave us tins of food. The greengrocers gave us
fruit and vegetables. The butchers gave mincemeat for the mince
and dumplings. Other shops just gave what they could, because
every shop in Horden was hit badly.

'There was about five women did most of the cooking. I helped,
but they really did it. I more looked after the financial side. I got

delegated treasurer at the start. Then when the secretary packed in, I got her job to do as well. Every tin that came in, every penny we were given, was written down in a book. And everything that went out was noted down, as it was used in the kitchen. The books were audited at least once a month, by a different person in the community. Because we never knew when the strike was going to end, and over the year we had thousands and thousands of pounds going through.

'I'd never done anything like it before. I had no confidence. But my husband said, "You can do it." And it just took off. It's fantastic where you get the energy from. Because I had no energy like that before. My life was just sitting in this house. I often wonder what I did with myself. All those wasted hours!

'I hardly saw my husband during the strike. He was doing his part through the union, and I was doing mine. We just met going in and out the door.'

Had this created strains on their family life, as one had heard about in other cases?

The recumbent form suddenly sprang to life.

'I was a problem,' it said brightly.

'You were playing up at school, weren't you pet?'

'I wasn't getting any attention off her, see.'

'He was dyslexic. But we didn't know that. He was getting frustrated because he couldn't learn anything. The teachers didn't realise. They just thought he was a troublemaker. Me and me husband were so involved in the strike, we didn't have any time for him, did we, pet? Anyway, they found out he's not stupid. He's just dyslexic. He's good with his hands though, aren't you pet?'

'Do you know of any jobs going with cars?' he asked.

Unfortunately not.

'He loves working with cars, but there's nothing going for him at the moment, is there, pet?'

'There's nowt going for anyone round here. I just lie here. I can't go out. 'Cause when I was younger I had a bit of a reputation. So every time I go out some hard nut tries it on with me, to try to prove themselves. I could sort them out with one hand tied behind my back, but I can't be bothered.' He leapt to his feet, and pulled out his wallet. 'Look, I've got a membership card for every club in Hartlepool.'

'Steve! He's not interested in that!'

'Have you been up The Trust [the "wine bar" in Horden]? It's fucking cack! Last time I went in there a thirteen year old asked me to go out the back for a quick one.'

'Steve! He's not married,' hissed Ada, as though a southern accent were an index of sexual innocence.

'It's true,' protested Steve. 'A thirteen year old.' Then he remembered he had to go and see someone. 'Taraa, marra,' he said, and was gone.

Ada shook her head.

How had the men on the union reacted to the women in the support group?

'How does men react to women in anything?' asked Ada. 'They put us down – even though it was them that asked us to start the kitchen in the first place. The way some of them reacted was like they didn't want us to succeed. They didn't want to see us doing a better job than they were. But when we were well into it, they saw they couldn't do without us, and after that anything we wanted from the union, we got.

'But the women worked well together. And they worked *hard*! If tempers got frayed from time to time, they had every right to. Nobody could have worked under them conditions without feeling strain and stress. As I say, often there'd be only five women there to feed five hundred people. The cookers we were using were old, and the rings kept going off. When we did the dumplings and the Yorkshire puddings, we had to do them at the Community Centre, that old school down on the corner, and transport them back up, because we didn't have enough rings. So we were forever running backwards and forwards up and down that street. Then you'd get a miner coming in saying, "Can you put the kettle on for a cup of coffee . . . ?"

'The kitchen could only hold so many people, so we couldn't have done with every miner's wife in the kitchen. But we never had enough people. A lot of women had small children which made it difficult for them to come. A lot of people said they'd like to come but just didn't. A few people came once and never bothered to come back. Whether we worked them too hard, I don't know. The men coming off the picket line generally did the washing up. But if they didn't do it, the women who'd done the cooking had to do it. Then the whole place had to be scrubbed out every day.

'But I always thought we would win. Right up to the last minute, even after the strike was over, I thought we would win. See, we weren't just doing it for the strike itself. We were fighting to keep our pit open, for our husbands to keep their jobs. That's what we made all that effort for. Because we believed Horden pit was still viable.

'But even before they took it to the review, a lot of the men were going to get their redundancies. We kept up like a picket line outside the colliery office, to try to persuade them not to do it.'

When Joe Summers told me with some amusement of the men having to run the gauntlet of the women, I'd imagined a raucous rabble, like the great crowds of women and howling children, all banging on household utensils, that used to 'tin pan' undesirables – strike breakers, women of ill-fame – from the colliery villages in the olden days. Ada seemed surprised at the assumption.

'We just stood there as they came off the shift, about twelve of us. And we asked them, would they just wait to see the outcome of the review procedure. They said they'd've loved to, but they'd been offered other jobs. And you could understand it. They were only young most of them. They had their whole lives ahead of them, and they had the chance to get out. They'd been on strike for a year. What more could you ask?

'The way you felt when you found out the pit was going to close, you just can't describe it. It was like something had come down over you. You knew that was it. You couldn't do any more. The day my husband got made redundant, I sat in here and wept. Because they'd fought for so long, and they'd got nothing. And the last time they marched into Durham for the Big Meeting as a working lodge, it was very emotional. When the band stopped and played in front of the County Hotel, you know, where the speakers stand, the feeling that came up in yer. And when they came back into Horden . . . Whenever the banner comes out, people are outside their houses, and on Big Meeting Day, they wait for the banner to come back into the village from Durham, and they march behind it. The band stood for ages playing, outside the Miners' Hall. And they were dancing. Everybody was joining in. It was July, about six o' clock. On a fine day.'

For me, the militants, the lefties, the 'headbangers', as Joe Summers liked to call them, had been shadowy, anonymous figures, part of the remote world of Arthur Scargill and the media conception of miners and strikes. It never occurred to me that some of them might be living near by, that I might be passing them every day in the street.

After the strike there were a number of incidents in which men who were very visibly involved in picketing were set upon by police on the thinnest of excuses, given a good hiding and charged with assault – charges that were later, inevitably, dropped. Such an incident had taken place in Horden, by the bus stop, just round the corner from where I lived. According to Joe Summers, one of the people involved was the lippy type, who wouldn't be able to resist answering back. The other, however, was very quiet. He wouldn't say anything to anybody. He'd transferred to Monkwearmouth when the pit closed, and was now, if Joe remembered rightly, studying for a degree in sociology at Durham University.

A degree in sociology, indeed. This was a person I was immediately keen to meet. One often heard about miners and women from the support groups who had not only been so politicised by the strike, but had their conception of themselves and life's possibilities so dramatically broadened that they'd been impelled to pursue their new found breadth of vision through concrete courses of study. But this was the first such person I'd come across in Horden.

Joe, however, had not seen the man for years, and had no idea how to contact him. He doubted furthermore that I'd get much sense out of him, as his father, a communist, had brainwashed him from an early age, and he only ever talked 'left-wing bull'.

No one else seemed to have heard of him for years either; though most seemed to think he was still living in his parents' old house, down the bottom of Horden, towards the beach. One night in the Big Club, I asked Jackie Hudspith about him.

'I knar 'im,' he said darkly. 'He's a communist, mind. His fattha was a communist 'n arl. He was one of the biggest communists in the world! They used to meet in 'ere in a Frida' night. They used to stand there.' He pointed to a spot two-thirds of the way along the bar, towards the Pigeon End. 'Aye,' he said, shaking his head meaningfully. 'But the committee put a stop to it.'

Why was that, I wondered.

He looked at me, incredulous. 'They were communists!'

'They were communists,' Ernie Wilding told me, referring to old Stan Best and his mates, 'without knowing what communism was. They didn't know there were different types and levels of communism. They just looked at the Soviet Union, and for them that was the be all and end all.'

'I think my father understood very well what communism was,' said Keith Best, as we sat in the very tidy living room of his parents' house, where he still lived when he wasn't at his girlfriend's place. 'Them's his library,' he said, pointing to a row of old and formidably *black* volumes in a corner of the room. There were solidly upholstered novels by Herman Melville and Jack London, as well as classic communist texts. Keith's hobby must have been ornithology, judging by the large number of books on the subject, all over the house, and there were several of those immensely detailed, quasi-scientific pen-and-ink drawings so beloved of bird watchers. And there were various Russian artefacts – modest tourist souvenirs – a wooden model of a house, a set of *babooshka* dolls. And, positioned on an otherwise bare wall, so that his steely gaze radiated sun-ray-like across it, a tiny sculpted head of Lenin.

Keith sat in the middle of the room, in the rather meagre pool of light thrown down by the overhead light. He sat forward in his chair, focused and alert, a stocky figure in jeans, with a close cropped grey beard, about forty-five, soft spoken. The last communist in Horden. He'd finally left the Party shortly after the last miners' strike, when the practical and physical developments taking place around him had rendered such theoretical allegiances irrelevant. The Party, as it had existed then, had simply not had anything more to offer.

It was true he was doing a degree at Durham University, but he was nonchalant about the distinction. Far from seeming grateful for this opportunity to broaden himself intellectually, far from feeling reverence and awe for the established processes of learning, as an older generation of trade unionists might have done, it was as though he were lending the course a greater validity, a greater reality, by agreeing to take part in it. Not, however, that he found the work easy. Not at all. He found it extremely difficult. They were having to get to grips with some exceedingly dense texts by the likes of Marx, Weber and Durkheim. He would be lucky, he reckoned, to pass.

'I always knew there was something different about my father compared to other men. But I didn't know what it was. When I was a very small child in the playground, the other children used to say, "Don't talk to him, his father's a comyoonist." That was the way they used to say it.

'There was quite a thriving Communist Party in Horden at one time – during the 1926 strike and after. Harry Pollit stood in this constituency against Ramsay MacDonald, and he polled about 7,000 votes. In my parents' day, there was a group of about twelve or thirteen communists in the village. My mother and father used to sell the *Daily Worker* outside the colliery offices on a Friday. I became very aware that there was something different about my parents, but I still didn't understand what it was. My father never took me aside and told me what was what. He never sat down and explained why, that he was a communist, that he believed in the social emancipation of men and women. It was only after he died that I began to think about what he'd been and what he'd said and what he'd done. I think that what he was talking about was complete freedom – that people could be released from this drudgery and darkness in their lives, so that they could know and experience the finer points of life – not just through art or music or things like that, but to be able to be aware of what the real world was about, of the forces that were controlling their lives.

'It was quite a while after he died that I joined the Party myself. It was during the coup in Chile, when Allende's Marxist regime was ousted. I still hadn't thought very seriously about my parents' politics, but their position in the village had been such that I found myself constantly having to defend their point of view. People used to say to me in the pit, How can you talk about democracy when communism's never been elected? Well, in Chile, for the first time, Marxism had been elected. The people had approved its programme. Yet it was thrown out by the army, and most of the people involved with it destroyed. I was so horrified by this, I wanted to do something about it. So I joined the CP.

'Communism had petered out, it had totally collapsed in Horden by then. I mean we're talking about a party that's been in decline since the late-Forties. I realised it was futile to try to operate as a solitary CP member in Horden. I used to go to party meetings in Durham, and I was on the district committee in Newcastle.

'Arguments at the pit and in the Club bar tended to fall back on the subject of the Soviet Union, or at least the people of Horden's understanding of what the Soviet Union was. They thought the Soviet Union was such a terrible place, yet they couldn't see the misery and degradation in their own lives.

'When I went to the Soviet Union myself in 1978, I saw an obvious lack of material possessions. But material possessions weren't what I was looking for. I was wanting to see a quality of life. I went back in 1985 with a trade union delegation. In Moscow, the standard of living looked good. At least, it was no worse than you'd see in a place like this, or in Newcastle. But moving outside, about two hundred miles south of Moscow, to a mining town called Novostimost, I saw people in abject poverty. I was walking through the streets with a Welshman from the Cokemen's Union, and we saw in this shop window a child's coat in mink, with a hat, gloves and boots. It was beautiful – really good quality. The price was 75 roubles. The Welshman had been changing money on the black market, and he had roubles bursting out of every pocket. He decided he was going to have it. We went in, and he put 75 roubles on the counter. The woman behind the counter just said, no. He thought she hadn't understood, so he went and got the coat and hat and laid them on the counter. But she just said, no. So he said, how much? And he just kept putting money on the counter till there was hundreds of roubles piled up. But she just said no, and she put the coat back on the rack.

'Now what significance you want to attribute to that, I don't know. But to me, it meant they were keeping that coat for someone in the community, and they weren't going to let some outsider walk in and take it just because they had more money. To me, that was a quality of life. In that way, I still think the former Soviet Union was one-tenth of the way towards socialising people into a basic respect for ... humanity.

'People here have a relative standard of life. They have cars, TVs, nice clothes. But they don't belong to them. Their cars are on HP. The clothes are out of catalogues. They have to hock themselves to live at a certain standard, to be able to emulate the middle class who can afford to buy these things outright. That to me is a misery. They're dehumanised by this process. When they put their wage packet on the table, they find that that money doesn't belong to them.

'I wouldn't say the Communist Party really educated me. There were a few lectures in Durham, on Marxism. But basically I was left to my own devices here. I just read and read, and a lot of what I read I didn't understand. Things like Marx and Lenin. I used to read it over and over again, for weeks, and I'd convince myself I didn't know what they were talking about. But I kept on, and I developed a theory of my own – like what I've been saying just now.

'The process of moving the union to the left started around the mid-Fifties, when the CP started up the Broad Left organisation. It was aimed at the Yorkshire coalfield, because at the time it was not only the biggest coalfield, it was also the most right wing. From there it spread to the peripheral coalfields like Durham. Scotland's always had a left orientation, same as Wales and Kent. But Durham was something different. It had a right-wing leadership, even before I was born. But by about the late-Seventies, the union nationally had shifted from the right to the left. And because of the position in the country at large, the attacks upon the unions and the welfare state, the run-down of industry, the conditions were there for some support for the left, even in Durham. The left was like a community within the NUM. There were other people in Horden who were part of it. People who supported me at meetings, but had their own idea of what socialism meant. They felt they were part of this community – a national community within the NUM.

'There was a newssheet coming out of Yorkshire called the *Yorkshire Miner*, and before I was on the committee, before I'd even stood for election, I used to go to union meetings, and one day I got a bunch of these newssheets and took them in. The lodge secretary said, "Who's brought these in here?" I said, "Well, I have." And he said, "Who's given you permission?" I said, "I didn't knar I had to have permission to give the men something to read." I couldn't see that that was anti-democratic. But that was the attitude. They didn't want to see anything else. They wanted that particular way that they'd been brought into the union, that consensus that operated in the union movement, to continue. They didn't want any confrontation with the management or the Coal Board. So there was a confrontation between the so-called moderates and the newer people coming into the union – mostly people of my generation, who were in their late twenties, early thirties at the time – who had this left-wing stance.

'There were some, mind, of that age, who came in with us, who sharp got out again. Because they wanted to fit in with the old structures, because that was the way you got on – got respected in the community and all the rest of it. I wouldn't put them down for it. But for me, it wasn't a question of getting on in the union, of making a career out of it. It was a question of shifting the union from that position it had always been in, towards recognising what was happening around it. The situation in the industry was desperate. But they didn't want to face that. They thought the way things had been at Horden was going to go on for ever. To put it crudely, the shit was coming down on their heads, and they didn't see it till the very last minute.'

Charlie Kemp answered the door, his shirt hanging out of his shell-suit bottom, a slight, rumpled figure with twinkly blue eyes and a ginger brush of a moustache. He lived in one of the so-called Big Houses – the houses built for deputies on the streets off the Top Road, just over the back lane from where my great-grandparents had lived. 'The Broad Left,' he said, as we went into the big back living room where the big black range would have been, and where the greater part of the talking and eating and watching telly was still done. 'It was just a group of lads who wanted to see maer democracy in the union.'

He sat back in his armchair and flicked the telly off. He'd been looking at the FT Index on Ceefax, to see how his shares were doing. He'd invested his redundancy, and quite well too, judging by his foxily contented expression. No, he hadn't wanted to transfer to another pit. He'd had a heart attack and was only fit for light work anyway. It had been the stress and strain of the strike and the closure of the pit that had caused it. It was his own fault. He'd taken it all upon himself. He knew he shouldn't have done. But what could he do? It was like saying to someone, 'Don't worry', wasn't it? He smiled and sighed.

'How I got involved with the Broad Left was because I was disgusted at the way the Productivity Bonus Scheme was brought in.

'See, the Power Loading Agreement, which came in with mechanisation in the early-Sixties, created parity between the different coalfields. All the power loaders at the different pits were on the same wage regardless of what they produced, which was in accordance with the aims of the union, which since time immemorial had been to eradicate piecework.

'Under the Bonus Scheme, which was supposedly an inducement to get the men to work harder, the power loaders – the face workers – got a percentage of what they produced. The back-bye workers got 75 per cent of that, and the datal lads got 50 per cent. The way I looked at it, it was a case of the poor being penalised as usual. Because these people were only being paid according to what the power loaders earnt. They had no opportunity to improve their own situation. Each district underground was negotiated separately. So you had some men earning fortunes, while others were getting nowt. And of course it affected people's attitude towards safety. They were concerned solely with getting coal out. All they thought about was the bonus. Safety went by the board – which was the way it had been under piecework.

'When the Bonus Scheme was first put before the national membership in 1979, it was overwhelmingly rejected. All the way through the last strike, the government and the media were banging on about how a national ballot should have been held. A national ballot was held in 1979, and it rejected the Productivity Bonus Scheme. But that decision was overturned by Joe Gormley and the national leadership, who had agreed to the Bonus Scheme to keep the Labour government in power. They saw it as a way of giving the men a rise through the back door, without breaking Jim Callaghan's wage freeze. So Gormley got the different area leaders to force it through on a show of hands – which was exactly what Scargill and the left were vilified for doing in the last strike – forcing through national policy at area level. That, to my mind, was the day democracy was destroyed in the NUM.

'Of course at Horden they were all in favour of it. At least the leaders were ... I wouldn't say they were corrupt. But the way certain decisions were taken definitely wasn't fair. They'd gan ahead without a quorum. But they got away with it, because like at most places, the average member didn't give a fuck.

'At Horden, the leadership didn't really lead. They'd listen out in the pit to find out what the majority of men thought, and act on that. They'd probably say that was democracy. But to me it was a failure of leadership.

'The information coming to the Lodge through the normal channels of the union never filtered through to the ordinary members. The Lodge officials only gave out information that it was to their advantage for the members to know.

'The aim of the Broad Left was to provide rank-and-file members at the different pits with information provided by the left wing in the higher echelons of the union, that they could use to combat the right-wing leadership of their lodges.

'For example, some of your officials might be members of Area or National bodies. You didn't know what they were saying and doing at these meetings. But the Broad Left provided you with that information.

'They used to hold the Broad Left meetings in an old people's lock-up on an estate in Sunderland. You know, where the old fellers meet to play cards. Me and Besty were the first to go through from this area. He had this old Caravette called the "battle wagon". We'd pick up Billy Stobbs, the chairman of Easington, and gan through.

'There were no membership procedures. Anyone who was a member of the NUM could gan. And at first there was no hierarchy. They chose a different chairman every week. There were never very many members. Even at its height, there were only about fifteen or twenty people going to the Broad Left meetings. But those few people were taking the gospel back to every pit in the coalfield.

'For a few weeks, we had the leadership on the run in Horden. They couldn't understand where we were getting this information from. They were used to just telling people what was what, and it being passively accepted. But now we were able to counteract their arguments. And because there was so little interest in the union, it was easy to swing a meeting. You only needed ten to do it, and we had a number of lads who weren't active members of the Broad Left, but who'd turn up and vote with us if we asked them to.

'Joe Summers was totally knocked off balance. He said, "If you cunts don't stop, I'm ganna give the fucker up!" – which was exactly what we wanted him to do. But of course he didn't. Instead, you had other people turning up at the meetings – dozens of 'em. People who'd never shown any interest in the union. A couple of them were even known to vote Conservative. Why, that was it. We were on to a losser by then. The left managed to gain control of most of the pits in Durham. But Horden? No chance. There never was a hope in hell that the left were going to take over Horden.

'Mind, towards the end it did start to get a bit more militant. After the strike, when the closure was announced, and they realised they had nowt left to lose, quite a number of lads started gannin' to the left meetings. But I'd dropped out a long way before then. As soon as they started electing chairmen, secretaries and the rest of it, it became a matter of cliques and rivalries. You had people coming to you canvassing for your support for their nomination as the Broad Left's candidate for this or that position in the Area hierarchy. Then they all started falling out with each other. You found that people were having meetings before the main meeting to decide which way it was ganna gan. And they were holding information back from the rest of the group. You got more and more opportunists coming in – people who didn't give a damn about democracy. I realised it was time to get out. I hadn't gone there to get a position. I've never wanted to be the leader of anything.'

15

The Wand of Authority

I SAT knee to knee with the under-managers in the dimness of the tiny set. Two men had been killed on this stretch of roadway about two months before – crushed to death when the inbound set hit the wrong points and the wagon in which they were travelling was rammed into the roof. Today, however, such things were far from people's minds. It was the day of the general election and everyone was talking about the bastards, the fuckers, the fucking slimy cunts, the daft cunts, the useless cunts. And the Green Party. 'Imagine what would happen to this industry if *them* fuckers got in!' Outside, the rock through which we were grinding and trundling was obscured by corrugated-iron, layers of plastic sheeting, or by white slats slotted in neat rows between the great arch girders. In well-lit recesses, rows of what looked like fridges, but which were probably part of the pit's sophisticated computer apparatus, stood whirring and bleeping.

I turned to the under-manager opposite me, and asked him what the slats were made of. He looked at me, his eyes narrowing, as if to say, 'Who do you think you are to address a question to me? You fucking insect!' But after a pause he said, 'As a matter of fact in this instance, they're concrete.' Then without expression, he turned back to his fellows.

The succession of strip-lights that had stood at right angles over the earlier sections of tunnel was gone. Now there was only the fragile gleam of our helmet lamps on the rock, visible between the girders, scoured and scarred with the marks of the machines that had ripped the roadway out, dusted with a fine glittering of quartz

– the pale lines of the strata wriggling with the motion of the truck. When we got off in the light of the landing, I could see the quartz glittering blood red in the rock. All the way in-bye stalactites a yard long hung like streamers, at times indistinguishable from the myriad wires – except that if you stopped still long enough you could see them dripping. According to Mr Grimshaw, the under-manager who was taking me in-bye, they were not real stalactites, but saline deposits which, as he demonstrated, crumbled at the touch. The water coming through from the permian above was, he said, five times saltier than sea water.

As we got off the second man-riding belt, the air was thick and dense – like getting off a plane at some steaming tropical airport. A great machine, a fan, kept up a deafening roar. We were joined by three other men – two in vests, shorts and wellingtons. The other appeared at a glance to be dressed in black patent-leather, but was in fact covered from head to foot in thick black slime, a fact which didn't seem to trouble him at all. Lank, sodden curls hung from beneath his helmet. Unlike Mr Grimshaw, he had a measured, unhurried, nonchalant gait. We pushed through a trap-door into another tunnel of total blackness. Mr Grimshaw forged ahead, and in the gleam of my lamp, I could see one of the miners in shorts and wellingtons, quite dwarfed by him, a shovel in his hand, a rucksack on his back, like an eager schoolboy trotting along beside his teacher, having almost to run to keep up with him. Soon I was very much behind. 'Is he still with us?' I heard Mr Grimshaw barking in the distance. I eventually caught up with the ringleted miner and danced behind him along the sleepers, clearly outlined by their coating of white stone dust, trying to avoid the steel rope which constantly changed its height and position relative to me, and might at any moment whirr into movement, slicing into my thigh or ankle. In the stories of the mines, people were constantly being grabbed or crushed or bisected by bits of machinery that came hurtling out of nowhere.

The moment one of the paths on either side of the track appeared to become more even, I would skip off on to it, attempting to avoid the bits of rock and debris, the pockets of white dust that exploded at the touch of a boot, the inscrutable bits of plant left lying about – and all the other unnameable and, to a stranger, mysterious forms of solid, liquid and atmospheric matter that make up the physicality of a mine: the ambiguous, half solid encrustations of dust and slime, the fetid liquids of every colour. Soon we were wading up to our knees in feculent black water on which the white stone dust floated like fat. Then after what seemed like a very long walk, we arrived at a crossroads, where by the light of many swivelling helmet lamps, we could see a dozen or more virtually naked miners standing or moving on a great heap of black slime and grit – their pallid flesh gleaming where sweat and water coursed through the dust and filth. Ahead and to the left, two immense machines stood idle, while to the right a mechanical dumper was attempting, to little avail, to move backwards and forwards over the great mound of black slurry it was supposed to be shifting on to a conveyor belt. A spotlight illuminating the machine on the left sent a spectral glow over the miners, who stood in a state of numbed dazedness, leaning on their spades, as they watched this apparently futile procedure, one casually urinating where he stood.

Overhead, water poured from the side of a huge pipe – though whether from the pipe itself or the roof above it was impossible to tell, and there wasn't time to ask.

Mr Grimshaw clambered up on to the illuminated machine, and I followed. At its head was a horizontal cylinder about ten-feet wide with stumpy flanges projecting from it, which would, when it could be got working, be driving the roadway – the GG1 Tailgate – into the high coal. Ahead of us was the high coal itself, glittering through a mesh. Eight and a half feet of it. Two four-foot seams with a few inches of stone between them: the F seam and the G seam, known at Horden as the Main Coal and the Yard Seam – running together for almost 20 square miles. It was said to be the biggest block of coal less than 2,000 feet under the ground in the whole of Britain. If it worked, and they could get it out easily, it would keep Wearmouth Colliery busy for thirty years. If there were serious problems, as they suspected, and there was a major fault running through it which would prevent them from getting to the best coal, it would be the end of the pit.

Mr Grimshaw was talking to the mechanics who were trying to get the roadway moving again. Their leaders, a deprecating Yorkshireman and a Durham lad with a great sweat- and dust-stained belly, listened with a certain amount of sympathetic deference as he told them how urgently he needed to get things moving. It was obvious that he commanded a certain amount of slightly pained respect, and equally obvious they were not going to be able to get it moving for some time.

Ahead of us was the Titan – the sight of which was the ostensible purpose of my visit – a great drill head on wheels like some medieval instrument of siege demolition. The great 'pineapple' head, as it was known, set about thirty degrees from the horizontal, must have been about six feet in diameter. If it had been in operation, we wouldn't have been able to see it, as no one was allowed to stand ahead of it, ever since a man who had been shouting instructions to the driver, who could not see ahead of the great beast, had been crushed to death.

There were quite a lot of Yorkshire and other Northern accents at Wearmouth. It was known as a 'cosmopolitan' pit. There, all the different accents and dialects of the North came together. Even if you were a miner, you were constantly hearing words you'd never heard before. All had brought with them their different words for the different things in the pit to this pitmatic Babel. Dating from 1826, Wearmouth was one of the older pits in the area, but unlike at Easington, everything at the pit was now new. You could walk from the carpeted computer room with its huge banks of VDUs right into the coal face itself without setting foot outdoors. As I'd stood in the lamp cabin, the sunlight streaming through from the skylights overhead, a big man came striding through the throng of miners strapping on their powerpacks and rescuers. He wore a donkey jacket, and with his closely cropped black beard and his pallid, but blue-stained, skin he looked a figure from an older and more brutal age. Around his neck he wore a white silk scarf, and in his hand he carried a stick about a yard long, narrow, rather pointed, and elaborately turned like the leg of an old-fashioned chair. It stood out amid the modern surroundings, this ancient and embarrassingly naked symbol of potency and authority, as something eccentric and strange, but none the less *real*. This, I thought, must be the under-manager, because as he moved he seemed to herd everyone naturally around him – the miners milling and eddying, without even seeming to realise it, around his overbearing but not unkindly presence. I noticed another stick, plain and slightly more pointed. These sticks, I was told by Dave, the training officer, who had arranged my visit, showed that these men were under-managers or overmen. They were called the 'wand of authority' or the 'yard of authority', and they were a relic of the coal owners' days, when the managers used literally to wield the big stick; though he said, with a slight smirk, that not everyone used them now.

This, however, was not the under-manager – Mr Grimshaw – who was to take me down. Mr Grimshaw was coming towards us now, and he was quite a different kind of man from any I had encountered before in the pits. No silk scarf, no turned wand of authority for him. Yet there was that insistence, even from the training officer, on the term 'Mister' ... In that world, where from the stranger's first phone call he is put automatically on first-name terms, this was not a mere form of address, this was an honorific title, a symbol of power no less ancient and esoteric than the scarf and stick. And no matter where we went in the pit, I heard this anticipatory buzz around the man – *Mister Grimshaw, Mister Grimshaw.* Even his surname had a Dickensian ring about it. Yet there was nothing Dickensian about Mr Grimshaw.

He seemed in his *crasher* – his helmet – to be about a foot taller than me, with a narrow face, a jutting jaw, a reddish beard and lively blue eyes appraising my insignificance. This was the man who had twice previously cancelled my visits. He gave me a very firm handshake, but there was reserve there, and I sensed that here was a man remote from the feudal familiarity of the Durham pit world. The very unconcern of his dress – why bother with encumbrances like scarves and sticks? He even slouched slightly, the weight of the objects on his belt making his hips jut forward – seemed to demonstrate concerns beyond that world of work as ritual. Was that a trace of Yorkshire I detected in his tones? There was a sense of freedom about him – the sense of an overview. And his overview at that moment was that I was a liability, who had to be got into the pit and out again as quickly as possible. He hooked his brass official's lamp on to his belt and we squeezed into the packed cage.

As we left the Titan area, he said we must be quick, as he wanted to get the first shift set back to the shaft bottom. The man-riding belts, the longest of which had taken us four kilometres, had been speeded up to save work time. Each man was now able to work an extra two minutes a day, though it meant the belts did go rather fast. At Easington, I had been told to lie on my stomach. But Mr Grimshaw sat up a few yards ahead of me, cross-legged like a goblin on a toadstool. I imitated him, though it meant having to lean forward to avoid girders from time to time.

He soon left me behind, with his determined forward-leaning stride – characteristic of miners, and caused by the weight of the appliances at their waists. Soon he was just a faint light far off in the distant dimness, with me having to run over the difficult ground to keep him in view at all. As I came off the last riding belt, I heard a great scream ahead of me: '*Fucking bastard!*' And he suddenly disappeared from view. Such was the frenzy of the cry, I thought that maybe Mr Grimshaw had been hurt. Then as I approached the junction, he came running into view, smashing his crasher and lamp together with ferocious force. 'The *cunt*!' he roared, quite oblivious of my presence.

He turned to me, calming slightly. 'The bastard set's left early.' He turned and looked the way it had gone. 'I'm sorry,' I said. 'But I couldn't walk any faster.' 'You're all right,' he said. 'It's not your fault, lad.' He called me 'lad' or 'Mark, lad', though he might well have been younger than me.

He got on the phone and told them to send a locomotive, as he had a visitor who had to be got out as soon as possible. We walked a bit further, turned a corner, and there stood a loco. We hoisted ourselves aboard, and Mr Grimshaw's spirits lifted as he got the driver to send a message through cancelling the other loco. 'I apologise,' he said with a magnanimous smile. 'My watch must've been slow.'

'Aye,' said the driver to his mate. 'He should be buying more than a new fucking watch on what he's getting.'

Mr Grimshaw examined his helmet mock ruefully. 'I've smashed my lamp prong out of alignment.'

He was, he told me, from Scarborough. His family had moved to Ashington in Northumberland, and he had spent a year in the local pit straight from school. He had then gone to university – off his own bat, he was keen to stress – and taken a degree in mining. He had been under-manager at another pit, before coming to Wearmouth a year or so before. He was schooled minutely in the geological and technical aspects of mining. He could see with chilling clarity the economic ramifications of everything that was taking place around him. But at the same time he had that first year's experience of life on the other side of the process, which helped him understand the feelings and concerns of the men under him. Mr Grimshaw had it all ways.

They had, Mr Grimshaw said, been mining the narrow seams very badly, and they were now totally reliant on the high coal to save the pit. To me, those seams had looked at least twelve feet high. Compared to the seams through which I had crawled at Easington and Willington, it was as though I were in a cathedral of coal. 'We'll be standing up!' a man who was going to be working there had told me. 'We won't know we're born!' But the seams were, I was assured, no more than eight and a half feet. The pit had been making severe losses, and it had not, Dave the training manager told me over a cup of coffee in his office, been a good time.

He had arrived there at the same time as Mr Grimshaw – about a year before. He was a small, dark, soft-spoken man, with an almost Welsh lilt in his vowels. After beginning as an electrician at Ryton in Northumberland, he had become involved in training, going to work at the Nack, the training pit at Seaham – called the Nickety-nack, after the rattling of the winding gear. The Nack had closed in 1986, and the men were now trained at the individual pits – a matter of regret for Dave since at Seaham they had had the whole pit and its equipment to use whenever they wanted, whereas now they had to wait for the equipment to become free. Now, to reduce the amount of man hours lost to the industry through training, 'open learning' was being promoted. Men took packages of books and videos home to work through in their spare time. Dave showed me one: a folder of booklets of multiple choice questions on 'safe slinging' – whatever that was. A miner would be paid £40 for completing this in his own time.

For all his affability, indeed the kindness and concern with which he had arranged my visit, Dave remained distant. He had a way of looking at me sideways, as if to make it easier to turn his head away and withdraw into his melancholy thoughts. He seemed at such moments to cut off from my presence altogether. He seemed a man adrift; a man cut off from the things that had drawn him into the industry in the first place. Sitting there in his portacabin, bewildered among his booklets, he was perhaps not long for the industry. But then the industry itself was perhaps not long for this world. At the end of our conversation he led me out into the sunlit yard, pointed off in the direction of the town and turned away without a word.

It was a balmy spring day. The centre of Sunderland lay only a few hundred yards from the pit head, across the Wearmouth Bridge. But walking in the utterly characterless shopping precinct with the same chain-stores to be found the length and breadth of the land, from which one felt that the important things – the great clamour of activity around the 'old' industries that had created the town – had been and gone, it was difficult to imagine that the world of the pit was continuing so near under the rock beneath our feet. The men of the night shift would now be getting into the sets to go the thirteen kilometres out under the sea, and would continue to do so, twenty-four hours a day, for the time being at least.

How remote that world of 'marra' – and all the other terms – seemed in the antiseptic mundanity of these streets. Such words were rarely heard there now. They were simply the vernacular of a marginal and dying industry. But in East Durham, even in Peterlee, you were still called marra as a matter of course. There, the language and ethos of the mines were still inescapable. It was easy to conceive of the world below as an inverse image, dark and hellish, of the world above. But listening to the miners, who had created the upper and lower worlds for me with their words, one often felt that it was the subterranean world that had the greater reality, while the daylight hours which one drank and gambled away were the illusion – carefree but insignificant.

16

The Labour Woman

T HERE WERE two old fellers, who every evening sat in the snooker end of the Big Club, their caps pulled down over their foreheads, intently watching the play. They never drank anything, they just sat there, like 'spuggies on a wal'. And every night at eight-thirty, virtually by the clock, they'd get up and head for home. One day, however, I got talking to one of them.

'It was a hell of a place, this – once ower. The biggest single colliery in the world! But there was nowt rough. Nobody could say this was a rough place. During the 1926 strike it was very quiet here.

'There was a big bloke come here, before the strike. Called him Claude. But he did nowt. He was naybody. Then there was Walker; and he had three or four behind him – big lads. They were price cutters. Brought in by the bosses to work the hewers' price off. You were working marras, see, and if you had three ha'pence a tub, they were doing the bugger for a ha'penny. They were paid by the bosses to do it, and when they'd worked the price down they'd move on. But there was nay rough stuff. Nowt happened. That was before the 1926 strike, that.

'The Big Club was mortgaged during the strike. Every member was paid five pund ten shillun out of the mortgage, to keep them gannin'. You had to gan to the Store [the Co-op] for your groceries. You agreed to pay them back, one and a tanner a week, when the strike was over. Everyone paid, bar a few that left the colliery. But that was the only way you could gan. Without that you had nowt.

'That shop down Sixth Street, on the corner by the Post Office. The communists took that over in 1926, and they tried to get a start here. One or two lads joined. They got different people in to speak, and they asked you to sign on.

'There were two lads – communists – used to gan around speaking. Harry Pollit was one, and there was his little cross-marra, his understudy, like. I forget his name. They used to come here spoutin', trying to get a membership for their party. But they never went in the Miners' Hall. Oh, no. They always kept the communists out of there. Anyone had communist ideas, they always managed to force them out, somehow.

'The communists did manage to get a bit of a foothold in the DMA after the '26 strike. But it came to nowt, because the Labour Party ruled the roost by then.

'I went to a meeting or two, but I never joined, because I didn't believe in it at the time. But looking back on it, the communists did nowt wrong. I mean they agitated. They'd tell you how to get at the bosses, how to bring them down. And there were some rotten bloody bosses in them days. I was a mechanic, and these engineers and under-engineers, if they didn't like you, they made life hell for you.

'J. P. Hall was the manager here. The coke ovens had their manager, but he was under J. P. Hall. He was the boss of the whole colliery. A big, tall feller. But I cared nowt for 'im. He was a manager, and no manager was popular with the working class.

'In them times, if the bosses got down on a man or a lad, they kept him down. If he was a bit of an agitator, the buggers used to nail him down. They used to quiet him. They'd give him the worst jobs. And if he hadn't a job, they'd make him wait. My boss, the Engineer, he knew I was on the union. I was on the committee. I was in the Labour Party. So he gave me the worst jobs. But after nationalisation, you had more say to the gaffer. If they knew you were on the union, they knew you might be able to do them some harm, so they were careful how they treated you.

'I never paid much attention to the last strike. It was after my time, like. Not that I thought it was a waste of time. They were only fighting for something they were entitled tee. What did they call that lad from Yorkshire, the leader . . . ? I mean, I never followed him. I never read any of his writings or owt, but he was a good leader as far as the men from Yorkshire were concerned. He was a bloody agitator, I know that.'

At one time it was only at the behest of the chairman of the local Miners' Lodge that anyone became a district or county councillor in East Durham. And if the chairman wanted to become a councillor himself, as many had done, there was virtually no way he could be stopped. Since it was, in those days, a foregone conclusion that whoever had the Labour Party nomination would be elected, the real struggles took place at the nomination meetings, rather than at the elections themselves. Easington Constituency Labour Party had 23,000 members affiliated through the NUM, all of whom had voting rights, and it was quite common to see a hundred miners walk into a ward meeting and carry the Lodge's nomination.

Eventually party rules were changed so that only individual members could vote at meetings, along with voting representatives from the Lodges. If a Lodge particularly wanted someone on the council, it was not unknown for the chairman to use union funds to pay the individual membership fees of however many miners it took to get that person on – up to a hundred.

Each Lodge was allocated seats, according to the size of its membership, on the Management Committee of the District Labour Party. On the Executive Committee, there was one seat for each County Council area (Horden, for example, represented one County Council Area, Peterlee two) and one seat representing the union for each area – though it was likely, as a matter of course, that both representatives would be Lodge officials. Generally about 70 per cent of the Management Committee were union people, while the union 'almost totally controlled' the Executive. It was said that the real decisions affecting Easington Labour Party were taken in Durham, when the chairmen and secretaries of the various lodges got together after their meetings at Red Hill.

Perhaps this was the kind of thing people were referring to when they said that the Durham Labour Party was the most corrupt in the country. On the other hand, when one considered that at one time nearly 90 per cent of the total insured population of East Durham were employed in the mining industry, these facts were hardly surprising. The union was the main avenue for the furtherance of the interests, for the collective self-improvement of the working class. The union had created the Labour Party. Anyone with any ability or political ambition became involved in the union as a matter of course. 'The Union,' I was told by one veteran Labour activist, 'was *everything*. The Labour Party was an afterthought.'

In those days, the Labour Party's Women's Sections were also a force to be reckoned with. They too could flood a meeting with members affiliated through the women's section, but not otherwise active in the Party, to carry their nomination, who was usually a woman. In most villages an *entente* had been established whereby the women were guaranteed one District Council seat in return for supporting the miners' nominations for all of the others. In Horden, the miners took four seats, the mechanics one and the women one. In each village there was a powerful woman who naturally filled this latter position, and who ruled over the Women's Section for decades. In Horden, there was Mrs Winter, wife of the famously left-wing Lodge Secretary Joe Winter. She was Horden's county councillor for many years, until the men decided to replace her, a year before she would have become an alderman. Then there was Mrs Beaumont, and then Mrs Salmon. In Easington Colliery, there was Renie Macmanners.

'Every year on the first Saturday in June, all the women's sections in the county would gather in Durham, for the Women's Gala. In those days there were sixteen women's sections in this constituency alone. We'd march through the city with our banners, and as many bands as we could get, up to Wharton Park. I can remember presiding over the meeting there when Nye Bevan and Jennie Lee were the speakers, and the chief of police told me there were well over 10,000 people in the park. The miners realised how important we were. That's why they helped us in all ways – financially, and loaning us their Redhills headquarters whenever we wanted it. They even bought a silver chain of office for the chairman of the Women's Advisory Council. Now, of course, there's no Advisory Council, no Gala, and hardly any women's sections functioning in the constituency at all. There's no sections in Seaham or Peterlee. Horden are down to about five members. There's only Easington that really functions.

'Women today contend, and they're right in a way, that there shouldn't be separate women's organisations. They're all members of the Labour Party, and they should be there on an equal basis with men. But in the past it was absolutely necessary to have women's sections, because the men got their experience of speaking and organising through the union. They decided what was going to happen at their union meetings. The different unions, the miners, the mechanics, the cokemen and all the rest, did deals with each other and put them into effect at the Labour Party meetings. So if the women hadn't been organised, they'd have been left totally out in the cold. Even today there's an attitude that women are good for making tea and taking leaflets round and not much else ...

'I was born in a little village near Chester-le-Street, called Wald-ridge Fell, where my father was Lodge Secretary. Both my father and my grandfather were from the Miners' Union and the Methodist Chapel. There was the pit, and along the street was the little Methodist chapel. The chapel elders and the union committee were, literally, the same people. And then there was the Labour Party. At election time me and my brothers were sent out to put the leaflets through the doors. We didn't really understand it, but we naturally assumed that anyone who was a Methodist was a Socialist. We didn't know where the one ended and the other began.

'I first took my Party card out in 1931, but I was married with a little daughter. I was busy with amateur dramatics and the chapel choir, and I didn't have much time for the Labour Party. Then one day, I was standing in the main street in Easington, and a big election parade came marching up from the colliery. It was 1936, and the Labour Party was running Manny Shinwell to try to get rid of Ramsay MacDonald who they reckoned had ratted on them by forming the National Government. The miners had the band and banner out, and I was standing in a shop doorway with the shopkeeper, a man I knew well, because he was the choirmaster at the chapel. Then a man came along with a collection box saying, "Help the International Brigade fight the fascists in Spain." And this man I was standing beside said, "And you're running a Jew to be your member of parliament!" This other man said, "He's the best man we could find." And the shopkeeper said, "Grand day when a place like Easington is represented by a yid!" And this man was a Methodist, the choir leader! I was so upset, I was almost in tears, and I went and told my father. A grown woman running home to her father to unburden herself! He said, "You're old enough to make your own decisions. You'll have to do what you think is right." I said, "I'll never go back to his choir again. Never!" And I never did. I spent all my time working for the Labour Party instead. And that was the time when we got Manny Shinwell into parliament.

'I went to conferences wherever I could, and I joined the Left Book Club, which was just a few coppers. During the war, the chairman of the local Miners' Lodge and I ran the National Council for Labour Colleges in Easington. We had this weekly class to discuss politics. It was during the blackout. The air raids would be going on overhead, and we would just carry on with our discussions. I was the only woman. I just became part of it, and in the end I think they forgot I was a woman.

'I was on the District Council for twenty years and the County

Council for ten years. I was a magistrate, and I was voted on to the International Committee for Local Authorities with representatives from all over the world.

'Every three years they had the nominations for the District Council. I'd meet men in the streets and they'd say, "Dig yer toes in! We'll be there." I knew the men would be in the Club buying those men drinks for their votes. But they still voted for me.

'I can picture the old ward meeting in Easington, where the women would be sitting up one side of the room and the men up the other. And you'd be sitting there counting them to see which way the vote would go. But it's different now. Women get where they want to now. But there's a lot of women who've gone on to the Council who've come off of their own accord. They realised it wasn't what they wanted. You've got to be committed. Because from a woman's point of view, there's a lot in doing that work that is really wasted time.'

In a book on local history published nearly a quarter of a century ago, I had found a map of Easington Constituency that showed the different County Council areas, such as Horden, Peterlee, Easington Colliery, Blackhall, and listed the names of the district councillors who then served them. I was astonished to find not only how many of the names were familiar to me through my researches of the last few months, but that many of the incumbents still held these seats. Apart from the many other considerations that sprang to mind, I could not imagine why anyone would *want* to be a local councillor for nearly thirty years.

'It was a bit of power for them,' somebody familiar with local politics told me. 'It meant that they were someone of consequence when they went out in the pubs and the clubs. And particularly in those days, when they controlled the housing, the district councillors did have quite a bit of power. If a councillor wanted to give someone a house, he could, and that was it.'

In most villages, the women's sections no longer functioned. The union was in the process of disappearing altogether. There were now only two pits working in East Durham, for both of which imminent closure was predicted. And while the councillors still had their strongholds in the different clubs, the old mass canvassing grounds like the Big Club, where nomination battles could be won or lost in epic pint-buying sessions were now so little patronised it was hardly worth an aspiring councillor even bothering to go into them. Yet although Horden was now represented by an Independent on the County Council, and there had even been a *Conservative* on the District Council for Horden, the ossified remains of the political system created by the pit still held sway over the area, simply because nothing had yet emerged to replace it.

Critics loved to scoff at how this system had elevated miners barely able to write their names to the position of councillor, to tell stories of their huge entertainment bills, of their drunk and disorderly behaviour on Easington Village green, of how the Education Committee interviewing teachers for a headship had been able to think of no criteria for selection other than to put the candidates' names in a hat. But whether an outsider liked it or not, these people *were* the people. They were the neighbours and the workmates and the relatives of the people who were electing them, in a way that local politicians in most other parts of the country are not.

It was only in Peterlee that the pattern had been broken. In Peterlee, it was muttered darkly, they had *teachers* and all sorts running the Labour Party. Teachers were figures of peculiar mistrust and resentment in the political world of East Durham. Since in the past they had been among the few representatives of the professional classes in the area, there was now some suspicion at their presence in the party of the workers, a feeling that they might try to use their superior knowledge to pull the wool over the eyes of their less educated fellows, and – although education had long since devolved to County authority – a sense that they were only there for their own professional advancement.

My uncle Fred, who had taken me round Horden on that first visit, had been a headmaster. He had started his political career in Easington Village, and whenever he raised something at a meeting, he would sense a 'reaction' from those present who weren't teachers. Not that he had found this an absolute obstacle. He'd been secretary of Easington Constituency Labour Party for more than a decade, and it had been the miners who had put him there. Fred had had no inkling that he might achieve such a position until he was approached by the chairman of one of the Lodges. And they had put him there in place of a miner!

There were once five sisters who were all members of the Labour Party. Three married, and two became mayors of Peterlee; though the ones that became mayors were not necessarily the ones that didn't marry.

'There were nine of us – the four boys and us girls. Our father was Labour, but he never joined the Party. The same with our lads.

They never joined the Party. It was just us girls – and Mother of course. We've always been in the Party.

'You couldn't call us religious, but we had to go somewhere. And my mother had always liked the Salvation Army, so we went there. You had to learn a piece of poetry for the anniversary, and everyone used to come and hear you say your "piece" as it was called. On Good Friday, you got all dressed up, and all the chapels and the Salvation Army got together and went through the streets singing hymns. And at the end of the morning you got an orange to take home.

'Every year they used to have a trip. At first they used to go to what was called Simpson's Field, at the top of Ellison's Bank, where it continued down into the Dene. It was like a sports day, and you got a bag with a sandwich, a sausage roll and a cake in it. But then as the funds got better we went to Seaton. And then as things got really good, we went to Redcar, and we got a shilling to spend. We used to think we were everybody for to have that shillun.

'Every year the Labour Party had a float on May Day, and us girls would all be dressed in white with green sashes and green and white rosettes – because green and white were the Labour Party colours in those days. And they had a trip for us as well. They started at Seaton Carew, then they used to take us to South Shields or Redcar. We used to think we were the bee's knees when we got away like that, because you hardly ever went on a bus in those days.

'Our father was a stoneman, on the ten o'clock shift at the pit. It never occurred to me at the time that we were poor, though looking back on it, I suppose we were very poor. But my mother always encouraged us. She always tried to get us to speak properly. The men could talk as rough as they liked, but you hadn't to. Even before we went to Henry Smith's, the grammar school, we had a proper tunic and blouse for school. But as soon as we got home, off it came, and we got our rags on. That was the way it was for most people in those days.

'I used to go round the doors and sell the women's section magazine for my mother – *The Labour Woman* I think they called it. It cost tuppence. And at election time we used to take the leaflets round for her. The Labour Party used to hold dances in the Miners' Hall and my mother was always cloakroom woman. When Shinwell was elected, I went to the victory dance with our Jenny. Ramsay MacDonald of course had got beat. He came to speak at the Empress Cinema, but he got shouted down. They wouldn't let him speak. He was our MP, but they said he was a turncoat. I can't really remember what it was about. I can just remember being there in the crowd as he came out, and everybody shouting at him.

'My mother had been in service at Wardley Colliery. But when she was young she'd been sent to work on the farms. They used to queue up, and the farmers used to come and feel them to see who they were going to hire – just like they do with animals. But mother was always a big woman.

'I don't know how she got involved in the Labour Party, but to me she always just was. She went to the Co-operative Women's Guild one Tuesday, and the women's section of the Labour Party the next. I think those are the only times she went out unless she was visiting my auntie. The Co-operative Guild was like a women's section of the Co-op. It was something like the Women's Institute – except that was for the better off sort of person, and the Co-operative Guild was for the worse off. Different recipes. How to make cheap food. How to get the best out of your oven. The best things to buy at the Co-op. Of course, everyone was in the Co-op then. You could get practically everything at the Co-op.

'When I was fifteen, my parents took me out of the grammar school, because they couldn't afford to keep me there. My mother had to pay £5 to get me released before I was sixteen. I went into service – to "place", as they called it – in Manchester, as a maid. We all went, all the four elder sisters – to different parts of the country. It was only our Joyce, the youngest, who finished her education, because by that time there were four of us sending money home. She ended up Mayor of Peterlee. But then, so did I.'

We were in a small terraced house, dating probably from the 1960s, right up the other end of Peterlee, near the A19. The speaker was Peggy Bryan, née Jackson, a stocky person, her voice, in the flow of mid-afternoon recollection, even and reassuring.

'In my mother's day there would have been about sixty women took *The Labour Woman*. Then there would be those that were members but didn't take it, and a lot of people who just went occasionally. They used to hold the meetings in the Miners' Hall. The seven officials sat at the top table. But we didn't have that in our day, because I didn't get fully involved in the Labour Party till we came to Peterlee, about 1960.'

The back door suddenly swung open. 'Here's another of our lot,' said Peggy. 'Howay in, Mavis!' She carried on telling me how she'd become active in the Labour Party, and how in the early days, Peterlee had been ruled by Horden Parish Council, as Mavis staggered in, a bundle of slender birdlike energy, compared with Peggy's more solid presence, and maybe four or five years younger. 'Are yer tired, now?' asked Peggy.

'Ee, aa'm crippled!'

When Peggy had finished her story, Mavis told me how she'd come to join the Labour Party.

'I put in for a job, serving school meals, and it was supposed to be for single women and widows. Well, all the married women got picked, and I was left out. And I'd been assured by the union man that I'd walk it. 'Cause I'd already worked in the canteen at Alexandra – the clothing factory, you see. Well, I went to his house, and he was out walking the dog. So I told his wife what had happened. She said, "You're kidding? Wait till Jack hears about this!" So he came round our house and he said, "Is it true what I've heard?" And he made me tell him all the members of the panel – the school governors. And they were all members of Horden Labour Party – Mrs Beaumont, Mrs Winter . . .'

'All good friends of our mother's, mind,' said Peggy. 'All good friends!'

'Anyway, he looked into it. And he said would I be prepared to go to a meeting of Horden Labour Party to face these people. He was going to collect me to take me down. Seven o'clock at the Miners' Hall, I think it was. But it never came to that. Because in the meantime I got a letter, *begging* to offer me the post, subject to references. I was there for twenty-three years. I was shop steward for a lot of years, and in the end I got made a governor myself. At Acre Rigg School, just up the back here.'

I wanted to make sure I'd understood the story correctly. 'So you were a single person at the time?'

'She still is,' said Peggy.

'Yes,' said Mavis. 'Anyway, when I told the caretaker how I'd got there, he said, "Well, you know what to do, don't you?" I said, "No, what's that?" "Join the Labour Party!"'

'You went on the council just after Peterlee Parish Council was formed, didn't you?' said Peggy.

'That's right. We started off as parish councillors. Then we got made governors. And I always made sure that no one who came in front of me had to beg and grovel. See, in those days, if the head teacher liked your face, you could get in by the back door. But we put a stop to that! When I got made governor, I said, "You get in by the proper way or not at all!" Of course, you got badly liked by the head teachers, but I couldn't care less about that.

'Oh, but Labour, mind – when we were little, we ate and slept it.'

'Mother never went anywhere except the Labour Party and the Co-operative Women's Guild. She didn't even go to the Labour Party, did she? The proper Labour Party, where the men go.'

'What we call "the ward"? No.'

'I've got a photograph of her with the other officials, sitting there at the top table with the cakes they'd made.'

'I could name them all,' said Mavis. 'And they were all characters. And she was never going to go back, was she? Oh no, she was never going back!'

'She used to come in so annoyed,' said Peggy.

'And then the next thing. Do me hair! Get me good coat out! And she'd be first there! But they seemed to have more get up and go in those days.'

'We're genteel compared to what they were,' said Peggy.

'I'm retired now, like,' said Mavis. 'But if anyone's going through to the union meeting at Easington in a car, I still go along and have my say.'

'When I lost my seat on the District Council,' said Peggy, 'I went to Dewhirst's clothing factory in Peterlee, and I got made shop steward there. I didn't know anything about industry, but I learnt as I went along.' She chuckled to herself. 'I soon picked up the rules!'

17

The Lads in the Middle

I'D BEEN INVITED to contribute my 'areas of expertise' to the production of a magazine at Horden Youth Centre, part of the old
school down the street from the Miners' Hall. It would be entered
for a competition organised by Comic Relief designed to promote
young people's awareness of the wide range of the charity's work:
development in Africa, drug abuse, homelessness, help for the elderly.
Hundreds of schools and youth organisations throughout the country
would be participating. Linda, one of the youth workers, and a relative
newcomer to the centre, wanted to pursue the project with a girls'
group she had started, to try to encourage them to do something more
than play table tennis to the accompaniment of thundering rave music.

The first meeting was rowdy but inspirational; rowdy partly
because everyone had to shout to be heard over the rave music thundering from the main hall. Tracey and Michelle, two rumbunctious
thirteen year olds who sat draped in each other's arms, wanted to
do everything. Rachel, a quiet fourteen year old, was confident
of her contribution on the art side. Caroline, fifteen, amiable
but uncertain, wanted to do anything connected with red noses.
Tracey and Michelle, it was decided, would write articles on drugs
and homelessness respectively. Rachel would design the magazine's
logo, while Caroline would produce a recipe for a red nose cake.
Two older girls who arrived later volunteered to write words for a
humorous rap song about Comic Relief.

The idea that we might write something connected with the
elderly met with a forceful response.

'They just sit there in their old people's homes,' said Michelle, 'waiting for other people to do everything for them!'

'Yeh,' said Tracey. 'If you go near their houses, they just come out and wrong yer. They've always got a real *twisty* look on their face!'

'Someone should write something on what should be *done* about old people,' said Michelle.

'We're supposed to be helping them,' I said, 'not exterminating them.'

Clearly the young in this part of the world had no more sympathy for the old than the old had for them. The idea of writing about Comic Relief's work in the Third World received even shorter shrift. Starving Africans should look to their own governments for help, not the West.

'I'd forget that,' said Linda. 'If it doesn't relate directly to them they're not interested.'

In the 'press kit' provided by Comic Relief, it recommended that aspirant journalists should listen to African music and read African novels, so that they could get a fuller perspective on the charity's work in the continent, which placed a high premium on the involvement of the recipients. While I was sure there were schools and youth centres where this challenge would be taken up, the plane of consciousness on which they existed was so removed from the reality of Horden Youth Centre it was almost heartrending. Even if these children had wanted to read African novels, where would they have got them from? The library would have to order them. Apart from a rack of paperback thrillers and romances in the Asda supermarket, it was impossible to buy books of any description in East Durham.

The next week, Linda was away at a meeting, and of the girls, only Tracey was there. She'd written an article on drugs. It wasn't bad, but needed work. It had, for example, only two punctuation marks. When I pointed this out, she informed me rather sniffily that she was top of her class in English. Realising I was foisting an activity on her equivalent to more homework, I let her go back to the table tennis.

The week after that the place was completely silent. The cavernous old classrooms, painted in brilliant colours, were brightly lit, but empty except for the deserted table-tennis tables. I found Linda sitting nervously in her office. 'Something's happened,' she said.

A fifteen-year-old girl had been raped the previous Saturday night, on the area of waste ground behind The Trust – the only one of Horden's three 'wine bars' still functioning – by two boys, aged fourteen and fifteen.

'No one's been in here for nights,' said Linda. 'Whether they prefer to stay out on street corners talking about it, or whether their parents are keeping them away ... It's ironic if they are, because the two lads who did it are barred out of here. Either way, the membership's plummeted. We had thirty-eight. Now we've got less than twenty.'

Who was the girl?

'They're not saying. I only hope it wasn't one of my little girls,' she said, referring to Tracey and Michelle. 'They've got such confidence, those two. I'd hate to see anything dent it.'

A couple of days later, I mentioned the matter when I was interviewing one of the district councillors. He lowered his voice, wincing, as was his continual habit, wheezing his words out. 'The two lads have been given a conditional discharge by the court, obviously to appear again. I did hear they've been sent up to stay with their grandparents in Peterlee, to keep them out of the road. Because there's people that are crying out for ...' He winced meaningfully.

'Blood?'

'Something of that nature. There's going to be some kind of retribution the way people feel. You've got to imagine the family ... We'd all feel the same.' He lowered his voice even further, grinding the words breathily from the sides of his mouth. 'They say a screwdriver was held to her throat while they were doing it ... Thankfully her name hasn't been bandied about.'

There was no retribution, however. No one bayed for blood. Not in my presence anyway. Asking people about it point blank, I could elicit no response stronger than a sigh or a shrug. There's something inherently repulsive about vigilantism. But there's something even more sinister, something eerie about total silence – about no response whatsoever.

A similar incident had taken place the year before, when a girl was violated on the playing field of the local comprehensive school, during the dinner hour, by a group of her fellow pupils. Everyone knew who had done it. The ringleader and his friends 'only' got time at a remand centre, I was told by one of their contemporaries, 'and not long either'.

When I'd first planned my project in Horden, I'd had such difficulties finding somewhere to live – the private rented sector in

East Durham being virtually non-existent – that I'd applied to the council for a house. Finally I was offered one, in Hawthorn Crescent, two streets up from Oak Terrace, where my father had grown up, on the other side of the Top Road, where it began to dip down towards Blackhall. Hawthorn Crescent had once been the most sought after street in Horden, one of the first with bathrooms and inside toilets. The great Hedley Mason, the first JP from Horden, and an alderman, had lived in Hawthorn Crescent. But Fred's friend Jack, who had worked in the council's maintenance department for years, told me not to touch it. 'That street was all right once over, but it's been run ragged.'

'Who by?'

He laughed at the naivety of the question. 'Why, them that live there!'

I made my way cautiously round the long curve of the Crescent. A thin drizzle hung in the cold late autumn air. The place was deserted. As I got closer to where my house was, the gardens became less and less well cared for. Some did not have fences, were merely patches of dead grass and weeds. The familiar draped curtains and rows of assiduously dusted ornaments gave way to blank and filthy nets, or no curtains at all. But appearances could be deceptive. The house of the family that were destroying the lives of the people around them might not look any more sinister than any other. In the summer, I had seen oil-stained neanderthal types sprawled black eyed on their porches, as their fellows tinkered with motorbikes and bits of vehicles spread all over the garden and pavement. But so what? They might have been canny enough lads who'd do owt fer yer.

And then I saw the house. Every door and window was clamped over with a steel grille – as was normal practice for any house left empty in that part of the world. Otherwise, every possible fitting would be ripped from it within hours – small boys doing most of the work, shoved in by their fathers and uncles through narrow bathroom windows – and the remaining shell burnt out by children.

The grille over the front door was covered in graffiti. Two teenage girls and a boy leant against it in conversation. Did they come with the house? I wondered. I noticed a middle-aged man watching me from the living room of one of the few 'respectable' houses left at that end of the street. Then he disappeared.

A couple of nights later, I bumped into one of the councillors in the Miners' Hall. 'Oh aye,' he said, in his dry, deliberate voice. 'We're really looking for someone seven foot tall and about twenty stone, to sort the next-door neighbours out.' I was not able to

establish exactly what these people had done, but the police had
organised a public meeting on the matter. The initiative had fizzled
out because no one was prepared to give evidence in court.

It was a surprise to me that a community that had cohered
so effectively to provide for itself during times of trial such as
the '84–85 strike could not find a collective method of dealing
with a problem as relatively minor as Hawthorn Crescent. For no
matter how much people decried the breakdown of the old ways,
Horden still was a community. It was still virtually impossible to be
anonymous in Horden. I didn't know any of the people that lived in
my street, but I frequently came across people I'd never met before
who knew all about me and where I lived. You couldn't 'just live'
in Horden the way you might in certain parts of London, without
being implicated in any way in the lives of the people around you.
The bad estates of Horden were not vast impersonal forests of otherness. They were ordinary rows of little houses minutes from your
back door. The scale of everything was still so close and so intimate.
Why did the people of Horden tolerate the behaviour of people like
'them'?

There was, the more I learnt and the more I reflected on it,
a scarcely definable ambivalence among the people towards such
things. For virtually everyone you met lived near 'terrible' people
who were ruining their streets or their back lane or the next street.
But there was a curious reluctance to confront this problem as part
of the reality of 'Horden' – as something that might be latent in the
organism of the place itself.

The Angels, the notorious wine bar situated on the Top Road
directly opposite the old people's sheltered housing, scene of massive
punch-ups and horrendous traffic accidents virtually every Friday
and Saturday night, that was closed down after drugs raids by the
police, had attracted bad elements 'from all over'. The Bradford
and Northern Housing Association, which had taken the remaining colliery houses over from the union, had, it was said, filled
the village with unmarried mothers – the scruffs of Birmingham
and Bristol. The causatory factors were always external – just as
the young people's appetite for every kind of solvent from Tippex
thinners to four-star petrol could be blamed on the willingness of
Asian shopkeepers to sell them glue. It may all have been true. But
I never heard the proliferation of 'odd' accents they described. The
only odd accent I heard was mine.

I was always hearing about 'rough' people. But most of the
people I passed in the street looked what I would term rough: the

blunt-faced women in shell-suits seizing on cancer sticks, the men in blackened army fatigues slipping shadow-like from their sea-coal lorries. For all I knew these were the people who had stood valiantly in the soup kitchens and on the picket lines. Or were they the 'terrible' people who were bringing the place down? Either way, whether you liked it or not, such people *were* Horden.

And while people loved to talk about the days when the bobby had clipped their ears with his gloves, it was an area, so I was told again and again, by people who represented some form of authority, that had always had a low level of co-operation with the police. In fact in the North-east as a whole, I was told, there was a greater tolerance towards things like receiving stolen goods than in the rest of the country. It was seen as socially acceptable over a far broader range of society. People knew the pubs to go to, and the people to ask, to get whatever they wanted.

There had always been bad families in Horden. Families where the parents and the grandparents before them were no good. But you lived beside them, because you had no choice. You knew them. You knew who they were. And they knew that if they overstepped the mark, you would come and sort them out. They took odd things. They might nick things out of your garden shed. But they wouldn't come in the house. They'd always been there. You'd been to school, or not been to school, with them. And your kids went to school, or didn't go to school, with their kids. You'd lived for a time in a street with more than its fair share of families like that. It had been OK. You wouldn't want to move back there, mind. But dealing with people like that was all part of what living in a place like Horden was about. And you didn't ask anyone else to live your life for you. It was in a way a measure of the virility of Horden that it could contain such people.

'I think what's happened in a place like Horden,' said an ex-policeman of my acquaintance, who was himself from a mining family, 'is that there's always been a slight tolerance of this type of thing. You know, they say, "Oh, they're Horden people. We know who they are." They're relatives of relatives, or distant cousins of people you know. There's a reluctance to take it very seriously. They feel that it can be contained in the community. What's happened is that this tolerance of what's acceptable has been stretched further and further over say the last two decades, without people noticing, until it's got totally out of control.'

In the days when the women drew their husbands' pay at the

colliery office, the centre of Horden would be milling with people on
a Friday. There were queues in all the shops, and it would take hours
to get round because you kept bumping into people you knew, and
everyone stopped to talk. Now of course it was deserted. But Peterlee
was still frantic on a Friday. Old pitmen in caps and car-coats. Young
couples trailing their squawling bairns. Middle-aged women striding
out determinedly with their shopping bags. There were queues at the
building societies and the banks, everyone desperate for tenners for
the weekend. There was a market in the square beneath the tower
block of the magistrates court: mostly Asian traders selling cheap
clothes, budget CDs, video games, Hulk Hogan calendars. Gangs of
lads hung over the parapet of the overhead walkways. It seemed as
though the whole of the East Durham world was there. And everyone
was talking, bursting into loud and animated conversations where
they stood. The forecourt of Safeways, where it went round under
the raised shopping area, was raucous with acknowledgement and
acclamation, the flashing eyes and gaping mouths of people in the
full flow of encounters with people they hadn't seen since at least last
week. Meanwhile hundreds of other people, loaded with shopping,
their bairns bawling or stuffing themselves from plastic packets, tried
to fight their way round or through these full-blooded engagements.

In the centre of it all, an old pitman, a massive fellow with
a great red face, sat on a bench eating yogurt from one of those
subdivided cartons, where you flavour the yogurt yourself with a
portion of fruit. He did this with great delicacy and deliberation,
looking round at the crowd as he sucked contentedly on the spoon,
enjoying the feel of the sun on his face.

I sat in the dense, smoke-filled interior of Sparks' Bakery, the
most congenial of Peterlee's three cafés, watching the myriad throng
streaming past. If I'd paused to think about it, I would hardly have
been able to breathe. I'd just eaten a large and rather good dumpling
adrift in a plate of glutinous mince of a rich but faintly unnatural
brown. The girl who'd served me at the counter had an oppressed,
benumbed air, as though she were on day release from a labour
camp, while behind her, a young woman who was supposed to be
defrosting a sack of peas and carrots was describing her previous
night's hilarity to an older woman. 'We were on wa backs!' she
crooned.

'Oh aye,' said the other.

'We were wettun waselves!'

'Charming.'

The young woman opposite me, who had achieved the kind of

glamour to which the girls who work in the banks and building societies and travel agents of Peterlee aspire – the glamour of celebrity guests on game shows I've never heard of: tight skirt, elaborately streaked and crinkled perm, overzealous attention of the sun-ray lamp, boatloads of make-up – the sort of girl who in London would be lunching on two lettuce leaves, if at all, was tucking into a plate of chips and gravy. People here ordered chips as a kind of cultural rite. 'I'll just have chips,' they said, as though this were a gesture of tremendous originality.

Beyond her, through the cigarette smoke and the glass front of the café, I could see the crowds of shoppers and promenaders milling past in the streaming sunlight. There were among them a fair number of people it didn't seem wise to stare at. Not just the lads, who sat on every concrete ledge with their legs apart in baggy jeans, or huge pyjama-like shell-bottoms, their hair crew cut, or shaved at the sides and slicked to a point at the back, as though they were balancing a wet fish on their heads. Not that ginger lad who seemed to have no neck or wrists or waist, his jersey tucked into massively baggy jeans, his face beneath a curly quiff like a bursting red potato. You could tell by the care and attention with which he was leading his tiny daughter through the crowd that he was all right. No. Them were just the lads.

There were other young men who slunk quickly through the throng, feral by two and threes. And there were men who seemed to bear in the way they carried themselves the marks of a kind of internal bruising. Such people, often trailing exhausted-looking wives and children, had a blackness, a seeping fury about their jowls and temples, which bore to the world a festering compulsion to pass that bruising on.

In *Viz*, the Newcastle-based 'adult' parody of traditional comics like *Dandy* and *The Beano*, there is a character called Biffa Bacon, a good-hearted lad dressed in shorts and bovver boots, with a round red nose, eyes permanently hidden by a bobble hat, and a mother even hairier and more grotesquely muscled than his father. The basic point of the strip is that the parents continually beat the shit out of their ever credulous son. When the doorbell rings, Biffa is loathe to answer it. 'It'll be wor fattha, an he'll hoof us in the knackaaz!' It is, however, a social worker come to find out why Biffa has not been to school for fifteen years. 'School,' says Biffa, 'is for lasses an' queers.' When the social worker threatens to report the parents for child abuse, the mother tells Biffa, 'This 'un reckons yer fattha's been queerin' y'up.' 'Aye,' says the father, 'an' that makes yer muttha a

friggin' lezza!' The strip ends with Biffa giving the interfering official
a good towzing.

From where I was sitting, this seemed not so much a grotesque
caricature of a certain type of working-class life, as a perspicacious
piece of social realism. These kind of people were out there. They
were walking past in the crowd. They were living up there on the
worst estates of Peterlee – letting their dogs defaecate in their living
rooms, not bothering with carpets or curtains, letting their gardens
run wild, shouting and banging around till all hours, and landing
the neighbours one if they complained. They were *them*.

Then there were the types who seemed to drift on the margins of
the crowds: the father unshaven and ashamed, the mother drained
and a bit shaky, gaunt or overweight, as though it were only the
dragging on her cigarette that were keeping her upright, oblivious
to the half-hearted whining of their grubby, starved-looking children.
These people too had always been there. They had been there in the
1820s. They had been there in the 1930s. They hadn't been able to
cope then, and they couldn't cope now. Such people existed everywhere, but you were more aware of them in East Durham. They
seemed to make up a larger proportion of the population. When
the crowds had gone on Wednesday and Friday afternoons, they
lingered in the precinct, hanging around the cafés sucking listlessly
on their cigarettes, their children running around the tables to the
annoyance of the staff – till it was time for the chairs to go up on the
tables, the steel screens to come down, and honest people departed
the precinct with all due speed.

From the Save the Children Fund Office, one could look down
on what was reputed to be the worst street in Peterlee. We were in
the Eden Hill area, one of the oldest estates, near the highest point
of the town site. The first street of the new town had been right
down beside the Dene at the bottom of Horden. Then this estate
was begun, behind the old Horden manager's house, which now
served as its community centre. For years the two areas had not been
connected even by road. But as other estates grew up, this area and
the pub after which the whole locale came to be known, The Royal
Arms, gathered a reputation as having the highest crime rate in the
whole of County Durham. The last landlord had departed overnight
after someone put the barrel of a shotgun in his mouth. Shortly
afterwards the premises were burnt out, and the boarded-up shell of
the building was now thickly covered with the spray-painted names
of the local youth.

When someone asked me if I'd like to meet the woman who ran the Save the Children Fund in Peterlee, I couldn't quite see the relevance to what I was trying to do. I imagined a middle-class woman raising money for the starving of the Third World. It never occurred to me that the Save the Children Fund would actually be working in Peterlee itself. The road in which this office lay had once been the most notorious in Peterlee. Those who had made the mistake of buying their houses, or who had not been able obtain transfers, lived among the blackened shells of dozens of burnt-out dwellings. Over the last couple of years, however, the area had been vastly improved. The PRIDE project initiated by the police in conjunction with the District Council, Durham Voluntary Service and local people, had led to the refurbishment of the derelict houses, and the setting up of a community centre in the house in which the SCF office was located. Downstairs was a women's group that organised trips for its members and their familes, none of whom could otherwise afford to go on holiday. They'd set up a credit union to try to cut out the small-time moneylenders who thrived on the estate. The 'village green' area between The Royal Arms and Pride House was assiduously maintained, and a mural of parrots painted on the bus shelter. The police had lost interest in the project as it had not led to the reduction in crime they had hoped for, but it continued through the enthusiasm of local people.

It was a brilliant day in late May, and everything looked tranquil enough from the office window. The roofs of the rows of old-fashioned council houses glistened in the mid-morning sun. The two women to whom I was talking, however, Sandra, the organiser, and Sally-Anne, the outreach worker, both seemed palpably on edge. Or was it me?

Sandra sat beside her desk, tanned, plumpish, masses of permed hair, smiling enigmatically. Was I, she was perhaps wondering, going to write anything that would seriously inconvenience them? Sally-Anne, tall, rangily muscular, blunt face, stood near the door, as though ready to make a quick exit.

Three streets parallel down the hill was Smith Crescent, now supposedly the worst street in Peterlee. It was a curious sort of crescent, being three sides of a rectangle, the two end pieces running up the hill towards us. 'They had a fight down there with fire bombs last weekend,' said Sally-Anne. 'There's a feud on between two families. They were just hoying them at each other along the street.' She looked at me earnestly. From her desk Sandra smiled her enigmatic smile. Every Friday night, the kids were down there

doing hand-brake turns in cars they'd 'twocked' – Taken Without
Owner's Consent.

Sandra lived on an estate on the other side of Peterlee, Sally-Anne
a few doors away. She did 'detached work' – going out on to the
streets to talk to the kids on their own territory. It was, she said,
very dangerous, because although you weren't trying to persuade
them not to take drugs, you were trying to get them to do other
things. And the dealers didn't like that. It was bad for business.
She was also seen as having links with the police through Pride
House. Both women had been 'circled' – followed by dealers in
their cars. Sally-Anne had had her windows put in. There had also
been an attempted arson attack on her house. Neighbours had seen
two teenagers, a boy and a girl, painting creosote on to the doors –
presumably with the intention of setting light to it. But they had run
away on being spotted.

She had worked as a bouncer, or 'door person' as she put
it, at Nimmo's, the huge old pub in Third Street in Horden,
that had recently closed. Drugs had been sold there openly –
mainly blow, speed and acid – and she had observed the effects
they had. Blow made the kids passive, speed and acid made them
aggressive. She had, however, enjoyed working there and thought
it a real pity the place had closed. Because if there were, say, two
hundred of them in there, you at least knew where they were. They
were at least contained for the time they were there. Anyway, the
place had calmed down a lot since the Easington Lane lads started
going there.

Why was that? I speculated. Were they hard or something?

She exhaled and smirked at the same time. 'Hard?'

Easington Lane and Blackhall would be at one end of the room,
Horden and Peterlee at the other. An uneasy peace prevailed.

The place had closed down because the owner, a man from
Sunderland known as Belly the Brick, had not paid the electricity
bills. He had owned a string of nightclubs, but was now bankrupt.
Kids had got in the place and were in the process of destroying it.
All the windows had gone. But it had not as yet been burnt out.

The previous summer, when the riots were on in Elswick and
Meadowell, a group of lads had gathered outside the shops by The
Royal Arms. One minute there were ten, then there were twenty,
then there were ninety. One of them had had a difference with one
of the shopkeepers. Sally-Anne had apparently had to go over there
and persuade them not to torch the place. She asked them to think
of all the people living above the shops who had children, and had

no part in any of it. The police had kept driving up and down in
their riot van which hadn't helped. But in the end it had all just
died away.

Sally-Anne pointed to a string of washing two or three gardens
along in the row backing on to ours. 'He's a real bastard, in there.
He's big! Thinks he's it!' I was surprised by the conjunction of the
Big Bastard and the line of demure sunlit washing. I didn't realise
the lives of Big Bastards could accommodate such placidly domestic
activities as washing clothes. But behind many a Big Bastard there
was probably a competent, but frightened little woman.

'He put my windows in,' said Sally-Anne.

'Why?'

'He felt like it.'

Peterlee Youth Centre was situated in the middle of the town, a
low, flat-roofed, unintentionally bunker-like building, just over the
walkway from Safeway. At lunchtimes it functioned as a café, and
members of the public were free to go in for a bowl of soup, a pie
or one of the 'specials'. A tall young man stood at the counter, lolling
his head forward between lunging bites at a toasted sandwich, that
he dipped in Daddy's Sauce. He looked neither to the left nor to the
right, but at some point low behind the bar, as though disassociating
himself from the act of eating – as though to sit down to the task
would have been an admission of weakness or effeminacy. Like a
warrior, who simply accepts whatever his women provide, offering
neither praise nor thanks for what is rightly his.

At one of the tables, I got talking to two lads, both one year out
of school. One, boyishly florid, smiling easily, was happy to talk
since there was nothing else to do. The other, detached, sprawled
back in his seat, in voluminous track-suit bottoms, the waistband
of which seemed to come almost to his neck, gave half an ear to
the conversation.

What was it like round here?

Crap.

Why was that?

There was nothing here. Except The Trust. And that was crap.

Did he go there much?

No. First he couldn't afford it, and second he didn't like to
go down Horden, because of the way people stared at you.

How did they stare at you?

As though they were trying to frighten you.

Was that in the streets, or just in the pubs and clubs?

He laughed. Both. He liked to go to Sunderland on the bus with his mates. Go to a club, come back by taxi. But he hardly ever did this, it cost a lot. Could only get money if his parents gave it to him. His father had been invalided out of the steelworks at Hartlepool with 'white finger'. His mother worked in a shop.

Used to nick sweets in shops, but wouldn't do it now, as he was sure he'd get caught. Not particularly interested in alcohol; too expensive. Had smoked blow, but never taken ecstasy. Too scared. A lad he knew had got in the habit of taking it regularly over a six-month period. At first he thought it wasn't affecting him, but he found he was losing his memory, getting hideous spots, and his hair was falling out. He'd stopped taking it and was now OK.

Was on a training scheme at Peterlee Tech. It was crap. Had been on a course in bricklaying at a college in Durham, but he'd walked out when the tutor told him the wall he was making was crap. A pity, as it had been a good course. He'd enjoyed school, but he hadn't learned anything. Had heard the school was improving; the teachers were getting stricter. But that was too late for him. Had no idea what he was going to do. Would like to get out of the area, but had no idea where to. Ideally, he'd like a job with the council, as the workload was very light, and it was easy to skive. If all else failed, he would consider the army.

The second lad had passed his army medical and was going in in three months' time. He wasn't bothered about drinking either. If it was a special occasion, say a wedding, he'd get drunk. But he didn't particularly like it. He preferred drugs. There were 'rives' of drugs in the area. Most came in via Sunderland. He'd taken acid for a year and a half. It made him feel happy. He saw colours and patterns. You got it on a piece of blotting-paper with a transfer, maybe a strawberry, on it. Bad trips made you feel frightened. Made you feel as though everything was closing in on you – as though everybody could tell what you were thinking. Acid was better than ecstasy as it was only £3 as opposed to £15 a time. He had stopped taking it, as he wanted to get fit to go in the army. His parents had noticed he was becoming moody. He hadn't noticed it, but when they pointed it out, he realised that he had. He'd managed to persuade his parents that he hadn't been taking drugs – just about. He was now fit, and had passed his army medical A1.

Neither had seen violence caused by drugs. They made everyone really friendly – except when people tried to sell drugs in the wrong places, or small dealers didn't pay up to big dealers. A bloke had been stabbed to death outside The Blue Monkey in Sunderland. But neither had seen or heard of anything like that happening in Peterlee or Horden.

Both had heard of the rape in Horden. The people who'd done the previous rape were from The Royal Arms area. They were all thugs up there. Their parents were slags – car thieves and that. You got ten- or twelve-year-old kids nicking cars up there. The first lad pointed to two crew-cut, shell-suited bairns effortfully wielding the full-sized cues at the pool table. They were the very ones. Their elder brothers didn't come in the Youth Centre. They were all barred out. The kind of people who came in the Youth Centre were neither the good kids nor the bad kids. They were the middle.

One day, sitting in the table-tennis area at the centre, I came across a lad who, though slight and quietly spoken, had about him a kind of weight, a presence that marked him out from his fellows, many of whom were still at school. He'd been in the army, but had taken a voluntary discharge.

'There was this particular sergeant, who was on to me from day one, and he wouldn't let up. Anything you did that wasn't your best, they'd slap you or kick you. I can see why they did it. They were just trying to bring you up to scratch. But I couldn't apply myself. I was homesick. I missed my mates. I wasn't ready. I was physically ready, but I wasn't mentally ready. If I could do it again, I'd be able to do it. But it's too late. They won't let me back in now. I tried to get in the RAF, but I failed the test . . .

'There's nothing round here. Only chew. In the pubs, in the clubs, in the street – everywhere. Chew all the time. Particularly in the clubs down Horden, Nimmos and The Trust. If someone's in a bad mood down there, they'll just lash out at anyone.

'You get these gangs that just go around looking for trouble. There's these lads from Thornley that go around in a white Transit van with baseball bats. They came in here once. People didn't know what was going on. Everyone was running outside, but they came after them and got them out there. They got this one lad on the ground, a crowd of them. He was only fifteen and they were beating him with bits of two-by-one. He was all right. He got up afterwards, and he was laughing. That's what you have to do for a bit of fun round here.

'How many young people round here have taken drugs? All of them. All the lads anyway. I've never taken anything stronger than acid. I've taken it quite a few times. But it only affected me once the way its supposed to. I looked up at the stars, and I could see them all moving. The sky was like water. Other times it just makes you feel daft. You laugh till it hurts. You laugh at anything. You'll be up all night laughing. If you smoke dope, you just sit around and talk. We might go and light a fire in the Dene and sit around all night talking.

'You know the Shell petrol station? Behind there, there's like a block of flats, with all the windows broken. The bloke who did it, Alfie Cummings, he's the only one left in there. They're supposed to be pulling the place down, but they can't get him out. He's a bit crackers. He's been in Sedgefield a couple of times. He's about forty. There's a mate of mine, Tony, who lives over the way from there. His family are Catholics, and Alfie got the idea they were in the IRA. So he started putting their windows in. He cut their telephone wires, and then he tried to set fire to their house. So some of the lads decided to go over there and sort him out. They threw bricks at his flat to get him to come out, then they got him on the ground and kicked him to shit.

'These lads? Oh, they're some of the lads I hang around with at the garage. That's where we go. There's two garages opposite each other, by the roundabout where it leads up to Horden. Shell and BP We like to sit on the wall by the BP, but the police keep moving us from there.

'On the fine nights, when it's warm, we'll go over and provoke Alfie. We chuck bricks at his door. We just do it to get the police out to give us a bit of a chase. On foot, by car. Any way. We usually head for the Dene. They never follow us into the Dene. They'll shine their lights into it to try and see where we've gone, but they never go in.

'Sometimes, I borrow my dad's car. I'd never get chased in my father's car. I'd never do anything stupid in my father's car. If I can afford the petrol, I'll ask him if I can borrow it, and I'll just drive, just for the fun of it. I'll drive to Hartlepool or Sunderland or Newcastle. Sunderland's about the best place round here. There's not too much chew at the clubs. Sometimes I'll go to the Bridge. That's where everyone goes after the clubs have all emptied. There's a car park by the pub at the end of Queen Alexandra Bridge, and everyone just goes there in their cars after the clubs have closed and dances till about eight in the morning. They started taking a generator there, but they had to stop because the police moved them on because of the noise.

'Sometimes if we drink, we get a bit carried away. We'll get up on the garage roof and start throwing bricks off. Just to get the police out. It's something to do. Early in the morning you feel like you want to do something. Some of the police aren't bad lads, but some are real dickheads. Think they're hard.

'We must have had about three or four thousand pounds worth of gear out of that place. There was one bloke, a little bloke, about forty, used to work there. He used to get so frightened, he used to let us nick stuff out of there. But the reason we were taking the stuff was just to get the police down there anyway. You can't do it now. They've made it all closed off so you can't get in.

'Sometimes we'd chuck bricks and bottles at the garage. When the police came with the riot van, we'd chuck them at them too. Then we'd run. They came with dogs once, but they didn't need to use them. As soon as we saw the van coming with them, we were away.

'I've had a lot of chew. I've looked for it, and it's come looking for me. You get a lot of people coming up to the garage looking for trouble. This one lad tried to run into me. He was parked at the garage. I went over towards him, and he just drove straight at me. They came back later with three cars. There were eighteen of them. I was with my girlfriend. I was walking her home. I told her to run. But she wanted to stay with me. I was really impressed by that. We got to my brother's place, and we stayed there till they'd gone.

'These lads live at the other end of Peterlee. They're like a gang. Once they came over with Big Lads. Their brothers and their brothers' friends. Lads in their twenties. We ran.

'There always used to be trouble at Shotton Hall [a community centre]. They used to hold discos there. We'd go down there to cause trouble, because that was their area. When you're fighting, you go as far as you need to. Until they say, "That's enough!" Once I went too far. I had this lad in hospital for a month. I broke two of his ribs and punched him in the kidneys. I didn't like it. I felt bad about it, because I knew I'd gone too far. But I was angry at some of the things they said, calling us "BP pussies" and that.

'These lads, when they come past the garage in their cars, they shout things at us, and we chuck things at them. They wouldn't walk by the garage. They'd never come in here, because they know what they'd get. They're not The Royal Arms. They're different again. They're just car thieves. And I don't support any car thieves.

'It's normally summer when things happen at the garage. Every summer something happens. But I don't think anything will this summer. There's too much dope about. Oh aye, things are very quiet at the garage these days.

'I was never at school. When I was in the third year, I stopped off a day. And when I'd done it once, I just wanted to keep doing it. I just wanted to be on my own. Now if you do it, they'll take you to court. But then nobody bothered. When I went in, the teachers just used to joke. They'd say, "What are you doing here?" Oh aye, the teachers were all right. And I didn't mind the work. It was just the school. Eventually they got the Nickyboardman round, and I couldn't explain why it was I didn't want to go to school. I couldn't ever tell anybody. Now, if I take any tests I fail them, because I'm forgetting the little I learnt at school. I haven't read a book since I left. I'm just wasting myself.

'The Dene's the only place round here where you can go and forget everything. I just go in there and walk. When I was training for the army, I used to go running in there at two o'clock in the morning. I'm trying to keep off drink and drugs because I can't afford them. If I ask my parents for money, they give it to me. But I don't like to ask them. I'm unemployed now. I was on a YTS, spraying gates. It was all right, but it only lasted six months. I come in here, but it gets boring. Even the garage gets boring.'

One morning I went to see Betty, who lived in Hawthorn Crescent, next door to *them*. The houses were semi-detached, each sharing its driveway and effectively its front and back garden with the first house of the next two – which in Betty's case was where *they* lived. She couldn't sleep because they were out there all night, screaming and shouting in the driveway, drinking, firing off air rifles. The eldest son wasn't so bad, and the youngest was too small to be much trouble. It was the middle two and their relatives and friends that were the problem.

They lived off lines. Everything they wore was stolen off other people's washing-lines. The other residents had a meeting with the police, but no one would agree to give evidence in court, or they'd have their windows put in and their houses smashed up. Half the street were related to them. The other half were terrified of them, and on waiting-lists to be transferred. Those who'd bought their houses were stuck.

Betty was twenty-four and lived with her two children and her boyfriend, who was on a YTS. She worked at a clothing factory in Peterlee, pressing shirts.

'My family belong Wingate, Station Town, but we've lived in

Peterlee as long as I can remember. My husband is from Horden, and when I left him, I was homeless, and I had to be rehoused in Horden. I liked living in Horden where I was before, in Seventh Street. You could leave your doors unlocked, and sit out on the step. Here, I don't even let the children play in the garden, never mind the street. They're only out there today because only Darren the youngest one's there. Normally by now there's a crowd of them. All their relatives and friends come in their cars, and just sit there, camping out in their front garden or on my driveway. I go out and scream at them, and they move away. I look out five minutes later and they're back again. Even little Darren, he's only nine, but you saw, he's been spitting on them, swearing and breaking their things.

'No one comes to see me any more, because their cars get damaged if they leave them outside. Dave's sister came. She was only in here half an hour, and when she got out there, all the locks were smashed and it was covered in indelible marker from front to back. One of the neighbours saw them doing it, but he wouldn't make a statement to the police.

'Their parents don't do anything, because they're out drinking all day. I think the father must be bit gone. When the sons got their heads cropped, he got his done too. Tramlines, the lot. Alcohol must've dulled his brain.

'I was talking to some of the girls that were hanging around out there. There were four of them – one twelve, two thirteen, one fourteen. They were talking about how many boys in the group they'd slept with. They've all had sex with each other. And they're all related.

'Where do they do it? Anywhere. In that big shed in their garden.

'I can't do anything with my garden because of the cans. That house that was empty two doors down, the one you were offered. They moved one of their friends into it. If the father wants to see him, he just walks straight through the back gardens. Never mind who owns them.

'The old woman who was in here before me was terrified of them. But she had to wait five years to be moved. The house this side was empty. They used to go in there at night. One night they were in the loft. They knocked through the connecting wall, and dropped into her house. Scared the life out of her.'

18

The Pitted Track

ONE AFTERNOON, I came out of the house in Hardwick Street, to notice what appeared to be traces of smoke in the air, as though someone nearby had lit a bonfire. Then, as I went through the lane into the Parish Council park, I saw clouds of thick white vapour rolling up over the bare sward, till within moments I could not see more than a few yards in any direction. A few days later, I was shopping in Peterlee town centre in brilliant sunshine, when I looked up and saw that the tower block of the council offices had disappeared. A few seconds later the whole precinct was muffled by a thick blanket of white mist. This was known as the fret; caused by sea breezes blowing low cloud on to the relatively warm land. It was very common in early summer, and just one of the many conditions, climatic and otherwise, that made that area, so its inhabitants believed, different from anywhere else in the world.

The razing of places of instruction by the people they are supposed to be serving has become a national pastime – so common it is almost *de rigueur*. In Horden, even the infants had had a go, while on the other side of Peterlee, Shotton Hall Comprehensive had been almost destroyed by arsonists.

At Deneside Comprehensive, one of the two secondary schools serving Horden, Mr Donaldson was showing me the harvest of the weekend's damage. Eight broken windows. Nowadays schools had to pay for such damage from their own budgets, and seven or so windows a night became quite expensive. There had been three fires at the school.

He showed me where there had been a recess – a door set back a couple of feet into the wall. The kind of sheltered place where it was easy to get a blaze going. The fire had partially destroyed that corner of the building, and the smoke had done considerable damage to the science labs. The door had since been replaced, flush to the wall. But the worst damage had occurred just around the corner. They stuffed burning paper into the library. Everything was destroyed.

'At my last school we used to leave the tennis nets out and the kids used to come into the grounds and play tennis in the summer evenings. You can't do that here. The second anything's finished its official use, it's locked away.'

It was misty the day I visited Deneside – not the temperatureless smoke-like cloak of the fret, but cold and grey and drizzling. I passed the school almost every day, its playing field sweeping down in a succession of broad grassy steps beside the main road from Horden up to Peterlee. A collection of box-like buildings with an anonymous prefabricated air. When the secondary school in Horden was closed, people had complained that their children would now have to go to Peterlee to school. The school's playing field, however, touched the edge of Horden. It merged with the grove of trees behind the Durham bus stop, where a single stone marked the site of Horden's original graveyard – the place where my great-grandparents had been buried, and where, about a year before, a fifteen year old from the school had been raped by her fellow pupils during the dinner hour.

As I made my way up the muddy pathway on to the plateau of the playing fields, I could see a group of figures trudging wanly about in the drizzle, engaged in some kind of dispirited team game. Suddenly a nasal, whining sound could be heard, and a dark shape appeared out of the mist – a motorcycle and rider moving towards the figures at considerable speed. As it grew closer I could see that the helmetless rider was wearing a camouflage jacket and a knitted face mask. It went tearing past, within a few yards of the players. But neither they, nor the teacher in charge, appeared to pay the slightest attention.

The bell rang for break as I entered the building, and immediately I was back in the world of my early teens. The hammering of desk lids. The shoving, the jostling, the pounding of feet on shuddering metallic staircases. The endless dragging of overladen duffel bags, rucksacks and briefcases along draughty corridors echoing with hormonally overcharged voices. How I loathed the prison of childhood!

They sat in their tracksuits, sprawled with an arrogant indolence, their feet on the tables, fixing me with an intent and hostile gaze. Geography and PE, I surmised, and headed for the other end of the staff room.

I sat down with a thin bespectacled woman and a huge sallow man slurping coffee from a Biffa Bacon mug, whom Mr Donaldson introduced as Bennett the Bastard, someone having sprayed a message concerning the master's parenthood in huge letters on the side of a nearby bus shelter. Together with the coolly earnest R E master, they obviously formed a coterie, a community of interest in the staff room, but exactly what this represented it was difficult to tell, as they seemed inhibited by my presence – all except Mr Donaldson, who sat beside me, smoothly composed and benignly inscrutable in a silky tweed jacket, like a rather glamorous bank manager. He was, I had been told by many lads I had met at the various youth centres, by far the best teacher in the school. At every such establishment there are one or two people who manage to achieve this kind of position through a mysterious inner dignity that is perhaps perceptible only to children.

After break, I walked down to Horden with Mr Bennett and a group of fourth-formers, to undertake a 'Personal Investigation of Third Street'. The drizzle had cleared, but although it was nearly June everyone was wearing coats or thick ski jackets. The group soon characterised me as 'the mad author', but otherwise paid me no particular attention, seeming quite happy to be shepherded along by Bennett's benignly overbearing presence, absorbed in their own conversations. He had prepared a list of questions and tasks, some of which seemed daunting even to me, who had been studying the place for the best part of nine months. 'Describe what Third Street was like before 1919, in 1919, and 1939; and sum up the changes over the years.' They must have done a considerable amount of background work to be able to answer a question like that. 'Why is Fourth Street gone, but not Third Street?' 'Why is the pub "Nimmo's" where it is?' I wasn't sure of the answers to these latter questions myself. Neither was Mr Bennett. He shrugged his shoulders with a deprecating snort. 'They're just there to encourage them to think.'

Most of the 'bottom' of Horden – all of First and Second Streets, most of Third Street, and the lower two-thirds of Fourth Street – had been demolished in the late-Sixties. But if you cut down the steep lane at the bottom of Hardwick Street, between the gable ends of the numbered streets, you came to the long green space where Fourth Street used to be. On the other side of that were two short lengths of terrace mysteriously left standing, at the end of Third Street. Most of the lower side of the street was taken up with the vast bulk of Nimmo's, an unlovely but imposing edifice of grey-green brick, in an Edwardian 'railway manorial' style, its lower portions boarded-up. Until recently the most notorious 'wine bar' in Horden, it was now becalmed, redundant on the edge of the piece of ground where Paddy's Market had been held.

The children sat down on the wall in front of Nimmo's, and settled themselves contentedly to do large and detailed drawings of the houses opposite. They were relatively large with gardens at the front – tiny gardens, extending barely six feet, but even that was unusual for a colliery house. Bennett and I speculated on whether they had been intended for colliery officials, and on whether or not the two-storey extensions at the back had been added later. Bennett thought they had, but they were so similar in the colour of the brick and the character of the detailing – the decorative lines of yellow brick, the moulded lintels over every window, I thought they must be original. Bennett had been unaware of the significance of the 'bottom' of the village, and he was fascinated. Having seen me as a southerner who had tagged along in the hope of finding out something about Old Horden, he now recast me as the resident expert.

'All right! Can you stop what you're doing a minute. Yes, that means *you* . . . ! Mark's got a couple of things to tell you about Third Street I think you may find quite interesting.'

So I told them all about how the streets went up through the different grades of workmen. The hewers at the bottom, the tradesmen – the mechanics, electricians and blacksmiths – in the 'new' streets above where we were now standing, the deputies and overmen in the 'big houses' along the Top Road, the under-managers and engineers in the posh houses at Yoden Crescent, and in his mansion high on the top of the bank, looking down on it all, the manager himself. I told them about the rough days of 'China Town' – about how the policeman used to start his beat in Fifth Street, I told them how the bricks for the Horden houses were made at Shotton Colliery, partly from pit waste, which explained the mottled, used appearance the village must have had, even when everything was new. I pointed out the concrete patches beside the front doors, where the knocking-up slates had once been.

A small boy with dark friendly eyes piped up that he lived in Eighth Street, and they still had the original slate on their house.

Bennett started a discussion on the sports and pastimes the people of Third Street would have indulged in fifty years ago.

I mentioned the children's version of pitch 'n' toss called 'mott'.

'I know mott,' said the boy from Eighth Street. While the other children were interested enough in the discussion, the world and environment we were discussing was no more relevant to them than that of a Roman amphitheatre. For this boy, however, we were talking about things he had experienced in his own life. He still somehow had a foot in the old Horden world – his father was perhaps a miner, or, though probably no older than me, had grown up in an environment through which the old rhythms still resonated. Yet the lad was removed from it enough to take pleasure in seeing himself the way we saw him, as a representative of a vanishing culture – like an Amazonian Indian in whom all traces of the ancestral lore had yet to be obliterated.

As we headed back to school, crossing the green space where Old Fourth Street had been, I caught a glimpse of a small motorcycle, with two young men slumped helmetless on the back, juddering out of a back lane, along the pavement, and then off along the street. There was something in the nonchalant ease of their postures that recalled the figures of bareback riders on ancient Greek vases. They were perhaps in their late teens, their expressions darkly and grimly closed off. None of the other people in our party seemed to notice them.

You saw these 'off the road' bikes all the time in Horden. You'd be walking along a quiet path through the allotments when there'd be a sudden roaring din and some twelve or thirteen year old would come bouncing along the pitted track towards you, hanging on like grim death – terrified but ecstatic. They appeared suddenly on grass verges, disappearing along the lanes and pedestrian walkways, coursing through the garden areas round the old people's bungalows. It was said that if you went at two in the morning to the area above the Pony Field estate, on the very top of Horden, where the new Peterlee cemetery was being built, you'd find it alive with people racing unlicensed motorbikes and stolen cars. All through the bank holiday just gone, there'd been the scything of police sirens through the white fret-laden air, sometimes far away, then terrifyingly near, as though they were about to come through the wall, then roaring off into the middle distance, hard on the tyres of cars festively twocked.

During my time in Horden, I'd worked my way through a pile of histories of the Durham miners and the North-eastern working class in general. At first these books, many of which described in detail conditions in the pit villages in the first half of the nineteenth century and the early struggles of the unions, had seemed remote in their significance to the world I was experiencing day by day. Events and experiences that were part of the Industrial Revolution as seen in engravings of women on all fours, dragging tubs of coal through the subterranean roadways, the time of child chimney sweeps, when coal owners wore top hats and frock coats, a world before Dickens, contemporaneous with Thackeray and Stendahl, a handful of years after Waterloo – a world banished forever to the history books by the legislation of the second half of the century.

The longer I spent in Horden, however, and the more I read, the narrower seemed the gulf in comprehension and consciousness between the two worlds. I realised that the real breakthroughs achieved by the unions in the relations between the employer and employed, took place not in our own century, as I had ignorantly assumed, but in the second half of the nineteenth. And the more I learned about them, the more painfully recent these struggles and the ensuing triumphs seemed.

While women had not worked in the Durham mines since the eighteenth century, boys of five and six were immersed for up to eighteen hours a day 'in the dark abyss of the lower worlds', not seeing sunlight, except on Sundays, for six months of the year. No safety precautions were required by law, and next to none taken. Fatal accidents were so frequent a coroner's inquest was normally not performed if the corpse were 'only that of a pitman'.

Every year the miners made their mark – very few of them could read or write – on 'the bond', a document that bound them not only to work at a particular colliery for the whole year without absenting themselves for a single day – on pain of imprisonment – but to submit to an almost unbelievable range of punitive fines and conditions. If a tub were set aside for having too high a stone content, the miner would be fined, while the coal content would be sold for the owner's profit. At some pits the keekers were bribed by the owners to arbitrarily set tubs aside. So a miner could slave for a week and end up in the owner's debt.

Supposedly a contract of employment, the bond did not guarantee the miners anything. If the pit stood idle they received no payment, and they could be discharged and evicted from the wretched hovels provided for their habitation at any moment, without reason being given.

Set apart from the old feudal settlements and the traditional structures of religion, the pit villages of the early nineteenth century had no churches, no schools – virtually no social institutions of any kind, other than an unrestricted number of beer shops. Most other shops were run by the colliery companies, who in those isolated places were able to dictate prices. Credit was stopped back from the miners' wages, ensnaring many in a cycle of debt from which they could rarely free themselves.

Epidemics of cholera and diphtheria were frequent in the 'unspeakably insanitary' conditions in which the miners lived. Life expectancy was short, the death rate high, even by the standards of the time.

Isolated in their benighted villages, 'sitting', as a Methodist chronicler – himself a miner – put it, 'in darkness and in the region of the shadow of death', the miners took their pleasures with a fierce zest. Gambling on dog fights, cock fights, on bare-knuckle boxing and foot races were the favourite holiday pastimes; drunkenness, brawling and wife beating were endemic all the year round. Even after the coming of the Methodists, the building of chapels, the creation of Sunday schools, which were for decades the only places of education in many of the villages, there were many who clung to the old ways of dissipation, who showed no signs of wanting to be raised from the condition of degradation in which the 'first wave of industrialization' had left them.

Now I could only too clearly envision these people, the 'sinners' of the old pit world. They were many of the people I saw around me daily, with whom I lived in uneasy proximity in Horden. They were *them*.

People like the two lads I'd seen earlier on the motorbike. Or the kind of men you saw tearing up to the tobacconists for tabs, working the vehicles with a Mongolian disdain for the longevity of the gearbox, the back windows, for some reason, always piled high with furry animals of fluorescent hue. They themselves, though not necessarily particularly young, moving with an eye-deterring fierceness, their expressions tight, sealed off from the everyday preoccupations of the respectable world.

Or were the descendants of those times, the denizens of 'China Town' – rough lads with hearts o' gold? Or were these people all really one and the same?

Into the world of the old Durham pit villages, the itinerant preachers had descended from their North Yorkshire circuits in the early 1820s. 'The Word ran like fire among dry stubble,' wrote the old chronicler, 'and many evildoers were turned into workers in the Master's vineyard.'

The Society of Primitive Methodists, founded in Staffordshire by a carpenter in 1811, had had to secede from the Wesleyan mainstream, because of its members' insistence on speaking and singing as they pleased. By the mid-Twenties, 'Primitivism' was established in the North-east as a religion dominated by miners and their families. By the end of the decade, it was 'notorious' that the leading part in the nascent unions was taken by Primitive lay preachers – avowedly 'plain', self-disciplined men who had 'hurt themselves sore to gain scholarship'. When it came to negotiation, one colliery owner noted, 'the men professing to be Methodists or Ranters are the spokesmen, and the most difficult to deal with. These men may be superior to the rest in intelligence and show great skill, cunning and circumvention.' Union meetings began with prayers, and during strikes special prayer meetings were organised by the union. 'Everything that could be collected from the Bible about slavery and tyranny, such as Pharoah ordering bricks to be made without straw' was used at these times. The coal owners were driven apoplectic with fury not only by the tough bargaining, but the self confidence and air of being privy to 'special knowledge' of these 'slick headed ranting knaves'. Men like Tommy Hepburn, leader of the United Colliers during the strike of 1831–2, who had enjoined Lord Londonderry to kneel with him in prayer before their negotiations, though it had 'burned the marquis's knees to do so'. Or John Wilson, a founder member of the DMA who became Member of Parliament for Houghton in 1885; Peter Lee, President of the Miner's Federation of Great Britain, of the International Miners' Conference at Lille, and Chairman of the first Labour-controlled County Council in the country. All these men were Primitive Methodist lay preachers, as was Hedley Mason, checkweighman at Horden Colliery, the first JP and the first alderman from the village.

Hepburn had been largely responsible for the lack of violence on the part of the miners during the struggles of 1831–2, during which thousands of miners were evicted from their homes and forced to camp out on the moors in freezing conditions, while labourers and their families were brought from all over the country to break the strike. After the union's collapse, Hepburn was spurned by his former members, and left to wander from village to village during the terrible winter that followed, vainly trying to sell tea. Finally, close to starvation, he was forced to beg for a job at his old colliery, Felling, which he obtained only on the promise that he would never again involve himself in any form of union activity – a promise he, of course, kept.

By the dawn of the new century, however, those who in their youth had been hounded from homes and jobs were the grandees of a huge movement with highly organised welfare structures and great financial power. Child labour and the Bond had long since been abolished, and standards of safety improved beyond recognition. Sitting magisterially back in the splendid fastness of the newly built Red Hill headquarters, with their neatly combed whiskers, weskits and gold watches, men like John Wilson could look back almost complacently on the fact that they had 'seen the great revolution in the relations between employer and employed. The gulf which divided the industrial community has narrowed beyond the dream of forty years ago.'

By the time the coastal collieries of East Durham came into being, Methodism had run out of energy as a transforming force in the coalfield. In Horden, the Primitives were just one sect among many, less numerous than the Catholics, let alone the Anglicans, and after the First World War dwindling numbers caused them to reunite with the Wesleyans.

In Horden, I heard a lay preacher – one of the district councillors – telling a very small congregation of how the need to live for others as well as one's self had led him to join 'a certain political party'. But afterwards, he was unable to explain how the connection between Methodism and socialism had arisen, or indeed, the distinguishing characteristics of Primitive and Wesleyan Methodists. They were simply words he had heard in his youth. Like the 'powerful times', the great revivals, when thousands of miners turned up at open-air meetings in the hope of achieving a Damascene moment of 'liberty', the factors whereby a faith that stressed man's sinful nature – that appealed to a sense of guilt, embracing cholera as a 'metaphysical sign' – had become the major force in the politicisation of a culture, now seemed unimaginably remote in time and consciousness. They were available to us only through interpretation.

But with the hardness and the harshness of that world of work, there had been no break in consciousness. Of how a boy aged six was dragged from sleep at three in the morning, descending the thousand feet of the pit shaft in his father's arms, hanging from the chain on which the 'corves' – the baskets of coal – were brought to bank. Of how each hewer put a leg through a loop in the chain, clasping to him a boy, who clung with him to the chain, as the spaces between the loops were filled with lads clinging with arms and legs, and how 'above the top loop,' as the Methodist chronicler told it, 'ten or twenty more lads would catch the chain, till fathoms of rope and chain covered with human beings dangled over the dark abyss'. And of how since the boys trapping doors worked longer hours than the men, a man would have to leave his son in the pit with only a flickering candle for company ... A man aged fifty today might have to read a book to find out the precise details, but he could in essence identify far more with that boy's life than he could with the youth of the present generation.

I sat with Mr Donaldson in the cupboard that served as the history department office. Mr Donaldson was from Crook in the west of Durham, where his father had been a miner.

'I've been here for sixteen years, and I find the outlook very insular – more insular even than where I was brought up. In those days, there was the idea that if you got to the grammar school, you were away. It was accepted that a certain proportion of people would go to college and move on. But that seems harder now, because of the system we've set up, where the children themselves don't aspire highly. Obviously there is a small proportion of children who go to technical college and then university. But I'm not talking about those few. All the time we see very able children who don't consider further education as an option because they feel the cultural gap is too great. They've set their eyes on a job at a local garage or the Nissan factory in Sunderland. And if they achieve that, they're applauded, because in this society that is an achievement.

'It often seems to me that the local community has set limits – culturally, economically, emotionally – on what it wants to do. And the fact that it is a highly structured society makes it easier in some ways to impose discipline. Coming from a very middle-class area where pupils were used to questioning and analysing everything you said, here it seemed much easier to get them to do things. They'd do them, without bothering to question.

'But every year, we're getting more pupils who we know will never get a job. They'll get on a training scheme – maybe. But that's about it. There's nothing on the horizon for them; and they themselves perceive it. So what can we hold out to them as an inducement to study?

'They look around, and they see unemployment around them everywhere in the community. They've got no challenge that they're being deprived of – no burning ambition to be a vet or an astronaut. So it's not such a shock to them as it might be to other people – the fact that there's no job for them, the fact that there's really nothing on the horizon.'

Six o'clock on a Friday evening, and Horden Parish Council
was in session at the Miners' Hall. The newly elected chairman,
one of these tough-seeming types in beard and glasses who are a
lot warmer than you think on the inside, set a cracking pace on
the agenda, reining in hard on waffle before it had even had a
chance to raise its head. Also chairman of Horden Labour Party,
he was a teacher at the local primary school. But he was born in
Horden, where his father was a well-known character at the pit.
The outgoing chairman, a raw slab of a man in Wrangler jeans,
was Secretary of NACODS, the officials' union, at Horden, now
an overman at Easington. His father, seated on the other side of
the table, had been an overman at Horden. The young-looking man
drawing intently on his pad was a power loader at Wearmouth. The
stocky fellow with the hook nose and the swirling moustache who
seemed to feel obliged to take the opposite line to everyone else, was
a deputy at Horden, where he was known as the Turk. Three other
male members, all now retired, were power loaders at Horden, while
Ernie Wilding, of course, was secretary of Horden Lodge for over
a decade. The three lady members, were the wives of the Turk and
two of the power loaders.

The main item on the agenda was the question of destruction
to the Welfare Ground through vandalism. They didn't want to
tar all young people with the same brush, but there was a small,
but determined nucleus of young 'uns who were costing the council
£20–30,000 a year. Most of this was recuperable through insurance,
but obviously the premiums were getting higher and higher, and there
was the evident inconvenience. In the case of the burning down of the
bowls pavilion – a pretty wooden structure dating from the creation
of the ground – arson was suspected, but nothing had so far been
proven. In the case of the smashing down of fences, however,
the breaking of windows, the riding of bicycles and off-the-road
motorbikes across the once-hallowed cricket square and into old
people and pregnant women, they knew exactly who was doing it.
But they were, it seemed, powerless to do anything about it.

There were only three police constables on the beat at any
one time to cover the whole of Horden and Blackhall. If an
arrest was made, charges were seldom brought, because of the
prevailing policy of keeping young offenders out of the courts
for fear the 'staining of character' would push them further into
a life of crime. Those cases that did reach the courts seemed
trivial in comparison with the crimes being committed by the
culprits' peers – rape, assault, car theft, burglary – and they received

derisory fines. Whereupon they came straight back and did it again.

A security firm had briefly been employed to patrol the ground with guard dogs and walkie-talkies, but it had proved prohibitively expensive. Anti-vandal paint had been applied to all the gates, to no effect. They'd even thought of getting a group of people together to sort these kids out physically. But several of the councillors were also JPs, so obviously that was out of the question.

They'd come to the conclusion that the only way to get through to them was through their parents. Because these children weren't scruffs. They weren't from poor homes. They weren't the Hawthorn Crescent type of people. Oh, no. Children from those entrenched, semi-criminal backgrounds didn't tend to be involved in vandalism. They'd rather nick a car radio than smash a fence down. The children who were wrecking the Welfare Ground were from relatively respectable backgrounds. To look at them you'd never think they'd do something like that. But their parents didn't want to know. When they were approached, they just said, 'Our Tommy wouldn't dee that.' They weren't interested.

Now a leaflet had been prepared, explaining the problem and how much it was costing the community, in the strongest possible terms. A copy was to be delivered to every house in Horden, in the hope that raising public awareness would have some influence on the children's parents.

The question remained as to whether the campaign would have greater impact if carried out in two phases – the north part of the village one month, giving time for the word to get round, and the southern part the next – or all in one go. But there was a half-hearted feeling about the discussion – as though all there had already acknowledged the futility of this gesture.

'Twenty or even ten years ago, we'd have had a way of dealing with this problem,' said the outgoing chairman. 'Because the pit was open, and if these kids' fathers didn't work there, their brothers or their uncles would have done, and they'd have been left in no doubt about what was going on, and how people felt about it – and they'd sharp have done something about it.

'Down there, if there's owt to be said it's said. If you've been down the pit you'll know that down there there's very few words minced. If someone goes against the will of the people, they're not allowed to forget it till they've done something about it.'

19

Quiet as a bit o'bread

W HEN JOE SUMMERS started on the belts, he'd come home from work on a Monday afternoon, go straight to bed and sleep right round till four o'clock the next morning, when it was time to go to work again. On Tuesday, he slept round again. On Wednesday, he'd get up in the evening. Then on Thursday, he'd get up earlier still. On Friday afternoon, he'd go to the Miners' Hall for a game of snooker. But by four o'clock he'd be asleep on his feet.

In those days, when men wore their pit boots from home, you could identify people by the sound of their footsteps. Lying in bed, you could put names and faces to the different rhythms of the hard encrusted soles, heavy with segs, echoing on the cobbles outside; and you could tell what time it was, by who was coming or going from which shift.

The men who couldn't afford a drink would gather on the corners, squatting on their hunkers, or more recently, just standing, to listen to the crack. Many were on the Stone Shift, sleeping all morning, and coming out to while away the afternoons on the corner opposite Nimmo's, or in Eden Street, a block down from the Miners' Hall.

There was one old feller turned up every day at three o'clock, in his pit clothes, ready to go down the pit at ten o'clock. He was always there at exactly the same time, and he always stood on the same step.

Ernie Renshaw liked to stand on the North-Eastern Corner, outside the North-Eastern Hotel, a premises at the end of Third

Street, long since boarded-up. One afternoon, a man came by in a car, and asked him if he'd seen a man passing at about four o'clock. Ernie said he hadn't. Some time later the man returned and said was he sure he hadn't seen anyone. Ernie said he was. The man became irritated. 'Why, 'ow long's tha been standin' 'ere?'

'About thirty-four years,' said Ernie.

Ernie Renshaw was a name that came up again and again in connection with 'the school' – the great crowds that gathered on the beach banks for the pitch'n'toss. When the men came out of the Big Club on a Sunday afternoon, there'd be as many as two hundred men forming a circle to watch the pennies go up.

One man, the pitcher, would throw two pennies – the 'hoyers' – high into the air, and bets were placed on the way they'd land. The pitcher, usually the person who had won the last toss, was generally betting heads, and he was expected to keep doubling his stake. If he kept winning, by the time he'd made, say, £12, it would take five or six men to club together to bet against him. And there would of course be dozens of side bets – men in the crowd betting a few shillings against each other.

When a man 'skint the school' – cleaned everybody out – he'd throw the pennies over his shoulder and walk away over the beach banks, a great crowd of men following – some of whom would have lost their entire week's wages. He might toss odd half crowns to his particular mates who he drank with, and they'd go back and start the school up again.

Lookouts were placed on all the pathways, and if a policeman approached the crowd would melt away along the cliff tops and down on to the beach.

And so it went on, week in, week out. In the pouring rain. In the middle of winter, with the wind blasting off the sea. If it was snowing, they still went down there.

'It was good if it was raining,' said Joe, 'because the pennies came down flat. If the ground was hard, one of them would always roll away, and you'd have a crowd running after it to see which way it fell.

'I loved it when I first went down there. I was magnetised, I was hypnotised by it. I couldn't drag myself away. I was courting our lass by then, and I was supposed to go to her parents for Sunday dinner. I used to turn up there at half past three. Her parents would say, 'Where've you been? She's been crying her eyes out!' If I'd won, I'd be full of it! I'd throw the money down on the table in front of her. That'd cheer her up! The sight of all that money! She'd still be annoyed. But it'd cheer her up. If I'd lost, I'd have to borrow money off her parents.

'There was a way of pitching, where you rested one penny on your thumb and you flicked them over, which made one coin go up in a proper spin, and the other fell to the ground sideways. For some reason that made it easier for this second coin to be heads. It was called "flamming", but it was really cheating. Both coins had to spin when they went up. If a throw wasn't acceptable to the person betting against the pitcher, he could shout "bar it" before the coins hit the ground, and the bet would be cancelled.

'There was a little feller with glasses called Saville, and he always skint the school. He was a pumpman at the pit. He worked as a chucker-outer at the Deluxe Cinema in his spare time, and he used a little polished wooden bat to pitch. He always bet heads, and the pennies always came down perfectly flat. Whether or not it was technique, whether he was able to judge exactly how much force to use to make them go so high and come down the way he wanted – but he always skint the school. He'd stay there till no one had any money left, then he went home.'

Every village had its school. The one at Blackhall was quite small. But the school at Easington was twice the size of Horden's. You had professional bookies going there on a Sunday. And every year there was a massive school on the river bank at the Durham Big Meeting. If you didn't honour your bet there, you went straight in the river. But although there were often fights down on the beach banks – most of the men being well tanked-up by the time they got there – they were rarely because of people not honouring bets; and those involved were relatively old – in their thirties, forties and fifties. A young man in those days wasn't important enough to draw attention to himself in that way.

'Ernie Renshaw,' said Joe. 'He's the one who knows about the pitch'n'toss.' But he was vague as to how the old man could be approached, or if he'd even be prepared to talk.

The Renshaws were one of those families to whom everyone in Horden seemed to be related. Ernie was the younger brother of the old park keeper, the one I'd spoken to about Percy all those months ago, who had died just after Christmas. Their sister Ria had been married to my great-uncle Hal.

'Ernie Renshaw?' said Jackie Hudspith, roaring with laughter. ''E's a *toucher*, 'im!'

A *toucher*? What did he mean, a *toucher*?

''E'll try anything. 'Im and his brother Yewie, that's just died.

They were like chalk and cheese. Yew? 'E was a gentleman, 'im. But Ernie . . . ? The coal cart went to 'is 'ouse every week. He sold it all! Got all his coal off the beach. 'E still does! They built the pithead baths. 'E never used'm! Walked yem black every day – along the railway line! True, that!' He roared with laughter, and was then suddenly serious. 'Good worker, mind. In the pit. Naybody better!'

Everyone had heard of Ernie Renshaw, but there was, as well as amusement, a slight wariness in the way they spoke about him – a sense of something if not dangerous, at least unpredictable.

'We used to lost our pocket money at the school,' said Joe Summers. 'Ernie Renshaw used to lost his wages. Or, he'd skint the school on a Friday, and then lost it all on the Saturday. He never pitched the pennies himself, mind. And he always bet tails!'

He'd lived down Cotsford Park, an estate off the beach road, for a good fifty years. When he retired there was a 'leading fee' of £20 that had to be paid before he got his free coal. Ernie was buggered if he was going to pay that. He'd go down the beach for his coal! Later he decided to pay his leading fee and he got his backlog of coal, which he sold. Now he was nearly eighty, but he still sold his coal, and burnt what he got off the beach. He'd bought an electric cooker, but then thought better of it. He made his wife carry on with the fire, because he didn't want to pay the electricity bills. They ended up using the cooker as a fridge.

His son Jackie still lived with him down Cotsford Park. He'd bought a video, but although he was now paying the bills, his father wouldn't let him plug the fucker in.

He'd remained a putter at the pit all his working life. And he always wore his 'crasher' – his protective helmet – back to front. He wore his shirt open at the chest, with just a jacket over the top, even in the middle of winter. And whatever the weather, he always had a drip at the end of his nose. He'd never worn a tie, not even to his own wedding. If he skint the school on a Friday, he might go out and buy himself a new pair of shoes. Then he'd lose the rest on the Saturday. That was the way he was – win all or lose all. Even today, he'd go out and blow his pension on the horses.

How did his wife and children survive? What did they eat, the weeks he lost?

'Their relatives would help them,' said Jimmy, the treasurer. 'Because in them days, they grew all their own vegetables.'

But didn't they get fed up helping him, week in, week out?

Jimmy looked at me, incredulous. 'He was they arn, wasn't he?'

Ernie's mate Blondie Ward had also bet tails. But he never won.

He used to keep his money in the pit to stop his wife getting at it. One day when they were coming out-bye, they'd reached the shaft bottom, when Blondie suddenly said he'd forgotten something. It took him an hour and half to get back in-bye and out again. But he'd left his life savings hidden under a stone at the coal face.

He used to work overtime every weekend without fail. He used to work all the worst shifts, just to get the money. But he once confided to Jimmy that of all he'd earnt, he didn't have a penny left. He'd lost it all at the school.

'He never had any luck, him. One day the canch tipped over and broke his leg. When the canch – the stone over the coal – had been fired down, the walls and roof were always really rough. Some of the stone fell away from the wall and crushed his leg. The water was pouring through. The only dry place we could find for him was on the conveyor. We lifted him on there, laid him out, then a stone came down from the roof and smashed his cheek. No, he never had any luck, Blondie Ward.'

I had been told that Jackie, Ernie Renshaw's son, had the big pigeon crees, just down past the back of the Officials' Club. Like all the allotments, it was fenced with corrugated iron, bits of board and a great number of old doors. I had always wondered how the gardeners of Horden had managed to come by so many doors. They were apparently left over from the demolition of the old colliery streets – not only the front and back doors, but the internal doors and the big cupboard doors.

Many of the allotments were filled with rotten and rusting furniture among which the weeds grew to the height of a man. But the area in front of Jackie's crees was neatly paved with flag-stones, and the crees themselves, three long low sheds, done out in brown-stained wood with white palings along the top to attract the birds home, were nothing short of palatial. The gate, however, was padlocked, and a dense silence reigned over the crees and the area of the allotments in general.

When I returned, the gate was unlocked, and the door of the far cree was open. Leaning over the gate, I could hear the murmur of voices. I did not enter, in case like many of the men he had a half-wild cur resident on the premises. It seemed unlikely, given the presence of so many timorous valuable birds, but I didn't want to take any chances. When I had been calling for some time, the voices suddenly stopped. There was a pause, then a red face, with a halo of unruly curls and wild blue eyes, peeked round the door before venturing out. A thin watchful man with shaggy, sandy hair stood behind him. What the fuck was going on? they must have been wondering.

'Can I come in?' I asked.

'Aye.'

'Are you Mr Renshaw?'

'Aye.'

'Is Ernie Renshaw your father?'

'Ernie's mi fattha.'

I explained the familial connection. He said Ria had died two years ago, and his father was now seventy-nine. He gave me their address, and said I'd find his father there till one every day. If I went to the Welfare Ground any afternoon, I'd likely find him watching the bowls.

Encouraged, I asked him how old his father was. 'Seventy-nine,' he said. 'I just tellt yer!'

Cotsford Park was a long street that looped round off the road down to the beach. Between the houses at the end you could see out over the treetops of the Dene towards Blackhall. Jackie, relaxed, almost genial, answered the door. In the shadows behind him, a slight man stood regarding me quizzically. He wore a very old double-breasted suit, the waistband of which came halfway up his chest. His collar, needless to say, was undone. He had fine, birdlike features, his dark thinning hair, Brylcreemed back, and small currant-like eyes above cheeks that were red and oddly shiny, as though vigorously polished. He had a way of lowering his chin to look up at you – not exactly suspicious, but searching.

They sat me on the sofa in the bare, bright living room. On the walls were paintings by local amateurs of Jackie's pigeons; in pride of place over the mantelpiece, was a picture of the Mean Machine, the bird that had won him more prizes than any other. The video was now clearly all wired-up, and Jackie, sprawled back on the sofa, was watching a tape on pigeon rearing. Ernie, standing over me, talked in a deep, flat and deceptively slow voice. His eyes, however, regarding every detail of my behaviour, seemed to function several minutes ahead of the rest of him. But they had no lustre or sparkle – indeed they appeared not to have any whites at all, like lumps of rubber or liquorice embedded in his face, which was pale except for the oddly polished cheeks. 'Does tha want to see tha relatives?' he asked, pulling a pile of small and well-thumbed photographs from his pocket. He had obviously prepared well for my visit.

The first was a black-and-white picture of three middle-aged people sitting on a rock on some beach. Two men in suits on either side of a rather good-looking dark-haired woman. 'That's thi grandfattha,' said Ernie, pointing to the mild-looking man on the right, who, I deduced, must have been Hal.

'Percy was my grandfather,' I said.

'Aye, Percy,' said Ernie, unperturbed at this slight shift in our relationship. He pointed to the figure on the left, a big faced narrow-eyed man who seemed to dominate the photograph, partly because he was nearest the camera, and partly through the blunt unsmiling forcefulness of his features. 'Ria died two years agan, on New Year's Day. That's her friend Richardson. You'll know him, won't you? Big, tall feller.' Ria sat slightly beyond him, in a smart 1950s costume, lifting her chin in a faint and slightly enigmatic smirk. Beyond her, Hal appeared rather out on a limb, but not at all troubled by it – a sweet and contented smile playing across his placid features.

I asked Ernie what Hal was like. I said I'd heard he was quiet.

'Aye. He was quiet.'

'He wasn't lively?'

'Oh, aye. He was lively. He was lively, but he was quiet.'

Hal had gone to Rugby in 1939, to work in a factory. He must have died some time in the Fifties.

The weight of significance however, not only in the photograph, but in the emphasis of Ernie's tone – was away from Hal and towards Richardson. Once again my own tenuous links with Horden, with the characters and dramas I saw before me, were being pushed to the rear, were being made even more tenuous. 'They never did marry,' said Ernie, referring to Ria and Richardson. 'He died on Christmas Day, and she died a week later on New Year's Day.' There was some story here, I could tell. Richardson had, I felt sure, usurped Hal's position in some way. But of the exact details it was difficult to enquire further, as Jackie was constantly drawing my attention towards the video, which was about some Dutch brothers who were something like champion pigeon breeders of the world.

The next photograph showed a cheeky fresh-faced lad in an oversized cloth cap. Ernie's brother Hugh, about to start work before the 1921 strike, standing with his legs apart, his eyes brimming over with indomitable, cocky confidence, the proverbial bonny pit lad, sure of the inevitability and appropriateness of his destiny – to be a pitman.

'I was thirteen in the 1926 strike,' said Ernie. 'Digging coal on the stone heap. It was almost pure coal that heap. A man was killed there. He was nigh on twenty feet in, and it closed in on him. Twelve went like that in a day at Thornley. It's a wonder there weren't maer killed.'

But as for the pitch and toss, he appeared not to want to broach the subject – as though I had mentioned something faintly indecent. Certainly he was dismissive of his own efforts in the field.

Was there any skill involved, or was it pure luck?

'Pure luck. There's nowt tee it. I never hoyed the coins, but anyone can dee it, as lang as they boozz oop – yi knar, spin . . .'

Did he remember that man Saville, the chucker-outer who always skint the school?

'Billy Saville? I knarred 'im. He was just lucky. There's some men that's lucky, and some that aren't. He was lucky.'

Had he been lucky, himself?

'Nooh!' The syllable boomed from its subterranean depths of anti-aspiration, as though being lucky were somehow discreditable, like showing off. And he headed off into the back kitchen.

Meanwhile, on the video, the Dutch brothers were taking the cameras on a tour round their crees, which were about the size of a council estate in South London. Jackie had visited them, with a group of other North-eastern pigeon fanciers. They'd been taken all over, given free beer, snacks and all sorts. The video went into the history of the family, who, it seemed, had been the gaffers of the pigeon world for generations.

Meanwhile Ernie continued our conversation from the kitchen, his low, lugubrious droning just audible above the spitting and roaring of the fire and the clattering of utensils. Jackie was up at four each day, to go to the crees. So although it wasn't yet eleven, he was ready for his dinner. He didn't work. He was 'on the invalidity' – as about half the population of East Durham seemed to be.

Both men talked as though they had my undivided attention, each ignoring the fact that the other was speaking – Jackie with ardent boyish enthusiasm, automatically assuming a similar level of interest on my part, Ernie in his droning monotone.

'Aad Bob, yer grandad's brother, he liked to get down the school. But not yer grandad, Hal or any o' them. They were maer futbarl. Why, Jack, he trained the Horden team. Hal played for Horden. And Charlie was a canny runner.

'Wasn't there an aad feller, used to come up from Yorkshire?' Ernie appeared in the doorway. 'Little stocky feller with a white beard.' This would be Grandad Feather, my great-grandfather's elder brother, Jack. A painter and decorator in Leeds, in his later years he had gone to live with his son George, a farm manager at Copmanthorpe near York. As a boy my father was sent down there in the school holidays and put to work in the fields, stooking with the men. This was how he had developed the remarkable muscles, on which, he said, everyone always commented. Grandad Feather had also taught him to shoot.

'Aye,' said Ernie. 'He came a few times, that aad feller. They had a farm somewhere down near York. I went to stay there once with our Hugh. They made you work, mind!' He gave a mirthless laugh and headed back into the kitchen.

Here I was, with one of the most notorious characters in Horden, and he turned out to know more about my family than virtually anyone I'd met.

'Nan was the tallest of the girls,' he went on from the kitchen. 'She was smart, she was. They were all tall, but she was the tallest. The mother, mind, she was a canny size. The men were stocky. Except Charlie. He was maer slim.'

Had Charlie ever worked at the pit?

'Why, aye. They were arl at the pit.'

On the surface or underground?

'They were yewers, man. The four Hudson brothers and the two Milson brothers.'

They were marras?

'Why, aye. But not arl on the same shift.'

I thought Bob hadn't worked much because of his illness.

'Oh, aye. He was arlwus a helluva worker, before he got bad. He had nay norves in the pit. When the stone was coming down, he was always the last one out.

'He was tall till he got bad.' Ernie appeared again in the doorway. 'He got black round here.' He squeezed his chin with his fingers, and went back into the kitchen. 'Must have had a bad shave, see. What they used to call a bad shave. Must've got it off the barber. Went all like scabs. Cleared up. But it left the marks. Good worker, mind. Always a good worker, Bob . . . Before he got bad.'

He came into the room with a plate of mince and tatties that he handed to his son. Jackie ate sat back on the sofa, still absorbed in his video.

Ernie continued talking as he ate in the kitchen, but I had to strain to hear what he was saying, his even tones obscured by the video and the sound of his ruminant mastication.

If he'd known my great-grandmother, he must have known my great-grandfather James Hudson too.

'Aye. He was a chargeman at the pit.'

What was that?

'Why, a deputy was in charge of the yewers. A chargeman was on the ten o'clock shift, in charge of the stonemen an' arl. He was a quaer feller, mind . . . Aad 'Oodson. He liked the women. He had a woman through here he was knocking about with for years. Just through here, Murray Street.'

Jackie got up to go. Time to get back to the crees. He turned the video off and headed for the door. When he'd gone, Ernie went back into the kitchen. I felt I'd been there for a long time. But I couldn't go yet. There were things I needed to know.

Suddenly much that had been obscured for me had become clear. Hal and Charlie had been part of the great social and industrial machine of Horden, as I'd always known they must have been. They'd been cogs close to the centre of the great mechanism. They'd been hewers. Real men of Horden. And the four brothers had all been marras together. Of course they had. How could I ever have doubted it?

But what of my great-grandfather? Had he had another woman as Ernie was now suggesting? Mrs Graham, who had known my grandparents well, had intimated that she had heard as much, when I spoke to her during my first week in Horden. But I had put it out of my mind. That wasn't the story I'd come there to hear at all. Now however, the idea had a peculiar and painful logic. In my mind's eye, I saw again the old man's face. Was there not, perhaps a glint of arrogant roguishness in those eyes sliced like clefts into a cliff of granite? Somehow I had never quite accepted all that about politics. Had a man like that really cared so much that his son was organising a trade union? No. They had quarrelled because Percy had spoken in defence of his mother's honour. And much else, like the coolness between Percy and his brother Jack, was somehow bound up with this.

And yet, it was still not possible to quite accept it. What sort of woman would have gone with a married man in the 1930s? It was difficult to imagine that my great-grandfather would have lowered himself in this way. I'd always seen him as a figure of dignity: inhuman, even absurd dignity, but dignity none the less.

The woman, I asked tentatively, was she married?

'Why, aye. But they were knocking about together for years. Neither of 'em were young, mind. And she was nay jawbreaker.'

What did he mean by that?

'She wasn't much to look at . . .' He laughed. 'She liked her beer!'

What did my great-grandmother think?

'I don't suppose she was too bothered.' He gave a throaty chuckle. 'What did they call him? Jim? Aad Jim.'

I would have liked to have probed him further but I could sense a reluctance in him to say much more on the subject. His voice now, as it came through from the kitchen, was distracted, as though he now had more important things to occupy him. I decided it was time to go, and moved towards the kitchen door.

On the left was the black-leaded range where he'd done the cooking. On the right, Ernie sat on the back step. And to my astonishment, close in the shadows beside him sat a painted woman. A woman of thirteen, fourteen? No more than fifteen, possibly even twelve. But a woman. A woman who had slipped silently in through the back door to visit her grandfather. Ernie looked back at me, his cheeks flushed, a look of rakish and ironic triumph on his features. 'Are you going home?' he asked, clearly enunciating the last two words. Did I detect a faint note of mockery in the use of this alien expression – rather than the traditional Northern 'gannin' yem'.

Could I believe Ernie Renshaw? Maybe he was confusing my great-grandfather with someone else. But his memory for other details was too sharp. He had remembered my great-grandfather's name over a period of sixty odd years. He remembered the existence of people like Grandad Feather, who even most members of my own family did not know about. Perhaps he was making it up. But what for?

Yet it seemed that to accept such things too casually from someone who was really a complete stranger, would be quite wrong. These people were my own ancestors, and they were not here to speak for themselves.

'Let them rest,' a woman had said to me months before, when I told her I was trying to find out about my forebears in Horden. 'Let them rest.' Maybe she was right. If James Hudson had had a liaison with another woman, however discreditable, however pathetic, of what consequence was it now?

And yet, I couldn't leave the matter there. I had staked so much of my sense of the past of Horden and my family and a whole culture on the obdurate sense of honour and pride, absurd and destructive though they might have been, of certain individuals. We weren't talking about Hampstead in the 1970s. This woman had supposedly been married. It was inconceivable that an affair with a married woman in 1920s' or 30s' Horden would not be squalid and demeaning as well as an unforgivable betrayal of family and duty. These allegations coloured my sense of the past so strongly that I could not afford to simply let them pass.

And yet, how could the truth be ascertained? These were people who had died nearly sixty years ago. Who had left no written records of any sort. The number of people who could remember them at all was very few. The people who would have been able to corroborate the intimate details of their lives – even if they'd wished to – had long since departed the earth.

As I walked along the grey and empty street back up to Hardwick Street, the very pavement seemed haunted by the resonance of possibility. If my great-grandfather had been going to see his woman in Murray Street, this is the way he would have come. I could see him now, padding grim-faced towards me, his eyes on the pavement – another stocky little man in a cloth cap, attracting neither interest nor attention. But where would he be meeting her? At home? She was supposedly married. In the pub? Ernie had said she liked her beer. But in those days, a woman who frequented such places was putting herself virtually on the level of a prostitute. Ernie had said that my great-grandfather had 'knocked about' with her for years. But from what I understood of the old man, he didn't really 'knock about' with anyone, let alone associate himself publicly with 'strange' women.

But perhaps the impression I had formed of him – the taciturn patriarch dourly rumpling the pages of the *Daily Mail* in his chair beside the fire – was a false one. Or perhaps, more likely, this persona had more than one aspect. Perhaps, like all of these people, he had greater complexity than I had given him credit for. He was said to have been an intelligent man. Perhaps bound for decades in a punishing cycle of labour well beneath the level of his talents, trapped in a monosyllabic marriage by an accidental pregnancy, the odd hour of jovial warmth, snatched when the woman's husband was on another shift, had seemed a small and not unreasonable recompense. Or perhaps he had just liked to 'put it about'. Looking into his eyes, in the one photograph I had of him, I wondered if I did not now detect a glint of mocking slyness in the dark slits compressed above those granite jowls. Perhaps, perhaps . . . There was the whole world of another human being in there. How had I had the arrogance to suppose I could so easily reduce someone, someone with whom I had had no personal contact, into a few glib paragraphs?

I went to see Mrs Graham, the woman I had visited shortly after my arrival in Horden, who had been close friends with Jenny and known Percy's mother well. 'Oh, it's you,' she said, as the care assistant announced me in the doorway of her room in Wilding Lodge, the old people's home on the Top Road. 'I'd forgotten about you.'

When we'd exchanged pleasantries, I asked her if she knew why Percy had quarrelled with his father.

'No, I don't. But I know they never spoke. We lived in with them for a time, you know. The mother often used to call round, but the old man never went near. There was another brother, I can't remember his name, but him and Percy never bothered each other either.'

That would be Jack. But did she know why that was?

'No.'

Had she ever heard that the father had had another woman?

'Oh, he did. It was the old woman, you know, the mother, who told us. She used to come to Jenny's sometimes, on the fine nights.

'Jenny was very upset when she told us. I think she must have known about it already. Maybe people had been talking about it. Because she said, "Yes, we know about that, Grandma." She always called her Grandma. I never knew her name, because everyone always called her Grandma Hudson.'

Did she think the old woman had been upset by it?

'Well, she wasn't a woman to show her feelings, you know. She had a funny eye. You could never tell what she thinking. But maybe she grieved inwardly, because she aged terribly after that. She'd been a big woman, you know. Bigger than the husband. She was tall, and she always carried herself very well. But after that she aged terribly.'

Sue Whiffen was my great-grandmother's niece. I had seen photographs of her father, Jack Wilson, a stiff-limbed, poker-faced man, with huge jug ears. A master bricklayer at the pit, he had worked on the cooling towers of the colliery power station, and he had built that wall of drear, ineluctable blankness that surrounded the Welfare Ground.

Auntie Sue, the third of his four daughters, lived with her daughter Sadie in a small close of terraced houses just around the corner from Fred in Peterlee, though until I called, both had been totally unaware of the other's proximity.

She looked to me, as I entered the house, exactly as I had seen my great-grandmother in photographs. Her face had that same round-featured composure and imperturbability; though she was smaller and lacked the overlay of stoic sternness. She was only eighty.

Her mother's family had owned the Robin Hood Hotel in Darlington and the furniture in Jack's house was of a standard remarkable in Horden in those days. There was a horsehair *chaise longue* and a black mahogony dresser, huge and ornate, like a baroque altar, known as the 'press'. 'How it came we had all that lovely furniture, was through my mother,' said Sue. 'She had money, you know. When my parents got married, they had one of the best weddings ever out of Ushaw Moor Colliery. And she went into her own house that she'd bought with her own money. She had carpet and curtains to match, and when she came to have her babies, the nightdresses and that! Everything was gorgeous! Mind, my dad was a drinker, but it never made him any worse. He got a bit tight, but he never badly used us or anything. But my mam died when he was thirty-nine, and I think it was through him being left young a widower, see, that he took to drinking.

'My grandmother, my father's mother, was a very nice woman. Very stern, but good. Just like her daughter, your great-grandmother – my Auntie Belle. They were out of the same mould. They looked the same: big, tall, upstanding. And they behaved the same: strict, but good.

'My grandmother owned several houses in Ushaw Moor. Three or four in Dale Street where we lived, and two or three in other streets. I don't know how she came to have them. She must have bought them somehow. But when I was little, I used to have to go round collecting the rents.

'They were very "Church", the Wilsons. Same as the Hudsons. They were all very "Church". Oh, yes.'

And had they been Labour or Conservative, these people?

'They were all Conservatives! When I went to school, every child was Labour, except us. At election time, everyone used to wear their party colours. And they were all wearing green rosettes. We had our little Conservative badges on, but we used to hide them under our collars, or we'd have been beaten up.

'When the strikes were on, all the other children had their dinners at the soup kitchens. They used to have a cup of cocoa and a bun at breakfast time, and soup and dumplings for their dinners. We couldn't have it and I could never understand why.

But our parents were officials, you see. They had their jobs.

'When I got married, my husband was Labour. So I became Labour too. But I've never been very interested in politics.'

Had her husband been a miner?

'Oh, yes. They were all miners.'

Had she ever heard that my great-grandfather had had another woman?

She paused, but only momentarily.

'No, dear. I've never heard that. I've never heard it, and I don't believe it. No, I definitely don't believe that. If it had happened we'd have heard about it. And they were all very nice people, the Hudsons. You've got nothing to be ashamed of there.

'I've always said that if you're going to marry a miner, you'll be all right if you can find one that doesn't drink. My husband was very quiet. Oh, yes. Quiet as a bit o' bread, he was.'

For me Horden had always been my father. So powerful was the association that at first I could not approach the place except through the medium of my father's personality. Now, however, having lived in Horden for nine and a half months, I couldn't imagine him in the place at all.

'I last saw yer dad about three years ago,' said his cousin Joyce. 'He came up when Mollie was ill. I was working in the bakers in Peterlee, and Mollie told him to pop in and have a word with me. I hadn't seen him for about thirty years, and I didn't recognise him. He was wearing a grey silk suit with a pink tie and a pink handkerchief in his breast pocket. The manageress let me go outside for a chat with him. When I came back in, she said, "Who was *that*?" She thought she was God's gift to men, you know. I said it was my cousin. She said, "He was the handsomest man I've ever seen." I said, "Forget it. You couldn't even get *near*!"'

When I saw my father for the first time since I'd thought of writing about Horden, it was not in Horden or Peterlee, but in London, in the cell-like room of the hotel where he always stayed, alongside the British Museum. As soon as I was in the presence of his voice, much of the almost morbid obsession I'd come to have with the familial past of Horden fell away. It resonated with a harsh metallic echo, as though scraped along the miles of passage from the centre of his stocky blocklike person. He found it impossible to whisper, difficult even to adjust the volume of this formidable instrument. Often in restaurants I'd ask him to talk more quietly, because the rest of the establishment didn't necessarily want to hear what he had to say. 'I *am* talking quietly!' he would protest, grinding hard on to the syllables in that inimitable twang, part suppressed pitmatic, part inadvertently acquired North American. And if feeling belligerent he would add in a hoarse and furious growl, 'I've worked hard all my bloody life. I've got a right to talk if I want to!'

Although he seemed to be getting smaller as he got older, and he loved to recite the litany of his aches and pains, he still packed a certain amount of power. If someone was in his way, he simply walked through them. If you were walking abreast with him along a pavement and he decided he wanted to cross the street or look at something in a shop window, he'd simply knock you out of the way, without even realising he'd done it. He was still personable in that narrow-eyed, rather exotic way that had made everyone think he must be foreign, or at least Jewish, though his hair and beard were now completely white. After his long flight, he looked like a rather exhausted Afghan warlord.

Grey silk suit, indeed! I thought.

I asked him if he was suffering from jetlag.

'No,' he said, dismissively, as though a hundredweight of gravel were being shifted in his nasal cavity. 'I never get that. I don't have time for it.'

A few seconds later he was nodding off.

Horden seemed far way. And now that my father was actually here in front of me, the obsessive interest I had felt in Horden, about the past of our family, about the world of my father's childhood and the youthful exploits of Tommy 'Oodson, was strangely absent. It could all be accommodated by the fact that he was my dad. They were his family, and that was that. It occurred to me that if he had come over from Canada the previous summer as was his annual habit, I probably wouldn't have bothered to have gone to Horden at all.

But I still felt a certain residual curiosity about Grandad Hudson and his alleged other woman. I asked my father if he'd ever heard anything to that effect.

'No!' he said, scraping the thought contemptuously from the surface of his mind. 'And I don't believe it either.'

Why not?

'Well ...' he lolled, still half-stupefied on the edge of his bed, trying to cast his mind back fifty, sixty years. 'He never went out! He was either at work or at home. He'd walk along to The Bell for a couple of pints, but that was about it.'

So why should people want to say these things, if they weren't true?

'I don't know. They're maybes inadequate.' The inadequacy of the great majority of people was one of his principal themes. 'So they think up these fantasies. But I never heard anything like that.'

He went on talking about my great-grandfather. About his slow and painful death. About how he had to write all his messages on a child's slate, because he couldn't speak. About the house in Cowell Street, and how Hal and Charlie would put the crabs they'd caught in the back yard, and then hang him out of the window by his ankles, as the crabs with their enormous claws sidled around him. I'd heard it all before, but I listened carefully, in case there were any details I'd missed. There were, of course, many.

20

Rock of Ages

I DID GO to the Durham Big Meeting that year. I went with my father and my friend Julia. Or rather I went in on the coach with the Horden band and banner, and they came later in Julia's car. Before I left, I warned my father that Julia had never been to the Big Meeting before and she didn't want to hear endlessly about how fantastic it was forty years ago and what a downer it was now. 'Of course not,' he said.

In the old days, every miner was given ten shillings 'Durham money' by the union, and by six o'clock on the morning of Big Meeting Day, the bar of the Big Club would be packed. Beer was only four pence a pint then, and by the age of fifteen Joe Summers was carrying the banner out of Durham as the men designated 'banner carriers' could hardly stand. 'They'd be rolling down the street after us,' recalled Joe. 'The pavements were packed with men with pints as the banners came out. You couldn't get in the pubs. Then as the bands stopped to play for the speakers at the County Hotel, the lads and lasses would dance in front of the banners. You don't see that any more.'

Even three years ago, the union provided four double-deckers to take people into Durham. But the drunken behaviour of a minority had got too much, and Joe put a stop to it. 'I'm not laying on buses for idiots,' he growled.

Now there was only one small single-decker for the brass band, and Joe was not sure I'd get a seat, because of the union members and their wives who'd be wanting to go.

By 8.30 am most of the band members were already at the
Miners' Hall, standing around the hallway and the pavement outside
in their navy and orange uniforms, expressions of self-conscious dis-
gruntlement on their faces. In the old days, when the union 'owned'
the band, turning out on Big Meeting Day was one of the band's
most crucial obligations. In those days of course, every bandsman
was a miner. Now, there were people from all walks of life, and
even a few *girls* in the band, and as they were at pains to make
clear, they were there only as a favour; though none of them, of
course, would have missed it.

At the cloakroom desk, Johnny Fairclough was taking names for
banner carriers. It used to be a matter of great pride to carry even
one of the silken tasselled ropes that ran fore and aft of the great
banner, and while the pit was still working, each carrier, like each
bandsman, received the equivalent of a full shift on power loading.
Now, however, there was only £5 in it, and so far only a large and
rather nervous-looking skinhead, who had been there since early
morning to be sure of the post, had shown any interest.

Joe Summers strode in, still working his breakfast round his
gums. 'Keen as mustard!' he taunted the band master. Eventually, a
few passers-by having been pressed into acting as banner carriers, the
band did the ritual rendition of 'Gresford', the solemn miners' hymn,
in the middle of the street between the Miners' Hall and the Big Club,
and we marched quickly off along Seventh Street, and then round the
corner up South Terrace, beside the blank red wall of the Welfare
Ground that my great-great-uncle Jack Wilson had built all those
years ago. The women, the kids wrapped in blankets, still groggy
with sleep, or standing cocooned in sleeping bags, stood watching
from the doorways. As we cut along the bottom of the Big Houses –
the deputies' streets, Hamilton, Hanley and Cowell, where the three
generations of Hudsons had lived, more people came out and stood
smiling and waving, stimulated by the booming, confident sound of
the band, and the fact that it was Big Meeting Day, and something
at least was happening as it should. But few of them followed. It had
fallen on Joe Summers to lead the procession. Johnny Fairclough,
the only other Lodge Committee member, marched in front of the
banner, and there were, apart from the rope carriers, only a handful
of people marching behind – an oldish man, a couple of women with
pushchairs, assorted kids, and myself. By the time we reached the bus
stop on the Top Road where the coach would pick us up, it had
became painfully obvious that far from having to fight to get on,
no one else was even interested in coming. As someone had warned

me in the Big Club the night before, no one in Horden gave a fuck about the Big Meeting any more.

About 8,000 people turned up that year to the Miners' Gala which many, in tones of luxuriant maudlin masochism, predicted (wrongly) would be the last. But, as the banners descended Silver Street, and slowly waited for their turn to cross the Elvet Bridge and play in front of the County Hotel, from the balcony of which the speakers and other worthies – local MPs, union bigwigs – stood watching, the diehard spectators who had been there since early morning pressed up against the crash barrier opposite, you could, if you looked from a certain angle, still get an impression of a brimming, multitudinous crush of people.

I bumped into my father and Julia, as Seaham Band played their chosen selection beneath the speakers' balcony – a number from *Joseph and the Amazing Technicolor Dreamcoat*. 'What are they playing this for?' my father asked for all to hear. 'They should be playing proper band music!'

In the event, however, my father did enjoy the Big Meeting, as did Julia, as did I, as did everybody there – because as the bands and banners marched out, Murton, led by a big, upstanding, red-faced man, in bowler hat and bright yellow buttonhole, breathing carefully and punctiliously in time with his stately tread, and the band stopped beneath the speakers' balcony, the snare drummer with his long shank of silver hair, crouching over his instrument as he added a bouncing syncopation to the old time blaring – like blues refracted through the Salvation Army and the Coldstream Guards – and the huge miners of Murton colliery, that had closed only the year before, danced a jig beneath the dark and thunderous sky, with Tony Benn smiling behind the glass above and attempting to shake in time, it was still possible to feel some of the old revivalist magic of the days of hope, the visions of betterment and co-fraternity ground out in the dark bruised notes of the sounding brass. And in the cathedral, as the first beat of the bass drum was heard outside, and the band slowly entered – the first notes surging with a mournful solemnity into the vast dark interior, the huge drum-like columns, with their stark, abstract decorations standing over the packed congregation, the musicians passing up the aisle, their instruments glistening with rainwater, the great banner swaying slowly above its huge bedenimed carriers and its gaggle of drenched and bedraggled followers – a woman with a pushchair and a few kids in shell-suits – the bands and banners of Murton, Sacriston and last of all Easington, hung with the Yugoslavian flag, in remembrance of the moment at the mass funeral of the disaster victims in 1951, when the Yugoslav delegate had draped his national flag over one of the coffins – it was as Fred had said it would be, impossible not to be moved and to feel that all of this still represented something that was not totally insignificant.

'It always used to be,' said Joe Summers, 'that when the band and banner got back to Horden, the Lodge would pay for all the drinks from the bar in the Big Club for about an hour. Then you'd go home for your tea about half-past six, seven.

'1985, the first Big Meeting after the Strike, I had the daughter up from London, with her boyfriend. He's got a degree in African politics or summat. They're both real lefties – even more left-wing than this lot we've got up here. As we walked into the Big Club, everyone started singing, "Jo-oe Sum-mers, Jo-oe Sum-mers! We'll support you ever more!" The daughter and her boyfriend couldn't believe it. I had tears in me eyes – all these lads who'd been on strike with us for a year, singing for me like that.

'The year after was the last time we went into Durham as a working lodge. When we got back in the Big Club, they were all shouting, "Come to the bar! Come to the bar!" I said, "Sorry lads. There's no pit. There's no Lodge. We've got no money coming in. We can't pay for anything any more." They were all going, "You fucking lousy bastards!" They were ready to beat me and Jimmy the treasurer up. Probably they were the same ones who'd been singing about us the year before.'

From Tyneside, the A19 runs south beneath the blackened outline of Penshaw Monument, the preposterous but inspiring acropolean monument to an earlier Lord Lambton, atop its hill, around which the Lambton Worm, a monster from Anglo-Saxon myth, is said to have lain curled. Beyond that, to the right, one can see through into the heart of Durham and the blue outlines of the Pennines beyond.

To the left, below the road, the sprawl of South Tyneside – South Shields, Jarrow, Hebburn – stretching almost as far as the eye can see, fades imperceptibly into the endless conurbation of Wearside – Boldon, Silksworth, Ryhope, Hylton, Sunderland. From up on the high road, the sun is still flooding the landscape to the west. But down there on the endless plain of the housing estates, the street lights were already coming on through the brown haze of urban murk.

And one could imagine all too easily the life that was going on down there: the lights being turned on in the little rows of aged miners' cottages, in the snooker rooms of the working men's clubs, in the huge old people's homes, in pubs with names like The Bonny Pit Lad with the blue star of Newcastle Brewery illuminated outside. Wine bars with names like 'The Batcave' boarded-up on street corners, closed down because of drugs or bad finance. It was Friday evening and one could sense the incipient energy of the lads and lasses preparing for their respective nights out. The last-minute crimping of perms, the queuing up for bathrooms; and outside, the little gangs gathering on street corners, by the bins or the garages, in the doorways of derelict buildings. And far away, in the faint distant haze on the sea's edge, standing up like a pin-head, the winding gear of Westoe Colliery – virtually all that remained of the old industries – the heavy industries – that had created the character and culture of that part of the world.

Easington and Vane Tempest collieries had been among those earmarked for immediate closure in the measures for the coal industry announced by the Board of Trade in the autumn of 1992. Production at Wearmouth was to stop, its reserves 'mothballed' for possible future exploitation.

Following an immense public outcry, twenty pits throughout the country, including Easington and Wearmouth, were reprieved. But over the following six months, the 'market shift' in favour of coal that would have allowed these collieries to continue working, did not occur, and one by one they closed – Easington in May, Wearmouth in December, 1993. From one hundred and eighty-eight at the time of nationalisation, there were now no pits working in the old Durham Area. The great Miners' Hall at Red Hill in Durham was up for sale, and early in 1994 the Big Club in Horden was sold and gutted prior to redevelopment as a multi-bar complex aimed at the youth of the area.

'I shouldn't have been a man,' said Harry Sugden, the old pitman, who had shown me his paintings and told me about the days of the handbarl alley, that dark afternoon, all those months before. 'I should have been a skylark. I'll sing a song anywhere. And I'm up each day, soon as it breaks light. I wish there were thirty-six hours in a day.

'Enjoy yourself, as long as you can get out for a pint and up for a game of dominoes or a game of bowls. You hear some men saying, "Why, lad, it's murder. Since I finished work, I feel rotten." I say, "What about the poor buggers lying in hospital that cannut get the pints in? Think yourselves lucky for what you've got.'"

People called the likes of Harry and Jackie Hudspith *characters*. But they were just men of sixty or seventy years ago. They didn't own their houses. They didn't have cars (few of these people could drive). They had no investments, no savings to speak of. They didn't really own anything apart from the clothes they stood in, and it was of no importance to them to own anything. They weren't greedy people. They had asked nothing more than to be able to pit themselves, as their fathers had done, against the darkness and the drudgery and the danger – the travails of the old industries that had given such intoxicating zest to their few hours of leisure and the modest pastimes with which they filled them. In the old bargain of the age of labour, they'd been racked and strained day in day out, torn, slowly drained, or suddenly disfigured, maimed and killed – all for profits that were not theirs. All they got was the feeling of having *deserved* – to live, to be able to support their families, to call themselves men.

The stoic cheerfulness, the unassuming generosity and gallantry of people like Harry and Jackie – indexes not of stupidity, as some might suppose, but of dignity and resilience – were now factors of almost antique quaintness – since the world of the old industries, in reaction to which they had come into being, now scarcely existed. But while the old structures of mutual assistance were breaking down at varying speeds, and the old world of self-entertainment had long since been replaced by the consumerism of Nike trainers and Nintendo games – things most people in that part of the world could ill afford – many of the fundamental attitudes of the old industrial world, the values and attitudes – anti-aspirational, fundamentally passive, as Orwell described them – of traditional working-class life, still underlay life in East Durham.

Education between the wars, I was told by an academic at Durham University – a man who had grown up in Wingate during that period – was for the majority of people in East Durham, 'largely an exercise in containment'. They merely sat out their schooling, because they understood precisely its value to their future life of unskilled endurance. And though even their parents had grown up in a world where the possibilities for that way of life were dwindling, the conception of education as something alien, something other, still underlay the attitudes of the present generation. There was, I was told, no shortage of jobs for skilled workers in Peterlee, yet I heard time and again from teachers in East Durham that the vast majority even of their able pupils, did not consider further education as an option. They weren't even thinking about it. They were much more concerned with 'going out' – the boys; while the girls wanted a boyfriend, because everyone else had one. And though the divorce figures were rocketing there as they were everywhere else, they were already thinking about marriage.

The only hope for the area, I had been told by one former Horden miner, was if in the wake of Easington's closure, someone brought some new heavy industry to East Durham. Heavy industry? I heard the syllables rise in my mind with the indignant incredulity characteristic of the region. *Heavy industry*? The heavy industry would be going to Taiwan, Singapore, China, India, South Africa. Even the hi-tech Nissan plant at Sunderland, said to be one of the most efficient in Europe, would, it was predicted, be shedding jobs in the near future. Heavy industry, the effects of which we all grew up with, is becoming a matter of folklore as much as historical memory. Even the stories of the struggles between the left and right in the union, which I had heard rehearsed so passionately – and at far greater length and more frequently than I have recorded here – though they had taken place so recently, were part of a world that was already almost quaintly historic. The great British public had rallied to the defence of the miners in the autumn of 1992, because the power of organised labour was no longer a threat to them. Meanwhile, the lads were still sitting at the garage in Peterlee, waiting to fulfil their part in the old bargain of unskilled labour, a bargain that no longer existed, in a world that had no use for them.

Rummaging in some old boxes, I found a roll of old standard 8mm film – just a small four-minute roll. I got the projector out, and after two and a half minutes of my two-and-a-half-year-old self trying to manhandle a plank round the garden of our house in Leeds, the film suddenly cut to the image of a grey-haired and obviously frail woman, sitting in the garden of a quite different house. My grandmother, Jenny Hudson, the skin tightening over her fragile bird-like features, close to death. My father, who has studied the fiercely objective drawings of the Renaissance masters, catches her in full profile, and she, stupefied by the drugs, or merely by the illness and the pain, appears not to notice. The image cuts to the greenhouse beyond. A man in a cloth cap is attending to tomato plants. The camera is furtive, surreptitious. The cameraman doesn't want to disturb the subject, make him self-conscious. Then he half turns. It's Percy.

These people I've fought so hard to visualise – to imagine as though they are actually *there* – there they are, before my very eyes.

Percy, ruddier in complexion than I expected him, a bit thicker set, becoming a bit slacker in the jowls, in a collarless shirt and an old dark suit – the sort of clothes that no longer exist – and, of course, a cloth cap. He doesn't look too pleased at having been caught in this way, isn't sure how to act, but at the same time, doesn't want to disappoint his son. There's a gentle sadness in his eyes. He moves towards his wife. You can see the tenderness, slightly gauche in front of the camera. 'Now, Mam.' He always called her 'Mam'. He leans forward. The film flies off the reel . . .

So that was Percy. To have come so far, to ask so many questions, to find out what I had in my heart of hearts known all along, that Percy was just a bloke in a collarless shirt and a cloth cap who liked his garden. What did a man like that know about education? Probably not very much. 'Art?' he had said, all those years before, when he learnt that my father was hell-bent on a career in that sphere. 'That's for shopkeepers' daughters and middle-class tarts!'

'Now, now,' said Mam. She was after all a shopkeeper's daughter herself.

Yet Percy had long before acquired a belief in the value of education. He understood its crucial, its overriding importance. There was nay other bloody hope!

So during the darkest days of the Thirties, he'd kept my father and Mollie at the grammar school. Although, by that time, there were places allocated for 11 per cent of the village's children, they went mainly to the offspring of Horden's small middle class – the doctor, the top colliery officials, the managers of the Co-operative Stores and the three cinemas. Most of the miners' children who made it to the grammar school were taken out by their parents at fourteen or fifteen to work and support their families. By the time my father reached the sixth form, he was virtually the only one left in his class from an ordinary mining family.

When he got home from school on the day his grandfather James Hudson died, my father found Percy sitting in the kitchen, freshly shaven, in a collar and tie and his best tweed jacket, his shoes highly polished – immaculately groomed, as he always was when he went to his union meetings. But there was no union meeting that night. He was waiting to be called to his father's bedside, as he was a few minutes later, and as he'd always known he would be; though my father had the feeling that even if he hadn't been called, he would have gone anyway.

It was no coincidence that my father was the favourite grandchild. It was the old man's way of keeping in touch with the son he never spoke to, who he turned away from in the street, who he refused to acknowledge right up to the very last moment. And Percy, until the end of his own life, had nurtured the hope that his father had harboured some faint grain of regard for the efforts he'd made on behalf of his fellow workers. Not just the going away as a delegate to the Cokemen's National Conference and the TUC, which he had of course done. Not just the preparing of compensation claims and negotiations with the owners' representatives. But all the endless hours of mundane administrative work required to keep a union branch in operation. Efforts he had maintained over decades, for little thanks or recognition, and which he had undertaken like all local union officials in the earlier part of the century, entirely in his own time, and for the most meagre of honorariums. It is only those closest to such people – their wives, their children, their intimate friends – who know the sacrifices they make, for a cause to which they have committed themselves.

Often during my time in Horden, I had felt there was a kind of priggishness, a lack of 'authenticity' in Percy's obsession with aspiration and improvement. I had almost resented the way he had distanced himself and his family, and thus me, from the warm old world of the Big Club, and of people like Harry and Jackie – the world I had found myself seeking out in Horden. Percy's chosen path had seemed to lack the authenticity, the vitality of Harry's way. But he had not been prepared to let things lie, the way Harry had, the way Jackie had, the way his own brothers had, and the way most people in Horden had.

Now there was for me no choice between Percy's way and Harry's way. Harry's way no longer even existed.

To raise themselves? What other option was open to them?

THE HUDSON FAMILY AS MENTIONED IN THIS BOOK

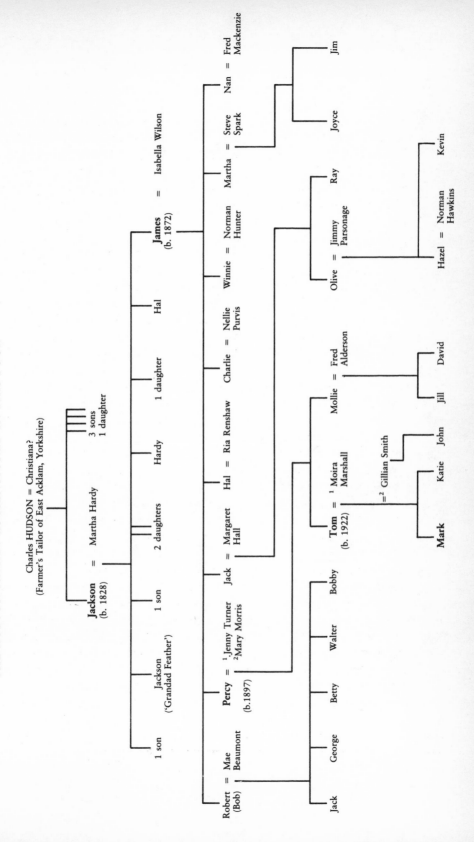

Charles HUDSON = Christiana?
(Farmer's Tailor of East Acklam, Yorkshire)

Acknowledgments

I would like to thank the many people in Horden and the surrounding area who took the time to share their thoughts and memories with me. Without them this book could not have been written. I would particularly like to thank Bob Naisbett, Ralph Porter, Erving Lyons, Bill Davis, John Turnbull, Fred Watson, Frank Smallwood, Joe Macguiness, Pop Porter, Fred Rogers, Stan Langley, J. D. Hesler, Brian Williams, Brian Walsh, Alec Turnbull, Harold Morrison, Nan Salmon, Monna Riley, Elsie and Ronnie Howden, Renie Macmanners, Edie Scholick, Dora Byron, Ethel Thompson, Jonty Camick, John Fairhurst, Gordon Tindle, Gordon Thom, Arthur Carling and Bobby Baker.

Also, Steve Cummings, Ted Maclean, Matty Prisk, John O'Donnell, Derek Gray, Joe Wilson, Norma Blevens, Birgit Hoppe, May and Jim Bell, Paddy, Arthur Robbins, Alan Cummings, Mick Carr, George Brennan, Billy Stobbs, Harry Miller, Lawrence Miller, Artie Cooper, Barry Chambers, Jack Hardley, Steve and Mary Thompson, Connie Hudspith, Heather Wood, Paul Stradlin, Mosey Kirkup, Bob Johnson, Dave and Ruby Larmer, Irene Lincoln, PRIDE Women's Group, Horden Women's Patchwork Group, Bill Dowding, Les Williams, Ronnie Rooney, Doug Langan, Ada Naisbitt, Norman Mackie, David Taylor-Gooby, Derek Armstrong, Lily Allen, Jimmy Hails, Jimmy Gray, Walter Hudspith, Ronnie Scott, Bella Turner, Walter Malt, Mr Garside, Paul Hebron, Linda King.

In researching the book, four texts proved invaluable: *True Stories of Durham Pit Life* by G. E. Parkinson, *The Story of the Durham Miners* by Sidney Webb, *Mostly Mining* by William A. Moyes and *The Pitmen of the Northern Coalfield* by Robert Colls.

I would also like to thank my editors, Dan Franklin and Jenny Cottom, and my agent, Gill Coleridge.

I would, finally, like to thank various members of my family: my uncle, Fred Alderson, for his unfailing generosity and support, Aunt Nan for introducing me to another world, Don and Mary Hudson, Joyce Stephenson, Hazel and Norman Hawkins, Ray and Sheila Hudson, Karen and Adie Milner, Gordon Hudson, Sue and Sadie Whiffen, Andrea Watson, my sister Kate, my mother, and, of course, my father for so generously sharing his memories.

M.H.